# TRADE UNIONS AND SUSTAINABLE DEMOCRACY IN AFRICA

# Trade Unions and Sustainable Democracy in Africa

*Edited by*
GÉRARD KESTER and
OUSMANE OUMAROU SIDIBÉ

Translated by Michael Cunningham

Trade unions and sustainable democracy in Africa

# Ashgate
Aldershot • Brookfield USA • Singapore • Sydney

© Gérard Kester and Ousmane Oumarou Sidibé 1997

Published by
Ashgate Publishing Limited
Gower House
Croft Road
Aldershot
Hants GU11 3HR
England

HD
6858.5
. S9513
1997

Ashgate Publishing Company
Old Post Road
Brookfield
Vermont 05036
USA

**British Library Cataloguing in Publication Data**
Trade unions and sustainable democracy in Africa
 1.Trade-unions - Africa 2.Trade-unions - Africa - Political
 activity 3.Democracy - Africa 4.Africa - Politics and
 government - 1960-
 I.Kester, Gérard II.Oumarou Sidibé, Ousmane
 322.2'096'09049

**Library of Congress Catalog Card Number:** 97-74263

Reprinted 1997

ISBN    184014 323 1

Printed in Great Britain by the Ipswich Book Company, Suffolk

# Contents

# List of Contributors

*The editors*

*Gérard Kester* is Associate Professor of Sociology and Labour Relations at the Institute of Social Studies in The Hague (The Netherlands), and Programme Director of the African Workers' Participation and Development Programme (APADEP).

*Ousmane Oumarou Sidibé* is Professor of Law at the University of Mali and General Coordinator of APADEP-Mali. He was Mali's Minister of Labour between 1993 and 1995. He is now Director General of the Malian National Administration School, and Dean of Law and Economics at the University of Mali.

*The authors*

*Florent Valère Adegbidi* is Consultant-Researcher at the Beninese Centre of Scientific and Technical Research, Cotonou, Benin.

*Jean Sourou Agossou* is a trade unionist and Head of Town Planning and Development in the Town Planning and Housing Directorate, Cotonou, Benin.

*Kwasi Adu-Amankwah* is Deputy-General Secretary of the Ghana Trades Union Congress, Accra, Ghana.

*Niki Best* is Associate Expert at the International Labour Office, currently based in Antananarivo, Madagascar.

*Nadedjo Bigou-Laré* is Executive Director of the University Institute of Technology-Management at the University of Benin, Lomé, Togo.

*Samuel E. Chambua* is Senior Lecturer at the University of Dar-es-Salaam, Tanzania.

*Raoul Galarraga* is Scientific Assistant at APADEP, Institute of Social Studies, The Hague, The Netherlands.

*David Ginsburg* is Senior Lecturer in the Department of Sociology, University of Natal, Durban, South Africa.

*Aimé Tchabouré Gogué*, a former Minister of Planning, is now Director of the third Inter-University Cycle Programme in Economics at the Conference of Education, Economic Research and Management Institutions in Africa, Ouagadougou, Burkina Faso.

*Ken Hansen* is a trade union adviser. He is currently working on two projects with the OTM and SLIM in Maputo, Mozambique.

*El-Khider Ali Musa* is Professor of Accountancy and Finance in the Faculty of Economics and Rural Development, University of Gezira, Sudan.

*Guillaume Silga* is Researcher at the National School of Administration and Law in Ouagadougou, Burkina Faso.

*Kwadwo Tutu* is Professor of Economics at the University of Ghana, Legon, Ghana.

*Brigitte Venturi* is in charge of French-Language Publications at APADEP, Institute of Social Studies, The Hague, The Netherlands.

*Eddie Webster* is Professor of Sociology at the University of Witwatersrand, Johannesburg, South Africa.

# Acknowledgements

We would like to extend our warmest thanks to all who have made this book possible:

*Raoul Galarraga, Nicole Vendange* and *Brigitte Venturi* for their valuable editorial support, for reading first and subsequent drafts of the chapters and offering essential criticisms and suggestions, and for their bibliographical support;

*Hélène Boender Quiniou* for writing the introductory paragraphs to the chapters on the ten African countries;

The Dutch Federation of Trade Unions (FNV) and the Dutch Ministry of International Cooperation (DGIS/IO) for the moral and financial support they have given to APADEP;

*Michael Cunningham* for his translations into English and editorial work of some chapters;

and *Antoinette Otto* for the layout and type-setting of the book.

# Foreword

Yet another book on democratisation in Africa. Yes, but this one is different. Different because the great debate on democratisation rarely gives credit of any sort to the trade union movement. And that is quite wrong, because trade unions in many countries have played crucial roles in the establishment of political democracy. One of the biggest challenges facing the future of Africa is how to maintain, consolidate and deepen democracy - in other words, how to establish Africa in a framework of genuine sustainable democracy. However, that is only feasible if the effect that democracy has on development is positive and visible. If standards of living continue to fall, and if the gap between rich and poor continues to get wider, it will become almost impossible to take democracy forward. Even with periodic elections - whether they are above board or not - democracy will not lay any sustainable foundation in society unless citizens control their future through significant participation in decisions both at work and at national level. Formal democracy that keeps citizens, particularly workers, outside the decision-making process is unacceptable to the trade union movement. The role that unions have played in the democratisation process means that civil society as a whole, and the trade union movement in particular, have acquired new responsibilities. The big question is how to establish participative democracy, first by constructing concertation mechanisms that take account of the sensibilities of all social groups, and then by applying them in all areas of society including the economic sector. In such a scenario, trade unions self-evidently have a key role to play.

APADEP, the African Workers' Participation Development Programme, is a cooperative university-trade union project that aims to strengthen participation. How trade unions can involve themselves in development, and contribute to the survival of democracy, has been a key issue for APADEP; as many as 20 researchers have been working on it since 1993.

It has been an uphill struggle. Data and documentation are in very short supply, and even when it comes down to basic facts like trade union membership figures, the information is far from reliable. We hesitated about undertaking the study in the first place, and hesitated even further about publishing it; however, in the end, we realised how critical the challenge was, and decided to go ahead. In our view, it is vital for the trade union dimension to be added to the democratisation debate; we trust that this study, albeit incomplete, will open the door to new research fields.

The book is in two parts. Part I consists of an overview of sub-Saharan Africa (SSA) based on selected documentation. We stress that the analyses cannot be extrapolated to incorporate the whole of SSA Africa. We only seek to ask general questions, and acknowledge that they need to be analysed in the present-day context of each country. That is why Part II is given over to an analysis of the specific situations obtaining in ten African countries in different geographical and language areas. Each case study provides its own democratisation scenario.

The authors, all of whom work closely with APADEP, have drawn on their personal experience and have been guided by a simple, yet flexible, theme: trends in the last few decades in their countries, with the accent on transition over the last five years. They have analysed the process of democratisation and developments in trade unionism and in the field of participation, and all within a context of socio-economic development. We also encouraged them to focus on factors relating to the specificities of their chosen country, after making allowances for the paucity of information available. The authors come from a variety of backgrounds; they include economists, sociologists, psychologists, lawyers and trade unionists. This has ensured a multi-disciplinary approach incorporating a wide range of perspectives on the process of democratisation. Most of them were able to meet on two occasions - once at Mopti (Mali) in 1993, and later in Bobo Dioulasso (Burkina Faso) in 1995 - to exchange draft chapters.

This book does not set out to provide answers, let alone prescriptions. Instead, it opens a dialogue with the trade union movement and its social partners including civil society, political leaders and the scientific community. We expect it will be controversial, and that is hardly surprising. For one thing, our stock of data is not complete; for another, the authors themselves are partners - some of them are even players - in the democratisation process. Opinions and expectations are not always shared. That is the very essence of democracy; it is also the basis of our desire to stimulate serious discussion on the future of trade unionism, participation and democracy in Africa.

The Hague/Bamako, January 1997
*Gérard Kester* and *Ousmane Oumarou Sidibé*

'I watched and learned a lot from the tribal meetings ... all Thembus were free to come - and a great many did, on horseback or by foot ... Everyone who wanted to speak did so. *It was democracy in its purest form.* There may have been a hierarchy of importance among the speakers, but everyone was heard: chief and subject, warrior and medicine man, shopkeeper and farmer, landowner and labourer. People spoke without interruption and the meetings lasted for many hours. The foundation of self-government was that all men were free to voice their opinions and were equal in their value as citizens ... at first, I was astonished by the vehemence - and candour - with which people criticized the regent. He was not above criticism - in fact, he was often the principal target of it ... the meetings would continue until some kind of consensus was reached. They ended in unanimity or not at all. Unanimity, however, might be an agreement to disagree, to wait for a more propitious time to propose a solution. Democracy meant all men were to be heard, and a decision was not to be crushed by a majority ... If no agreement could be reached, another meeting would be held.'

NELSON MANDELA, *Long Walk to Freedom* (1994:24-25)

# Part I

# Trade Unions, Democracy and Development

Sub-Saharan Africa is made up of a large number of countries. They each have their own history, culture, society and economy. In trade union terms, they each have their own separate issues - but there are common issues as well.

Part I of this book opens up a general discussion on the trade union movement and democratisation in sub-Saharan Africa. This discussion takes its inspiration from research conducted in ten African countries set out in Part II, and from general literature on the subject.

What role has the trade union movement played in the establishment of political democracy? Surely a bigger role than one has been led to believe. And what influence has it had on the structural adjustment of the African economy? Probably less than one would have liked.

The fourth and last chapter in Part I examines the potential role that African trade unions have in making democracy sustainable. It is a provocative chapter because the trade union movement has reached its meeting-place with history just as it is having to cope with some serious problems of its own. If trade unions are unable to democratise the economy, can democracy itself survive?

# Part 1

# Trade Unions, Democracy and Development

# 1 Trade Unions, It's Your Turn!

GÉRARD KESTER AND OUSMANE OUMAROU SIDIBÉ

Africa had been preparing the ground for major change for many years when structural adjustment and its stablemate, neo-liberalism, came onto the scene in the early 1980s. They have dominated the continent's economic and social development ever since. Economic reform may have been long overdue, but these two have made their combined presence felt with quite unmistakeable force. Suffering has increased and the debts have piled up, and privileges have continued to be showered on a tiny élite who seize the property of the State claiming that they can manage it better themselves. Open protest has been relatively muted, but this has been mainly due to the tanks that dictators have sent onto the streets: the people's sense of injustice has certainly been deep-seated enough. Finally, the end of the Cold War gave neo-liberalism the extra boost it needed, and provided a justification for unrestrained capitalism.

Hopes soared once again when 'democracy' became the new principle underpinning the organisation of change, and most of the people who poured onto the streets to call for democracy did so because they were weary of bad management, nepotism, embezzlement of public funds and a failure to observe human rights. This intensification of popular pressure indicated that people no longer had confidence in the State. Demonstrations, too, revealed that people were aware of the issues, and were keen to demonstrate their ability to do whatever was necessary to survive, to make their voices heard, and to be involved in decision-making - even if there were others who found it discomfiting (Sidibé et al, 1994: 83).

## Democracy in Africa: a brief history

It is not our intention here to recount the great debate that has surrounded democracy; there is an abundant literature on the subject of democratisation in Africa, and it is to this that the reader should refer (see Bibliography). Instead, we shall confine ourselves to some comments that are particularly relevant to this study.

Africa has a long and varied history of democracy. Indeed, we have preceded this chapter with a quotation of Nelson Mandela that expresses the best in a wholly African tradition, even though it cannot be applied to

1

the entire continent. In some pre-colonial African States such as the Ghana, Mali and Songhoi Empires, people exercised their sovereignty through representatives appointed according to strictly enforced rules. Even sovereigns themselves were assisted by assemblies designated in accordance with well-tried mechanisms. At the level of more scattered units such as villages, direct democracy was also exercised through the arbre à palabre, or 'palaver tree', a form of open, undiluted democracy still to be found in francophone Africa.

It would be a mistake to paint too romantic a picture of participative democracy in pre-colonial Africa. The substantial literature on the subject boasts a wide variety of viewpoints ranging from the positive to the cynical (see Buijtenhuis et al, 1993). There is also an impressive range of African political systems, but there is no hiding the fact that nearly all of them excluded women and slaves from their decision-making structures (Codesria, 1992: 15-16).

## The confiscation of freedoms

The one-party interlude - in which one man, as Head of State, wielded total power by combining the Presidency of both the government and the single party - is not a throwback to pre-colonial days. On the contrary, it is in many ways a consequence of the hiatus filled by colonisation. Indeed, the first three decades of independence in African countries were marked by a shameful lack of democracy and the confiscation of freedoms.

During this period, trade unions - usually single organisations covering an entire country - were centralised, they had to pledge their allegiance to the single party and operated as an instrument for keeping workers in check. Young people and women were similarly organised into monolithic organisations similarly attached to the party. Even in countries like Côte-d'Ivoire which openly took their inspiration from economic liberalism, economies were planned and extensively nationalised.

As a result, a deep chasm opened up between the people and their leaders, the latter revealing themselves incapable of comprehending the problems of the former, let alone find solution to them.

Military régimes were also unable to fulfill promises that they would inject a note of morality into public life and the management of public affairs; in the end, they exhausted the good will of their people, whose hopes had evaporated as a result of corruption, nepotism and the confiscation of freedoms. A deepening of the economic crisis also caused this general discontent with ruling political régimes to crystallise.

From the 1980s onwards, African governments were forced to agree Structural Adjustment Programmes (SAPs) with international funders. The social consequences of these programmes were dramatic and governments gradually lost control; in particular, SAPs undermined the social bases that governments had in the towns and cities. Factors that combined to swell the numbers of the excluded in urban areas included early retirement schemes in the public sector, massive lay-off programmes in public enterprises and a shortage of jobs for many young graduates. This expanding army of excluded found new hope in an opposition organised within political associations that were mostly illegal, but which were beginning to demonstrate increasing support for urban revolt.

*The turning point*

The growing discontent orchestrated by well-structured organisations fed into the movement then promoting democratisation, but we should not underestimate the impact of events taking place in eastern countries, or of positions adopted by external partners; all of these factors acted as catalysts for democratisation. For example, in 'From Crisis to Sustainable Development' (1989), the World Bank stated that political legitimacy and consensus were essential conditions for sustainable development in Africa; the Bretton Woods Institutions, too, were convinced that democracy provided an environment favourable to economic development, and Mauritius and Botswana were held up as examples for other African countries to follow. Then, in 1990, at the La Baule Summit, the French President, François Mitterrand, announced his intention of linking development aid to democratisation in African countries; finally, in 1991, the idea was adopted by USAID after the US Congress directed that progress towards democracy should be taken into account when granting aid.

Many African countries, to a greater or lesser extent - and with varying degrees of fortune - committed themselves to a process of democratisation. However, it all happened in a climate marked by a radicalisation of internal demands and external pressure for more democracy and freedoms, and these pressures were given an extra impetus by the end of the Cold War.

Some countries, including Benin, Zambia, Malawi, the Central African Republic, Congo and South Africa, achieved peaceful transformation, while others underwent more violent change. An example of the latter was Mali where democratic transition was only achieved in the wake of several insurrections and a military coup d'état.

For many countries, such as Côte d'Ivoire, Burkina Faso, Gabon, Togo and Cameroon, the democratic opening was largely controlled after elections led to the re-installation of groups that had previously held power; these elections were often notable for their lack of transparency. Some countries, like Zaïre and Chad, are still engaged in transitions that never reach a conclusion, or else they have totally rejected a real democratic opening (Nigeria, Sudan and, to a lesser extent, Kenya). Others are in a state of civil war and are still searching for peace (Angola, Somalia and Liberia) or are attempting to consolidate it (Mozambique). Finally, we must not forget Rwanda and Burundi where the democratising process has caused a major ethnic conflict leading to genocide in Rwanda, and making the whole issue of democratisation much more complex.

*Anger*

The type of democracy that Africans have chosen is close to the European model, that is to say it is a political system that allows the people to elect their leaders freely and ensures a separation of powers and executive control. A system of this sort also incorporates respect for individual and collective freedoms, and the existence of counter-powers such as a free press and a strong civil society.

In a brilliant exposition, Mafeje has developed the idea that Africa has borrowed the vocabulary of democracy from Europe, with the caveat that these words only become functional if they are structured by a common grammar (Mafeje, 1995). It was, in his view, 'folly' to try and transplant elaborate democratic systems developed across 200 years of history in a specific historical climate. The debate on democratisation in Africa has, in many places, given a new dimension to Afro-pessimism. Intermediary assessments of democratisation are often negative (see Lemarchand's summary, 1992), and indicate big differences between African countries.

In his summaries of progress on democratisation in 15 francophone countries, Monga uses a large number of criteria to measure the democratic 'design' and, above all, the implementation of the concept of democracy; his conclusion is that the prospects in most countries are gloomy (Monga, 1995: 63 ff). The fragility of democracy is all the more striking if one recalls the fact that, only months before the military coup d'état in Niamey, Monga's 'democratic classification' had Niger in second place, and only just behind Benin.

More interestingly and more hopefully, however, the advent of democracy has opened the floodgates to a tidal wave of ideas, proposals, theories and actions. Democracy has come under the close scrutiny of the intellectual world, of women, of politicians and the public at large; all acknowledge that its present form is only a beginning, and that democracy needs to be adapted to African realities.

'For Africans,' writes Monga in his captivating 'Anthropologie de la colère' (Anthropology of Anger), 'it is all about reappropriating words that have been confiscated for too long by the official institutions of power'

(Monga, 1994: 99). 'How can we manage the collective anger and, behind the façade of an informal civil society, prevent it from degenerating into some sort of anarchistic cacophony? How can we restore the credibility of the State by simultaneously bolstering the structures of "private" society?' (ibid: 117). The challenge is to develop a form of democracy that meets African needs in an African context, and which varies from one country to the next. The thirst for democracy must be translated into an appropriate form; the vocabulary is in need of a grammar. Democracy is not simply System X or System Y; it is a dynamic phenomenon ('A developmental concept', Sklar, 1987). African countries have not yet rooted themselves irreversibly in democracy. The nascent movement is undermined by too many factors; one of them is the need simply to survive in a harsh economic climate. To achieve that alone, enormous sacrifices will have to be made.

## Democracy and development

Democracy has made huge strides in Africa during the last five years, but sadly the concluding years of the 20th century have also been marked by a persistent decline in African people's living conditions. The coincidence of these two facts has revived the debate on the nature of the relationship between democracy and development. However, the debate is now even more critical as this catastrophic fall in living conditions in sub-Saharan Africa (SSA) simply cannot be tolerated; a still burgeoning democracy still needs urgent support. Many commentators have remarked that any debate on democracy that excludes economic issues completely misses the point. As Newbury has pointed out:

> '... rural dwellers in Africa and the urban underclasses want more than social peace, due process in the judicial system and political accountability. They hope for justice, as well as legal order; they want improved opportunities to feed their families and educate their children, as well as the opportunity to vote for one or another elite. Authoritarian regimes are being rejected because for the most part they have failed to meet these needs; democratic regimes will be judged (in the popular mind) on their ability to respond to such concerns.' (Newbury, 1994: 2)

Before we move on to the question of whether development is a necessary condition for democracy, or whether democracy should precede development, let us first be clear about what we mean by development. In our view, all development must be sustainable development; in other words, it must lead to an improvement in the physical and moral well-being of the population who, in addition to preserving the environment, must participate both in the production and distribution of the profits of that production, and in the transparent management of the State and the rule of law.

This definition implies a distinction between economic growth and development, and these days we use Human Development Indicators as well as per capita GDP to describe a country's level of development; these usefully illustrate the limitations of economic growth as a criterion for identifying the well-being of a country's inhabitants. Otherwise, even if the country enjoys a high rate of economic growth, it cannot achieve development without equitable distribution of this addition wealth - an improvement in the well-being of the people, and a structural change in production. Growth rates say nothing about the level of a population's well-being: for example, is the emphasis on investment or on consumption - and, if the former, where is the money being invested? An eloquent example is provided by the former USSR where the level of the population's well-being fell away just as the country was enjoying a relatively high rate of growth based largely on priority investments in arms.

Clearly, we cannot talk of development in Zaïre if the price of copper continues to rise and the national wealth continues to grow, but without any perceptible effects on the living conditions of the majority of Zaïrians. If there is to be development, people must participate in production. In practice, a population that lives solely on foreign exploitation of its natural resources cannot claim to be developing; it is over-dependent on the foreigner and not in control of its own destiny. As Ki-Zerbo puts it so well, a people is not developed, it develops itself (Ki-Zerbo, 1992). When 'they develop us', we play a passive role; we are unable to participate in drawing up the country's overall directions and priorities, and we have to endure the sectoral allocation of resources as defined by the people who are doing the developing.

*Self-development*

Self-development, as distinct from development carried out by someone else, implies that one is also a player in the development process oneself, a participant in drawing up the country's overall directions and priorities and in managing the State. Development in its broadest sense, therefore, needs democracy; it cannot be restricted to the notion of growth, because growth does not necessarily place constraints on rulers.

If development means a flourishing of the human condition, there can be no question that democracy is essential to development. Ten years ago, Anyang'Nyong'o argued that the absence of democracy was the main reason for the absence of development in Africa (Anyang'Nyong'o, 1987). Nowadays, this idea arouses controversy, although it is more likely to be defended than opposed (Buijtenhuis et al, 1993). More recently, Anyang'Nyong'o has replied that democracy is worth defending in Africa on the grounds that the cause is philosophical and moral in the first instance; only later does it become political and economic 1995: 38). Writing in the same spirit as Ki-Zerbo, Alain Touraine adds that, in his view, 'development is not the cause but the result of democracy' (Touraine, 1994: 222).

Democracy allows each person to feel involved and his/her views taken into account, and thus allows each person to give of his/her best; democracy will therefore make it possible to mobilise the resources a country needs for its development. Structural economic reforms will also be more sustainable and more relevant if they flow from a democratic process involving concertation with the organisations of civil society (Torres, 1995: 53). Democracy is essential if a country desires sustainable development.

The example of the countries of south-east Asia proves there is nothing coincidental about calamities such as poverty, under-nourishment, malnutrition and high rates of infant mortality; it also shows that they can be resolved by the right policies. However, as our definition of development suggests, these economic policies assume that there is consultation and concertation with the populations concerned, and this method of political management has not been applied to the SAPs that have dominated economic policies in Africa since the early 1980s. We shall examine SAP policies in detail in Chapter 3.

## Democratic participation[1]

Participation is not easy to define as it affects all dimensions of society: economic, political, social and cultural. In labour relations, the notion of 'workers' participation' normally refers to the taking of decisions; this phenomenon needs to be defined within a dynamic perspective. Workers' participation is a process that involves the gradual transformation of labour relations and, through the accumulation and institutionalisation of participative practices, workers acquire an independent, significant and effective influence over decision-taking at various levels of company management and/or policy. This influence may, through trade unions, extend to all decision-taking levels outside the enterprise as well (Kester, 1995: 61).

The notion of participation most frequently refers to the sharing of power, but it can also be understood in a broader sense, that is to say sharing in the distribution of profits and work (economic democracy), and sharing in production (a better use of human resources). The concept of 'people's participation' is the most far-reaching and refers to the sharing of power, profits, employment and production.

After achieving independence, many Third World countries adopted participation policies partly as an integral part of their development strategy for creating a new political, economic and social order, and partly as a measure to accompany nationalisation. Various forms of participation and self-management have been influenced by European theory and practice; these have sought to set up democratic institutions and practices in the process of socio-economic development, and to instigate a rapid move towards self-determination and self-sufficiency.

In this context, we recall the Chilean experience in which Allende introduced co-determination and self-management into nationalised industries (Raptis, 1974; Espinosa & Zimbalist, 1978), the transition to self-management in State-owned concerns in Peru (Lowenthal, 1975; Stephens, 1980) literally introduced by people 'in uniform' (Meister, 1981), workers' committees in the Sri Lankan public sector (Abeyasekera, 1977), the Ecevit plan in Turkey which transformed the entire public sector into one self-managed by workers (Uca, 1983), and other experiments in Asia and Latin America (Spirianni, 1987; Prasnikar, 1991; Bayat, 1991).

## Participation confiscated as well

There have been experiments of this sort in Africa, too. The 'humanist philosophy' of Zambia's President Kaunda involved transition from one society in which capitalist enterprises were in the hands of the few towards another society characterised by human dignity and social justice, and the ultimate objective of workers managing enterprises themselves (Fincham & Zulu, 1980). Similarly, human-centred development was key to the approach to development adopted in Tanzania; this involved the introduction of various forms of workers' participation (Mihyo, 1983). Self-management was official policy in Algeria in the first few years of independence (Clegg, 1971), and Egypt introduced major, formal structures of workers' participation at middle and senior management levels in public enterprises (El-Sayed, 1978). Charismatic African leaders such as Nasser, Nyerere and Kaunda all played leading roles in introducing and implementing policies of this type.

The fate of these régimes after independence is well documented. Power achieved through democratic means initially corrupted the leaders; later on, utopia became a slogan, the slogan converted into dogma, dogma grew into repression, and repression turned into dictatorship or even tyranny. Participation reflected this course of events and ended up the loser: it had originally been a source of economic and social liberation; as time passed, it fell prey to manipulation and exploitation.

'Responsible participation' became the key slogan in numerous francophone countries, and even trade unions gave the policy their support in many places including Togo (Barnabo, 1981; see also Nadedjo Bigou-Laré's chapter on Togo in this book), Senegal (Fall, 1987) and Mali (Dicko, Sidibé & Touré, 1985). It sought to co-opt civil society, in particular the trade unions, with a view to procuring their backing for objectives already determined by the single party or the military régime. In other words, it was a purely manipulative policy, and participation was confiscated.

The explanation for the failure of experiments in participation and self-management does not lie in any inherent weakness of the idea, but rather in the fact that the conditions for the development of participation were simply not there. Participation itself did not fail; what failed was the way it was implemented. Predictably, of course, conservative forces developed their own counter-strategies, but the talks that prepared the ground for participation simply did not provide the necessary support (e.g. there was a crucial shortage of training) and politicians and trade union leaders opted instead for rhetoric (Stephens, 1980; Kester, 1992: 237 ff).

*The participation controversy*

The African economy 'broke down' (Giri, 1986). However, to be fair, SAPs were not introduced for the pleasure of 'restructuring' but out of necessity; they were intended to put an end to bad management of the economy. A change in economic policy was clearly called for, but what was utterly unacceptable was the way in which new economic policies, and SAPs in particular, were decided on and enforced (see Chapter 3). The broad aims of the new economic policy are contraction of the public sector, privatisation, the introduction of market forces into the economy, and a reduced role for the State in general; trade unionism or participation do not get a mention. This prompts the notion that these two ideas are associated with bad management. In fact, it is not an unreasonable conclusion as governments no longer support the kind of participation they themselves introduced; these governments also pass new labour law to attract local or foreign private investors, thereby guaranteeing them 'carte blanche' in running their enterprises. Democracy is now restricted to multi-annual elections, and the economy is in the hands of the bosses. Trade unionism is also seen as a form of harassment, and participation as an error for which previous governments are to blame.

This trend is not confined to Africa. In Europe, workers' participation was a dynamic phenomenon back in the 1960s and 1970s; at the time, it was welcomed by the trade union movement, and was often backed up by legislation. However, even in Europe, the new neo-liberal tendency has prevented further evolution of participation in decision-making. It has been replaced by a series of employer initiatives designed to develop organisational and financial participation (they are later seen for what they are - anti-union strategies) and block interference in management prerogatives (Pinaud, 1995: 33-48).

Surprisingly, when the winds of change swept over Africa, workers' participation was not jettisoned together with the old leaders, ideologies and systems. It was quite a different matter in eastern Europe where 'participation' had become a dirty word in political debate. The African Charter of Popular Participation in Development and Transformation (Arusha, 1991) was adopted at a conference of heads of government and national and international NGOs; it rehabilitated the values and objectives of participation, but did not formulate any practical policy and strategy to go with it. For a short while, the Arusha Declaration breathed new life into participation rhetoric, but it all came to nothing. Today, the political debate, like the trade union debate, on participation in Africa is almost non-existent.

Nonetheless, as we shall see in Chapter 4, interest in participation has not faded among workers and rank-and-file trade union activists. APADEP studies confirm that most worker representatives have a need - not to say a thirst - for participation. And it is not simply a thirst to express ideas, criticise and share; worker and trade union representatives are also eager to contribute to workplace productivity and efficiency.

This book sets out to revive that debate. Responsible participation must be replaced by a kind of democratic participation that has new aims, values and objectives. A democratic form of workers' participation must create the conditions for a new type of economic and social justice, and that in turn will constitute the necessary foundation for any real democracy.

## Democracy, participation and development

Participation is a key player in the struggle for democracy. The position put forward by Pateman (1970) - a classic that no political scientist has called into question - defends the idea that, in daily life, and particularly at the workplace, participation is a necessary condition for the sustainability and deepening of political democracy and the development of a democratic culture. This view has recently been restated by Touraine (1994) and Dahrendorf (1996). Moreover, by applying it specifically to labour relations, Albert has been able to argue that industrialised countries with the best combined economic and social records have a co-determination structure. They are the countries of so-called 'Rhineland' capitalism: Germany, Benelux and the Scandinavian countries (Albert, 1991).

Several African analysts are thinking along the same lines. Monga, for instance, believes that social groups, including trade unions, 'are moved by a thirst to express themselves, to participate, and to be represented in the places that matter ... the main issue is enlarging the scope of popular participation' (Monga, 1994: 106 & 126). Ake claims that the basic problem facing government is the absence of participation, and 'only participation can ensure deep democracy' (Ake, 1995: 89). And according to Ayesha Imam, democracy needs to be defined in relation to the day-to-day lives of all citizens, and must include the right for all to take part in decisions that are important for them (Imam, 1991: 5).

Underlying this book is an assumption that democracy can only survive if it is participative, and that participative democracy is a necessary condition for development; as we demonstrate in Chapter 4, this position is currently shared by the World Bank, UNDP, OECD and others. In an African context, it is extremely important to know which ideas South Africans developed when they were preparing for political democracy; it was, after all, one of the most remarkable achievements of the 20th century. As the Reconstruction and Development Programme states, 'Democracy is not confined to periodic elections, but is an active process enabling everyone to contribute to reconstruction and development' (§ 1.3.7, 9) and 'The Government's central goal ... is to ... democratise the economy and empower the historically oppressed, particularly the workers and their organisations, by encouraging broader participation in decisions about the economy in both the private and public sector' (§ 3.2.1 20). We deal with South African matters in more detail in Chapters 4 and 5.

Being able to cast one's vote is not the same thing as democracy. If we define the word more broadly, democracy becomes a political phenomenon, a phenomenon with economic, social and cultural dimensions, and these dimensions form part of the broader concept of 'participative democracy'. Participation is the cement between general elections and grass roots democracy; it is also a necessary complement of political democracy because it enables people to express themselves without interruption, and participate in decisions on the allocation and distribution of wealth. The Arusha Declaration also subscribed to this broader vision of democracy.

The Universal Declaration of Human Rights also sees participation as a fundamental right, and views the right to freedom of expression and the right to vote as components of human integrity and dignity.


## African trade unionism

African trade unions played an important part in the struggle for independence in African countries, and collaborated closely with African political parties. In doing so, they imagined that independence would guarantee enhanced freedom for trade union action, and that it would promote development and, by the same token, better living and working conditions for their members. That was why they evinced so much interest in, and devoted so much of their time to, participation in the economic and social development of young African countries. However, once independence was won, political leaders started to distrust trade unions which, in their view, were beginning to put in too many claims. And when drawing up and implementing economic and social development programmes, African governments, both civil and military, did not give unions enough scope for independent, democratic participation. When they did agree to let them take part, it was within the framework of a pseudo-policy of 'responsible participation' which relegated unions to the status of government poodle, or mouthpiece for passing on instructions to the workforce. Unions accepting this role did so to avoid isolation, banning or brutal repression; if nothing else, they did so just to survive. They then hoped to find room for manoeuvre that would give them a minimum of autonomy and credibility with workers.

As a result, thanks to the resilience one might expect from the trade union movement, and with support from international trade union organisations, African unions were able to maintain a degree of independence, although it varied from country to country. This autonomy was extremely limited, not to say non-existent, in Communist régimes (e.g. Guinea under Sékou-Touré) and openly dictatorial countries such as Togo; it was average in many other countries (e.g. Mali, Senegal and Nigeria) and substantial in a small number including Burkina Faso and Zambia. However, there were no instances of governments silencing trade unions altogether or controlling all structures - which is what they would like to have done. True, high-level union committees were controlled by governments to a greater or lesser extent, but intermediary structures, and particularly the grass roots, frequently had more autonomy.

Trade union democracy was often stronger among the rank and file than at the top, the upper échelons having long been notable for 'pre-fabricated' committees influenced, or even imposed, by the State. Unsurprisingly, there has been fierce pressure from the branches since the early 1980s to challenge the relations between trade union centres and governments, on the grounds that they did not operate on behalf of workers. Excessive organisational and operational dependence on the State angered workers as they saw their living standards plummet and their jobs come under threat, notwithstanding union claims that they were party to the decision-making. In fact, when we talk of trade unions being bought off by the government of the day, what we are often referring to are the actions of local and national leaders. It is easy to forget that unions are criss-crossed by numerous internal forces and currents that do not share the same view of union policy. Furthermore, governments sometimes attack currents that are hostile to a union line on positions already adopted by the party; they then promote trends that enable them to take over the leadership of the union through rigged elections.

## Trade unions and democratisation

If trade unions have made a stronger commitment to the process of democratisation than other social forces, this is because they are a unique component of civil society and are well equipped for the task. They are important players because of their position in the economy, and their views cannot be ignored by the State; as they have demonstrated during the democratisation process, unions can paralyse a large section of the economy by calling strikes in strategic sectors such as energy, transport or telecommunications. Moreover, thanks to the international protection that they enjoy, unions are part of an international solidarity chain; other social groups do not have access to anything comparable. Moreover, protests from international centres and ILO condemnations are feared by all governments, and have often helped to get trade unionists out of prison, or preserve a minimum of trade union freedoms under dictatorships.

Trade unions also developed a culture which, during the colonial period, fostered solidarity, combated economic and social injustice, and promoted human rights. Although they did not always have the necessary independence or strength to defend these values effectively, at least they consistently incorporated them into everything they said.

Today, when governments have turned their backs on participation, and are instead promoting economic liberalism and a reduction in the role of the State, trade unions have to take a new stand. If participation is seen as a way of guaranteeing social cohesion and harmonious development within a negotiated framework, and aimed at avoiding social devastation, nobody is better placed than trade unions to promote it. After all, on a continent such as Africa where so much profound change is taking place, who else can produce democracy in an insecure economic and social climate when political parties think of nothing but the conquest of power? Who else can propose a vision or model of society that has a reasonable chance of being accepted by the various social forces?

These days, it is no longer enough for trade unions to fire off salvoes of protests about SAPs. They need to develop alternative proposals through a new social pact negotiated by all social players including political parties, governments and employers; such a pact might take the form of a charter for managing the great problems of the nation, thus providing the foundation of sustainable democracy. Democratic participation, which trade unions appear to have abandoned, could be the instrument for such a policy.

One big question remains: are trade unions capable of meeting this challenge?

*Trade unions in a process of change - not of erosion*

A recent, ambitious study of the current situation of Third World unionism concludes that it is undergoing a process of erosion, and is even close to 'almost total elimination as a significant social institution' (Thomas, 1995: 3). In the view of Thomas and his fellow writers, the unions were particularly strong in Africa in the years that followed independence, and secured major economic benefits for their members by remaining in legitimate contact with the grass roots (ibid: 15); the book is implying that the trade union movement has now lost its economic, social and political power (ibid: 235).

This is based on a serious, and widely shared, misconception. It is also regrettable that a study claiming to use a rigorous scientific method (ibid: 20) should neither define the notion of erosion nor look at criteria for assessing the nature and degree of the alleged erosion. The three criteria implicit in the study - loss of trade union influence, loss of legitimacy and loss of members - are all invalid. It is true that membership has declined, but this needs to be examined with care. In most countries, members used to be automatically recruited under the 'check-off' system, and this gave a false impression of the true figures: 'Unions were widely seen as recruitment offices set up by the single parties in power' (Monga, 1994, 102). As time passed, Structural Adjustment Programmes led to numerous retrenchment measures and contributed to a further reduction in trade union membership.

There is certainly erosion if we look no further than the statistics of dues-paying members, but who exactly are we talking about? Nominal, symbolic members, or people who have freely chosen to join the union? Events of the last few years have shown conclusively that unions have spent far too long organising the formal sector (i.e. the public sector) to the exclusion of all else.

They are now paying the price for such neglect, but this particular cloud may have a silver lining. As unions are now experiencing a shortfall in contributions (in many countries, State subsidies are still linked to union docility going back to the time of the single party), they are obliged to take more interest in new areas of recruitment and, as we learn from a study of Zimbabwe in the same book as Thomas's article, the type and range of trade union membership is already expanding. For example, the ZCTU (Zimbabwe Congress of Trade Unions) has not only been able to reorganise itself, attract new categories of worker and develop alliances with other unions in civil society; it has also impacted on the process of democratisation, particularly in non-urban areas (Schiphorst, 1995, 229). Moreover, over the last few years, a great deal of effort has gone into making trade union activity appealing to women, encouraging them to join, and generally turning trade unionism into a battle zone for women's issues. Nearly all African countries now run projects that involve women. Is this erosion, or a candid acknowledgement of current reality?

Nor is it true to say that trade unions have lost their legitimacy vis-à-vis their members and workers in general; on the contrary, their legitimacy has broadened. At one time, unions in most African countries were largely integrated into the single political party, their leaders were appointed rather than elected, and trade union training consisted of dogmatism and indoctrination in equal measure. This was 'State trade unionism' rather than any form of member-led trade unionism. However, over the last five years, as Chapters 8, 11, 13 and 14 show, divorce from the single party or the government has opened up a new space for democratisation. There is an increasingly audible call for bottom-up democratic control, and trade union legitimacy and strength have grown as a result; inevitably, it has also led to multi-trade unionism, which in turn poses the question of union unity, or at least unity of action. Trade unions have moved away from an uneasy situation where they enjoyed pseudo-importance, and into a new situation where they have wrenched, or otherwise obtained, independence from political parties and governments. After decades of choosing their leaders by appointment, designation or acclamation, they are well down the road to democratisation.

To what extent have trade unions lost their influence? As we have seen, trade union structures were largely plundered by single political parties and military régimes, and unions themselves were often unable to negotiate on behalf of workers: new working conditions were announced by the political leaders, and all trade union leaders could do was applaud. Unions were neither autonomous nor democratic, let alone free. One only has to read the section on Mozambique (Chapter 11) to see what the situation was like in certain African countries only recently; the authors even wonder whether it was possible to speak of trade unionism at all in Mozambique. More generally, Chapter 3 shows that trade union influence over SAPs was almost non-existent during the 1980s, although this has begun to change over the last few years. Clearly, trade unions have come out of their corner fighting!

When people say that trade unions have almost been eliminated, they are referring to some point in the distant past and not to the last few years. In fact, for some time now, there has been no trade union erosion; in fact, unions are actually going through a period of far-reaching change. They underwent a process of fundamental transformation which weakened them, above all materially, when 'check-off' was abolished and subsidies suspended or withdrawn. That was a serious body-blow to the trade union movement, but it is not the same thing as erosion. Unions are now experiencing change; they are reorganising and taking fresh bearings. As we can see from the descriptions in this book of the situation in ten African countries, trade unions are coming to grips with problems. There is no question of them throwing in the towel.

## Trade unions and their appointment with history

Other analyses, including the work of Akwetey (1994), do not share this pessimism over the future of trade unions. Akwetey's analysis shows that unions constitute the largest force in civil society, and have major responsibility for the defence of democracy. We return to Akwetey's theories in Chapter 2. In her account of South Africa, Torres describes unions as 'schools for democracy'; here, leadership training and the knowledge and experiences acquired in the course of trade union work are key to obtaining a general democratic competence and to nurturing democratic values. She also says that, as workers gain a measure of control over their workplaces, they want to have more say in the decisions that determine their lives outside work (Torres, 1995).

The main objective of this book is to examine how trade unions can help to make democracy in Africa sustainable. Accordingly, we propose the following hypothesis: that trade unions are among the best placed to promote the effective and significant participation of workers at the workplace and in the economy, and that they thereby contribute substantially to the establishment of political democracy. When one-party or no-party States collapse - when the dictators have fled, leaving the single party dissolved and the army discredited - trade unions are the only force left standing. For all its organisational and financial shortcomings, the trade union movement constitutes a major interest group with structures scattered throughout the country; it is also typically non-ethnic in its composition. Zambia and Mali have emerged as the best known examples of trade unions to have successfully intervened in the establishment of a political democracy. However, by fighting for both trade union and human rights, unions have played a much bigger part in the process of democratisation in many other African countries. Their actions have added much substance to the defence of democracy.

However, trade unions are essentially facing the long-term challenge of how to make democracy sustainable once it has been established. The argument underpinning this study is that democracy constitutes a necessary condition for development, but that it is not enough on its own; complementary conditions are citizens' participation through civil society and workers' participation through trade unions. Unions can play a vital role in the establishment and perpetuation of democracy, particularly in economic and social matters. They are the agents of participative democracy.

The first part of this book is followed by three further chapters dealing with the African situation overall, and it then passes on to specific analyses of the situation in ten African countries. Chapter 2 describes and analyses the role that unions are playing in the transition to political democracy. It poses the question: What impact have unions had on the establishment on political democracy? It then asks the same question in reverse: What impact has the new political situation had on trade unions? Chapter 2 includes a broad range of examples.

Chapter 3 contains an examination of the contribution that democracy has made to economic development, and SAPs in particular. Trade unions speak eloquently in national and international settings when protesting against economic policy, and above all against the social consequences of structural adjustment. However, words are not enough. We need to know what practical steps trade unions are taking to have a decisive influence on the formulation and execution of economic policy.

If trade unions really wish to exert greater control over the economy, one possible answer is through participative democracy. Chapter 4 looks at the necessary conditions for the effective and significant participation of workers, and the role that unions can play in this participation.

## Note

1   Some of the arguments used in this section appear in already published material (Kester, 1992).

# 2 Trade Unions and the Process of Democratisation

OUSMANE OUMAROU SIDIBÉ AND BRIGITTE VENTURI

For many years now, a substantial literature has been given over to the theme of democratisation in Africa, but closer examination reveals a major lacuna relating to the role played by certain social players, and trade unions in particular (Buijtenhuis et al, 1995). This shortcoming has not come about by chance; indeed, the opprobrium customarily reserved for trade unions has ensured that their role in the process of democratisation is regularly disregarded. What has happened is that, over the last few decades, unions have been censured either for being the subjects of authoritarian governments or else for defending only the corporatist interests of a 'working class élite' - otherwise known as the 'labour aristocracy' (Konings, 1993) - and to the detriment of other sectors of the population, notably rural dwellers.

They have also been criticised for not carrying out certain tasks allocated to them, including duties that governments have imposed relating to their participation in the development of the nation. This negative appraisal has cast the role of trade unions in civil society in an unfavourable light, and has obstructed consideration of changes they are currently carrying out and of their potential for change. The role of civil society in general has frequently been neglected in studies of players involved in African democratisation (Buijtenhuis et al, 1995), and any consideration of the trade union contribution has been totally ignored.

However, we are now seeing a trend towards a rehabilitation of the role that African society has played in recent events concerning democratisation. It is now acknowledged that certain social groups played decisive roles in the struggle for democracy; they include students (frequently in the vanguard of democratic action), political associations and underground political parties, youth groups, human rights associations, the Church, women (who have spontaneously come onto the streets in the wake of violent repressions whose casualties have included family members), professional bodies (such as lawyers' associations) - and, of course, trade unions.

In this chapter, we assess action that the trade union movement has undertaken in the democratisation process. We do not simply study the role that trade unions have played in pro-democracy movements in different SSA countries; we also examine exactly what it was that predisposed them

19

to play such a role in the first place, and the means that they employed. In particular, we look at their current strengths and weaknesses to illuminate the role they are currently playing in the establishment of true sustainable democracy in Africa.

It is a difficult subject, if only because of the paucity of available information, and the empirical nature of what little documentation exists. However, we have endeavoured to highlight what has happened, and hope to throw new light on trade union activity in SSA Africa.

## Why have trade unions often been key players in the democratisation process?

The trade union movement's commitment to democracy over the last few years has not been evenly spread across the whole continent of Africa; the impact has also varied substantially from one country to the next. However, an impressive number of trade unions in many countries have been actively involved.

This activity has not come out of nothing. The potential was always there, and in some countries it has flourished thanks to a favourable political climate and circumstances. We shall now attempt to understand the factors that positively determined the role of the trade unions in certain countries during the process of democratisation.

In addition to the democratic principles that underpin trade unionism - their implementation often leaves much to be desired, but let us leave that to one side for the moment - there are three major factors which, in our view, explain the commitment of African unions to the struggle for democracy: long experience of struggle, a massive potential for organisation and action, and the expectation that democratisation will have a positive outcome for workers and unions.

The African trade union movement developed slowly as a result of hostile colonial legislation and a numerically small proletariat. For example, the right to organise was not recognised in Ghana and Nigeria until 1941; elsewhere, in West Africa and French Equatorial Africa, the Popular Front granted the right to organise in 1936. The establishment of real unions was also impeded by numerous obstacles that were placed in the way of freedom of association; these included an obligation to be literate to set up a union, and discrimination between French citizens in the Senegal's Four Communes and the indigenous population. In fact, the trade union movement did not properly come of age until the Code du travail des Territoires d'outre-mer (Overseas Territories Labour Code) was drawn up in 1952. In Belgian territories, the right to organise had not been recognised until 1946.

*Obstacles robustly countered*

Trade unions ran into numerous difficulties almost as soon as they were set up. For a long time, their financial base and ability to mobilise workers were undermined by low membership; this reflected not only under-industrialisation and sluggish economic performance, but also a fear of management reprisals. Furthermore, the lack of training of union officers among miners and skilled and unskilled manual workers proved a handicap in the context of drawing up basic union policy; this was particularly significant at a time when French unions were exporting their ideological feuds to Africa, and to francophone Africa in particular.

Despite these drawbacks, the combativeness of African unions never faltered. Given their numerical weakness, they concentrated their efforts on key workplaces, and were responsible for a number of major actions including indefinite General Strikes in Nigeria in 1945 and the Gold Coast (later Ghana) in 1950, and the Dakar-Niger railway workers' strike of 1947.

Throughout these now legendary strikes, African workers demonstrated a capacity for tenacity and solidarity that took their colonial masters by surprise. Indeed, it was in the course of these strikes that African nationalism was developed, and trusting relationships were forged between union and political leaders brought together by a common struggle for political independence. To take just one example, at the 1957 Congress of the Rassemblement Démocratique Africain (RDA - African Democratic Assembly) held in Bamako, the delegate of the Union Générale des Travailleurs Africains (UGTA - General Union of African Workers), Alioune Cissé, looked forward to the day when an alliance of all democratic forces would rid the continent of colonial rule; it was this that African nationalists and trade unionists saw as the root-cause of all their misfortunes. The harsh punishments that trade unionists were forced to endure (e.g. arbitrary relocations, imprisonment and torture) only stiffened their resolve to challenge both their colonial rulers and, after independence, authoritarian African governments.

*A combination of allegiance and resistance*

The way that trade unions were inextricably bound to single political parties through a process of incorporation is just one aspect of African trade union history. The long union struggle for emancipation is another.

Firstly, we need to remember that governments in some countries never succeeded in incorporating the unions; a typical example is Burkina Faso, formerly Upper Volta. This country has known nothing but trade union pluralism, and over the years the unions have been responsible for toppling a number of governments through strikes and popular demonstrations; these slowly weakened the governments in question, and prepared the ground for military coups d'état. The chapter on Burkina Faso in Part II shows how, after a period of marked hostility between unions and government following independence, the trade union movement was successful in developing unity of action and in creating the conditions for the fall of the first two Republics in 1966 and 1974. A General Strike in 1975 calling for a pluralist democracy led to the adoption of a multi-party Constitution and pluralist elections. In fact, the Burkina Faso trade union movement frequently made a name for itself by rounding on the government of the day in the defence of democracy and human rights.

Individual unions were frequently divided on ideological grounds, but they managed to broker agreements in the struggle for democracy, and sometimes even constructed approaches which, in more recent years, have proved useful in the campaign to democratise the whole country. In the Sudan, as a later chapter on this country shows, trade unions have often been involved in bringing the government down, and in the Congo, too, the most important changes since independence have been instigated by the unions (Tedga, 1991: 85). Unions in other countries have attempted to a greater or lesser extent to establish an identity and articulate their autonomy from government. For instance, as the chapter on Mali describes, the Union Nationale des Travailleurs Maliens (UNTM - National Union of Malian Workers) was one of the most important organisations to condemn the military coup d'état of 1968; as a result, the centre was closed down and many of its leaders were thrown into prison. However, even though it could rely on its 'responsible participation' policy, the single party founded by General Moussa Traoré, the Union Démocratique du Peuple Malien (UDPM - Democratic Union of Malian People) never succeeded in fully incorporating the UNTM. UNTM members who did not hold mainstream opinions consistently opposed the military régime and called for a democratic opening. For example, after the referendum on the 2 June 1974 Constitution, which also established the UDPM as the single Constitutional party of government, trade unionists denounced it as an 'electoral farce'; they were sentenced to long terms of imprisonment in the Malian desert for their pains. Nonetheless, the UNTM continued to be feared by government, and this partly explains its role in the struggle for democracy and the demise of the single party in March 1991.

## Unions did not take things for granted

South Africa is, of course, the most celebrated and most striking example of trade union resistance to a hostile government. Ghana is equally fascinating, and the chapter devoted to that country details the relations between trade unions and the State. They enjoyed a close working relationship at the time of independence, but that did not stop the government from amending the freedom of association law in 1965, with the ultimate intention of limiting the right to strike. Many unions, particularly those with membership on the railways, protested vigorously. Then in 1971, the confederation of Ghanaian unions, the Trades Union Congress (TUC), locked horns with the government of the 2nd Republic on the question on minimum pay and wage differentials. This confrontation led the government to push emergency legislation through parliament dissolving the TUC. The crisis created the conditions for the 1972 military coup d'état, and for the suspension to be lifted.

Unions did not take things for granted even in countries where they had close links with the single party. Mozambique is an exception, but later chapters show that, in countries like Cape Verde, Tanzania, Togo and Benin where unions were incorporated into the State apparatus, brave men and women continued to fight overtly and covertly for democracy and freedoms, often putting their own lives at risk. Their often unsung heroism helped to keep the flame of liberty alight, and ensured that progressive forces stood united. Nascent democracies owe them a great debt of gratitude. Their work deserves to be chronicled in great detail; sadly, however, external forces are all too often given excessive credit for establishing democracy in Africa.

## Great potential for organisation and action

In many African countries, unions have ensured a united struggle for democracy. To a significant extent, this ability of the trade union movement to keep the various components of civil society in harness comes from its potential for organisation and action.

### *Trade union membership in strategic sectors of the economy*

Union members in some countries work in strategic sectors of the economy, and have therefore been able to bring a substantial proportion of economic and social activity to its knees. Good examples of this have occurred in Zambia, the Congo, Niger and South Africa.

The prime example is Zambia. During the period of political democratisation, the trade union movement, which is affiliated to the Zambia Congress of Trade Unions (ZCTU), was extremely strong. In fact, it is one of the strongest in the whole of Africa; its influence is based on its large membership (25% of the country's total workforce of 352,000 in 1990) and strength in mining regions. The latter enjoy exceptional strategic importance as copper mines account for 90% of State revenues (Simutanyi, 1992).

The Congolese trade union movement, and its national centre, the Confédération Syndicale Congolaise (CSC - Congolese Trade Union Confederation), also has substantial membership and wields great influence in the towns and cities; the vast majority of the 73,000 State employees are union members. What is more, the Congo is one of Africa's most urbanised countries - almost 60% of the population lives in the towns and cities - and CSC decisions therefore exert a considerable influence on the economy and the government (De Jong, 1993).

The Union des Syndicats des Travailleurs du Niger (USTN - Workers' Trade Unions of Niger) has been a leading force in the campaign for multipartyism in that country; much of its strength lies in the fact that nearly all civil servants ('Le Monde' of 7 February 1995 quotes a figure of 39,000) are members. In Mali, union premises became the headquarters of the campaign to bring down the régime of Moussa Traoré. They were also the meeting-place of the democratic movement's coordinating group; this was made up of associations and organisations fighting for democratisation, and included political associations, bodies representing youth and lawyers, trade unions and human rights organisations. The union headquarters was also where preparations were made for marches and other demonstrations, and was the venue for numerous meetings. In short, the UNTM acted as coordinator and protector to the democratic movement (Chapter 10).

Authoritarian régimes sought to keep trade union activities and structures under control through new labour legislation, decentralisation policies and State funding, but paradoxically this endowed the movement with an organisational capacity that it was subsequently able to make use of (Akwetey, 1994).

*A nationwide structure*

Another factor that explains the influence of the trade union movement is that, unlike other social groups that operate predominantly in capital cities, unions are frequently established the length and breadth of the country. This means that they can call on thousands of workers from all over the nation for marches, meetings and other events. Through the principles of democratic centralism which provide the basis for the African trade union movement, unions have had little difficulty in ensuring that decisions were taken up at different levels of individual organisations and implemented by the appropriate bodies.

The trade union movement's capacity for mobilisation is perfectly illustrated in Mali, where the unions are among the most important organisations of civil society (see Chapter 10). The authors of that chapter describe how Operation 'Ghost Towns', launched by the opposition in 1994, fell by the wayside through lack of trade union support. By contrast, the indefinite General Strike called by the UNTM in March 1991, which had a turnout of close to 100%, led to the army's decision to intervene and arrest General Moussa Traoré. It is worth noting in passing that strike calls have also been supported by self-employed workers such as artisans and shopkeepers.

In certain countries, the potential for trade union activity has not been fulfilled. There are a number of reasons for this, and this is not an appropriate place to examine them in full. However, it is worth looking briefly at a disturbing example of trade union impotence which occurred when the Togolese government stepped up coercive action. Chapter 14 describes how a well-supported General Strike lasting several months in 1992 failed to depose President Eyadema. The Togolese army largely supported the President, and crushed demonstrations with the utmost brutality; as a result, Eyadema has been able to hang onto power, although his control has, to all intents and purposes, ceased to exist in terms of either legitimacy or effectiveness. The same happened in the Sudan where, as Chapter 14 shows, the trade union movement, after occupying a position of strength for many decades, was eliminated by the military government in 1992.

## An expectation that democratisation will produce positive outcomes

Trade unions agree to make sacrifices in the struggle for democracy because they feel the latter offers a framework that is well suited to, not to say essential for, for the exercise of their freedoms. The right to organise and freedom of association are tangible barometers of the state of democracy in a given country. Unions have also observed that democratisation and the establishment of a pluralist government provide opportunities to halt the repression they have endured for decades, to obtain institutional autonomy, and to participate fully in national decision-making fora, particularly those that deal with economic matters.

### The need for autonomy and participation

For many years, the majority of African trade unions have had to endure State control and a manipulative 'responsible participation' policy that crudely incorporates unions into the single party. Calls for trade union autonomy are fairly meaningless in such a climate. In fact, the desire for autonomy grew as relations between the unions and the State soured.

Additionally, the crisis of the State's legitimacy, the economic crisis and popular resistance to SAP-imposed restrictions slowly built up a conjunctural climate that led to a flourishing of trade union activity.

As for the trade union demand for autonomy and for participation in decision-making bodies, a debate has opened up between those who see it as a simple matter of the unions disengaging from the life of the nation, and others, like Akwetey (1994), who claim that it shows the unions were hoping for a change of government to realise their political and social aspirations.

Akwetey's argument is interesting because it insists that democratisation may also be analyzed from the viewpoint of existing relations between corporatist régimes and unions; he demonstrates that, even when they are incorporated into the apparatus of the State, unions have been able to develop organisationally thanks to centralised structures, legislation and State funding. Limitations imposed by corporatist governments on the organisational activities of centralised trade unions have caused major tensions, and led unions to step up their demands for more autonomy and participation in decision-making at the highest governmental level.

Akwetey uses Zambian and Ghanaian examples to develop his thesis. Trade union demands and struggles have sometimes resulted in corporatist régimes bringing in reforms aimed at introducing more democracy. Then, when these governments tried to re-establish control over the unions - or, failing that, when they sought at least to undermine them by a strategy of decentralisation - the centres found their unity under threat, and their desire to participate in the country's main decision-making bodies blocked. This reverse further fuelled their demands for autonomy, and accordingly encouraged them to form alliances with other groups opposed to authoritarian régimes. Akwetey's thesis, which is based on events in Ghana and Zambia, finds support in the chapters on Cape Verde and Tanzania.

## Trade union centres shaken up by grass-roots activity

Responsible participation clearly caused the trade union movement to ossify in some countries. It also helped to isolate leaders - already seen as corrupt, and thought to have been 'bought off' by the government - from the rank and file; ordinary trade union members had nothing to show for this superficial participation. A deepening of the economic crisis, together with the introduction of SAPs and the impact they had on jobs and purchasing power, ultimately placed union leaders in a totally untenable position as far as their members were concerned.

In practice, it was impossible for them to remain on various decision-making bodies of State - such as National Commissions, political bureaux of single parties, and even the government and National Assembly in the case of the CNTT in Togo and the CNTS in Senegal - and at the same time argue against the social consequences of the SAP. It was also becoming increasingly difficult for union leaders to carry on being government mouthpieces: on a continent that had already become too used to the all-embracing State (le tout État), public enterprises, which had long been (inaccurately) presented as belonging to the people, were in the process of being dismantled. Often it was the rank and file who urged the hierarchy to abandon responsible participation and seek more autonomy through political pluralism and the rule of law. Survival instinct also told union leaders to distance themselves from governments if they wanted their pronouncements to have any credibility. In Mali, for instance, members of the UNTM Executive Bureau only decided to commit themselves to the battle for democracy at the last moment, and even then it was only because of grass-roots pressure. In the Congo, Jean-Michel Bokamba Yangouma, General Secretary of the Confédération Syndicale Congolaise (CSC - Congolese Trade Union Confederation), announced on 20 February 1990 that multipartyism had no place in his country; only a few months later, his centre called a General Strike to demand the multiparty system he had previously spoken out against (Tedga, 1991: 93).

*Democracy for global change*

Given the colossal economic problems facing their countries, trade unions hope that democratisation will at last enable them to participate significantly in a better managed economy and help to improve workers' living conditions. It is nowadays accepted that part of the explanation for the disappointing economic results of African countries is a bureaucratic form of economic management that has excluded concertation with social and economic players, particularly employers and workers. The lack of a consensus on economic programmes has a disheartening effect on economic players, whereas involving trade unions in wide-ranging concertation exercises helps them to win members' support, and guarantees that the programmes will be successful. Democracy can reverse negative trends and introduce more rigour and greater transparency into managing the economy. In short, trade unionists believe that it creates an ideal environment for improving workers' conditions of employment.

To put it in another way, trade unions argue that socio-economic development is closely linked to democracy, and that participation is a vital ingredient. Having endured poorly managed economies for so long, trade unions are now beginning to see that they need a change of government if they are going to win improved living conditions for workers. Moreover, they must install democracy and open up spaces for freedom if they are ever to facilitate serious negotiations within a labour relations framework. As the trade unions see it, therefore, the struggle for democracy is tantamount to a struggle for global change.

## The role of the trade unions in the process of democratisation

As we have seen, trade union action aimed at achieving democracy goes back to a time before the 1980s. In the preceding decades, unions may have had little room for manoeuvre, but they still managed to organise strikes in defence of workers' interests and political demands. In this way, they demonstrated their rejection of corrupt, élitist, authoritarian post-colonial States.

Trade unions responded decisively to the events of the late 1980s and early 1990s; this time, the climate was more favourable, and their action was often very effective. It is no exaggeration to say that trade unions frequently helped to rid countries of their single-party systems and bring down authoritarian régimes: the trade union movement played a significant role in seven of the eleven countries where the process of democratisation led to multi-party elections and the possibility of political alternation. The first countries to hold multi-party elections were Benin, Zambia, Mali, Niger, the Congo, the Central African Republic and South Africa.

In other countries such as Côte d'Ivoire, Burkina Faso, Gabon and Togo, where pluralist elections did not result in political alternation, trade unions still played an important role in the opposition movement. However, when they found themselves caught in a crossfire between angry workers and the government, they predictably sought to recapture their independence and establish autonomy from authoritarian governments and the single party. In this way, trade unions influenced events from the outset by campaigning on two fronts: firstly, by orchestrating dissatisfaction, and supporting popular and workers' demands for democracy and the rule of law; and secondly, by calling for trade union autonomy from the State and the single party.

Much of the struggle for political change took place at street level. These protest movements were inspired by economic and political hardships in equal measure, and the unions often played important roles in the fields of organisation, orchestration and coordination. This maximised the impact of the protest actions, marches, strikes and demonstrations, and governments came under considerable pressure as a result.

The demand for autonomy made by trade union centres affiliated to the single party, or controlled by the State, was of particular importance in that it underlined the extent to which the State faced a crisis of legitimacy. The very structures of the State were now under attack. Was it not a sign of great weakness and of internal contradiction for a régime to find itself disowned by one of its quasi-institutional props? Unions employed all manner of verbal and written means to make their views known in the media, for example using Congresses and addressing open letters to Heads of State. This enabled them to increase public awareness and keep governments under pressure.

## *The actions of trade unions affiliated to one-party régimes*

Single trade union centres hitherto affiliated to the single party, particularly in the Congo, Mali and Niger, have announced their autonomy from the single party; they have also pressed their governments to carry out political reforms aimed at establishing multipartyism and holding elections. Their demands were all the more effective for being backed up by mass action.

We have already referred briefly to Mali; the trade union contribution to the fall of the Moussa Traoré government is described in the second part of this book. In the Congo, the government of Sassou Nguesso announced a series of measures in July 1990 aimed at democratisation and the establishment of political pluralism; however, the government simultaneously outlawed people wishing to found their own parties prior to the Extraordinary Congress of the single party, the PCT (Parti Congolais du Travail - Congolese Labour Party). At that point, the Confédération Syndicale Congolaise (CSC) announced its independence from the government and called for a review of certain economic measures and a National Conference. The response of the Parti Congolais du Travail (PCT - Congolese Labour Party) was characteristically blunt: reject the independence demanded by the CSC, and appoint a new leadership. The PCT subsequently halted the CSC's move towards democratisation. The response of workers was no less unambiguous; it took the form of a General Strike that shut the economy down for several days and forced the President to give way on several political, economic and social counts. Three days later, the PCT Central Committee decided on the immediate introduction of multipartyism, and on a National Conference to which political parties, associations and religious organisations were to be invited (Tedga, 1991: 85-94; BFTU (Botswana Federation of Trade Unions)/ICFTU, 1991: 29).

The Union des Syndicats des Travailleurs du Niger (USTN - National Union of Niger Workers) has long been in the vanguard of the struggle for multi-party government in that country. The union was brought brutally face to face with the crisis of the 1980s and the government's austerity plan (together with the innumerable retrenchments that accompanied it) when school and high school students took part in demonstrations and strikes in February 1990.

The excessive violence that marked those few days (the 'Kennedy Bridge events') sparked off a fresh series of demonstrations, and throughout the rest of the year, the USTN organised numerous General Strikes in protest against the government's economic austerity measures. The union also campaigned for democratisation and called for the perpetrators of crimes and human rights violations to be punished; offences of this type included the violent repression of demonstrations and strikes and the arbitrary arrests of USTN leaders. In his 1 May speech, the USTN General Secretary, Laouali Moutari, appealed for political pluralism and demanded a debate on the political and economic situation.

In November of the same year, the Niger economy was paralysed by a well-supported General Strike. The USTN-USN (Union des Scolaires Nigériens - Niger Union of Teachers) alliance forced President Ali Seïbou to beat a retreat, and on 15 November he agreed to a plan to introduce multi-party government; he also called a National Conference for May 1991, and accepted the effective setting up of political parties. The USTN argued strongly for a role in the Conference preparations, and was a key player in the decision-making (Tedga, 1991: 144-146; BFTU/ICFTU, 1991: 29; Kotoudi, 1993).

*The activities of independent unions*

Independent unions were in the vanguard of the struggle for democracy in other countries, too. This was often because workers had become frustrated by the submissiveness and inertia of the single trade union centre affiliated to the single party, and had set up new independent unions; these all played leading roles in the protest movements. New unions were formed outside the single national organisations in Benin, Côte d'Ivoire, Senegal, the Central African Republic and Togo, and fought alongside workers in the defence of democracy. Occasionally, single trade union centres participated in the protests and strikes, but they tended to join late in the day.

In Benin, trade union mobilisation and union criticism of the Kérékou régime had their roots in an internal, procedural battle with the leadership of the UNSTB (Union Nationale des Syndicats des Travailleurs du Bénin - National Union of Beninese Trade Unions), the centre affiliated to the party in power; the dispute focused on allegations that the leadership was a government mouthpiece. The wildcat strikes of 1989 were a reaction to persistent economic stagnation aggravated by the rigours of the first SAP, and were organised by unrecognised parallel organisations that succeeded in setting up coordination structures. These provided the basis for an alternative trade union organisation, which ultimately emerged as a key government player (Banégas, 1995: 34-36).

These movements for independence and disaffiliation from the single national centre were therefore major catalysts in another movement - the one that brought down the government. In fact, the failure of UNSTB leaders to come up with any response persuaded strikers they had to restructure the political system totally and introduce institutional pluralism (Allen, 1992: 48). After a turbulent year of incessant strikes - particularly among teachers - and bloody repression, the government was forced to make concessions. These included abolishing single-party government, abandoning Marxism as the official ideology, and calling a National Conference of representative bodies to discuss the social and economic situation and the new Constitution. Researchers who have studied the process of democratisation in Benin (Allen 1992; Banégas, 1995) and the authors of the chapter on Benin in this book all agree that trade union action was decisive in helping the people to understand what democracy was all about.

The main trade union centre in Côte d'Ivoire, the Union Générale des Travailleurs de la Côte-d'Ivoire (UGTCI - General Union of Côte d'Ivoire Workers), was first affiliated to the single party in 1962, but took no part in the process of democratisation that led to de facto political pluralism in May 1990; multipartyism had been provided for in the Constitution, but was never implemented. By contrast, a number of autonomous centres were leading lights in the early demonstrations that preceded the political reforms. These actions included a protest march against the austerity policy and civil servants' pay cuts in April 1990. Demonstrators taking part were brutally attacked and trade union leaders were arrested, but one month later, political pluralism was established (De Jong, 1993: 20 & 53).

After a ten-year 'trade union truce' in the Central African Republic, the unions re-formed in 1988 and, alongside other movements committed to the defence of democracy, played an important role in events that marked the democratic process over a period of three years. In November 1990, the Union Syndicale des Travailleurs de Centrafrique (USTC - Union of CAF Workers) launched a general strike with economic and political objectives for the first time in its history. It produced no concrete gains; however, it made people realise they had power, and that accelerated the democratic process.

Fresh strikes were organised in the spring of 1991 following the arrests of political opponents; action began with teachers, who were owed considerable sums of back pay, and then spread to the private sector. Support also came from students who called for a resumption of Operation 'Ghost Towns'; this proved extremely successful. At that point, the government was obliged to release a number of political opponents, and it also introduced a law sanctioning the setting up of political parties; however, shortly afterwards, and despite a barrage of international protest, a number of trade union leaders were arrested, tried and imprisoned. All trade union activities were banned for a time - a sign of the extent to which the government feared the power of the unions - but in the end it was obliged to take democratic reforms on board. Constitutional reform was announced in 1993, and Presidential elections in September of the same year propelled Ange Patassé into power in place of André Kolingba (Tedga, 1991: 139-144; BFTU/ICFTU, 1991: 31; De Jong, 1993: 9-13).

## Alliances for democracy

In all the examples set out above, the ability of trade unions to forge alliances with other democratic forces was decisive. In Mali, we saw how the UNTM made common cause with a large democracy movement and allowed its meeting rooms to be used as the movement's headquarters. In Togo, an alliance was made between new unions which then formed themselves into the Collective of Independent Trade Unions; one of its objectives was to attend the National Conference due to take place in Lomé in July 1991. All of these unions were strong enough in combination to threaten a strike in the ports and the communications sector, and this was the springboard they needed to participate in the Conference. In the Central African Republic, the unions joined forces with political groups and student movements in calling for democratic reform and a National Conference. And in Niger, the alliance between the USTN and the teachers' organisation, the USN, played a key role in the introduction of multipartyism.

The trade union demand in certain countries for a National Conference, and for participation in the new democratic structures of transitional or newly elected governments, is clear evidence of the desire of some organisations to be fully involved in the affairs of the nation.

The purposes of holding a National Conference, a phenomenon peculiar to francophone countries, were twofold: firstly to ensure that the government did not manipulate the democratic process, and secondly to bring all players in civil society and the political opposition together and reach agreement on the implementation of democratic institutions; the latter included the conditions and operation of elections. The trade unions, for their part, saw it as an opportunity to hold discussions on changes they considered essential for the trade union movement, such as the right to organise and the basis for a labour relations structure. The National Conference in Benin, which is now held up by many countries as a model, was attended by numerous organisations of civil society including trade unions, but the official centre did not participate. The Conference led directly to the demise of General Kérékou, although he again became Head of State following the Presidential elections of March 1996. Trade unions also took part in National

Conferences in other countries including Zaïre, Gabon, Niger, the Congo and Togo; elsewhere, for example in the Central African Republic, Conferences were manipulated by the government and, in the end, unions refused to take part.

*Participation in the new democratic structures*

Trade union action did not always stop there. Some unions have been actively involved in the establishment of democratic institutions; examples include Burkina Faso where the unions took part in drawing up the Constitution of the 4th Republic, and Mali where three UNTM officials sat on the Transition Committee that ruled the country as it edged towards democracy. The Vice-President of the Transition Committee was the UNTM General Secretary, and the union's representatives had to take over the reins of government jointly with the military when political associations became over-preoccupied with the elections. Critically, the trade union centre was able to act as conciliator between the numerous claim-making movements that sprang up in various large Malian enterprises during the transitional period.

In Niger, too, the USTN participated in a number of transitional governments, and appears to have influenced several government decisions relating to such matters as the Tuareg crisis and demands emanating from the Niger army (Kotoudi, 1993); when transition came to an end, the USTN argued that a special forum should carry out an objective, critical assessment of the period. However, as the events of February 1996 showed, the USTN's impact on political life was such that its radical ideas, particularly on the SAP and the payment of public sector salaries, had a negative effect on the operation of the democratic and political life of the nation.

*Trade unions 'in power'*

It is impossible to talk of the influence that trade unions had on the processes of democratisation without reference to South Africa and Zambia. In both countries, unions forged close alliances with opposition parties, and in the case of Zambia they were involved in founding a political party that came to power in the wake of pluralist elections.

The example of Zambia and the role played by the trade union movement in democratisation is well documented (Rakner, 1992; Akwetey, 1994), but it is worth taking another look at them if only because the case of Zambia clearly shows how union activity on the political stage was shaped by limited trade union autonomy and a low level of institutional representation in labour relations.

The single-party régime had worked hard at keeping the trade union movement under control since 1972, and had hoped to convert it into an official wing of the party, in the manner of other grass roots organisations and traditional institutions. The Zambian movement, constituted by the Zambia Congress of Trade Unions (ZCTU), steadfastly refused to be controlled. After years of struggle against incorporation into the government and the one-party structures, the ZCTU had become a social and political force to be reckoned with.

The government made one more attempt to undermine the ZCTU's organisational cohesion by the introduction of new labour law. The ZCTU saw it as a direct threat to its very existence and this, according to Akwetey, forced the Confederation to call for the restoration of multipartyism on 30 December 1989. A conference then brought groups opposed to the Kaunda government together, and it decided to form the Movement for Multi-Party Democracy (MMD). The ZCTU had a big hand in setting up the MMD, and placed its organisational structures and communications network at the Movement's disposal; this enabled the campaign to extend across the whole country. During the following year, 1991, there were numerous demonstrations organised by unions and by students, in particular, these included mobilisations triggered by a 100% rise in the price of cornflour and an attempted coup d'état; the Kaunda government responded by announcing a General Election for October of that year. It proved a triumph for Frederick Chiluba, General Secretary of the ZCTU and leader of the MMD.

South Africa (see Chapter 5) provides a different, and quite remarkable, scenario in which the strength of the trade union movement lay in its grass-roots organisations and in its alliance with the political opposition. COSATU (Congress of South African Trade Unions) was founded in 1985 and consistently linked the political battle to rid the country of apartheid and the struggle to defend workers' interests. It was affiliated to the United Democratic Front (UDF), which acted as a front for the ANC during the time the latter was outlawed, and was a member of a tripartite alliance with the ANC and the banned SACP (South African Communist Party).

Observers agree that COSATU was mainly responsible for keeping the democratic movement alive during the State of Emergency from mid-1986 to mid-1988, and organised unions played a central role in bringing the State of Emergency to a close; at no stage was the State able to enforce the banning of COSATU in 1988. In the workplace, the Shop Stewards' Councils (shopfloor councils) that COSATU established played a crucial role in the day-to-day resistance of the government's authoritarian practices; they were frequently the first line of defence against repression, and saved many leaders from imprisonment (Baskin, 1991: 450).

COSATU's campaign against the new labour legislation carried the battle to the government, and even after February 1990, when the ANC was unbanned and Nelson Mandela was freed, COSATU maintained the pressure and the whole country was convulsed by a long series of strikes. When non-racial elections were held in 1994, COSATU played a key role in encouraging people to vote for the ANC, and contributed its own members as part of the triple alliance. The union also organised education sessions inside companies (Buhlungu, 1994).

This picture of trade union activity should not blind us to the fact that the trade union movement often played a less influential role. In some countries, although unions helped to destabilise the government, trade union action was much less visible.

*Less spectacular trade union activity - but no less important for all that*

Little is known about the activities of trade unions in Mauritania, but the national centre was nonetheless behind a number of political reforms promoting democracy. Relations between the Union des Travailleurs Mauritaniens (UTM - Union of Mauritanian Workers) and the military government had been stormy since 1978, but the union went onto the offensive in June 1991 when its General Secretary appealed to the government for political reforms and a National Conference. His appeal was accompanied by demands for improved living conditions and by pay claims on behalf of civil servants.

When the negotiations came to nothing, the national centre organised a short General Strike; a number of strikers were arrested, but the action helped to increase the pressure on a government now coming under pressure from opposition groups to stand down. One month later, in July 1991, a referendum led to a new Constitution that brought in political pluralism and granted greater freedom of expression and communication. In January 1992, Colonel Maaouya Sid'Ahmed Ould Taya, who had been Head of State since the coup d'état of 1984, was democratically elected President of Mauritania. Then, following lengthy, internal debates that the UTM held throughout the summer of 1991, the General Secretary, who faced criticism for playing politics, was forced to resign. With that, trade union action ground to a halt (De Jong, 1993: 48).

The Zimbabwean union confederation, the Zimbabwe Congress of Trade Unions, was established in 1980, the year of the country's independence. President Mugabe tried to integrate it into his political party during the 1980s, but the ZCTU came under pressure from its strongest federations and robustly protected and nurtured its autonomy. In order to achieve internal democracy, the ZCTU acquired a more professional and credible leadership, and set up regional structures with a view to dealing more effectively with workers' problems at the workplace. It also fought off an attempt by the government to co-opt union leaders, and adopted a position of strict neutrality during elections. The ZCTU also became increasingly critical of the government on economic and political matters, notably by openly condemning the government's repression of the student movement's campaign against corruption and the single-party régime. Owing to the ZCTU's sparse membership - public sector workers, for instance, were not allowed to join trade unions - and the weakness of its alliances with other organisations, the trade union movement was not able to play a decisive role in the country's democratisation; as a result, the ruling party, that is to say the single party, did not feel greatly threatened by its existence (Schiphorst, 1995; Raftopoulos, 1992).

It is not really possible to speak in terms of democratisation in the Sudan at the present time, but admirable efforts were made in this direction between 1985 and 1989 and the unions played an important role in them. Chapter 12 shows how the trade union movement, constituted in the Sudan Workers' Trade Union Federation (SWTUF), was instrumental in bringing down the authoritarian régime of Jaafar Nimieri, and fought hard to sustain the fragile level of democratisation that ensued; it also involved itself closely in the national process of decision-making by putting its signature to a Social Contract. The coup d'état of 1989 aimed to put a stop to the numerous strikes, and neutralise trade union action by banning unions - and political parties - altogether. The government that emerged after the coup d'état unified the trade union movement, and attempted to control it from the inside by organising elections by consensus. With the Federation now gagged, an illegal Sudanese trade union movement was set up in exile, and fought alongside opposition parties for the re-establishment of pluralist democracy.

*Trade union action under the "cosh"*

Trade unions that sought to establish democracy met with brutal repression in many countries; one such example is Nigeria, although the efforts of the country's trade unions have not slackened in recent years. Shortly before it was disbanded in 1988, the Nigerian trade union confederation, the Nigerian Labour Congress (NLC) tried to found a workers' party in order to play a leadership role in the transition to a multi-form, democratic society. However, when the 1993 election results were annulled, the unions attracted the attention of the military both by supporting a campaign for democracy run by a united front of human rights organisations and activists, and by organising broad-based strikes that took in other groups in addition to workers. This led to the implementation of a number of measures that the trade unions had been demanding, but it did not secure the release of the elected President, Moshood Abiola. Successive governments have responded to this trade union activity by persistently arresting its leaders, sentencing them to long terms of imprisonment, including life imprisonment, and arresting people who call for their release (Konings, 1993; Barrett, 1994).

Lastly, the Ghanaian trade union centre, the Ghana Trades Union Congress (GTUC), appears to have played no significant role in the movement for multi-party democracy between 1989 and 1992; what is more, its decision not to build alliances with forces opposing the Rawlings régime attracted criticism on the grounds that it deprived the country of any strong democratic movement that might have brought the government down. In the event, just as the campaign for pluralist elections was getting under way in the autumn of 1992, the GTUC rules were changed, and as a result the union was no longer able to make alliances or give official support to any political party with electoral ambitions. The decision was motivated by the lessons of the union's earlier political experience, and the GTUC decided that it would be more effective if it remained aloof from any link with political parties.

However, a number of observers, including Akwetey (Akwetey, 1994) and the authors of the chapter on Ghana in this book, reject the notion that trade unions did little to establish democracy. They argue that the unions tried to change the Constitutional rules from the inside, and sought to extend their scope for taking part in national decision-making processes through collective bargaining and other forms of representation. In fact, the GTUC was relatively successful in redefining the terms of its interaction with the government of the Provisional National Defence Council (PNDC), and in this way guaranteed its autonomy and institutional representation, particularly in labour relations. The PNDC believed that coercion was a legitimate form of government, and it was also becoming increasingly aware of the GTUC's organisational skills. Fearful that violent confrontation might jeopardise the adjustment process, the government tried to re-establish good relations with the more powerful urban groups, and the GTUC in particular. As a result, the GTUC achieved its objectives, and did not thereafter feel it was appropriate to involve itself any further in the democratisation process in terms of national policy.

All of these examples provide evidence of impressive trade union participation in the process of democratisation. They must now show that their activities are not limited to democratisation and that they are working for the installation of sustainable democracy.

## A new trade union dynamic

Today, the African trade union movement stands at a decisive turning point. True, most African countries enjoy one form of democracy or another; true, there are more spaces for freedom than there used to be, and that can only help to promote trade union action. Moreover, in countries characterised by the rule of law, and in which fundamental freedoms are respected, trade unions can (in principle) act freely to defend workers' rights. However, it would be a serious error to imagine that the battle is won. In the new dynamic now taking shape in Africa, the numerous challenges that trade unions are now having to confront are possibly more decisive than those of the past.

Breaking off relations with the single party brought autonomy; however, it also caused funds to dry up because newly elected governments often terminated existing systems of compulsory contributions, subsidies and other benefits. Burundi provides a good example of the impact of democratisation on the trade union movement. The country's trade union federation, the Union des Travailleurs du Burundi (UTB - Union of Burundi Workers), broke free from the single party in order to become an autonomous democratic union in the new pluralist democracy; it won its autonomy in 1990. The UTB had previously had a car fleet, a team of paid full-time officials, offices in every region of the country, and a system of all members paying their contributions by 'check-off'. Then, in the space of a few days, the union lost all of its income when the 'check-off' arrangement and State subsidies were withdrawn; what is more, the UTB no longer had any transport, the party having taken back all the vehicles the union had had at its disposal. The officials even had to look for new jobs, and trade union work continued, mostly in the evenings and at weekends, in a rented family flat in Bujumbura (APADEP Study Visit, 1991).

Democratisation has had serious consequences for African trade unions over and above the withdrawal of union facilities. Key issues requiring a response from the trade union movement include the setting up of autonomous unions and concurrent trade union centres (sometimes with government blessing), the demand for greater internal democracy inside unions themselves, and (in the context of the rule of law) an expanded form of freedom of association for which not all trade unionists were necessarily prepared. Unions had grown accustomed to working within a monolithic, dictatorial framework; it had encouraged them to develop strategies for defensive struggle which bordered on illegality. Now, they had to adopt a more open, more offensive strategy of action: this involved using both the legal ways and means provided by the rule of law, and the communications and management techniques used by governments and employers.

*Does freedom of association really exist?*

In strictly legal terms, freedom of association is recognised in nearly all Constitutions. However, in a number of countries, such as Benin, there are no laws and regulations backing up the conditions and operation of the right to organise and the right to strike, particularly as far as civil servants are concerned. Legislation in force in Chad and Niger prior to democratisation was rejected by the unions, and there was a similar response in Mali to a minimum service standard that workers had to provide in the event of a strike. More worryingly, existing law is sometimes breached by certain government departments, and unions are subjected to repressive measures that are a throwback to earlier times.

As an ICFTU publication reveals, government control or incorporation of trade unions appears to have continued after democratisation (ICFTU, 1995). Countries in this category include Angola, Burundi, Cameroon, the Congo, Ethiopia, Gabon, Kenya, Mali, Mauritania, Mozambique, Niger, Nigeria, Rwanda, the Seychelles, Somalia, Tanzania, Togo, Zaïre and Zambia. The ICFTU notes that governments interfere in union affairs either by overtly imposing single union structures that are (to a greater or lesser extent) incorporated into the single or dominant party, or by using various means to influence the elections of union leaders. The same ICFTU study also identifies serious limitations to the right to strike, and even the banning of strikes, in countries such as Angola, Cameroon, Chad, the Congo, Equatorial Guinea, Ethiopia, Mozambique, Rwanda, the Seychelles, Somalia and Tanzania.

Of the countries illustrated in Part II, it is interesting to look at the case of Cape Verde where, despite a process of democratisation widely held to be exemplary, the new government seems to have attempted to control the trade union movement by de-stabilising the old national centre on the grounds that it was still linked to the former single party, and by giving a new centre preferential treatment.

Time was when trade union freedoms were trampled underfoot, and trade unionists were arbitrarily prosecuted on facile, specious grounds like the fight against 'Communism', 'imperialism' or 'subversion'. Other arguments are deployed in today's democratic climate. Democratically elected African leaders still seem to think that all protests and demands, however banal, constitute a threat to political stability, and they continue to see trade union action as collusion with the opposition. Aware of the union movement's potential for destabilisation, these leaders often strive to divide unions and weaken them, sometimes by means of brutal repression.

*Trade union pluralism and an apolitical approach*

It would be an easy matter to quote examples of this scenario and denounce violations of trade union freedoms in Africa. However, what trade unions need to do these days is look beyond, and analyze the situation so as to find solutions. For instance, there are political leaders who have fought alongside trade unions - sometimes as union members - to establish democracy, and who then trample on trade union rights as soon as they get into power. This phenomenon needs to be examined very closely. It goes without saying that violations of human rights can never be justified on any grounds; Africa has no alternative at present but to invent a new social pact that will enable social players to act out their rightful roles in a climate of trust. To this end, an apolitical approach is essential if governments are not going to be given an excuse for declaring war on trade unions because of their political affiliation. This poses the whole problem of trade union pluralism; after all, it flourishes throughout the continent to the advantage of political pluralism.

For instance, Senegal and Burkina Faso were once the only francophone countries to have trade union pluralism. However, it is now the norm in most other countries (except Cameroon and Niger) through the setting up of concurrent trade union centres or the founding of autonomous unions alongside existing single union structures. Trade union practice over the last few years would appear to indicate that union pluralism has, if anything, weakened the trade union movement; in some countries, the need for freedom of association after years of a compulsory single union structure has led to a flood of new branch unions and federations. In Zaïre, for example, over 150 unions covering 1,500,000 employees in the formal sector have been established since 1990 (interview with Simon Tshimpangila N'Domba, General Secretary of the Confédération Démocratique du Travail du Zaïre (Zaïre Democratic Confederation of Labour).

A number of factors may explain the development of trade union pluralism. They include:
- Mimicry. Workers imagine that political pluralism necessarily goes with trade union pluralism. This belief is particularly strong in francophone countries where people tend to take their lead from France, without realising that trade union pluralism there hinders rather than helps trade union cohesion. In practice, they know little of the experience of Anglo-Saxon countries (e.g. Germany, the USA and Great Britain) where the trade union stage is dominated by large national centres and a small number of usually weak, autonomous unions.
- The personal ambitions of union leaders. Some union leaders want to set up new unions as soon as they reach the top of their own organisations. In recent years, there has been evidence for this in many

countries, including Guinea and Mali, where former officials of national unions have founded their own union following defeats in elections, or else because they wanted to settle old scores with former colleagues. One wonders whether some trade unionists are really motivated by the prospect of perquisites like free travel and per diem expenses.

- Interference by governments and by majority and opposition parties. Clearly, when the government controls and uses the single trade union structure, it is perfectly legitimate for the opposition to give into the temptation to set up its own trade unions. Equally, if the single union acts for political ends and supports the opposition, it cannot be too surprised if the government imposes repressive measures and tries to weaken it by setting up more sympathetic unions.

- The absence of democracy within the trade union movement and the lack of transparency in the managerial methods and behaviour of trade union leaders. This is the sort of thing that can push workers to set up their own unions, and is particularly likely when the union line manifestly runs counter to the workers' wishes.

- When a group of workers feels that its problems have not been adequately addressed by the union, they may well want to establish an autonomous union. This is what happened in Mali where magistrates set up an autonomous union to defend demands that they had made, and which had not been adequately addressed by Syntade, the union representing employees in various State administrations. In the case of Mali, the new unions were autonomous rather than concurrent.

Trade union pluralism, if we interpret that to mean concurrent unions, could well be a major factor in weakening the African trade union movement. Usually, it is only with the greatest of difficulty - if they are successful at all - that unions manage to establish unity of action, or determine a common platform of demands or a framework for concertation. They can also find themselves caught up in inter-union disputes that have nothing to do with workers' problems.

Certain governments exploit these divisions to the full in order to undermine strikes; unions opposed to the industrial action sometimes do the same. In Mali, for example, every time in recent years that one of the teachers' unions has called a strike, the other teachers' union has urged its members to carry on working. Interestingly, strike notices lodged by Malian teachers' unions after 1991 were frequently withdrawn following negotiations, despite the fact that the union had not got what it wanted. Did the union really want to reach agreement? Was it using the threat of a strike as blackmail to obtain a minimum demand? Or was it simply afraid that the troops could not be relied on? The answer is probably a combination of all three.

## Trade unions and sustainable democracy

For the millions of Africans who have fought for democracy, the democratic issue means a global change in society: new relations between the State and its citizens, new spaces for freedom, more scope for civil society, and democratic control over the rulers.

Taking our lead from Akwetey, we see that democratisation has been triggered by the economic crisis and external factors, and that there are two additional factors: the crisis of the State's legitimacy, and the fact that social groups have honed their organisational skills. We can therefore define democracy as 'a process that modifies the post-colonial, politico-institutional framework by institutionalising not only organisational autonomy and participation but also individual freedoms, and using them to hammer out the new terms of the relationship between civil society and the State' (Akwetey, 1994: 80).

Democracy cannot simply be reduced to a multi-party system in which the State apparatus, the political parties and the trade unions are prisoners of a tiny group of manipulators who use millions of men and women in struggles that are remote from their real interests. So what do we find? In many countries, the real players in the process of democratisation (i.e. the workers) are kept at a remove from decision-making processes either by new élites that have come to power through hard-fought, and sometimes disputed, elections, or by former dignitaries of single parties who are eleventh-hour converts to democracy. The defeat of President Nicéphore Soglo in the 1996 elections in Benin showed how resistant Africans have become to the old practices of nepotism, personal or clannish power, corruption, or contempt for the popular masses. However, all of these practices are still alive in all African countries to one extent or another. If they are not the preserve of the most senior officials, they are jealously guarded by other coteries of power that grab riches and privileges, and have no intention of accepting a system that involves political alternation.

It is scarcely surprising, therefore, that people should become disillusioned and turn their backs on the State, even before democracy is installed; however, this is exactly where the trade union movement is at its most effective as an organised social force representing broad sectors of the population. Today's economic crisis threatens the very foundations of democracy, and what is happening largely transcends the arguments between opposition parties and governments. The issue is one of identifying ways and means of establishing sustainable democracy in Africa for the benefit of all. In the view of Alain Touraine, criticism of an exclusively political conception of democracy has most frequently been born of an overwhelming need to transform society. Touraine argues that the 20th century has forced us to acknowledge that it is even more important to get the form of political power right than the social organisation of production, and that action aimed at workers' liberation can ensnare an entire people unless it is founded on political freedom (Touraine, 1994).

We are in a period that is effectively a democratic transition; we are still at an early stage of learning about democracy, and political parties are poorly structured and not yet well established; they are therefore weak. It follows that trade unions have a major role to play in founding a true democratic culture in society. To achieve this, certain conditions are required, and they are closely linked to trade unions, their organisational ability, and their understanding of society's problems.

The internal democratisation of trade unions is absolutely vital. The lack of democracy that prevents certain currents inside unions from making themselves heard and having their ideas articulated has ossified the trade union movement; in some cases, it has driven workers to break free and set up their own structures. This is therefore an appropriate time to query the validity of Executive Councils that have been set up quite arbitrarily, and the need to organise the free, transparent trade union elections that workers really want.

Any improvement to internal democracy will also take account of minority currents in decision-making. Obviously, if decisions taken at key committees do not reflect workers' wishes, those workers will feel betrayed and feel that the organisation has nothing to offer them. This need for democratisation has been articulated in a number of countries, and a new dynamic may now be observed. Internal democratisation is becoming a reality in many countries, and evidence for this is to be found in the chapters in Part II.

To take just one example, the Tanzanian trade union movement has undergone major internal changes in both its organisation and its relations with government. These changes have been made gradually since 1991 when the single trade union centre (JUWATA), which was affiliated to the single party, became independent (OTTU); in 1995, it became a federation whose leaders were elected by delegates from newly formed unions. During the last few years, this new form of organisation and relationship with the State has been reflected in the pressure that unions have exerted on government, and particularly in the functioning of labour relations institutions and collective bargaining.

Internal democracy also means better management of trade union resources. The question is a permanent item on the agenda of African trade union congresses and sparks off much controversy. At a time when unions are clamouring for sound management on the part of governments, they are aware that they cannot dodge the question themselves. The trade union position on the introduction of morality into public life will only gain credibility with governments and public opinion if the movement itself gives a good example. This lies at the foundation of the whole debate on sustainable democracy. There can be no social or political stability in Africa until African workers and populations see that public resources are being well managed. To a worker whose standard of living continues to tumble, democracy only makes any sense if it leads to both better management of resources, and eventually higher wages for the largest number of people.

Through its position in the economy and its record of commitment to social justice, the trade union movement is naturally one of the leading social forces capable of ensuring that public affairs are managed in a transparent manner. However, this is only true if, and only if, the unions give a good example by establishing new, reliable systems and administrative procedures that provide basic management controls.

These efforts also go hand in hand with the search for substantial sums of money. In a climate where the unions are striving for maximum autonomy from governments which previously gave them much of their funding, the question of managerial transparency is of paramount importance. It provides an opportunity not only to restore members' confidence, but also to organise the transfer of their contributions, and those of international funders; the latter are not totally unaware of certain unions' unorthodox practices. Transparent management leads to better use of resources and, therefore, to more efficient unions.

However, there is more to trade union democracy than that. In every part of Africa, there are instances of workers in different categories not being equitably represented in trade union structures; young people and women in particular are under-represented. A national seminar held in Porto Novo, Benin in July 1994 on women's participation in the process of democratisation argued that there was an urgent need to involve them more through vigorous action, and particularly through a platform of demands that might turn them into activists (see Chapter 6). The conclusion reached by the Porto Novo seminar has been confirmed by APADEP studies (to be published in 1998); these show quite clearly that when a union does not take account of the specific problems facing women, female members lose all interest in becoming activists and try to resolve their problems in their own way - unless, that is, they simply give up the unequal struggle.

One option gaining ground in some organisations is a policy of broadening the social base of trade unions. Traditional trade unionism based exclusively on a defence of interests of employees (a category steadily dwindling in number) simply does not measure up in present-day Africa; nowadays, increasing emphasis is being placed on the socially excluded, who are unorganised and ill-equipped to resolve their problems. The trade union movement is now facing a challenge from, on the one hand, millions of people working in the fast-developing informal sector and left to their own devices, and from the great mass of non-employed workers on the other. Trade unionism can bring them succour by influencing government training and employment policies, and by giving support to more vulnerable groups such as women and young people. In other words, trade unions are in a position to give active support to the least protected social groups through a global union strategy that extends beyond companies and the public sector, the trade union movement's traditional areas of competence. This point will be examined in more detail in Chapter 4.

Another challenge facing the trade union movement concerns the drafting of a new union policy that reconciles both a defence of workers' interests and the general interest and economic constraints. If trade unions wish to have credibility, it is no longer enough for them to brandish a list of grievances and give no thought to how they might be met. The new trade union dynamic now taking shape in Africa is forcing unions to be aware of short-term, medium-term and long-term socio-economic matters, and to be conversant with the main political, economic, legal and social issues, so that they can act in a fully responsible manner. All of this is vital if workers and the population in general are not to become disillusioned with the trade union movement as a whole.

To achieve this objective, the trade union movement will clearly have to become much more cohesive. The key question is how to prevent the kind of dissipation that sometimes accompanies trade union pluralism. How can agreement be reached on a joint platform of demands - and, particularly a platform of proposals - that demonstrates the trade union movement's strength, capacity for adaptation and constructive attitude? Trade union unity is already very difficult in many countries, and unity of action is therefore what they must aim for. This involves a united vision of trade union responsibilities for supporting democracy and representing the interests of large sections of the population.

Trade unions will be able to develop unity of action, and inject cohesion into the trade union movement as a whole, if they acknowledge that every single person is welcome to contribute all his/her characteristics and unique features to the defence of democracy, without which no free trade union can survive. It goes without saying that this will involve a root-and-branch reappraisal of how all the players - governments, employers and trade unions - have behaved in the past. At the end of the day, there can be no democracy without democrats, and everyone will have to make a huge effort to jettison old reflexes picked up over decades of authoritarian rule. The development of a democratic culture unquestionably relies on a democratised workplace.

# 3   Africa in a Period of Adjustment

RAOUL GALARRAGA AND AIMÉ TCHABOURÉ GOGUÉ

The social upheavals of the early 1990s suggest that the rejection of dictatorships and African peoples' aspirations for more democracy are now established facts. Obviously, one reason why people strive for democracy is that it hastens the attainment of certain aspects of their well-being; however, it often happens that they are also concerned with short-term gains, and therefore by a country's level of development. This is particularly important when we recall how fragile democracy can be in its early stages. There are always social groups that have done well out of the old system and, because they want to retain privileges, will oppose any social and political change. It is therefore essential that we do not swell the number of discontented people who have the means at their disposal to destabilise.

One of the strategies and conditions for ensuring the survival of democracy involves increasing the number of people who support this form of political and social organisation. However, it is only effective if democracy prevents the level of general well-being from falling, and halts the decline in the living conditions of all people in general - and of the leading players in the introduction of democracy in particular. It is therefore important to find ways in which democracy can foster development as defined in Chapter 1.

The process of democratisation in Africa got under way at a time when countries there were undergoing a major economic crisis - a crisis which, it should be said, is not yet over. The crisis is not so much conjunctural as structural; it therefore calls for measures that will make the economy more efficient and capable of generating growth, and will ultimately promote sustainable economic development. A country needs to be able to raise the level of domestic saving, re-direct resources and investment, and encourage certain sectors at the expense of others. It will also be necessary to make choices that are both unavoidable and difficult. Given the overall situation in, and the economic performances of, SSA countries since the latter half of the 1970s, economic reforms are absolutely essential.

Implementation of such reforms inevitably leads to a short-term fall in the level of private consumption. It is therefore necessary to persuade people, particularly those who made substantial contributions to the democratisation process, that these reforms, so long as they are correctly implemented, will eventually lead to economic growth and a more equitable distribution of income. Factors critical to the survival of democracy include the credibility of the reforms, their coherence with long-term growth and equitable distribution of income, and the ability of governments to persuade electorates to put up with a temporary drop in consumer levels in exchange for future growth. The question is therefore how to come up with good policies, and then carry them out in such a way as to ensure the country's sustainable economic development. We have to ask ourselves, therefore, what kind of political organisation is needed to draw up these reforms and see them through to a successful conclusion. African trade unions have already made decisive contributions to the introduction and installation of the democratic process, and they still have an important role to play.

## Economic management

Economic management in African countries needs to change course, if only because we know from the economic history of the last three decades how dictatorships in Africa have been responsible for an unimaginable waste of resources. The only two African countries to have experienced sustainable economic growth are Botswana and Mauritius; significantly, they have parliamentary systems that are up and running.

In the view of Alain Touraine, a sociologist and champion of a positive link between democracy and development, the thesis of a voluntarist State has not produced the results that some people had hoped for. According to this notion, there is a need for a 'voluntarist State in order to get moving, and particularly to make a break with the former oligarchies ... dictatorship is necessary at the moment of take-off, and it is only when you reach cruising speed that political control over social change can be defended, and democracy can be introduced before it becomes a condition of development' (Touraine: 222). Funders support this analysis, and have often supported totalitarian régimes on the grounds that they can:
- construct the nation;
- ensure compliance with laws and regulations currently in force, and guarantee that States function normally;
- mobilise investment finance, particularly in public infrastructures;
- modernise administration and economic structures, thereby encouraging the promotion of economic development.

In the view of those who believed in strong government, economic under-development and crisis therefore called for authoritarian régimes, because they alone were able to formulate coherent economic policies aimed at sustainable development. Consideration could be given to democratisation during the second phase.

Experience has shown that totalitarian régimes intrinsically contain the germs for dividing a country. The mobilising State may well construct the nation during the early stages, but it is the experience of virtually every country that dictatorships have soon been assailed by clientelism, corruption and internal dissent, and have only been able to maintain any semblance of an internally coherent society through brutal political repression. When the State is more preoccupied with its own survival and interests, it turns into an absolute power; at that point, development is ruled out because society is then paralysed and stifled by the repressive means that the state uses to control the people. The slowdown in growth, assuming there is any growth at all, then leads to a growing shortage of the resources which are accumulated for later distribution to 'activists'.

*Clientelism*

Where shortages occur, the group that controls the government and has best access to public resources - in countries with a significant public sector, it is also the group that has access to their distribution - will tend to look after its own interests and show partiality to its own ethnic and regional clans and groups; ethnic and regional social groups that are already under-privileged will lose out. What we then have is an absolute enrichment of the former sector of society, and an absolute impoverishment of the remainder. That is a potential source of conflict. The ruling class then turns in on itself, and that is a signal for clientelism to put down its roots. The case studies in Part II show clearly how the struggle against these evils has guided social movements in their search for freedom and democracy.

In countries like Benin, Mali, Nigeria, Togo and Zaïre, governments have been quick to turn their backs on the interests of the community. They have become much more preoccupied with their own interests and with remaining in power, and this has justified their use of repressive measures and recourse to violence. If that was not bad enough, this repression has also fuelled the brain drain, with well qualified African professionals - engineers, doctors and university teachers - being forced to take themselves off to developed countries where they become street cleaners, taxi drivers and night security guards. Africa also has the dubious honour of having the record number of political refugees. Moreover, the importance accorded to membership of political parties when appointing managers has led to a disastrous use of human resources. Another consequence is the flight of capital; this happens not only because of poor economic policies, but also for political reasons; typically, it happens just when governments are making their most energetic efforts to attract foreign capital. In the end, resources are expended not only on developing the country, but also on acquiring and maintaining a political clientele and obtaining security. This can be very expensive: we only have to look at the sums spent on the military and the security forces to see that. Later, as the strength of these régimes begins to wane, they become more demagogic as they battle to remain in power. The reason is very simple reason: they cannot come up with an alternative.

Of more serious concern is the fact that, unlike the governments of south-east Asian countries, these régimes were directly responsible for the major economic crises that rocked most African countries during the late 1970s and early 1980s. These crises forced countries to implement economic reforms, and the SAPs introduced through the offices of international financial bodies, mainly the Bretton Woods Institutions, with a view to correcting economic imbalances did not enable the economies to achieve growth. In most cases, the Programmes also led to substantial social costs.

## The whys and wherefores of SAPs

Since the relatively steady growth that marked the 1960s and early 1970s, most African economies have performed disastrously, particularly in the wake of the first oil crisis. In fact, the economic situation became so critical that most countries were obliged to implement Structural Adjustment Programmes with help from the World Bank and the IMF.

While average annual growth in GDP declined in all industrialised countries from 4.7% to 2.8% between 1965-1973 and 1973-1980, it fell in SSA countries during the same period from 6.4% to 3.2%. Between 1965 and 1973, per capita income climbed annually by 3.6% on average, but between 1973 and 1980 it rose by only 0.3%. Other economic aggregates performed even less well.

According to the World Bank (World Bank, 1994), agricultural production increased by about 2% every year between 1965 and 1980, but fell by an average of 0.6% annually between 1981 and 1985; by contrast, countries in the Far East enjoyed an average annual rise of 3.2% during the first half of the 1980s. During this time, return on investment in Africa was particularly low, poorly maintained physical infrastructures deteriorated fast, and education and health indicators, which had improved since independence, continued to be among the worst in the world.

Table 1:     Economic performance by African countries

| Indicators | 1965-1973 | 1974-1979 | 1980-1985 | 1986-1993 | 1990-1994 |
|---|---|---|---|---|---|
| dY/Y | 5,7 | 3,5 | 1,8 | 2,5 | 1,9 |
| dy/y | 3 | 0,7 | -1,1 | -0,5 | -1,1 |
| I/Y | 16,5 | 20,9 | 16,3 | 15,6 | 15,3 |
| dI/I | 9,6 | 6,9 | -4,8 | 1,2 | 0,8 |
| s/y | 16,2 | 19,7 | 14,9 | 13,8 | 12,7 |
| dX/X | 8,2 | 2,6 | 0,4 | 3 | 0,6 |
| dM/M | 7,4 | 6,2 | -2,4 | -0,7 | 0,4 |
| dG/G | - | -5,4 | -9 | -8,7 | -4,8 |
| dB/B | 1 (1965) | -3,6 (75-79) | -2,8 | - | -1,6 |
| dP/P | 5,8 | 13,8 | 18,8 | 21,7 | 27,2 |

*Source*: African Development Report, African Development Bank, 1995: 223

Y: GDP, y: Per capita GDP, I: Domestic investment, S: Domestic savings, X: Exports, M: Imports, G: Budget deficit, B: Current account; For any variable, dZ/Z indicates the rate of variation.

Data supplied by the African Development Bank (ADB, 1995) point to a slow but steady deterioration in the economic situation of African countries, particularly between 1965 and 1985. Inflation averaged 5.1% in 1965-1973, but then jumped to 13.8% during 1974-1979, and then to 18.8% in 1980-1985; during 1986-1993, it climbed further to 21.7%. Growth in gross investment fell from an average of 9.6% during 1985-1973 to 6.9% in 1974-1979, and dropped further to -4.8% in 1980-1985 before recovering to 1.2% in 1986-1993; after rising from 16.2% in 1965-1973 to 19.7% in 1974-1979, the gross savings rate (gross savings/GDP) fell to 14.9% in 1980-1985 and then to 13.8% in 1986-1993. The budget deficit, which accounted for -5.4% of GDP, widened to -9.0% in 1980-1985. Export growth also fell back, from 8.2% in 1965-1973 to 2.6% in 1974-1979, dropping further to 0.4% in 1980-1986.

At one time, the external debt of the entire African continent was USD 10,824, but in 1975 it rose to USD 31,169 and then to USD 113,920 and USD 186,195 in 1980 and 1985 respectively. Debt servicing became an increasingly intolerable burden despite the inflow of public development aid for countries whose exports were stagnating. According to the World Bank, external debt which had been estimated at 13.1% of GDP in 1970 climbed to 57.4% in 1980; debt servicing as a ratio of exports of goods and services rose from 5.3% in 1970 to 19.3% in 1980.

There are both internal and external reasons for these poor economic performances. Internally, the reasons most frequently adduced are inappropriate economic policies as follows:

- policies biased against exports and in favour of import subsidies; exchange control measures adopted to deal with an acute foreign currency crisis in countries outside the franc area indicate an overvaluation of the exchange rate, and have resulted in the existence of flourishing parallel exchange markets;
- a sprawling, inefficient public sector riven with corruption, and hampered by an inability to formulate appropriate economic policies;
- ever-increasing public deficits;
- an import substitution policy characterised by tariff and non-tariff obstacles (mainly the latter);
- political instability in certain countries (a succession of civil wars, inter-ethnic conflicts and coups d'état).

External reasons often given for worsening economic performances in African countries include the combined impact of higher interest rates and worsening exchange rates brought about by the world economic crisis. At a time when the exchange rates of African oil-exporting countries rose by 100%, those of the non-oil-exporting countries declined by 30% between 1970 and 1986; those of countries that export mining products fell by approximately 50%.

In this way, the combined effect of higher interest rates and worsening exchange rates led to a loss of USD 2.8bn in foreign currency in 1980 and USD 13.8bn in 1987, equivalent to 90% of the inflow of capital. However, the African Development Bank believes that there are two fundamental reasons for the economic situation in Africa. The first is that the vulnerability of African economies to external crises flows from a failure to diversify economic structures, particularly exports; the Bank argues that these countries should have taken advantage of the higher prices that raw materials commanded on international markets in the late 1960s and the second half of the 1970s to restructure their economies. The second reason is the inability of countries to undertake the internal economic reforms that proved necessary because of worsening economic aggregates and new macro-economic imbalances (African Development Report: 230-231).

*SAP objectives and prescriptions*

In view of the generalised decline in the economy, there was an urgent need for economic policies that targeted growth. As a result, SAPs were introduced to re-establish the major macro-economic balances (a reduction of budget deficits and the current account, particularly inflation, and paying off external debt on a regular basis) and promote an upturn in long-term economic growth. Countries turned to the IMF and the World Bank for appropriate economic policies, and agreement between governments and the Bretton Woods Institutions provided immediate access to external finance.

The prescribed economic policies are fundamentally monetarist and based on a monetary approach to the balance of payments. However, SAPs are becoming less and less monetarist, and are instead incorporating elements of the structuralist and neo-Marxist schools. As far as monetarism is concerned - the fundamental basis of SAPs is the IMF's concern - there are measures designed to control the money supply and reduce the budget deficit. Designers of SAPs say that the purpose of these measures is to correct conjunctural imbalances; they argue that the difficulties that these countries were facing were transitory, and that in these cases it was enough to finance the deficits in order to re-establish macro-economic balances.

However, in the light of their poor economic performances - and the relevance of structuralist criticism that rigidity and bottlenecks in developing economies cause stabilisation policies to fail - SAPs have been used to top up monetarist prescriptions during the second stage with medium- and long-term measures targeting institutional changes. SAPs contain measures that place special emphasis on public sector reform and liberalisation and, for example, remove any form of market distortion.

SAPs also take their inspiration from neo-Marxist theory of the 1970s. This discovered that the State had been taken hostage by a ruling class made up of foreign capitalists - and/or members of the local middle class as well as capitalists - and was incapable of acting in the general interests of society. For that reason, SAPs insisted on government having nothing to do with production and finance. Bretton Woods Institutions thought that governments acted on behalf of pressure groups with divergent interests, and that they therefore used economic policies to set up profit-making situations for their protégés. They also introduced incentive structures that caused a waste of scarce resources and distortions, and this in turn made the economy inefficient. Such an approach consistently served the interests of the government's own activists, including civil servants working in the towns and cities. SAPs also sought to counter the urban bias that had marked earlier policies; this took the form partly of subsidies that supported urban dwellers' consumption and provided high salaries in the towns and cities, and partly of excessive taxes imposed on the agricultural sector.

In this way, SAPs incorporated a combination of the following measures:

*monetary and fiscal measures*
- limits on ceilings for extending credit to the economy;
- selective allocation of credit;

- reduction in the growth of liquid assets;
- reforms in interest rates;
- an appropriate distribution of credit to the private sector;
- an improvement in the system and mechanisms for mobilising private saving;
- a high level of net foreign reserves.

*policies relating to the public sector*
- restrictions on current expenditure by central government (reduction in salaries and remuneration, transfers and subsidies, capital expenditures and net loans; improvement in the administration of expenditures and changes in priorities);
- tax systems (measures for improving tax revenues, reform of the administration of taxes);
- non-banking enterprises (improved performance and control of State-owned enterprises);
- budget (reduction of the deficit as a percentage of GDP, reduction of domestic arrears).

*policies relating to external debt*
- control over the level and settlement dates of external debt;
- other policies (e.g. reduction and rescheduling of the debt, finding loans on more favourable terms, reduction of arrears).

*policies relating to trade and commerce*
- liberalisation or reform of exchange rates;
- liberalisation or reform of the commercial system.

*policies relating to prices and incomes*
- reduction or abolition of subsidies and price controls;
- reform of pay scales and pay policies (aimed at keeping wage costs under control).

*other measures relating to structural adjustment*
- development and restructuring of sub-sectors;
- improved management of the economy;
- improved performance, and reduced public sector involvement to the advantage of the private sector;
- improved planning and procedures for investment.

Stabilisation measures are designed to achieve monetary and fiscal policies, particularly those covering the public sector and the external debt, an enhanced financial situation for the government, and control over inflation; by contrast, structural reforms aim to make the allocation of resources more efficient. Broadly speaking, stabilisation measures influence demand while structural reform measures affect supply.

## Criticism of SAPs

Although the need for economic reform is not in doubt, the interventions of international finance institutions, particularly the World Bank and the IMF, have come in for heavy criticism. The criticism has been political on the one hand, and economic and social on the other. Advocates of SAPs say that the poor results that African economies have achieved following the application of SAPs have been the result of faulty or insufficient adjustment; opponents argue that the reason for the poor economic performances of countries going through a period of adjustment is more likely to be the poor quality or unsuitability of the measures contained in the reforms.

*Political and institutional criticism*[1] For their part, governments think that these institutions are stepping outside their remit as set out in their Statutes: for instance, on 2 March 1979, the IMF Board of Executive Directors made it very clear that their organisation must take due account of a country's internal social and political objectives, of its economic priorities and the general situation. However, under the rules of adjustment, the World Bank and the International Monetary Fund insist that countries make alterations to their fundamental choices. Moreover, with regard to the desired economic efficiency, countries are required, for example, to privatise, reallocate resources between sectors, and liberalise the economy; it all depends on what kind of society they want to have. However imperfect they may be, the development plans of countries undergoing adjustment are carefully put to one side, and the objectives defined by, and for, society are totally ignored.

In the opinion of many critics, the conditionalities prove both that these institutions have no respect for a country's sovereignty, and that they practise an unacceptable degree of political interference. Rightly or wrongly, some people also think that these institutions sometimes defend the appointment of Ministers who agree with their proposals, and that they give governments a boost in the eyes of their people through the transfer of resources or 'good reports'.

*Economic and social criticism* Under this heading, critics focus equally on the suitability of SAP prescriptions to the economic climate of the countries concerned, the rationality of the economic players, the basic model that informs SAPs, and the results that are obtained.

For example, Wapenhans (1994) wonders if Structural Adjustment Programmes are appropriate when the imbalances they are supposed to correct reflect bad government, weak institutions, and external crises that simply reinforce the imbalances. In practice, a country cannot improve its economic performance and efficiency if the government is not accountable or if its administrative skills are of a low order. Moreover, any fall in the prices or quantity of exported goods also prevents the country from boosting its export revenues, thereby improving its balance of payments. Restricted elasticity in the supply of exports and in the demand for imports reduces the likelihood of improving the position of external imbalances after the currency has been devalued.

Kankwenda (1992) thinks that 'SAPs have extracted nothing from the crisis (i.e. the economic crisis in Africa) but its manifestations in terms of financial and external imbalances' (p 16), and that Africa's economic problems really result from the crisis of its accumulation model (p 10). There is no hope of re-establishing the main macro-economic imbalances if we disregard socio-political structures and the relationships that these countries maintain with the former colonial powers. In the view of these critics, the neo-colonial relationships underlying these countries' international economic relationships form insurmountable obstacles to the successful outcome of any adjustment policy.

Others claim that the prescriptions are not adapted to the socio-economic structures of African countries. For example, Henri Saby, former Chairman of the Committee on Development and Cooperation of the European Parliament, argues that 'the Bretton Woods criteria for structural adjustment are perfect for Sweden, but are completely wrong-headed for countries such as Zambia and Mozambique' (Saby, 1991: 60).

Although, as we have already pointed out, the designers of SAPs have noted the criticisms of structuralists and neo-Marxists that they should adapt their prescriptions to developing economies, the underlying hypotheses clearly continue to be those of the monetarist model developed by the Chicago School. In other words, what these critics are saying is that a monetary approach to the balance of payments is unsuited to the structures of African countries.

The prescriptions of international financial institutions and the IMF are largely based on the relationship between money and income. If we go along with the quantity theory of money whereby the velocity of money is stable and income is constant in the short term, the Polack model that has influenced SAPs deduces that any increase in the money supply will lead to an increase in imports and higher prices. Accordingly, budget deficits financed by the Central Bank are tantamount to an increase in internal credit, and therefore to an increase in the money supply. This situation then leads to an increase in imports and prices, which is exactly what the Polack model predicts. Domestic inflation makes the economy less competitive on the international market, thereby reducing the country's exports, and this, together with an initial increase in imports, worsens the balance of payments deficit. In conditions such as these, stabilisation policies for correcting macro-economic imbalances (e.g. inflation, balance of payments deficit and budget deficit) are the result of budget deficits financed by the printing of money.

It therefore makes sense to recommend a reduction in internal credit as this keeps the consumption of imports under control and brings inflation down. Recommendations to reduce the wage sum for public servants are designed to limit government deficits, and thereby the financing of public expenditure. Compulsory devaluations also lead to higher imports and lower export prices, and so balance the current account.

However, restricted elasticity of exports inhibits a country's ability to react to foreign sales, whereas a reduction in imports cannot be guaranteed because it is not possible to lower foreign expenditure by much. A more serious matter is that criticism has also been levelled at the basic hypothesis of the monetarist model. According to Yung Chul Park, 'the velocity of circulation of money is not stable in developing countries, and it follows that any prediction, or any economic policy based on such a policy, is incorrect' (Park, 1990: 149). Champions and detractors of SAPs alike have valid arguments to support their positions, so for a better understanding of the rationality of these policy reforms, we have to rely on what actually happens when SAPs are implemented.

## Outcomes of adjustment

Assessing the results of adjustment has sparked off much controversy. In fact, there is little unanimity of any sort surrounding the impact of SAPs on the economies of African countries. For one thing, it has proved difficult to agree on criteria; some say it is necessary to compare the current economic performances of countries undergoing adjustment with what they would have achieved if they had not adopted SAPs in the first place; others merely examine countries' economic indicators before and after adjustment.

Another difficulty is that the fact that a country commits itself to implementing reforms does not necessarily mean that the reforms will be put into practice effectively. A recent World Bank study (Adjustment in Africa: Reforms, Results and the Road Ahead, World Bank, 1994) placed African countries in three categories: countries that have significantly improved their economic policies (i.e. those that have rigorously applied

SAP prescriptions) (Group A), countries that have made slight improvements to their economic policies (Group B) and those whose economic policies have worsened (Group C).

Given the breadth and extent of the planned policy reforms, the effects of SAPs are bound to be very varied. They are designed to re-establish the main macro-economic balances, and will therefore have macro-economic effects. Furthermore, some measures like liberalisation of the economy, getting prices back onto a sounder economic basis, and a reduction in public deficits will have a mainly damaging effect on living standards and employment in countries in the process of adjustment.

Given the time-lags, one might expect the effects of stabilisation programmes to be felt before those of structural reforms.

Table 2:    Economic performance during a period of adjustment
(1981-1986 compared with 1987-1991)

| Country | Growth by per capita GPB | | Gross investment /GPD | | Public investment /GDP | |
|---|---|---|---|---|---|---|
| | 1981-1986 | 1987-1991 | 1981-1986 | 1987-1991 | 1981-1986 | 1987-1991 |
| Major improvements to policies | -0,7 | 1,1 | 19 | 20,7 | 6,8 | 8 |
| Minor improvements to policies | -0,9 | -0,2 | 16,4 | 16,6 | 7,1 | 6,7 |
| Less good policies | -2,1 | -2 | 15,8 | 12,6 | 9,1 | 6,8 |
| All countries | -0,7 | 0,1 | 17,2 | 16,3 | 8,7 | 6,4 |

*Source*: African Development Report, African Development Bank, 1995: 227

As the figures in Table 1 indicate (see p 51), growth in per capita GDP in African countries moved from -1.1% in 1980-1985 to -0.5% in 1986-1993 (i.e. the years of adjustment); this suggests that the SAPs managed to cushion the fall in people's standard of living. The budget deficit as a percentage of GDP also fell from -9% in 1980-1985 to -8.5% in 1986-1993. However, inflation rose from an average of 18.8% per annum in 1980-1985 to 21.7% in 1986-1993. These results conceal disparities in performances by different countries.

One preliminary observation is called for: a relatively high number of governments were unable - either for internal or external reasons - to implement SAPs, even though they had agreed to introduce them; that was for socio-political reasons or because of the quality and quantity of available skills.

The figures in Table 2 show that countries in Group A improved their economic performances; growth of per capita GDP in these countries rose from -0.7% in 1981-1986 to 1.1% in 1981-1991, and investment rates climbed from 19% to 20.7% in the same period. Countries in Group B achieved slightly improved economic performances, but economic performance declined in countries where economic policies deteriorated (Group C).

These conclusions have been challenged by many writers. In the view of Stefano Ponte (1994), for example, if countries are classified according to how far their economic policies have improved, SAPs cannot on their own explain:

- the difference between the performances of Group A countries and those of Group B countries;
- changes in countries' economic performances before and after the SAPs were implemented.

## The social costs of adjustment

Since 1987, researchers have been criticising the social costs of adjustment and calling for adjustment with a human face (Cornia et al, 1987; Jolly et al, 1991). By demanding both an increase in real interest rates (by raising interest rates or indirectly by controlling credit) and a reduction in government expenditure, SAPs should bring about a fall in consumer levels. What is more, the 'demonopolisation' of the economy, reduced subsidies to companies, the abolition of subsidies on the price of consumer products and privatisations will cause a fall in employment and, in so doing, reinforce the decline in consumer levels. However, the designers of SAPs thought that these costs would be short-term, and that an upturn in economic growth would lead to an improvement in the well-being of society. That was why nothing was done to protect the most vulnerable social groups when SAPs were introduced. The high social costs of SAPs also explain why institutions concerned with development, particularly UNESCO, have demanded adjustments with a human face; in due course, they have also encouraged governments and funders to draw up programmes that will absorb the damaging effects that SAPs have on the most under-privileged sections of society in particular.

However, there is no unanimity at all about the effects that SAPs have on poverty. When SAPs are introduced at times of crisis, the first thing to find out is whether poverty would have intensified or declined without the

SAP. What is more, the quality of statistics in developing countries makes it difficult to assess the impact of SAPs on households. Defenders of SAPs claim that criticism concentrates on the short-term effects, and ignores the longer term when economic upturn leads to an improvement in the general well-being of society. It is now acknowledged that the impact of SAPs on different social groups is not uniform, and that economic agents in the tradeable goods sector benefit from measures to liberalise the economy, to the detriment of the rest of the population. In short, some measures may have a negative impact while others may improve the level of well-being. It is therefore accepted that theoretical frameworks and available methodologies do not satisfactorily identify either the impact of macro-economic measures on different social groups or reactions at a micro-economic level.

A number of studies have looked into the social costs of SAPs; they include work by Jolly (et al, 1991), Gogué (1997a, 1997b), Kakwani (1995) and Killick (1995). In the view of Aimé Gogué (1997a), the fall in school rolls in Togo between 1981 and 1985 is only partly explained by the reduction of public spending on education; more influential factors include the introduction of more restrictive measures at the point of entry into education cycles, a fall in household incomes, and a more rigorous interpretation of the criteria for recruiting public sector employees and the conditions for taking retirement. Such measures were introduced as a result of SAPs. Gogué also discovered (1997b) that, although the government did not substantially reduce the percentage of resources devoted to the Ministry of Health's operating expenses, there was still a fall in expenditure on public investment. He also observed that the main impact of SAPs on health demand was linked to a fall in household incomes, itself a consequence of higher unemployment and the multiplier effects of falling government expenditures.

*The poor once again bear the brunt*

Kakwani (1995) has noted that countries which adjusted during the second half of the 1980s had performed less well during the 1960s in terms of living standards than those that did not adjust at all during the same period. He also found that countries which introduced SAPs made less headway in raising living standards than those that did not adjust. In the opinion of Killick (1995), poor people, particularly workers, have always been badly hit by SAPs, but the costs have been exaggerated.

The chapter on Ghana is equally clear that the social costs of adjustment are considerable. Real salaries in 1990 were 50% of the 1975 level, and real per capita income in 1990 was lower than in 1980. Furthermore, the percentage of poor people living in rural areas rose from 43% in 1970 to 54% in 1986. The number of citizens overall living below the poverty threshold climbed from 30-35% in the late 1970s to an average of 45-50% in the 1980s.

Broadly speaking, research shows that the people most affected by SAPs were workers in the towns and cities.

## SAPs and the trade union movement

In this section, we shall first examine the impact of Structural Adjustment Programmes on workers and their trade unions in SSA Africa; we shall then deal with the way that national and international unions have reacted to SAPs. For further information on this subject, the reader is referred to the bibliography at the end of this book.

Structural Adjustment Programmes have had a considerable influence on African workers and the trade union movement. The neo-classical paradigm underpinning SAPs, and supported by international financial institutions, has led to the policies set out above; moreover, to correct macro-economic imbalances, use has been made of policies such as 'stabilisation' and 'adjustment' measures with a view to reducing government interventions on the labour market. Market forces, rather than any objectives associated with equity, became the focal point of the process of economic restructuring; in this context, trade unions have long been seen as an obstacle to the smooth running of the free market, and therefore as a handicap to structural adjustment.

Particularly during the period of SAP stabilisation, that is to say the early 1980s, adjustment policies aimed to reduce public expenditure, and therefore the ability of the State to provide social welfare; this restricted the State's role in achieving an environment favourable to the private sector. One of the key measures in this context was the privatisation of a large number of State-owned enterprises. This change of ownership meant that private capital now controlled both companies and the salaries and profits that went with them. The new contractual relationship also gave capital the right to get rid of workers whenever their presence threatened profit margins (Bangura, 1989).

It follows that, during the first generation of SAPs in the early 1980s, few national or international trade unions were consulted about, let alone involved in, designing, negotiating, implementing and managing adjustment policies. A long time was to pass before the World Bank (World Bank, 1989) agreed that the State should play a more important role, and that steps should be taken to develop skills in Africa and to reinforce an institutional framework that might foster development. The World Bank finally recognised the positive role that could be played by trade unions in 1995. In its World Development

Report published that year, trade unions and particularly their role in collective bargaining were described as essential mechanisms for both the stability of democracy and the functioning of labour markets.

## Unemployment on the increase

Structural Adjustment Programmes have had a major impact on the level of unemployment in the formal sector, and have been basically responsible for massive retrenchments in both the private and the public sectors. Total unemployment in the formal sector rose from 7.75% in 1978 to 22.8% in 1990 (ILO/JASPA, 1992). The effect was particularly acute in the formal sector in the towns and cities: unemployment in this sector doubled between 1975 and 1990, rising in SSA countries from 10% to 20% (estimation by IILS, 1994: 2).

20% of workers in the public sector (the public sector in Africa accounts for about 40% of all employment) were laid off during the 1980s; in the early 1990s, dismissals in the pipeline or already taking place have been even more substantial, possibly rising to as much as 26-30% (Diejomaoh, 1993: 9). In Nigeria, for example, rationalisation processes in certain enterprises have reduced the workforce by 50% (Fashoyin, 1994). Across the board, this represents many thousands of job losses in the public sector: 209,000 in Ghana (see Chapter 9), 40,000 in Guinea, 27,000 in Tanzania and 16,000 in Cameroon (van der Moortele, 1991: 92). Jobs in the primary sector appear to have been less affected because of slow growth in employment (estimated by Bourguignon & Morrison, 1992).

## Expansion of the informal sector

One consequence of the decline of the formal sector has been an increase in the activities of the informal sector. An analysis of the impact of adjustment policies on employment in Kenya, Uganda, Zambia, Tanzania and Zimbabwe (van der Hoeven, 1996) reveals that the ratio of employment in the formal sector to the labour force has fallen in all countries since the early 1990s. Statistics confirm that the decline in public sector employment has not been sufficiently matched by an increase in private sector employment, and this has led to an expansion of the informal sector. The informal sectors in the national economies of the five countries considered to be Africa's best performers (World Bank, 1994) have grown during the last five years, and in 1995 the informal sector of all SSA countries employed over 60% of the total urban labour force (ILO, 1995: 65). Predictably, workers are more vulnerable in the informal sector because of poor conditions of employment.

*Serious repercussions for women*

Adjustment policies have impacted more severely on women than on men. African women were poorer than African men when SAPs were first introduced, and the poor are more reliant on public services than those living above the poverty threshold. Moreover, poor women are more numerous than poor men in urban areas, and this means they are excluded from access to social services (Turshen, 1994). Less well paid workers have been particularly prone to redundancy because the economic sectors that employ unskilled staff have been the first to be affected by dismissals and restrictions (ILO/JASPA, 1990). African women account for a high proportion of these workers. In Benin, Ghana and Senegal, women have been disproportionately affected by redundancy, and this has contributed to an increase in their rate of unemployment: in Benin, where a redundancy programme was introduced in 1987, women made redundant accounted for 21% of all redundancies despite the fact that they represent only 6% of the workforce in the public and private sector combined; in Senegal, where women account for 12% of the public sector workforce, 20% of them have been made redundant; in Ghana, although accounting for only 23.5% of the total employed workforce, 31.5% of those made redundant in 1987 were women (ILO/JASPA, 1990). Apart from these redundancy measures, the reduction in public services generally has affected women more than men, in the sense that it is women who have to cope with reductions in health and education services and other social services (Elson, 1991: 177).

Structural Adjustment Programmes have led to a considerable fall in real pay. Other factors contributing to this decline include pay freezes and pay cuts linked to currency devaluation, and the abolition of controls on food prices and subsidies. At the same time, purchasing power has been reduced by rising inflation. If we recall that salaries in Africa are the lowest on the world market (Toye, 1995), it is not difficult to imagine the horrendous situation that African workers now face. Their pay fell by 25% on average between 1980 and 1985, with Somalia (84%) and Tanzania (64%) being the worst hit (Mihyo & Schiphorst, 1995: 183). During the second half of the 1980s, the average decline in real pay was approximately 50% (Onimode, 1992: 64).

A key component of structural adjustment policies has been that new laws have been framed, or existing laws amended, so as to make the labour market more flexible. According to SAP philosophy, laws and procedures make the market inflexible and even hamper the process of adjustment and future employment growth. Measures to prop up conditions of employment and the minimum wage have also withered away in countries such as Burkina Faso, Cameroon, Côte d'Ivoire, Gabon, Guinea and Mali (ICFTU,

1995). To compound the problem, new forms of labour law have placed few restrictions on employment contracts, employment procedures, redundancy for economic reasons, or compensation for job loss or temporary employment. Restrictions relating to hiring and firing are seen as factors that push up redundancy compensation costs, discourage job creation, and cut down on mobility and productivity. Much employment legislation is now more liberal and flexible; it also makes it quite easy for employers to dismiss staff, and to ignore the conditions and benefits that workers have painstakingly won. Laws that might give workers a framework in which to improve their conditions of employment (particularly independent collective bargaining rights) are not encouraged, even though they are covered by regulations governing negotiations. In Tanzania, for example, where funds were once available for workers' participation, even though they only applied to public sector enterprises, these have not been automatically transferred to private companies (see Chapter 13).

SAPs have also affected trade union involvement in decision-taking at national level. Much of the time, they have not been able to participate in the framing of economic restructuring policies, or else they have not been able to do so effectively (Limmen, 1996). In francophone countries that recently introduced Labour Code reforms, consultation and dialogue between government, unions and employers' associations has often been non-existent, or else it has been poorly managed. In only three countries, Benin, Burkina Faso and the Congo, have Codes drawn up by the respective Ministers of Labour been submitted to unions and employers, and then it was only because they were sitting on ad hoc committees.

The impact of SAPs on employment, pay and the informalisation of the economy has caused trade union membership to fall. This has undermined their financial base and bargaining power. In 1994, under 10% of the economically population were employed in the formal sector, and of these only a minute percentage were unionised (Plant, 1994: 91).

As we have seen, SAPs have had a major impact on workers and trade unions. Negative factors over and above the consequences for employment, women and real pay have emerged; these include voluntary (unpaid) severance, pay cuts, a block on promotions and annual bonuses, and the introduction of limited work schedules.

It is also clear that the economic reforms prescribed by SAPs have not shown they could accelerate growth at a steady rate. For growth to be sustained, it is necessary to create macro-economic conditions and a favourable environment. For long-term development, a more global approach to economic reforms is clearly necessary, and formulas designed to mitigate the negative effects on social issues need to be found and approved by the peoples concerned. Organisations of civil society, such as trade unions, that have close links with the people must be consulted at different stages of the process; this contribution is essential if economic reforms are to be accepted and made effective.

According to Plant (ibid: 91), 'it has been commonplace to point to the limited role' played by SSA trade unions in employment and social protection policies ... As a result of declining trade union membership since the late 1980s, organised activities have had little effect on the dramatic fall in wages and widescale lay-offs in the public sector.[2]

Elsewhere, as an analysis of the ILO's 1992 World Labour Report points out, the role and impact of unions and collective bargaining are changing in a number of ways: 'Although labour relations in Africa are still strongly shaped by a history of one-party and often autocratic government, the wave of democratisation sweeping across the continent is beginning to take effect. There is a trend now for governments to reduce their level of involvement in labour issues and to allow or invite unions and employers to participate more or to resolve issues themselves ... In this new environment trade unions have also become more active. They are frequently the only mass organisations which cut across tribal lines, so they can offer a political focus in countries where opposition parties have previously been outlawed' (ILO, 1992: 63).

The positive role that many trade unions have been able to play in the processes of democratisation has been dealt with at length (see Chapter 2). In this new climate, therefore, unions have a key role to play, particularly in the economic arena. In most countries, despite the loss of membership and resources, trade unions have been capable of responding to structural adjustment, and of openly formulating criticism of the economic policies introduced by SAPs. In fact, unions have almost been totally united in their criticism of adjustment measures and of accompanying social injustices such as redundancies, discontinued subsidies and pay freezes. They have also censured the IMF and World Bank for forcing governments to adopt policies that impact negatively on workers' living and working conditions. In some countries, however, criticism by trade unions lacks robustness because they are too close to the government; they are not able to stand back and establish the autonomy needed to articulate criticism about the effects of SAPs, let alone come up with alternatives (see Chapters on the Sudan and Togo).

*Strike action across the board*

Trade unions activity ranges from the drawing up of memoranda to the organisation of strikes; these actions argue against the privatisation of public enterprises, call for pay rises to compensate for the effects of inflation, or protest at the withdrawal of subsidies on staple goods. For example, in Zambia, there were strikes in the late 1980s against a government decision to halt subsidies on maize (Simutanyi, 1992); and in Nigeria, after the government announced an increase in the price of petrol in 1988, nationwide strikes led to clashes with workers and students (Bangura et al, 1992). In Benin, students, teachers and public sector workers went on strike on several occasions in 1989 in protest against the non-payment of wages and grants (Allen, 1992). In Côte d'Ivoire, a government decision to introduce a strict economic policy that specifically targeted pay met with a series of strikes and demonstrations and a union-organised march (de Jong, 1993). In the Central African Republic, public sector and industrial workers were on strike for several weeks in 1990 and 1991 after talks with the government on pay rises, the regular payment of salaries and conditions of employment broke down (de Jong, 1993). The Ghanaian TUC has publicly condemned the implementation of adjustment measures, and organised a number of strikes (Konings, 1993), and strikes have also taken place in francophone countries (e.g. Benin, Burkina Faso, Gabon and Niger) against the effects of conditions imposed by international financial institutions and the devaluation of the CFA franc (Martens, 1996).

## Trade union resistance

Some meetings and conferences have eventually come up with resolutions; they include conferences organised by the ICFTU on The Trade Union Response to Devaluation of the CFA Franc in Dakar on 14-15 April 1994. The Malawi Congress of Trade Unions 'protested bitterly' at the increase in the price of maize in 1995, and when the government deferred pay rises for civil servants, the unions rebelled and called a General Strike; it cost the government millions of kwachas (Mtukulo, 1995: 13). And so the examples go on. In general terms, the protests took the form of riots, wildcat strikes and popular uprisings.

Unions have sometimes tried to head off the implementation of anti-worker adjustment measures, such as redundancies, by demanding consultation rights. In Kenya, for example, rapidly escalating unemployment has prompted campaigns for a fresh examination of public sector reforms (Ikiara et al, 1996); and in Tanzania, the trade union movement has just opposed redundancy measures and the privatisation of high-performing State-owned enterprises (see Chapter 13). In other countries like Burkina Faso, national trade union federations have organised meetings, and demanded a total halt to SAPs on the grounds that structural adjustment will never resolve problems of the economy and, worse, will always be to the detriment of workers (see Chapter 7).

In some countries, trade unions have had to grapple with political problems peculiar to the country in question (e.g. Nigeria), to SAPs that have been implemented in a peculiar way (e.g. Ghana), or where the unions have played specific roles, for example in Zambia and Zimbabwe.

The role played by the trade unions in Ghana has been important because this country is often presented as the SAP 'success story'. Some think that union criticisms and alternatives have been feeble and uninteresting (Herbst, 1991). In fact, the success of structural adjustment in Ghana has been attributed to the firm control that the government has exerted over the trade union opposition. There are three reasons for this: the first is that, when the government of Jerry Rawlings took over in 1981, the senior trade union officers in post were replaced by leaders who clearly sympathised with the new government; the second is that many workers trusted the charismatic Rawlings and his revolutionary rhetoric: the third was that many trade union members and officers were subjected to repression and intimidation (Konings, 1993). When the first SAP was put in place in the early 1980s, trade unions were too divided at both national and local level to put up joint resistance (Akwetey, 1994). Nonetheless, the TUC leadership criticised the arbitrary way in which the government took decisions affecting workers without prior consultation, negotiation or discussion. For the most part, the TUC made its positions known by means of memoranda addressed to the government, and through press releases designed for public consumption (Akwetey, 1994). However, this trade union resistance had little effect on the introduction of structural adjustment measures, and for the most part the government succeeded in persuading the unions to accept the negative effects of SAPs on incomes (see Chapter 9).

Towards the end of the 1980s, the TUC persuaded the government to revive tripartite institutions and set up bilateral consultation mechanisms. However, these consultations did not automatically lead to any improvement in workers' material conditions. At this point, the TUC threatened to call a General Strike in January 1995 because of the erratic way that the tripartite committee was operating; this led to a slight improvement.

A recent TUC initiative in 1995 suggested that the government should set up a National Forum on the current state of the Ghanaian economy, to which organisations of civil society and representatives of the tripartite committee would be invited. The Forum took place in May 1996, but sadly no agreement came out of it; all that emerged was an announcement that there would be further consultation with the various organisations of civil society in the future.[3]

When SAPs were first introduced into Nigeria, the trade union movement was already saddled with one of the most repressive military régimes in the country's history. However, when the government announced major adjustment measures in July 1986, strikes broke out spontaneously, and the union campaign against the SAPs enjoyed the support of the majority of workers. The government responded by imprisoning union leaders, and by disbanding the Nigerian Labour Congress (NLC) in 1988. Bangura and Beckman (in Olukoshi, 1993) discuss three strategies that Nigerian trade unions use in an attempt to influence SAPs in the workplace:

- activities of the unions within the logic of the SAPs, accusing employers of being responsible for the problem. They expose bosses and high-ranking bureaucrats as corrupt, inefficient and undisciplined, and the aim is to undermine employers' legitimacy and encourage broad-based popular support for the trade union struggle. Bangura and Beckman suggest that this strategy also enables unions to demand a role in the adjustment process;
- the struggle to institutionalise collective bargaining. By making employers responsible for the adjustment measures, they are able to open up lines of communication and offer alternatives. Contracts of employment - frequently used by employers as a pretext for dismissing workers and curtailing benefits - often come under the microscope. Bangura and Beckman believe that the collective bargaining strategy gives unions an opportunity to try to wring concessions from employers; examples include arguing for annual bonuses, sharing the burden of rationalisation, staggering redundancies (if they are unavoidable), paying redundancy compensation, and using non-discriminatory procedures (in the event of redundancies);
- the third strategy relates to strikes and demonstrations aimed at disrupting production. Such actions are carried out when employers refuse to negotiate with the unions or refuse to honour commitments; when there are SAPs in force, trade unions come under pressure from workers to develop a militant strategy.

Zambia is well known for the fierce criticism and opposition that structural adjustment measures have attracted from the unions; as a result, SAPs often proved difficult - or impossible - to implement. In fact, the government frequently had to terminate SAPs in the late 1970s and late 1980s because of trade union action. The Zambian trade union movement was in a position to exert this kind of influence because it was independent and because trade union members distrusted the government (Akwetey, 1994). However, after the 1991 General Election, which resulted in the former ZCTU (Zambia Congress of Trade Unions) General Secretary, Frederick Chiluba, becoming President, the new government adopted very wide-ranging SAPs (Fashoyin et al, 1996).

## A participative approach

The trade union confederation in Zimbabwe, also called the ZCTU, concluded that, although criticism concentrating on the negative side of SAPs was essential, it was not enough on its own (ZCTU, 1996). The ZCTU therefore brought together a team of experts to work closely with unions, universities and other groups in civil society with a view to promoting a second phase of SAPs. The ZCTU had expressed its misgivings about the poor results of SAPs introduced during the 1980s, and now came up with an alternative which involved an approach based on coordination; under this scheme, the trade union movement would work with the government and employers in a joint institutional structure, the Zimbabwe Economic Development Council (ZEDC). 'A truly national compromise can only be arrived at when all interest groups and stakeholders participate in policy formulation, decision making and implementation' (ZCTU, 1996: 8).

This system will enable representatives of the informal sector and other groups in civil society to become ZEDC members, and participation and decision-making at all levels of society will thus be guaranteed on the basis of a broad-based, decentralised participative approach. In 1996, the ZCTU drew up a long-term strategic development framework that went further than the economic Structural Adjustment Programme. It included a range of economic proposals and alternatives that were presented to the government; they dealt with agriculture, industry, commerce, finance and the labour market.

In most of the countries we have referred to, trade unions did not question the fundamental need to stabilise and restructure the economy. They questioned SAPs, which appeared to be the only existing method of economic reform. They felt that their organisation was not seriously involved in the process whereby SAP policy measures were determined, despite the fact that tripartite structures were sometimes in existence. They focused their criticism on the social consequences that SAP policies had on workers and society in general, and observed that little serious attention was accorded the social dimensions of SAPs.

During the time of the first generation of SAPs, criticism concentrated on protests at the negative impact on workers and their non-involvement in the process of introducing these SAPs. Some unions, like those in Zambia, were fiercely critical; others, for example those in Ghana, were less so. It was not until later SAPs came on stream that unions in some countries (e.g. Mali and Zimbabwe) began to be more *pro-active*, particularly by making suggestions about the way the Programmes were designed and the impact they had on workers. The new democratic climate also made governments less reluctant to involve unions in economic reform and social affairs. In Mali, for example, the government consulted the trade unions before adopting economic measures in 1996, and the union proposals helped to slow down the rate of inflation in that country (see Chapter 10). In Zimbabwe, unions were able to play a particularly active role because they have been involved in the proposal of alternatives.

## The international response

At an international level, there is a consensus among the various trade union organisations (e.g. the OATUU, ICFTU/AFRO, WCL, PSI and EI) and the ILO on the need for economic reform. The main opposition stems from the way SAPs are drawn up, negotiated and implemented. International trade union organisations have criticised not only governments but also international financial institutions such as the World Bank and the IMF, castigating them for not consulting the trade unions. The unions are only approached when there are problems. The most frequently articulated criticism has been that the first generation of SAPs were designed to redress the imbalance between the financial and fiscal sectors, and that no attention was paid to social issues and economic development. The social dimension should have been an integral component of SAPs from the outset because, as international trade union organisations point out, no country can develop as long as social indicators, such as education and health, are falling. Economic restructuring is important for growth, but a programme of social development needs to be run in tandem: without stability in the social arena, there is little likelihood of investment. Unions should therefore be involved in the design of SAPs. Criticism of certain adjustment measures set out in international trade union documentation may be summarised as follows:

### SAPs in general
- SAP policies need to be reviewed; markets play a key role in the economy, but in many cases these do not exist, or else they function imperfectly;
- the social partners need to be actively involved in negotiating, designing, implementing, controlling and evaluating SAPs;
- the broad outlines of Programmes should be more flexible; they should not impose the same measures on every country, and thereby fail to take account of their specific characteristics;
- costs should be shared out more equitably;
- SAPs should be extended over a long period of time, thereby providing the relative stability that economies need if they are going to adjust by developing production and employment;

- continuing education and short-term employment programmes should be an integral part of SAPs.

*Privatisation*
- consideration should be given to alternatives; if privatisation is introduced, individual case studies should be conducted into the managers' competence, market structure and the legislation governing competition;
- privatisation during austerity programmes is discouraged; if, however, it is decided to go ahead, provision must be made for compensation to cover unemployment; long-term measures are also needed to provide dismissed workers with opportunities for continuing education and to help them find new work;
- privatisation should not take place in all areas of economic activity; nor should it be taboo for the government to be involved in managing the economy. Many services are provided by the public sector because the private sector lacks the motivation to get involved in such activities as social welfare for the poor, work in remote districts, sound long-term investment (particularly in transport), education and health;
- in the event of privatisation, the employers who take over need to be supervised to prevent exploitation, and to ensure that the resources that emerge from the privatisation exercise are used for productive or social ends, including cash aid and training for workers who have been made redundant.

*Rationalisation and redundancy*
- when rationalisation measures are introduced into the public sector, the impact should be more evenly distributed among workers, and redundant employees should be offered new employment;
- because of the negative effects that redundancy programmes have on the public sector, efforts should focus on preventing the introduction of such measures in the first place; however, if redundancies cannot be prevented, certain principles should be adopted.[4]

*The ILO and international trade union organisations*

*International Labour Organisation (ILO)* The ILO has organised several meetings and symposia on SAPs. A 'High-Level Meeting on Employment and Structural Adjustment' was organised in 1987 and concluded that adjustment policies should be designed in such a way as to increase the production capacities of the poor in order to construct a basis for maintaining growth and meeting essential needs. Furthermore, the need for tripartite consultation when economic policies are designed was emphasised. In 1989, the ILO organised a Tripartite Symposium on Structural Adjustment and Employment in Africa. SAPs came in for some criticism during this conference, and it was agreed that structural adjustment should not focus solely on economic management. The sustainability of economic restructuring means involvement on a national scale, and therefore the involvement of all the social partners. The ILO has also stated that if governments, social partners and other socio-professional groups do not have the skills to come up with alternative programmes, they should make use of the ILO's expertise. The ILO's Employment Department recently mounted a project on SAPs and the role of labour market institutions (ILO, 1996); the objective is to conduct research into the impact of SAPs on the labour markets in certain African countries (Kenya, Uganda, Tanzania, Zambia and Zimbabwe). Changes needed in labour market institutions are also identified in order to give employment concerns priority on the agenda.

*Organisation of African Trade Union Unity (OATUU)* The OATUU's basic position on SAPs is based on the African Alternative Framework to Structural Adjustment Programmes (AAFSAP) set up by the Organisation of African Unity and the UN Economic Commission for Africa. AAFSAP recognises the need for restructuring exercises, but thinks they should have more social content than SAPs. The main OATUU programme that addresses the issue of SAPs is entitled 'OATUU Human Resources and Capacity Building Programme'; the role of trade unions with regard to democratisation, economic restructuring and the social dimension of SAPs is analysed in seminars organised at continental, national and regional levels. The main objective is to educate members and increase their awareness so that trade union leaders can react effectively to particular questions (Limmen, 1996: 15). Representatives from the World Bank and the IMF are invited to take part in the continental seminars. The OATUU also organises international seminars on this issue.[5]

*International Confederation of Free Trade Unions (ICFTU)* The ICFTU has taken part in meetings with the IMF and World Bank in the hope of changing their views on SAP policies. Regional conferences have also been organised on the subject to help trade unions deal with SAPs. The conferences were critical in their evaluation of World Bank and IMF SAPs, which have placed too great an emphasis on the development of market economies in Africa, while disregarding their institutional environment. It is argued that a pre-condition for the success of structural adjustment is a healthy, democratic institutional basis that inspires confidence in economic and social rules (ICFTU, 1991, 1993).

At national level, programmes have been organised to give assistance to trade unions, and national conferences on the social dimension of SAPs have been held in some fifteen countries; their aim has been to create a space for dialogue between trade unions, governments and international financial institutions. The ICFTU believes that the opening thus created can serve as a point of departure for unions to exert greater influence on governments in economic and social affairs. The ICFTU's RDTP (Research and Development Training Programme) projects (RDTP, 1994a, 1994b) run in cooperation with researchers and trade union leaders in various African countries have been studying the impact of SAPs on workers since 1991.

*International Trade Secretariats (ITSs)* Reductions in State expenditure have often led to privatisation and retrenchment measures in State-owned enterprises; the sectors most acutely affected included those represented by the Public Services International (PSI), the International Transport Workers' Federation (ITF), the Postal, Telegraph and Telephone International (PTTI) and the Education International (EI). Other sectors to be hit included those covered by the International Union of Food, Agricultural, Hotel, Restaurant, Catering, Tobacco and Allied Workers' Association (IUF), the International Federation of Commercial, Clerical, Professional and Technical Employees (FIET), the International Federation of Building and Woodworkers (IFBWW) and the International Federation of Chemical, Energy and General Workers' Union (ICEF). Of these, the PSI and the EI have been most active in the field of SAPs. The PSI has sometimes used experts to analyse the effects of SAPs on a given sector, both the PSI and the EI have published a number of documents, particularly educational workbooks, on the subject, and the EI has recently conducted research into the reaction of Ghanaian teaching unions to SAPs (Limmen, 1996).

The ICFTU approach to SAPs was criticised in a recent evaluation by the Dutch Federation of Trade Unions, the FNV (ibid, 1996). The FNV argues that the national conferences on structural adjustment have been merely informative, and there has been no in-depth debate between trade unions, governments and international financial institutions. What is more, the programmes are put together by the ICFTU and ICFTU/AFRO, often in collaboration with a trade union researcher. This means that the unions themselves did not develop a feeling of 'ownership' of the document. The internal and external problems of individual trade unions and a lack of adequate preparation and follow-up have meant that these conferences have largely been one-off events (ibid: 32).

Other weaknesses identified by the FNV evaluation concern the low level of coordination on various SAP activities (as described above) among members of the international trade union community (i.e. ICFTU, OATUU,

ITSs and ILO) (ibid:18). Improved coordination and cooperation among international trade union organisations could help to develop a long-term strategy for the ICFTU and other union bodies; the FNV recommends this with a view to exerting joint influence on international institutions.

Table 3:    Survey of conferences and activities organised by the ILO and trade unions on structural adjustment (1987-1996)

| | International conferences | National conferences | Research programmes | Documents |
|---|---|---|---|---|
| 1987 | ILO: Tripartite Preparatory Meeting on Employment and SAP | | | |
| 1989 | ILO: Tripartite Symposium on SAP and Employment in Africa: The Challenge of Adjustment in Africa | | | |
| 1991 | ICFTU: Pan-African Conference on Democracy Development and the Defence of Human and Trade Union Rights, Gaborone | | ICFTU/RDTP research reports from 1991 onwards | |
| 1992 | ICFTU/WCL Conference with the IMF and the World Bank | Zambia | | What is structural adjustment (OATUU) |
| 1993 | ICFTU Conference: Building Democracy and Equity into Adjustment and Development Harare<br><br>OATUU: High Level Trade Union Policy Conference on SAP and Trade Unions, Cairo | Ghana Mali Niger | OATUU R&D programmes and capacity for construction since 1993 | Harare Declaration |
| 1994 | ICFTU Conference: The Trade Union Response to Devaluation of the CFA Franc, Dakar<br><br>Conference organised ICFTU, OATUU, WCL, ETUC, EU, IMF, and World Bank: Expanding the Trade Unions' Role in the Lomé Convention IV, Lusaka | Chad Côte-d'Ivoire Uganda | | Structural Adjustment Programmes and the Public Sector in Africa (PSI)<br><br>Lusaka Trade Union Declaration |
| 1995 | ICFTU meetings with the IMF and World Bank | Burkina Faso Gabon Mozambique Senegal | ILO Employment Department Research Project: Adjustment, Employment and Labour Market, Institutions in Sub-Saharan Africa in the 1990s<br><br>EI: Research project on SAPs inGhana | Impact of SAP on public services (efficiency, quality improvement and working conditions) (ILO) |
| 1996 | | Kenya | FNV/ICFTU Evaluation | |

The above table is a summary of regular activities; it is not exhaustive.

# Three lessons

African trade unions now find themselves in a situation in which their continent is said to have the highest poverty levels in the world. It is estimated that 54% of the inhabitants of SSA Africa live in absolute poverty (UNDP, 1994). Underemployment affects nearly 100 million Africans (Rasheed, 1996), and open unemployment is further projected to increase to 30% by the year 200; forecasts show that SSA Africa will be the only region in the world where poverty levels are likely to worsen between 1990 and 2000 (UNDP, 1990). Bad management in the 1960s, 1970s and 1980s was responsible for catastrophic economic performances in sub-Saharan Africa, and made economic reform inevitable. SAPs were therefore adopted, designed and introduced after a fashion, and with the assistance of Bretton Woods Institutions. However, despite efforts to adapt to local economic conditions and structures, the measures that were ultimately adopted failed to correct the macro-economic imbalances that had developed.

Three lessons may be drawn from this experience. Firstly, even if the reforms had been unavoidable, the damaging effects resulted in a deterioration of people's living conditions. The examples referred to in this chapter and the case studies in the Part II of this book underline the colossal social costs borne by the most vulnerable social groups; these have included a decline in employment opportunities and workers' purchasing power, and a deterioration in social services. However, the sacrifices that people were forced to make did not go away, there was no improvement in public sector management, and the promised economic upturn failed to materialise; as a result, both on their own initiative and otherwise, trade union leaders argued for mobilisations. The international climate was favourable, and trade unions in Mali, Benin, Niger, Zambia and Togo fought hard to defend the interests of the most disadvantaged members and groups and promote democracy.

SAPs extolled the virtues of economic liberalism, but felt that trade unions were responsible for rigidities that found their way into the operation of markets. In short, marginalised by politicians and weakened by a substantial decline in their resources, trade unions have done little to provide alternative solutions to the prescriptions of the Bretton Woods Institutions.

The second lesson to emerge from this analysis is, as the case study on Mali shows, that successful transition towards more democracy has not necessarily guaranteed economic upturn. During the transitional phase - when the country commits itself to the process of democratisation and is thrust into a situation of profound economic crisis - a fall in revenue is inevitable. Social groups whose levels of well-being deteriorate are potentially inimical to democratisation, and it is therefore essential to find mechanisms that will ensure that democracy survives. One way might be to increase the number of supporters, by promoting a form of economic development that will ensure that democracy is consolidated.

As the most important and most dynamic component of civil society, the trade union movement will have an important role to play in the economic future of SSA countries. National and international trade union organisations must help to shape the social dimension and, even more important, come up with alternative economic policies.

## Involving the people

The third lesson to be drawn from this chapter is the similar way in which the various components of civil society are involved in managing the country before and during the SAP, and during the short period covered by the process of democratisation. Even in Benin and Togo, where a responsible participation policy has been adopted, and in Tanzania where they have espoused the principles of collective bargaining, the various components of society in general, and the trade unions in particular, have taken little part in the design, framing, implementation and control of economic policies. This is based on a belief that involving the people in consultation and concertation exercises leads to hold-ups, and can even prevent decisions being taken at all.

Some writers now believe that more involvement by people at different stages of economic policies could improve the technical quality of the programmes concerned. Concertation increases the likelihood of popular support, and of establishing a political base on which to implement the measures. It also makes it possible to come up with better policies by involving all the skills at the country's disposal. To quote Haggard and Webb, 'The allocation of the costs and benefits of reforms is the subject of bargaining among competitive groups. Sometimes such bargaining is inefficient and fails to produce economically optimal outcomes, which makes it tempting to limit or defer the democratic control of policy making. The history of the 1970s and 1980s shows, however, that authoritarian rule does not necessarily produce positive results and that, in any case, governments cannot suppress or marginalize indefinitely the interests of major groups' (Haggard & Webb, 1994: 31). Furthermore, 'structural adjustment is not complete until the public has voted for reform (p 32).

In the socio-economic context of SSA countries, any programme of reform that has serious repercussions for people who have not been consulted can quickly bring about a climate of violent opposition, and later anarchy and social disintegration. That much is clear. Social and political stability is therefore essential if economic restructuring is to succeed.

Reflating the economy in order to improve people's well-being needs more than coherent and well formulated economic policies; it also requires the country to be managed in a new way. In our view, if people are enabled to participate in political and economic life, economic policies can match their aspirations. If people are confident that the policies will foster their development and well-being, they will work to achieve the kind of economic development we have described in the introductory chapter.

It follows that participation cannot be dissociated from development. We now have to show that participation is essential for democracy, and that the introduction of democracy is necessary for development. Chapter 4 now examines this question in more detail.

## Notes

1  Blardone, 1990.
2  An example frequently quoted in this connection is the 50% devaluation of the CFA franc in January 1994; this had major implications for pay. The unions were neither consulted about what happened nor prepared for it in any way.
3  Based on an interview with the TUC's senior political officer in July 1996.
4  For example, the OATUU/ILO principles, 1993: 9-10.
5  In particular, Lomé Convention meetings that take place every year in Brussels between countries of the European Community and the ACP.

# 4 For Participative Democracy

GÉRARD KESTER, OUSMANE OUMAROU SIDIBÉ AND AIMÉ TCHABOURÉ GOGUÉ

If the pitiful destitution of its peoples, the decay of its economy and the dramatically low level of its social indicators are anything to go by, the continent of Africa appears to have little to show for its efforts. Despite encouraging signs, particularly in countries in the franc area since the devaluation of 1993, Africa has not yet properly set foot on the road to sustainable development.

Some people now attribute this to a technocratic style of managing the economy that gives people - and therefore the various development players - little scope for involvement. Indeed, it is clear that much of the explanation for the failure of numerous, high-spending development projects has been the fact that people have not been involved in designing them, and often not even in implementing them. Development is no more than a pipe-dream unless all political, economic and social players are involved in implementing policies at both national and workplace level. The chapter on Mali shows quite clearly how insufficient concertation in framing economic reform programmes is deemed to be one of the weaknesses in the drive for sustainable growth; similarly, the absence of participation is increasingly seen as a handicap in the search for sustainable development.

We saw in the last chapter how economic policies, particularly SAPs, that receive support from external partners are drawn up and implemented without the involvement of the most important social forces. The result is that workers reject them out of hand. Indeed, a crucial ingredient of the African malaise is the fact that African peoples - employed and unemployed, men and women, young and old - have no control over their own futures because they are excluded from the major decisions concerning them.

To quote from a study that has lost none of its validity, '[t]rue democracy is ultimately incompatible with economic underdevelopment and inequality ... for the overwhelming majority of people in Latin America, Africa and Asia. It seems to be a question of keeping people sick and oppressed in order to produce a "healthy" economy. For the submerged humanity, the masses of working men and women in the underdeveloped world, the real threat lies in remaining where they are, at levels close to or below subsistence, while their countries adorn themselves with industrial trappings for the benefit of local

79

minorities and groups tied to multinational concerns. However, identifying the present situation or structural tendencies of a social system does not signify foreseeing its future. Historical change is a process open to human action and aspirations to freedom, self-determination and self-realization. In the short term, these aspirations may be repressed. In the long run, they will inexorably emerge' (Espinosa & Zimbalist, 1978: 189).

Africa has now embarked on the democratic process, and new perspectives are the harbingers of fresh hope. However, as we pointed out in Chapter 1, democracy will only survive if the democratic landscape broadens to include people in the decisions that concern them. And we are not talking about 'ballot box' democracy here, but a form of democracy that incorporates participation at all levels, including economic matters. We showed in Chapter 3 how trade unions have expressed their misgivings about SAPs; however, they have not been able to exert any palpable influence, particularly on economic policy. There is therefore a need to find mechanisms to ensure that democracy affects the economy and other areas of society.

Trade unions now play a part in initiating democratic policies, but their task is far from completed; in fact, it has only just begun. Democracy not only has to be defended; it must also be deepened and institutionalised in all sectors of national life. Young, fragile African democracies still need to be defended, as recent events suggest, notably the coup d'état in Niger, and the violent oppression (including barbarous military clampdowns) perpetrated by the governments of Guinea, the Congo and the Central African Republic in 1996.

In Chapter 1, we stressed that democracy is a factor in development; in this chapter, we shall examine how trade unions can contribute to democracy. The challenge concerns preserving and deepening democracy, and trade unions have an immensely important part to play in both arenas.

In Chapter 2, we described the key role that trade unions played in civil society in achieving democracy. What can be done to ensure that, with support from the whole of civil society, they realise their potential? Political parties still lack structure; they are not yet fully established and are therefore weak, and civil society therefore has an important role to play as a counter-power, and even more as a school for democracy. Every union and association can enable its members to learn the ways of democracy through its own democratic activities, and ultimately contribute to the development of a democratic culture of societal proportions. In this respect, trade unions have a major responsibility. The trade union movement is both a social player and a horizontal institution representing broad social groups, and unlike other, transitory elements of civil society, it is particularly involved in the defence of democracy. The defence of human rights and fundamental liberties, and the sound management of public resources within a transparent democratic framework, are permanent battlegrounds of the trade union movement.

As soon as formal democracy has been achieved, certain elements of civil society customarily depart and take refuge in corporatist demands. However, any trade union conscious of its mission in an African context cannot permit itself such liberties without running the risk of forsaking its mission, and discarding an ideal for which it has mobilised millions of men and women. Trade unions should not be left to defend democracy on their own, while other players in civil society are free to focus exclusively on corporatist demands; indeed, these very players have themselves made vital, not to say decisive, contributions to the democratisation process. Examples include members of the Togolese Commission Nationale des Droits de l'Homme (National Human Rights Commission), the students of that country and the lawyers of Cameroon. Rather it is for trade unions, where circumstances allow, to continue to bring the various protagonists together under a single umbrella - and motivate them. In other words, they need to act as a catalyst in an economic crisis where political parties seem to be more preoccupied with winning power than with developing the long-term vision that alone will guarantee sustainable democracy.

In most countries, once formal democratic change has come about, civil society falls apart, or at least loses its cohesion. Centripetal forces then take control and each group, the trade union movement included, finds itself locked into sectarian demands. This may well be one of the great problems for trade union leaders because, if civil society does disintegrate into different pressure groups, African States do not yet have the strength to muster much resistance. There is so little to share out that the most violent groups, or anyway those that occupy the most strategic sectors, will corner what meagre resources there are, and everybody else will go away empty-handed. Countries will then be catapulted into a vicious circle of demands, anarchy and repression, and the outcome will be the inexorable return of dictatorship.

## The deepening of democracy

In many African countries, democratic change 'has essentially occurred in form only and has not led to effective participation in governance or to meaningful political accountability ... multipartyism has not guaranteed broad-based participation in governance and development' (Rasheed, 1995: 340). Can we say we have achieved democracy when workers are barred from all decision-making processes in the workplace? Can we say we have real democracy when the opinions of trade unions and citizens are neither canvassed nor taken into account in the framing of economic and social policies? Can we say we have true democracy when women and young people continue to be marginalised?

In this respect, as Onimode points out, in addition to the restricted democratic rights that Africans enjoy, we also need to look into the question of citizenship rights related to economic democratisation, and also the right to life, the right to minimum levels of income, the question of redistribution of ownership, and control of resources (Codesria Bulletin, 1992, N 1/2: 23). A similar point is made by Zenebeworke Tadesse: 'In Africa today, and especially given the restructuring of the economy, the major social players are not organized at the economic level' (ibid: 18).

Democracy therefore needs to be extended throughout society and embedded into social, cultural and economic life. To use the language of sociology, democracy needs to be institutionalised. It needs to become rooted in people's hearts and minds, and become the major factor determining their future.

From this perspective, the trade union movement has a considerable role to play in the institutionalisation of democracy. Given the importance of the economy in people's commitment to the process of democratisation, trade unions in particular need to re-think their strategy if they want to play a new role in the economy and ensure that democracy survives. We set out below the various options open to them.

First of all, a plea that unions take a renewed interest in participation. Whereas a consensus is developing between the World Bank and associated institutions that participation is necessary for economic development, the response of the trade unions remains timid. We will present a selection of provisional APADEP research results which clearly show how keen workers and their representatives are to participate. We shall also look at recent developments in South Africa where participation has become a fundamental component of development strategy.

Participation at the workplace is on the wane despite the high expectations that workers' representatives once entertained. At national level, it has become a matter of urgency: What forms can participation take? How can trade unions produce an alternative vision of economic and social development, and therefore join the avant-garde of civil society? How can the trade union movement come up with a vision of society?

We shall also pose the following questions relating to feasibility: What conditions do there have to be for trade unions to play a key role in participation? And who will foot the bill?

*The rehabilitation of democratic participation*

Since the early 1990s and the heady days of the movement for political democratisation and economic liberalisation, the notion of participation has disappeared from the vocabulary not only of political parties and governments, but often of trade unions as well. In practice, governments and (new) employers have found it a lot easier to operate in a neo-liberal space provided by international institutions which rejected participation outright. In fact, workers were hardly consulted at all over privatisations sanctioned under economic reform programmes. In Africa, particularly, when governments modelled on east European régimes were finally brought down, features that had been closely associated with the latter, such as participation, were simultaneously jettisoned. In general terms, by adopting a 'no nonsense' approach, conservative forces did very nicely out of the new situation.

However, analysis of the social consequences of SAPs has increasingly persuaded even the most sceptical international organisations, such as the World Bank, that there is a need to address the social dimension of Programmes, and that participation is vital to their success (World Bank Annual Report 1993: 18 & 37; UNDP Human Development Report 1993: 22-23).[1] The Development Assistance Committee (DAC) unequivocally subscribes to the development of participation in that 'it strengthens civil society and the economy by empowering groups, communities and organisations ... [and] enhances the efficiency ... and sustainability of development programmes' (OECD, 1993: 8). However, declarations of intent are all very well; reality is a quite different matter. To date, there has not been a single full-blooded initiative to set up an institution involving consultation, let alone one based on co-determination.

More surprising is the trade union movement's lack of enthusiasm for participation. Perhaps the end of the Cold War is to blame. In the past, trade unions were frequently incorporated in single parties, but they are now autonomous and most of them are affiliated to AFRO, the ICFTU African Regional Organisation. The ICFTU used to argue strongly against the policies of east European countries, and consistently condemned participation, which it (wrongly) associated with these régimes. In Africa, AFRO campaigned for traditional trade union methods, that is to say for collective bargaining and trade union action rather than participation. True, with a nod in the direction of the Arusha Declaration, the OATUU made workers' participation one of the main planks of its trade union policy, but affiliates, many of which were also affiliated to AFRO, never translated its resolutions into participation.

As a result, 'responsible participation' gave way to 'rhetorical participation'. Nevertheless, a resurgence of enthusiasm for participation is needed for moral, political and practical reasons. Firstly, moral reasons because, by achieving dignity and self-respect, it can contribute to human development (essential for a people yearning for *self-development* (see Chapter 1)). Secondly, political reasons because democracy is not just about control of a country's administration, transparency and good governance at national level. These factors are equally necessary both in the workplace and for the economy, particularly at a time like the present when the State's role in the economy is in decline. Furthermore, who will exercise democratic control in this vast arena? Thirdly, there are practical reasons because human resources need to be mobilised for optimum performance and creativity.

Participation is simply not fashionable at the moment; it does not accord well with the neo-liberal spirit of our times. Participation, say managers and decision-makers, is unrealistic. However, realism that feeds on cynicism destroys society, whereas realism that feeds on an ideal is a progressive force. We appear to be living in an age when people almost seem to be ashamed of holding ideals. As Fukuyama (1992) suggests, the end of ideologies means the end of history.

Assuming they retain their realism, will trade unions slide into cynicism or idealism? Economic and political trends have forced them onto the defensive, and to a greater or lesser extent they are in crisis in both industrialised and developing countries. Loss of membership has restricted them to defending the rights of those who are still in membership, and high priority is given to campaigns that defend jobs, purchasing power and social security rights. This work is very important, but it exhausts much of the trade union movement's energy. And meanwhile, who is going to deal with the key social problems of the totality of workers (not to mention the unemployed, marginalised women and the socially excluded), whether or not they are trade union members? And if trade unions don't do it, who will?

An alternative strategy is participation, not as a replacement for confrontation - this is still essential, and it is also what gives trade unions their strength - but as a supplementary strategy. Collective bargaining only covers contractual aspects of employment, which may include many elements, but it allows other decision-makers to determine policy prerogatives relating to work organisation, production and (above all) company, community, regional and country policy. Negotiations are often based on the effects of previously made decisions, rather than on the decisions themselves. Criticism made from outside the decision-making forums is not sufficiently probing; trade union protests against SAPs (see Chapter 3) provide ample evidence of that. If one is to have any impact at all, one needs to get inside these forums and partake in the decision-making on the basis of statutory equality. One also needs to formulate appropriate institutions and instruments if one wants to be where the decisions of the future are taken.

Trade unions will have to make up their own minds about this, of course. They also have to ensure, though processes of internal democracy, that members' ambitions are translated into trade union policy and action. And one final element of ambiguity: does a trade union speak as representative of its members or of all workers?

*Yearning for participation*

We should now ask ourselves whether the picture we have drawn of participation is one that is shared by grass-roots activists. In fact, the results of APADEP research point to a quite different conclusion; we set out our provisional results below. Our current research is based on a comparative international questionnaire survey of trade union and workers' representatives, and a series of case studies and longitudinal studies. A questionnaire survey of 1960 trade union representatives was carried out between 1987 and 1990 in Guinea; a similar survey that commenced in Mali in 1993 is now being finalised (a sample of 1160 interviewees is available for the period 1993-1995); and in Tanzania, 835 workers' and trade union representatives replied to a questionnaire between 1993 and 1995. As for the other countries (Zimbabwe, Ghana, Burkina Faso and Mozambique), processing of the questionnaire is at different stages of completion and is not sufficiently advanced for results to be made public. In the cases of Guinea, Mali and Tanzania, the available data are based on a quasi-representative sample of local workers' representatives in all three countries combined.[2] Some twenty case studies on the functioning of trade unions and enterprise-level participation have been carried out in these three countries and South Africa; we refer to them later in this chapter.

Five dimensions of worker's representatives' views of participation were studied: acceptance of participation in general, evaluation of participation, militancy with regard to participation, participation propensity and participation confidence.

Acceptance of participation covers workers' general predisposition to participation. Table 1 indicates almost across-the-board (between 93% and 99%) acceptance in Guinea, Mali and Tanzania; one could not hope for a more eloquent research outcome. What do representatives value in participation (evaluation of participation)? To this open question about what participation meant for them, 75% of Tanzanian representatives and about 50% of Guinean and Malian representatives spontaneously replied 'democracy' (e.g. 'taking part in decisions', 'having things to say' and 'being able to express their views'). Other opinions ranged from better labour relations to productivity.

In a structured question, participants were asked to choose three from a total of eight opinions distributed evenly between four aspects of participation:

human relations, democracy, economic equity and production. As Table 2 shows, human relations scored particularly high in Tanzania; this may reflect the accent that this country has placed on 'Socialism with a human face' for so many decades. In Mali, scores were more evenly distributed: human relations ('getting more respect as a worker', 'better relations between workers and management'), democracy ('having more influence on important questions', 'more power for the working class'), equity ('getting a decent wage', 'fair distribution of work') and production ('working better and more' and 'assisting in the construction of the country').[3]

Table 1:    General attitude towards participation of trade union and workers' representatives in Guinea, Mali and Tanzania (%)

|  | Guinea (1987-1990 ; N=1960) | Mali (1993-1995 ; N=1160) | Tanzania (1993-1995 ; N= 825) |
|---|---|---|---|
| For participation | 98 | 93 | 99 |
| Against participation | 1 | 3 | 1 |
| No reply | 1 | 4 | 0 |
|  | 100 | 100 | 100 |

Table 2:    Priority values attributed to participation by trade union and workers' representatives in Mali and Tanzania (%)

|  | Mali (1993-1995 ; N=1160) | Tanzania (1993-1995 ; N=825) |
|---|---|---|
| **HUMAN RELATIONS** better employer/employee relations more respect from employers | 34 46 | 72 53 |
| **DEMOCRACY** more say in the workplace more power for workers | 53 6 | 34 9 |
| **EQUITY** better pay better distribution of jobs | 60 2 | 61 3 |
| **PRODUCTION** working better and more development of the country | 41 46 | 38 17 |

*    Percentages add up to more than 100 as interviewees were asked to prioritise three out of eight values.

Table 3:    Acceptance of participation by trade union and workers' representatives in Guinea, Mali and Tanzania (%)

|  | Guinea (1987-1990 ;N=1960) | Mali (1993-1995 ;N=1160) | Tanzania (1993-1995 ;N= 825) |
|---|---|---|---|
| Reject participation | 1 | 3 | 2 |
| Accept participation | 30 | 34 | 54 |
| Conditionally accept participation* | 69 | 63 | 44 |
|  | 100 | 100 | 100 |

* Only if the conditions for effective participation are present.

Table 4:    Participation militancy of trade union and workers' representatives in Guinea, Mali and Tanzania (%)*

| Workers are entitled to: | Guinea (1987-1990 ; N=1960) | Mali (1993-1995 ; N=1160) | Tanzania (1993-1995 ; N= 825) |
|---|---|---|---|
| Information | 79 | 91 | 93 |
| Consultation | 66 | 87 | 88 |
| Co-determination | 57 | 76 | 83 |
| Profit sharing | na** | 69 | 80 |
| Sharing of ownership | na | 46 | 68 |

*   This Table only presents percentages of those who believe they are 'entitled' to participation; other percentages ('it is a privilege' and 'we should not participate') are not included.

** The questionnaire used in Guinea did not include questions on militancy in respect of the sharing of profits or ownership.

**Table 5:**    **Participation propensity with respect to 18 types of decision of trade union and workers' representatives in Guinea, Mali and Tanzania (%)**

|  | Guinea (1987-1990 ; N=1960) | | Mali (1993-1995 ; N=1160) | | Tanzania (1993-1995 ; N= 825) | |
|---|---|---|---|---|---|---|
|  | Management prerogative | participation | Management prerogative | participation | Management prerogative | participation |
| **ECONOMY** | | | | | | |
| Investment | 35 | 65 | 20 | 80 | 5 | 95 |
| Profit allocation | 32 | 68 | 23 | 77 | 8 | 92 |
| Expansion | 51 | 49 | 31 | 69 | 9 | 91 |
| **PRODUCTION** | | | | | | |
| Maintenance | 30 | 70 | 18 | 82 | 9 | 91 |
| Purchase of machinery | 43 | 57 | 31 | 69 | 12 | 88 |
| New technology | 43 | 57 | 25 | 75 | 8 | 92 |
| **ORGANISATION** | | | | | | |
| Work | 36 | 64 | 26 | 74 | 17 | 83 |
| Job allocation | 48 | 52 | 39 | 61 | 19 | 81 |
| Working hours, breaks | 38 | 62 | 23 | 77 | 10 | 90 |
| **STAFFING** | | | | | | |
| Disciplinary procedures | 16 | 84 | 14 | 86 | 6 | 94 |
| Dismissal | 35 | 65 | 26 | 74 | 8 | 92 |
| Promotion | 41 | 59 | 36 | 64 | 16 | 84 |
| **CONTRACT** | | | | | | |
| Transport | na* | na* | 28 | 72 | 12 | 88 |
| Wages | na | na | 35 | 65 | 13 | 87 |
| Bonuses | na | na | 30 | 70 | 12 | 88 |
| **WELFARE** | | | | | | |
| Sports facilities | 15 | 85 | 20 | 80 | 10 | 90 |
| Health and safety | 33 | 67 | 24 | 76 | 10 | 90 |
| Canteen | 30 | 70 | 28 | 72 | 13 | 87 |

\*    The questionnaire used in Guinea did not include questions on the contract of employment.

Table 6:   Self-assessment of ability to participate by trade union and
workers' representatives in Guinea, Mali and Tanzania (%)

|  | Guinea (1987-1990 ; N=1960) | Mali (1993-1995 ; N=1160) | Tanzania (1993-1995 ; N= 825) |
|---|---|---|---|
| Capable of participation | 62 | 47 | 59 |
| It depends | 34 | 38 | 29 |
| Not capable | 4 | 15 | 12 |
|  | 100 | 100 | 100 |

Opinions on participation are remarkably diverse; they range from more
access to power and greater equity in income and employment, to more
human dignity and higher productivity and economic development.
Predictably, the last two opinions are highly esteemed by managers, and
were priority aspects in the manipulative application of 'responsible
participation'. Table 3 provides evidence of the courage and wisdom of
workers' representatives in Guinea, Mali and Tanzania (despite its relatively
low performance in participation (see Chapter 13)), where it is almost
universally accepted; this bears out the figures in Table 1. It would appear,
therefore, that workers set far too much store by participation for it to be
sidelined; this was the fate to which earlier schemes were consigned.
However, representatives are still wary: in Guinea, for example, seven out
of eight say they will only go for participation if it guarantees protection of
their interests; this view is also widely held in Mali.

In Tanzania, almost half of the representatives are prepared to opt for
participation unconditionally and, what is more, adopt a militant policy to
achieve it: most think that workers have an absolute entitlement to be
informed and consulted, to be involved in decision-making, and to have a
share of profits and ownership (see Table 4). In Mali and Guinea, militant
support for participation is only slightly less enthusiastic.

As often happens, 'political' orientations run into the buffers when they
encounter concrete, practical realities. As for the 18 different types of
company-level decision - they range from overall economic policy to staffing
issues and welfare - an average of one third of interviewees in Mali and
Guinea replied that such decisions were management prerogatives (Table
5); the fact that a substantially lower percentage of representatives in
Tanzania took this view is further evidence of a higher degree of militancy
in that country. At all events, the message contained in Table 5 is that the

majority of representatives want participation to cover a whole range of issues, and not to confine itself to welfare, contracts of employment and staffing matters. Their predisposition towards participation focuses on organisation and production, and even more critically on key economic decisions. Their position on this is quite unshakeable in all discussions on the future of participation in these three countries; this is probably, albeit hypothetically, reflected throughout the rest of Africa as well.

Questions relating to workers' predisposition to participation provide more information on the degree of participation under the 18 questions in Table 5. The most common reply was a demand for consultation on these decisions; a less widespread response (under 25%) called for the right to co-determination and the right of veto. Enthusiastic support for participation wanes when people begin to realise how little control they have.

The final question, which deals with representatives' confidence in participation, looks at the extent to which they feel capable of participating. Approximately one out of two feel capable; only 4-12% do not (Table 6).

The 20 or so case studies carried out up to 1995 suggest considerable interest in participation not only among representatives, but also among the workers they speak for. They are frequently aware of the qualities they have to offer, and feel bitter about the lack of consultation. One can only ponder the grim consequences of this for employers - and for the workers themselves.

## The enterprise as a micro-SAP

The neo-liberal ideology that currently pervades thinking across the globe, and particularly in Africa, seems to be saying that democracy was designed with politics, and not economics, in mind. Both in African countries in transition and in the countries of eastern Europe, the vestiges of participation inherited from earlier (Socialist) governments have been unceremoniously swept aside. Instead, encouragement has been given to forms of labour relations that are based on collective bargaining and which do not question management prerogatives. Structural adjustment and accompanying privatisations have also introduced this principle into both the new private sector and the reorganised public and parastate sectors. By way of corollary, private enterprise has re-introduced the key concept that employees must bow to the fluctuating demands of employers and managers (Fox, 1971). Management prerogatives relating to decision-making should not be challenged in such a way that managerial authority is based 'on the normative agreement that, in entering into a contract of employment, the employee legitimizes the employer in directing and controlling his activities' (Ross, 1969: 13). To put it more simply, as classical theoreticians have pointed out, collective bargaining determines what the contract of employment says, but beyond that, all decisions relating to organisation, staffing, production and commerce lie outside democratic control.

The enterprise is a micro-SAP. National and international structural adjustment policies are replicated in miniature at the workplace. In Africa, most participative structures that have been set up in workplaces are to be found in the public and parastate sectors. However, as soon as enterprises are privatised, as the chapters on Mali and Tanzania show, participation withers on the stem. There are also fewer practical examples of participation in what is left of the public sector, because government enthusiasm to defend it has evaporated. We have stressed on a number of occasions (see Chapter 1) that this lack of interest is a legacy from an earlier period when participation was synonymous with manipulation; moreover, trade union protests at the lack of participation have also been conspicuous by their absence over the last few years.

Political democracy has been a key dimension in the development process throughout the 1990s. However, if a country's policy is to be democratically controlled, there is no reason why a company's policy should not be controlled in the same way. 'Destatisation' was a consequence of poor management of public enterprises, and workers were the first to suffer, but who is to say that a company is necessarily better managed by a private individual? Case studies of private enterprises, particularly in Mali, point to exceptionally bad management (Mallé et al, 1992; 'Mopti Syndicalement', 1993; Coulibaly et al, 1993, 1994a, 1994b). Even if private companies happen to be better managed, workers and their representatives are not saying that democracy should stop at the factory gate. Moreover, grass-roots activists do not go along with the privatisation philosophy that employers have 'carte blanche' to do as they please just because the companies went bankrupt when they were in the public sector. The question of good governance needs to be addressed at both workplace and government level. Let us not forget that democratic control is part and parcel of good governance.

If democracy is to be deepened, given the resources to survive and made a permanent feature, the workplace is the battlefield par excellence; moreover, if workers' representatives are putting their faith in participation generally, it is because they are also putting their faith in democracy in their immediate surroundings. The institutionalisation of democracy through participation structures and mechanisms is in itself a way of nurturing a democratic culture. In Chapter 1, we referred both to Pateman's theory that participation at the workplace is an essential condition for the survival of democracy, and to Albert's theory which uses an international comparative study to show that co-determination economies (i.e. those characterised by co-determination) function better than those that eschew participation altogether. It is a lesson that post-apartheid South Africa has been quick to learn.

## The South African challenge

Of all countries on the continent of Africa, South Africa is most likely to make strides on the workers' participation front. Recent legislation on labour relations there is also considered to be the most modern in the whole of Africa, as is its overall conception of participation questions.[4]

The underlying aim of the new labour Bill is to promote cooperation in the country's reconstruction. Previously, relations between workers and management were exclusively marked by adversarialism, but trade union militancy and protest was a necessary component of the war on apartheid at the time. However, the new South Africa needed a different conception of labour relations, and one that gave new powers to workers. This was the key element of the platform that COSATU (Congress of South African Trade Unions) adopted in December 1993. COSATU leaders have also played a major role in the Reconstruction and Development Programme (RDP), the main political manifesto of the ANC that gave policy guidelines to transition in South Africa. Democracy, participation and development are the basic principles of the RDP whose main aim, as we saw in Chapter 1, has been to democratise the economy by encouraging participation in decisions on economic matters (Coetzee, 1996; Kester, 1995).

The latter objective has been achieved through the Labour Relations Act (LRA), and particularly through the setting up of 'workplace forums'; they are workers' councils in workplaces that employ more than 100 people. These forums can only be set up if a representative trade union expressly asks for one. A forum's structures, competence and procedures are determined by negotiation between the trade union and the employer, and employers have to consult the forums and involve them in decision-making. Forums also have a mandatory right to consultation over a company's most important economic decisions, and any other decisions affecting production, organisation and staffing. Contracts of employment continue to be covered exclusively by collective bargaining. The right to co-determination (i.e. the right to vote) only applies in respect of a small number of decisions: disciplinary codes and procedures and works rules (apart from those related to work performance), 'affirmative action' issues, changes to rules regulating social security schemes, and all measures dealing with acquired rights can only be invoked following consensus between the employer and the forums (LRA, Section 86). The union and the employer may extend the scope of participation by negotiated agreement.

Interestingly, the law gives considerable impetus to participation at the workplace and, although the parties still have very few agreements to show for it, the LRA has been responsible for the introduction of new democratic procedures. The law also provides for a wide range of supports; one example is training which is made available to enable employers and workers' representatives to acquire the necessary skills for effective participation in the forums (Explanatory Memorandum 1995: 38). Other forms of support provided under the new legislation include the right to invite experts to prepare and attend meetings, forum meetings during working hours, and employer-provided facilities (e.g. electoral expenses, administrative back-up, secretarial assistance and telephones) to enable forums to function effectively. Without going so far as to make it mandatory, the law also suggests that the employer should also bear training costs (Section 82).

The law offers much hope for the future, in the sense that it opens up new perspectives for participative democracy in South African labour relations. However, it has caused much controversy, sparking off stormy debates throughout the country when draft legislation was published in February 1995. It has now been adopted by parliament, but the dust has yet to settle. The role of the trade union 'trigger' (i.e. no forums unless the union expressly asks for one) and the 100-employee threshold (workplaces with fewer than 100 employees are excluded despite the fact that they are in the majority) both arouse much controversy. The 'trigger' clause hands all initiative and control over to the union, but there is even resistance in certain union circles where it is feared that participation might curb the aggressive tactics of shop stewards' committees, hitherto the bastion of the South African trade union movement (for an update on this controversy and discord, see du Toit, 1996).

## Participation and trade unions beyond the workplace

Trade unionism and participation have been designed for, and implemented in, workplaces, particularly enterprises. However, given the current conjuncture in African countries consisting of high unemployment and a large number of socially excluded (e.g. women and young people), trade unionism and participation also need to confront the numerous problems that workers face outside traditional places of work. Workers affected include not only those who have been laid off by public enterprises, but also employees who have precarious conditions of employment (e.g. part-time, seasonal and day work).

A great divide has opened up between those who are in work and those who are not, yet trade unions continue to concentrate on the formal sector and the workplace. More to the point, in industrialised countries, and increasingly in Third World countries, the structure of power in the workplace is becoming increasingly elusive as a result of relocation of capital ownership, and the internationalisation and globalisation of the economy. This also results in a relocation of centres of power, with the enterprise eluding all democratic control.

Moreover, there are key issues that are having a major impact on employment and, by extension, on labour relations, the trade union movement and participation. These mainly relate to energy supply, natural resources, the environment, technological change, migration and population growth. In other words, the company is no longer the place where all labour relations problems can be resolved. Because of major developments in the labour market, the technological revolution and changes in ownership structures, labour relations now have to deal with many quite different questions, and workers' problems have to be resolved at several levels.

Jacques Delors, himself a former trade unionist, has appealed to European trade unions to make a firmer commitment outside the workplace and to establish direct contact with workers. Otherwise, Delors believes, the trade union movement faces an bleak future (Delors, 1994: 44). Such an appeal has even more resonance in Africa because of the size of the informal sector and the number of socially excluded. We need answers to the following questions: Where and how are these marginalised groups going to participate in democracy? To what extent can they receive a fair share of national revenue within the framework of the shared fruits of an economy restructured for them? And where and how will they have an opportunity to co-determine their future?

## Agents of change and development

It is not unreasonable to believe that trade unions can be persuaded to play an innovative role. One of the main conclusions of the survey carried out in Guinea (completed 1990) was that trade union representatives are 'agents of change', and the results overall enable us to determine the characteristics of trade union representation throughout that country. Most Guinean workers' representatives employed in the formal sector - the implication is that they are relatively privileged, although the popular notion of a 'labour aristocracy' is a gross exaggeration - live in the countryside and come from peasant households; the members of these households are semi-skilled or skilled workers, mostly in the informal sector, and many of them are unemployed. Their share homes with people of all ages, virtually none of whom is in regular employment or has a wage or salary. All of them, without exception, including the workers' representative him/herself, have to engage in other economic activities (e.g. agriculture, cattle breeding, craft work and commerce) to make a living. The representative's wage then has to be shared among family members - perhaps even among inhabitants of the village - to pay for a marriage, a dowry, the education of his/her own or other children and medicine, and to help the handicapped and the unemployed. A job in the formal sector and the wage attached to it are linked to social security problems for large families; the wage is often the cash segment of total income from all sources, including a variety of jobs that these people perform just to survive (Diallo et al, 1992: 115). Research outcomes point to the same conclusions in Tanzania and Mali.

These trade union representatives have a dual perspective as far as labour relations are concerned. On the one hand, they are concerned about pay because they are desperately short of money and are unable to meet most of their basic expenses. On the other hand, their time is also taken up with work and their families; furthermore, as individuals responsible for people who, if they were living in industrialised countries, would be taken care of by social security, they are also concerned with development. This emerges clearly from their lists of priority problems (e.g. water supply and systems of communication). They also want development programmes to be better organised, and they criticise the waste of human and material resources, together with poor management of the civil service and of local development projects (Diallo et al, 1992: 100).

This awareness could provide the basis for a policy of democratic participation. However, we are left with the following circular question: How can this development 'conscience' be mobilised, developed and translated into concrete actions? That is where the trade unions come in.

In some African countries, local and regional trade union structures were put in place in the days of one-party government to act as lines of communication between the grass roots and the leadership. Unfortunately, their potential for representing workers' interests before local and regional administration officials was realised either not at all, or only to a limited extent. When the single parties were brought down, these trade union structures were not reoriented in such a way that they became legitimate partners in the administration, examining workers' grievances and passing them on to decision-makers at the top; the reason for this may have been that they were afraid of being associated with the previous régimes.

The argument for a trade union presence has again become a current and crucial issue due to the democratic void at local and regional level; when the single parties were replaced, the new political parties and other elements of civil society rarely made much of a mark. We saw in Chapter 2 how trade unions have acted as catalysts of the democratic movement in some countries. This is particularly true where unions have not been really dependent on the party, or where they have unambiguously kept their distance. It is therefore important to explore the different possible dimensions of trade union participation outside the workplace.

## National concertation

### *For a vision on society*

The citizens of every country need to develop a vision of their future, and reach a basic agreement on long-term political, economic and social objectives; in other words, they need to produce a vision on society. This vision will enable the country to define its priorities, and determine both the strategies that have to be implemented and the actions that need to be carried out.

In the euphoria that followed independence, African political leaders were unable to draw up a coherent society vision in a systematic way and with clear, realistic objectives. In the early 1960s, development policies were constructed within an economic and social development framework. In principle, plans are documents that provide direction and decisions, but these projects and plans were simply amalgams of non-prioritised objectives and took no account of the constraints facing society. In the event, everything was accorded priority: economic growth, rural development, industrial development, the development of human resources, the construction of infrastructures, self-sufficiency in food - and so the list goes on. To make matters worse, people were not consulted at the planning stage. Objectives and strategies were defined by political leaders and technicians with assistance from foreign experts, and their ideological inspiration was frequently out of kilter with the realities of the country in question. Moreover, the various plans were blatantly similar in content; this reflected the trend to use external experts who were usually UNDP-funded.

Quite simply, in the absence of any serious evaluation of the pros and cons, and with people not involved in planning their future, internal resources were never going to be mobilised to any significant extent. The plans eventually adopted were only implemented with assistance from external resources which, in most cases, accounted for over 60% of estimated investment earmarked for the duration of the plans. In fact, the efficiency of Ministers with responsibility for the plan was judged by their ability to tap external resources.

The situation remained unchanged throughout the 1980s and the early 1990s. Bretton Woods Institutions replaced the UNDP as chief partner as far as policy and sometimes economic assistance were concerned, although these days the economies and modes of operation of the various sectors are better known and the constraints are better understood.

Unless a country meticulously determines the directions it wishes to take, it is not safe from donors' whims. If a country does not define its long-term priorities, it leaves the door wide open for anyone to take advantage and for uncontrolled improvisation to take place. Any foreign economic agent - whether a bilateral or international aid donor or a private investor - who has the resources to invest can do so without giving a second thought to the country's real needs.

Then, external partners, whose objectives are sometimes very different, not to say divergent, inevitably become involved, and this leads to even more dependence; as a result, the external community begins to play an increasingly influential role in the country's economic, social and political management. With the country now firmly locked into this logic, it gradually strays from the need to draw up a society vision, and allows itself to be taken over - until the point comes when foreign partners eventually lose all interest.

When the first SAPs were put in place, the objectives, priorities and means were defined by the Bretton Woods Institutions; these included the macro-economic framework, movements of the various aggregates, sectoral policies, economic growth rates, allocation of resources, fixing the price scales of public sector goods and services, price and subsidy policies affecting income distribution, and privatisation policy.

In a multi-party system, it is the job of the political parties to formulate society visions for the benefit of the electorate. In the old western democracies, the traditional divide between conservative and left-wing parties is sufficiently well known, as are the shades that fill the spectrum from far left to far right. However, the worldwide triumph of liberalism has largely diluted the ideological differences between left and right; this has had major repercussions on society, and in particular it has deprived citizens of a point of reference.

However, the situation in Africa is radically different. The youthfulness of the political parties, their lack of roots and, in many cases, their regional or ethnic membership base - not to mention a scarcely concealed partiality for clientelism - make it almost impossible for them to come up with a coherent, acceptable society vision. By contrast, the various components of civil society have a close relationship with the people, and are better placed to understand their aspirations. It follows that civil society occupies a key position in the process of defining the vision.

The existence of several social groups - and, by the same token, of contradictory interests - makes unanimity on the future of society difficult, if not impossible. It is therefore important to accept the principle of the right to be different. In fact, unanimity is the exception. Accordingly, the problem is not the existence of disputes; the problem is how to resolve disputes in a way that is acceptable to all. A diversity of options is an inherent quality of living in society, and it is difficult to achieve divergent objectives simultaneously. That is why accepting arbitration between the visions of the various components of civil society is also essential to life in any society. It is therefore important to arbitrate between the aspirations of the various social groups. These aspirations vary in time and space. A good society vision will synthesise the aspirations of the various components of society, and the various groups will only feel they are part of this synthesis if they are sure, not that all their concerns have been dealt with, but that their aspirations have been, and continue to be, taken into consideration. Accordingly, the body charged with arbitrating between aspirations must have credibility and represent the various components of society.

## National concertation and trade unions

It is customary for political parties to consult their own activists, and no one else. However, if civil society and certain political parties have little, or no, parliamentary representation, it is very easy for their activists' aspirations to count for very little when the society vision is being developed. That is why some countries complement parliaments with Economic and Social Councils in order to promote social dialogue. If these Councils base their deliberations on concertation and consultation with other institutions and social groups, they will be able to produce a vision that has a chance of being accepted by everyone.

The trade union movement can also play a role of this type through its position in the economy and its horizontal position in society. This scenario is not some theoretical vision; it has already been tested experimentally in several countries, although on a modest scale and not systematically. In 1994, for example, when beset by enormous problems on the political, economic and social fronts and facing an ever-increasing wave of demands, the Malian government organised a series of regional concertations rounded off by a 'coming together' (synthèse nationale) in Bamako. These concertations were intended to identify issues underlying consensual solutions to critical problems such as the Tuareg rebellion in the north, the student crisis, economic problems arising out of the devaluation of the CFA franc and youth employment.

The concertations brought together all players in civil society and the political parties, although they were boycotted by one of the opposition parties; the meetings produced a consensus on all problems raised. They also lowered the level of social tension and facilitated solutions to certain delicate matters, such as the student crisis, which the government had not resolved. Although the trade unions took part, it is regrettable that they did not play a bigger role in identifying the problems discussed or in the scenarios suggested for dealing with them. If they had been more proactive, the concertations would undoubtedly have had more credibility; moreover, it would probably have headed off the petulant response of certain opposition parties which saw them as no more than a political manoeuvre to back the government as it put difficult decisions (e.g. criteria for granting scholarships in higher education) into practice.

The democratisation of African countries has opened up numerous spaces and frameworks for concertation which, if properly used, could gradually establish a tradition of resolving difficulties through open, frank dialogue. Examples of this include the Economic and Social Councils set up in Côte d'Ivoire, Burkina Faso, Mali, Senegal, Gabon, Guinea and South Africa. Now that African countries are learning to experience living democracy, and the means of expression are becoming more numerous and more available, there is a growing need to organise and listen to these institutions and groups in order to ensure that they both feed into political debate and have control over, and participate in, the economic, social and cultural affairs of their countries.

However, these structures have not played the roles that were expected of them, and for the most part they continue to be institutional ornaments; this is because the social groups that have seats on them - particularly trade unions, which are enviably well represented - appear to have neither the enterprise nor the energy to conjure up a dynamic for reform. In this respect, the trade union movement has a lot to answer for. This intensification of popular pressure in Africa means that people no longer have any confidence in the State when it comes to key issues like bad management, the economic crisis and the violation of human rights. Demonstrations of this sort have also revealed that people have an awareness, and also a wish to demonstrate that they are capable of mobilising to survive, to make themselves heard, and to take part in decision-making - even if it means upsetting a few people in power. The extent of this awareness and the range of movements that are often difficult to keep under control, underline the urgent need to reinforce the bases of civil society in such a way that the foundations of democracy, too, are reinforced (Sidibé et al, 1994: 83).

This is where trade union revival has the best chance of success. Because of the democratic void, unions should now listen to the problems of the unemployed, peasants, women, youth, the handicapped, migrants and everyone in the informal sector. These social groups are also potential members who might reinvigorate the trade union movement through infusions of new blood and by rejigging what trade unions do and say; both need to be adapted to a modern African context.

Trade unions could also broaden their base by establishing links with the numerous organisations and associations that came into being to promote democratisation; in this way, the trade union movement would acquire new allies as it seeks to strengthen democracy and the economy for the benefit of the majority. This struggle is not solely a matter of making protests and issuing demands. Internal democracy and transparency in management as mediated by the current democratic climate are also assets that could help trade unions to grow stronger.

If sustainable solutions are to be found, it is essential to develop forms of participation that are adapted to specific situations. Trade unions occupy a special position, and can act as bridge-builders in the participation process. They are also able to win the confidence of workers, both members and non-members, and can draw together the various levels, key moments and questions that are central to participative democracy. The challenge is how to direct and structure the presence of trade unions at local and regional levels.

*National policy*

At national level, civil society, and trade unions particularly, should be playing a key role in monitoring policy implementation. Control of public sector management and of actions carried out by the Executive is one of the most important ways of ensuring that the evils so loudly deprecated in African countries (e.g. corruption, nepotism, clientelism and regionalism) are eliminated. The sound management that is increasingly a condition of aid provided by donors seeks to achieve not only transparency and control of management but also sanctions. A well-drawn up society vision, together with coherent and well-formulated economic policies, can career completely out of control if the officials or Executive Power charged with implementing them are not accountable to anyone. In some countries, the Constitution even provides for institutions whose task it is to manage the public sector.

However, the State monitoring service often becomes a political weapon when placed in the hands of the supervisory authority: control is rarely systematic, and reports are not made public except when they concern disgraced senior officials or political opponents. Unfortunately, more autonomous institutions like the Revenue Court often lack resources: when they were set up under the Constitutions that came out of the democratic process, they appear not to have been a government priority. If the trade union leadership put more effort into drawing up a society vision and defining the country's priorities, unions could then press for these institutions to be given the independent resources they need.

**The trade union deficit**

Trade unions need to take up a number of challenges simultaneously both at the workplace and in national and international arenas. At the workplace, workers' representatives are looking to trade unions for support so that they can participate more effectively. This is what happened in the 1970s and 1980s when governments in certain countries contributed to the dynamic of the participation movement (Gogué et al, 1992: 171); this demand for support by trade unions continued when the governments ceased to be cooperative. The positive attitude shown by trade unions, when they have been sympathetic to participation, has rarely been translated into strong participation policies (ibid: 172). In fact, workers' representatives have often complained about the lack of time, and the absence of premises for meetings, secretarial back-up, transport and means of communication that would have helped them develop participative activities.

Representatives at the grass roots are keenly aware of education and training deficits, and are eagerly looking forward to trade union support in this area (Kester & Nangati, 1987: 71). More recent APADEP case studies show that the main reason for the relative failure of participation is an almost complete absence of training in this area. Topics that require examination include What is participation all about? and How can it play a significant role? (Coulibaly et al, 1993, 1994a, 1994b; Chambua et al, 1994). According to a case study conducted in Tanzania, this lack of education can lead to passivity among workers' council members and a sense of inferiority among workers' representatives (Kiduanga et al, 1994).

As we have made very clear in this chapter, the APADEP survey shows beyond all doubt that workers' representatives are eager to participate. What now needs to be done is ensure that their ambitions are translated into action, and defended and developed; the necessary resources must also be made available. Workers' representatives are in desperate need of trade union support; this is hardly surprising if we recall how closely the effectiveness and quality of workers' participation in Europe relies on trade union back-up. By and large, participation is more successful when it is supported by trade unions (Pinaud, 1995: 37 et seqq). Participation is a learning experience, and the trade unions now face the challenge of how to make good the deficit.

Participation by trade unions is also necessary at national level. The previous chapter on structural adjustment underlined the trade union deficit in this respect, too. The unions have been knocking on the doors of governments, the World Bank and the IMF, it is true, but without great success. Indeed, a report published under the auspices of the ICFTU has concluded that ICFTU affiliates' criticism of Structural Adjustment Programmes have had no real impact on macro-economic and social development; moreover, national conferences organised by the ICFTU have been well perceived but poorly prepared, and have contained neither critical debate on macro-economic questions nor follow-up (Limmen, 1996: 19-23). Instead, the accent has been on the social implications of structural adjustment, and therefore on remedying the symptoms rather than on formulating a trade union policy for economic and social issues; 'formulating a trade union vision and approach should be identified as a top priority for trade unions' (ibid: 23).

The same report argues that trade union influence should be channelled through participation structures at national level. As we have already described, structures of this sort already exist in certain francophone countries; for instance, South Africa's NEDLAC (National Economic Development and Labour Council) (see Chapter 5) is a major source of inspiration for surrounding countries (Seminar organised by SATUCC (Southern African Trade Union Coordinating Council), Harare, April 1996). In other words, an opening for more national concertation is beginning to emerge, and the World Bank and IMF appear to be more receptive; at least, they are more so than certain governments. This leaves the trade union movement with the formidable task of ensuring that these efforts are turned into reality. If they do nothing, and if the conditions in which they operate remain unchanged, trade unions cannot expect to meet the new challenges.

*Problems in profusion*

As we briefly indicated in Chapter 1, this immense task presents itself just at a time when the African trade union movement is going through a process of major change. Having shaken off political party or government control, unions in many countries are now fighting to find their place in the democratic order. They, too, are undergoing structural adjustment. The move towards autonomy and democracy goes hand in hand with trade union pluralism, which could in turn inflict harm on the movement generally: trade union rights have had to be redrawn and defended and, following the withdrawal of (official or disguised) government subsidies and the automatic 'check-off' system, widespread lay-offs have led to unions losing members and income. As a result, trade unions in many countries have lost much of their power, and where they have managed to avoid that fate to any extent, they have foreign funders to thank.

APADEP research shows that most local trade union committees in the countries examined have no income, no means of transport and no premises (APADEP, forthcoming). A case study of a Togolese mine describes how the management banned union representatives from meeting on site; they had to hold their meetings elsewhere outside working hours, and in the end, meetings became impossible to organise because of the distances that workers had to cover. The one file on the trade union was kept in the Personnel Office, and access to that was extremely difficult (APADEP, 1985).

One consequence of the opportunities opened up by donors is increased expenditure on international travel (i.e. to seminars, conferences and congresses) to the detriment of travel within the country; this has driven a wedge between rank-and-file representatives and national officers. There is a healthy demand for trade union information, but most grass-roots committees have no way of finding out about labour law in their countries and cannot even get hold of copies of their own union Statutes (APADEP, forthcoming). The content of education and training packages has changed now that indoctrination by the party is a thing of the past, but most representatives cannot attend the courses. Education programmes are beginning to take place in the cities and the more industrialised areas thanks to help from donors; away from urban centres, however, opportunities are few and far between. It is not unusual for the APADEP education programme to be first to be presented in a given region for many years; sometimes, it is the first ever.

The notion of a trade union deficit is also true of trade union organisations themselves; this stems from the residue of 'State trade unionism' that survives in the practices of many countries. The whole issue of internal democracy is a huge challenge. In this context, APADEP surveys have unearthed major disparities in trade union elections: in Guinea and Mali, for example, over 80% of shopfloor elections are 'by show of hand' or 'by acclamation', whereas in Tanzania 63% of representatives are elected by secret ballot (APADEP Research Report, to be published in 1998). Such 'discreet' elections do not happen automatically at national level either; in fact, as happened, for example, at the CNTG Congress in Guinea in 1996, leaders are often elected at union congresses by acclamation despite the fact that the rules stipulate a 'secret ballot'.

Like political democracy, trade union democracy is not just a matter of periodic elections. Unions will themselves have to demonstrate good practice in such areas as democratic culture, good governance and democratic control of governance if they wish to play a decisive role in consolidating African democratisation. Transparent management, and good communications between grass-roots representatives and workers (and between grass-roots representatives and regional and national leaders) are both major ingredients of democracy and key battle zones for the trade union movement.[5]

In Chapter 10, Bakary Karambé, the doyen of the Malian trade union movement, warns that trade unions are in urgent need of change, and that they must become more professional if they are to meet the challenges of the future. Similarly, the ICFTU report referred to above argues for trade union skills, research and expertise, on the grounds that they will enable trade unions to take an active part in framing macro-economic policies (Limmen, 1996, passim). The same also applies to the grass roots.

## Democratic participation: the cost

The main problem facing trade unions is funding. In most countries, members' contributions are not enough to ensure that unions function properly and can pay for things like premises, telephone bills and transport, let alone additional services such as education and training, research and the use of experts, a facility that all professional organisations have now come to expect.

Campaigns have been necessary in many countries to encourage members to pay their contributions, particularly where check-off has been abolished. A campaign of this sort costs a lot of money if it has to reach out to the full membership. In some countries, these campaigns are already running at full capacity, but any increase in resources will be nothing like enough to enable unions to function properly. This applies equally to increased membership in the informal sector, among women and peasants, and in the new service sectors. These campaigns are essential if only because they make unions more representative and more closely involved in economic and social development at national and international level.

Even when they are successful, these campaigns are not always synonymous with healthy bank balances. In fact, the opposite is much more likely to be the case. If trade unions want to move into sectors which they have hitherto neglected, they will need to develop a large number of professionally based activities.

### *Dancing to the donors' tune*

It follows that trade unions need to look hard for funding, and this has made them even more dependent on western donors and international trade union confederations. Often, trade union congresses cannot take place at all unless they run alongside seminars that the funders have financed, and most trade union activities are based on projects whose criteria have often been determined a long way from the country in question. These projects have become the linchpin of trade union activity and, depending on the creativity of the union concerned or donors' conscious flexibility, money freed up for projects is often used to fund union infrastructures or pay international dues. With money on offer, it would be churlish to take trade union leaders to task for speaking the language of funders as they attempt to obtain donations for their organisations.

International trade union cooperation is, of course, extremely welcome because it enables the African trade union movement not only to oversee its own democratisation, but also to run a grass-roots education programme and carry out research; in other words, it can manage its process of change. The philosophy underlying this cooperation is quite simple: the achievement of self-sufficiency. Aid needs to promote activities that will then be taken up by individual trade unions using their own resources.

Anyone moving in African trade union circles knows full well that, for the reasons set out above, self-sufficiency is an idle fancy; quite simply, trade unions are still run by people who have no money. Projects launched in the framework of international cooperation are accompanied by follow-up projects, and if there happens to be no external funding, nothing comes of them. A fear of unfinished projects may encourage donors to mount further follow-up projects. In these circumstances, cooperation could become addictive, and that is exactly the kind of pitfall that donors and trade unions need to avoid. The unions cannot carry on dancing to the donors' tune for ever.

In view of the generous, and frequently honest and disinterested, work of donors, criticism might appear churlish. However, there are grounds for concern. Why do donors not take more interest in the overall coordination of cooperation? Projects of all types are funded in many different places by various international trade union organisations. These include not only the ICFTU/AFRO, but also the WCL, WFTU, OATUU and CTUC, and a large number of International Trade Secretariats (e.g. Education International, FIET and PSI). Then, there are foundations (e.g. Friedrich Ebert, Hans Seidel and the AALC), and national trade union confederations based in Europe (e.g. LO (Norway), LO (Sweden), SASK (Finland), LO-FTF (Denmark), FNV and CNV (Netherlands), CFDT, CGT and Force Ouvrière (France) and the ISCOSS project (Italy)), and major projects undertaken by the International Labour Organisation (ILO).

Trade union affiliation was a strong argument in the project allocation that led to a showdown between the ICFTU/AFRO, OATUU, WCL and WFTU, and it could trigger a new balkanisation of the African trade union movement. As national trade union centres often cooperate with a large number of donors, it is not unusual for project target groups to overlap. Furthermore, as donors, too, want to cooperate with many countries despite limited finances, their respective funds only benefit the upper layer of the trade union structure in capital cities and urban areas. Donors organise numerous (often poorly prepared) international seminars and conferences in Africa and Europe, where the same trade unionists are to be found discussing the same agendas - and agreeing on the same resolutions. We estimate that the amount of money spent on international trade union travel is much higher than the total sum of trade union members' contributions in Africa. A moratorium lasting a few years could enable substantial sums of money to be put into the training of trade union representatives and into trade union research. However, beneficiary unions have little say over cooperation with donors, and they do not often control the use of available funds. Criteria and allocations are being determined by the north.

## Who is responsible?

Irrespective of the practical details of cooperation, the African trade union movement cannot continue to be funded by dipping into other people's wallets in the name of international trade union solidarity. For the trade unions themselves, the future looks difficult. They already lack the resources to meet the challenges of their own participation, despite considerable efforts to expand their financial base; an example of this is the Ghana TUC project to create and maintain jobs in enterprises set up through a trade union share fund (Ghana TUC, 1996: 76 et seqq).

A completely new set of opportunities could be explored. For example, in the course of collective bargaining exercises with private enterprises, there could be scope for negotiating support for both trade union activity and participation training. More to the point, taking our lead from South Africa (see above), one also needs to fight for national legislation compelling employers to fund activities linked to participation, possibly by fixing a sum of money proportional to payroll costs. This would enable trade unions to stop begging for money since they would receive funds for participation support as of right. It would also mirror what happens in Europe where participation could never function properly without financial support from employers.

However, responsibility also lies with society in general. If society recognises the positive role played by the trade union movement in promoting democracy and development, it must take steps to enable trade unions to play their part: the demand for legislation covering the launching and sustaining of participation should enjoy support from politicians. There is also the possibility of encouraging public institutions to strike up alliances with the unions.

A concrete problem is that of universities. One of the basic conditions for trade unions being able to play their role is the availability of training and resources to support high-quality research; it is an area that clearly involves universities. The whole field is marked by a wide range of perspectives. An important Codesria report on the role of social movements in the democratisation process came to the following conclusion: 'The alienation of academic institutions from social movements and the related practice of academics limiting academic freedom is a historical legacy. African academics should be beyond casual and distanced discussion of social movements and identify research themes in collaboration with popular movements with a view to devising a usable strategy for social movements and popular struggles ... Such a strategy requires a lot of creativity and implies moving away from the existing, very individualized and institutionally located research paradigms' (Codesria Bulletin, 1992,

1/2: 26). For the time being, the trend is moving in the opposite direction. Universities, too, are working through their own structural adjustment; this is founded on a privatised economy concerned with the marketing of services. In such a climate, trade unions with their empty wallets stand little chance of making any headway.

If we push the analysis a little further, we begin to realise that it is not only trade unions that are short of money, but also universities - and even governments. Trade unions are poor. All of Africa is poor. Debt is condemning an entire continent to the begging-bowl.

Structural adjustment is a good thing insofar as it facilitates a restructuring of both the economy and social affairs - in other words, if it facilitates true democracy. However, what do trade unions get out of accepting World Bank invitations to participate in concertations on macro-economic policies unless they do so as equal partners? And what do they get out of involving workers' representatives in decision-making in enterprises unless they can back them up with the necessary training and provide them with the necessary resources?

Participative democracy does not happen on its own. It requires a huge investment. The underlying argument running through this book is that democracy is a necessary condition for development. Even the international community has now come round to this way of thinking, but it will amount to nothing more than vain rhetoric if good intentions are not translated into real support. Democratic participation has to be budgeted for. It also needs to be a structural component of work on structural adjustment, preferably as a percentage of the budget for projects launched by the World Bank and other international organisations.

At the end of the day, what is the point of economic progress if this 'progress' is wrecked by revolution, civil war - or just war?

## Notes

1  According to the UNDP Human Development Report 1993, 'political parti-cipation is not just a casting of votes. It is a way of life' (p 23) and 'participation in economic life affords people a basis for self-respect and social dignity' (p 22).

2  Results of the survey are due to appear in a forthcoming publication that will also elaborate the methodology, including the sampling strategy, used in the research. Given the subject matter covered in this chapter, we have decided to publish certain statistics on Guinea, Mali and Tanzania early; consolidated results are expected in 1997 and will be published in 1998.

3  This question did not appear on the questionnaire in Guinea.

4   In February 1995, the South African Minister of Labour submitted a drafted Labour Relations Act, together with an Explanatory Memorandum. Both documents were publicly debated, and were negotiated by the various social partners concerned. The law was adopted in 1996. On debates relating to the law, see NALEDI, 1995; for a commentary, see du Toit, 1996. For the general process of transition in South Africa, see Chapter 5 of this book.

5   The next APADEP publication (1998) will cover this issue in more detail.

# Part II

# A Look at Ten African Countries

Ten countries, ten case studies, ten ways of dealing with reality. All of these countries big and small, English-, Portuguese- and French-speaking have been carried along by the same historic whirlwind known as 'democratisation'.

Today, the powerful gusts of neo-liberalism have brought most economies to their knees, and forced their peoples back on the defensive. Now, these people call out in a single voice, 'Let us look after our own affairs, and as far from Bretton Woods as possible! Let us create and evolve our own democratic culture!'

However, there are many routes to achieving these aims, and each country is following its own path at its own speed: some countries already boast a detailed balance sheet of benefits of democracy, while others are still at the stage of assessing their options.

In Part II, the authors have looked at four issues (democracy, development, trade unions and participation) and have adopted different positions on the specific characteristics of their respective countries. Some bluntly chronicle a spade a spade while others content themselves with posing questions.

# 5 South Africa
# A Negotiated Transition

DAVID GINSBURG AND EDDIE WEBSTER

*Using the transition theory as the basis, 'parleying' seems to be the key to a successful passage to democracy. In South Africa, apartheid is no more and, after years of struggle, the régime's opponents and reformers finally reached a negotiated solution. Trade unions like COSATU played a pivotal role in the fall of apartheid, and are now very active in implementing the process of transition. However, will the new democracy satisfy a civil society that has little experience of social, economic and political equality?*

The transition from apartheid to democracy in South Africa aroused immense enthusiasm and interest around the world. Massive global attention was devoted to the country's first genuinely democratic elections, held on April 27, 1994. The elections saw the triumph of the African National Congress (ANC) with nearly 63% of the vote, and replacement of the previous National Party government by a multi-party but ANC dominated Government of National Unity.

The truly remarkable transformation - what Adam and Moodley described in 1993 as a 'negotiated revolution' - has seen South Africa warmly welcomed back into the international community and widely cited as a model for other conflict torn states to emulate. Our particular interest is with the role of the labour movement in the transition process, and whether the nature and extent of the democratisation on offer will satisfy and contain the aspirations of South Africa's organised workers. If it does not, we may conclude either that the labour movement - and perhaps other popular social forces - will attempt to push beyond the boundaries of democracy as it has arrived in South Africa or, more alarmingly, that the newly democratic regime may resort to authoritarian means to re- impose a politics of order.

What lies at the base of this work is concern that South Africa's new democracy - if it is to be a democracy in more than just name - must bring both material benefits and a better quality of life to all people of all classes, creeds and races. That, after all, was what the struggle against apartheid was all about.

111

*Theorising transition*

The theorist whose work we use as a starting point is Adam Przeworski, whose Democracy and the Market (1991) provides a particularly succinct and systematic analysis of the transition process in recently democratised countries, elaborated further by Adler and Webster (1995: 83- 84).

Underlying this theory is the assumption that successful transition from authoritarianism to democracy can only be brought about as a result of negotiations, of pacts between reformers in the state and moderates in the opposition.

'The political implication is that pro-democratic forces must be prudent; they must be prepared to offer concessions in exchange for democracy.' (Przeworski 1991: 98)

Przeworski argues that very few transitions to democracy are the result of a revolutionary rupture where the ancien regime is overthrown by a popular insurrection. Instead, they more usually occur in contexts where existing power holders retain much of their control over the levers of power in society, property, the military and, not least, the state bureaucracy. At the same time, they are unable easily to eradicate opposition. Transition begins when there is a mutually perceived sense of stalemate, the continuation of which becomes untenable:

'Protagonists agree to terminate conflicts...because they fear a continuation of conflict may lead to civil war that will be collectively and individually threatening. The pressure to stabilise the situation is tremendous since governance must somehow continue. Chaos is the worst alternative for all.' (Przeworski 1991: 85)

Przeworski finds the solution to chaos in an alliance between reformers inside the authoritarian block and moderates in the pro-democracy opposition. Both distance themselves from extremists in their own camps: reformers from hardliners and moderates from radicals. Thus both seek a sub-optimal solution that will nonetheless allow themselves and their society to survive:

'Reformers face a strategic choice of remaining in an authoritarian alliance with hardliners, or seeking a democratic alliance with moderates. Moderates, in turn, can seek all out destruction of the political forces organised under the authoritarian regime by allying with radicals, or they can seek an accommodation by negotiating with reformers.' (Przeworski 1991: 69)

This solution is encouraged by the threat of chaos implicit in continued stalemate or maximalist solutions:

> 'Political actors calculate that whatever difference in their welfare could result from a more favourable institutional framework is not worth the risk inherent in continued conflict.' (Przeworski 1991: 85)

Reformers and moderates find common cause in a limited, or shrunken notion of democracy in which governments 'must be strong to govern effectively, but weak enough not to be able to govern against important interests'.

## An elitist character

The elitist aspects of liberal democratic theory find new currency as the alliance of reformers and moderates commits itself to a form of politics that preserves the central pillars of capitalist society, ensuring that entrenched power holders - especially the bourgeoisie - maintain a veto over the pace, content and institutional form of the new democracy. Hence Przeworski concludes that successful transitions require an arrangement which is 'inevitably conservative, economically and socially'. This is brought about through institutions of 'elite pacted democracy' which insulate the government from the broad mass of people by making politics the permanent business of a small number of specialised personnel.

Importantly, however, in such situations governments are confronted with two options in relation to social movements. They can either work to undermine them or they can work with them to garner support for their programme. Where there are strong social movements, the first path can only be pursued at great risk, as it threatens to compromise the democratic character of the transition. Consequently, most governments attempt to draw in social movements through corporatist type arrangements on the assumption that these will demobilise and moderate popular movements.

## South Africa's transition

In applying this framework to an analysis of the transition to democracy in South Africa, we may usefully start from the mid-1980s, by which time the crisis of apartheid had produced an impasse between the white controlled state and the popular organisations of the oppressed mass of the population.

No longer could the apartheid state secure the conditions for capital accumulation that it had once so effectively done. While previously apartheid provided the material conditions for profitability, the policy had come to engender a level of conflict in society that seriously jeopardised the future of capitalism in South Africa. Indeed, a low intensity civil war had emerged in the townships, with large parts rendered ungovernable, operating as 'no go areas' for the security forces and virtually under the control of what were, effectively, embryonic institutions of people's power. In the words of the United Democratic Front (UDF), the coordinating body which emerged in early 1983 and came to embody the exiled ANC in its enforced absence from above ground politics:

> 'Not only are we opposed to the present parliament because we are excluded, but because parliamentary type of representation in itself represents a limited and narrow idea of democracy... The rudimentary organs of people's power that have begun to emerge in South Africa...represent in many ways the beginnings of the kind of democracy we are striving for.' (Quoted in Lodge 1994: 24)

Grassroots democratic pressures could no longer be suppressed through the tried and tested states of emergency that once seemed to work so effectively. The regime had run out of repressive options and increasingly lacked the will, if not the resources, to suppress conflicts occasioned by armed struggle and mass action by unions and civics. The campaign to make the country ungovernable had stretched the resources of the state to a point where further repressive measures would have entailed costs that capital was increasingly unwilling to bear. Crucially, too, the global financial community had refused to 'roll over' the government's debt repayments and harsher sanctions had begun to take a toll. However, for all that the government faced mounting difficulties in pursuing apartheid, so too did the ANC in seeking to dislodge it. Although it could claim massive popular support, the principal liberation movement failed in its bid to unilaterally seize power because, while disruptive, neither the armed struggle nor the campaign to make the country ungovernable neared a point where the state was likely to be overthrown.

Labour struggles too - for all that latterly they were spearheaded by COSATU, a federation which proved strategically highly astute - had indicated what unions everywhere else have learned: that the withdrawal of labour alone, albeit over non-workplace issues, is only exceptionally sufficient to topple governments. Even South Africa, which by then had one of the strongest labour movements in the developing world, was no exception. The stalemate could only be broken when the major protagonists realised that their individual solutions to South Africa's crisis could not be imposed unilaterally on others and that a negotiated solution, with all sides involved, would be the only way to achieve some of their aims. More specifically, the regime had to accept that the demise of apartheid entailed a new, non-racial democracy in which minority interests were guaranteed by a Bill of Rights rather than race specific legislation.

On the other hand, the pro-democracy forces had to accept that the end to the stalemate would not be achieved through armed struggle and that they would have to enter the process of negotiating a new order that would leave key institutions of the old South Africa intact. It was only when the stalemate was finally and mutually acknowledged and when the military formations on both sides came to accept that they could not eliminate each other, that the main opposing parties to the conflict began to talk to each other. Key actors began to sense the stalemate in the mid-1980s when tentative and exploratory talks between quasi-official intermediaries began both inside the country and abroad.

An important moment occurred when Kobie Coetzee, Minister of Justice, Police and Prisons, began discussions with imprisoned ANC leader Nelson Mandela in 1986 (Sparks 1994). Initially, the talks made little headway because of the insistence by President PW Botha that Mandela publicly renounced armed struggle. However, the emergence of FW De Klerk as President in 1989 allowed reformists to move decisively in the direction of a negotiated solution. In February 1990, Nelson Mandela was released unconditionally and the ANC, the Pan Africanist Congress (PAC) and the South African Communist Party (SACP) were unbanned.

Over the last 12 months the ANC, SACP and COSATU forged a formal alliance that cautiously began to distance itself from the armed struggle and from more radical elements within their own ranks. In Przeworski terms, the preconditions for negotiations had been met.

*Vanishing ideologies*

Negotiations for a democratic alternative in South Africa began in earnest at precisely the moment when notions of alternative forms of democracy vanished. The collapse of Stalinist societies in Eastern Europe and the Soviet Union, and the bankruptcy of social democracy in Western Europe, had transformed the international climate, delegitimising radical notions of democracy and social change. This removed the apartheid regime's historic fear that the commandist version of democracy, long espoused by the SACP, would be imposed on the negotiating process.

It became imperative at this point that the ANC reassert its organisational and ideological hegemony over the radical and precocious grassroots social movements that emerged during the near insurrectionary period of the 1980s. During the 1980s high expectations were generated of a 'revolutionary rupture' that would usher in an egalitarian society. It was a period of hope, when activists in the labour movement and the civics were de facto leaders in the internal democratic movement.

The first step in the process of demobilisation was the unceremonious disbanding of the UDF. While many of its activists joined the ANC, a large number withdrew from political activism and were lost to the movement. At the same time, COSATU's leadership was increasingly drawn into tripartite corporatist type arrangements such as the National Manpower Commission, the National Economic Forum and many other forums that emerged during the period. Initially, COSATU entered the negotiations with a perception of itself as an equal partner in the transition process. Indeed, it applied to participate in the Convention for a Democratic South Africa (CODESA), which constituted the first round of formal negotiations after February 1990, in its own right. The application was rejected on the grounds that COSATU was not a political party of government, and it was informed that its interests would be represented indirectly through its ANC and SACP allies. Subsequently, the three organisations entered a formal Tripartite Alliance for the purpose of ensuring that each of their positions were accommodated in negotiations: ostensibly each party to the Alliance had equal status. COSATU entered into an electoral accord with the ANC on this understanding.

However, this was transformed during 1993 into participation in a broad based programme of national consensus, the Reconstruction and Development Programme (RDP). COSATU played a central role in the ANC's election campaign, and some 20 COSATU members stood as ANC national candidates. Two of its leading members - Alec Erwin, now Minister of Trade and Commerce and Minister of Telecommunications Jay Naidoo - were appointed to key ministerial posts in the new Government.

*Transition theory limitations*

At first glance it appears as if South Africa was a textbook case of democratisation along the lines of transition theory. There was indeed a meeting of minds between moderates and reformers, and pro-democratic forces were prudent in the version of democracy they were willing to settle for. In Przeworski's terms we have a parliamentary system based on an interim Constitution which effectively protects the interests of capital. In this sense, the system is economically and socially conservative.

But appearances can be deceptive. What transition theory neglects or downplays, and the South African case demonstrates, is the central role of social movements - of struggle - in shaping both the modalities and the outcomes of the transition process (Adler and Webster 1995: 76). This is our point of departure, and the rationale for our research. Although widely recognised as key actors in the transition, remarkably little research has been done on the expectations unionised workers have of the corporatist trends already visible and their relationship to parliamentary democracy. The central research question we were concerned with was whether the social movement character of the South African labour movement would be lost in the face of the new political dispensation, or whether its social movement character would significantly shape the transition process.

This chapter is based on the findings of a nationwide survey conducted among organised workers, and on interviews with key officials in COSATU and its affiliates. They allowed us to identify the persistence of a tradition of participatory democracy in the workplace and its transfer to the parliamentary arena. More significantly, we suggest that there are growing signs of a democratic rupture between trade union leaders drawn into corporatist type tripartite structures, and rank and file trade union members. Further, in contrast to the 'hegemonic' notion that South Africa has become a parliamentary democracy in which the elected majority party has a relatively free hand to govern the country as it likes between elections, our respondents appeared to be committed to a different notion of democracy. They tended to view democracy as an ongoing process of decision making in which all people affected should be continuously and actively engaged.

The survey identified a tradition of participatory democracy among COSATU members, whose elected leaders are expected to be accountable and report back to their members. Importantly, most were committed to the view that parliamentary democracy must be substantially the same and consist of elected members held regularly accountable to the citizens. If the new Government fails to deliver, workers claimed they would resort to ongoing mass action to force the Government to live up to its electoral promises. We argue that this - not a rightwing coup d'etat or demands for sovereign ethnic states - constitutes the greatest challenge facing the Government of National Unity: a challenge which could propel the Government towards redistributive policies by mobilising pressure from civil society, the community and the workplace. The South African case holds open the possibility of a less conservative outcome than transition theory would suggest.

## Taking democracy seriously

The transition from authoritarian rule to democracy is effected through a process of elite pacting in which reformers in the state and moderates in the democratic opposition negotiate a form of representative democracy which essentially conserves the pillars of a capitalist order. This conservative outcome is essentially attributable to the fact that neither the state nor its democratic opposition are able to impose their will on the other without inducing a level of chaos that is unacceptable to each. Thus the notion of democracy articulated by transition theory represents a compromise that holds few prospects for a more radical form of participation than is typically encountered in liberal, representative democratic systems. Put differently, it is a form of democracy that does not extend beyond the realm of parliamentary politics.

A case can clearly be made for viewing deputy president FW De Klerk's faction in the National Party as having a reformist bent while the alliance between the ANC, the SACP and COSATU has been committed to a moderate path of negotiating the demise of apartheid. It is also reasonable to conclude that neither the former South African Defence Force nor the armed formations in the democratic movement were able to achieve their respective objectives of suppressing resistance to apartheid, and of unilaterally seizing power, without plunging the country into Bosnian type civil war.

The apartheid order was thus dismantled - in line with the 'model' of transition - without engendering the chaos predicted by the numerous prophets of doom who, prior to the onset of negotiations, were convinced that any attempt to wrestle power away from the apartheid regime would trigger resistance and counter resistance that would end in the destruction of all.

It is equally clear that the form of democracy established on the basis of the Interim Constitution does accord closely with the form of limited representative democracy identified in transition theory. Thus while few could gainsay the fact that real democratic progress has been made in the past few years, we must question whether this particular form of democracy will prove capable of resolving the conflicts that persist in civil society, and of satisfying the aspirations of ordinary people demanding a say in the running of the new South Africa. In particular, the question arises as to whether this new democratic form can accommodate the demands emanating from civil society for greater equality at the social, economic and political levels.

There are, of course, those who would argue that the bourgeois state, whatever its form, is inherently incapable of meeting either the democratic aspirations of the working class, narrowly defined, or of civil society. The claim is that bourgeois states exist essentially to buttress the power of classes whose material interest lie in excluding workers and the masses from critical decision making processes and otherwise limiting their demands to those consistent with the ruling interests. In short the argument is that any form of bourgeois democracy is inherently incapable of meeting popular aspirations, and that even to work with it is to risk drawing the working classes into political practices that involve unacceptable compromises of their interests. From this perspective, the road to democracy lies in the revolutionary overthrow of capitalism and the establishment of a socialist society.

In our view - whatever the theoretical merits of the above argument - the radical scenario for the future of South Africa is unlikely to materialise. In the first place our data tend to suggest that organised workers are thus far willing to participate in parliamentary politics and evince no significant desire to embark on the kind of politics that would usher in a socialist order of the kind described.

Moreover, the Government of National Unity appears willing to deploy forces of law and order against worker militancy as was demonstrated in the strike wave and blockades in mid-1994. In addition, our reading of the current international environment suggests that the major powers would use all means at their disposal to prevent South Africa's workers from effecting a revolutionary overthrow of the capitalist order.

Contemporary democratic movements have the misfortune of entering the state when notions of alternative societies have vanished. The collapse of Stalinist societies in the Soviet Union and Eastern Europe and the bankruptcy of social democracy in Western Europe has transformed the international climate, delegitimising radical notions of democracy and social change. This has reinforced the apparent intellectual hegemony of liberal democracy and the free market - the 'limited democracy' favoured by transition theorists. It has opened up a gap between expectations developed by workers during the struggle against apartheid and the reality of the form of parliamentary democracy under a Government of National Unity. The findings from our survey illustrate this argument.

The vast majority of respondents subscribe to the notion of direct participatory democracy in the workplace, where they see their elected representative, the shop steward, as directly accountable to them. With this bottom up notion of democracy, most are firmly of the view that parliamentary democracy should be substantially the same and must consist of the following principles and practices:
- Members of Parliament must report back every time they make decisions in Parliament that affect their supporters.
- If Members of Parliament do not do what their supporters want, they should be recalled.
- If the new government fails to deliver, workers will participate in mass action to force the Government to deliver on its promises.

More significantly, there are growing signs of a 'democratic rupture' between leaders drawn into corporatist structures and rank and file members. We have entered a phase of parliamentary democracy in which the elected majority will have a relatively free hand to govern the country even if it means abandoning its election manifesto. Our respondents, on the other hand, appear to be committed to a different notion of democracy: they tend to view democracy as a continuing process of decision making that all people affected should actively engage in.

In a democratic South Africa contradictions are coming sharply to the fore as the Government of National Unity embarks upon the task of national development. The pressure on unions to identify with the goals of national development as defined by political leaders is considerable. In post-colonial Africa, governments have expected unions to play a dualistic role: firstly, that of sacrificing their narrow sectional interests to the overall demands of national development and, secondly, representing the job interests of rank and file members.

The argument for the reversal of the primary role of unions to be developmental rather than representational has been based on the belief that trade unions represent a small and privileged proportion of Africa's labour force. As a World Bank report recently argued:

> '...increased union activity raised African real wages in the formal sector by about 15% above what they otherwise would have been from 1979 to 1990. 'The evidence is clear that higher wages have led to lower demand for labour - although the magnitude of this effect remains in dispute...in the absence of the 15% induced increase, formal African employment would have been 200 000 to 400 000 above the present level of about five million.' (World Bank 1994: 7)

The study concludes that unions have contributed to slowing down the overall rate of economic growth.

Perhaps even more significant was the response of President Nelson Mandela and the Government of National Unity towards the 1994 wave of strikes in the retail industry: it was said that picketing created an environment which jeopardised foreign investment and in this sense put sectional interests of the working class ahead of national interest (Sunday Times July 24, 1994). Similarly, a six week strike in the motor industry was effectively collapsed by the Government when it announced a reduction in tariffs on car imports, thereby immediately undercutting workers' outstanding pay claims.

*Union-state relationships*

Robert Cohen (1974) has tried to capture various union-state relationships in post-colonial Africa by identifying four specific types of relationships. The first and most common involves an attempt to subordinate unions to the interests of government, where unions are expected to discipline their members to facilitate increases in productivity. The second type of relationship is a partnership between unions and the state, in which unions retain their independence but cooperate closely with government. In this relationship unions attempt to combine their right to collective bargaining with the goals of national development. A third type is one in which the union movement retains its independence from government and becomes an ally of the opposition. This leads to conflict with the government and the union emerges as an alternative locus of power. A final scenario is one in which the union movement is independent but remains non-aligned politically. The government tolerates this independence because unions confine themselves to collective bargaining and do not engage in political activity.

The strength of the labour movement, and the deep commitment to union democracy revealed in our survey, makes the first option of union subordination to the state unlikely. Before he became Minister of Labour, Tito Mboweni acknowledged the temptation of government to subordinate the trade union movement in post-colonial Africa. But, he argued:

> 'This temptation can best be avoided through the development of methods and institutions which seek to increase mutual cooperation and joint programmes whilst insuring the independence of the trade unions and other organs of civil society.' (Mboweni 1992: 28)

Clearly his approach points towards the second option, that of a partnership between an independent union movement and the state. This partnership is most visible in the RDP, in which the underlying idea is that social movements such as trade unions, civics, youth and student organisations, and associations of the unemployed and the aged, would all be part of an organised pact to reconstruct society.

> 'The democratic government, the trade union movement, business associations and relevant organisation of civil society must cooperate in formulating economic policy.' (ANC 1994: 81)

But the constraints on the new Government are considerable. There are constraints from business and international agencies such as the International Monetary Fund and the World Bank to follow structural adjustment policies and reduce the social wage (through reduced expenditure on social welfare), weakened wage setting arrangements (including trade union rights), and enforced laissez faire market systems. Attempts to forge social consensus, to prevent the flight of capital and scarce skills, and to encourage foreign investment are pressurising the new

Government to limit its redistributive efforts. The Government is likely to be long on promises but unable to meet all its commitments in the short term at least. In short, it is not difficult to imagine the Government expecting workers to sacrifice their 'narrow interests' to the demands of nation building and development on the grounds that workers represent a small and privileged proportion of the population. The Government might even enlist trade union leaders to restrain their members. This will open up conflict inside the labour movement between rank and file members and leaders, and place considerable strain on the partnership option.

The dilemma for the government is whether to try and accommodate organised labour and become a state in which the concerns of labour predominate, or to allow the interests of capital to dominate, accepting the inevitability of a labour dominated socialist opposition. This option - the third in Cohen's typology - involves unions entering into sharp conflict with the Government and becoming alternative loci of power. This is unlikely since our survey points towards a commitment to the ANC led Alliance not only in the April 1994 elections but also in the election scheduled for 1999.

The fourth option suggested by Cohen is for the labour movement to become completely independent of political parties, in the interest of forging a united trade union movement. In terms of this scenario COSATU, NACTU, FEDSAL and other trade union groupings would merge and labour would decide to concentrate on 'pure and simple' trade unionism. This option is attractive and substantial progress has been made since the election on unity between the trade union groupings. However, the problem raised by collective bargaining unionism is that its exclusive focus on workplace issues is likely to accelerate divisions between unionised and non-unionised workers, employed and unemployed.

Research on the labour market points to a growing stratification of the black labour force, and in particular the emergence of a skilled stratum of African workers (Crankshaw and Hindson 1990). This creates the real possibility of an increasingly divided African work force and a growing divide between a well paid unionised work force and a stratum of rural and urban poor.

Given these structural trends, unions face a choice: should they prioritise the narrow interests of their members or do they continue to try to combine workplace issues with broader developmental issues faced by labour in a developing society? By attempting to combine workplace issues with wider community and political issues, COSATU has already established a form of unionism which challenges the traditional division of labour between union and politics - a form of unionism that has been described social movement unionism.

This form of unionism points towards a scenario not foreseen in Cohen's typology of relations between union and state: a possibility that COSATU could become a radical pressure within the Alliance in the form of a left or socialist bloc that could propel the Government towards redistributive policies by mobilising pressure from civil society, communities and the workplace. The first signs of such a development emerged in the wave of strikes in July 1994, when COSATU general secretary Sam Shilowa denied that the strikes were a battle against the ANC. He said the wave of industrial action was aimed at reinforcing the ANC's hand to bring about change. By initiating and committing itself to the RDP, COSATU has made clear its commitment to broad national goals. What Sam Shilowa was pointing to was the need for COSATU to imprint workers' demands on national development. In this way, the possibility of deepening democracy by operating as a left pressure within the Alliance holds open the prospect that democracy in South Africa might transcend the conservative limits predicted by leading exponents of transition theory.

It will be difficult but not impossible for the labour movement to remain in the Alliance but not be coopted, and to neither alienate itself from its base nor lose its militancy. For this possibility to be realised tow conditions are necessary. Firstly, unions will have to shift from the antagonism that previously characterised their relations with the state to a closer working relationship with their allies in Parliament and the new Government. A priority will be legislation that enables management and labour to genuinely co-determine decisions in the workplace. A first step in this direction was taken in early 1995 when the Draft Labour Relations Bill was tabled. The Act which became law in August 1995 is expected to be effective late 1996, when all institutions foreseen in the Act will be functional. The Act introduces, through the concept of workplace forums, co-determination in the workplace.

Democracy, for our respondents, is not confined to periodic elections but is a direct means of empowering both unionised and non-unionised sectors of the working class within and beyond the factory gates. Because the civics, women's movements, youth and unemployed are the weakest, the poorest and the most marginalised, they will experience difficulty in developing their organisational capacity. If these organisations are to participate meaningfully in shaping social and economic policy in bodies such as NEDLAC, the development of their capacity will have to become a priority for the RDP and departments such as Labour.

The second condition required for a deepening of democracy is, in the words of Paul Hirst, 'a programme of reform that would supplement and extend rater than destroy representative democracy' (Hirst 1993:116).

In our view, this would require integrating the principles and practices of direct participatory democracy with indirect parliamentary democracy. Although it is unrealistic to run a modern industrial state through the principles of direct participatory democracy, it is clear that any programme of parliamentary reform must take seriously the practices and experiences of the mass movements that emerged in the 1980s, and especially of the labour movement. Mechanisms must be found to ensure that the direct will of the electorate is expressed in Parliament and that parliamentary representatives are made more accountable to the electorate. In Przeworski's words:

> 'If democracy is to be consolidated, that is, if all political forces are to learn to channel their demands and organise their conflicts within the framework of democratic institutions, these institutions must play a real role in shaping and implementing policies that influence living conditions.' (Przeworski 1991: 216)

# 6 Benin
# The Challenge

Florent Valère Adegbidi and Jean Sourou Agossou

*Six years on from the National Conference and the advent of an era of democratic revival, the leading players in the Beninese trade union movement are beginning to wonder: Since we have a government that invests itself with democratic and extravagantly liberal trappings, how can we bring into being a form of real democracy? Trade unions have succeeded in breaking free from State control, but they still have plenty to do. The road is long and littered with pitfalls.*

Given the manifest inability of investment, education and technology transfer policies to promote development, one question that has re-surfaced in recent years is whether there is a virtuous link between democracy and development; the issue was long ago dismissed by those who took little interest in the fundamental transformation of Africa. However, Western nations and international institutions like the IMF, World Bank and the UNDP are now coming round to the view that the reason for the African economy's poor showing in agriculture, industry and finance is the failure of the 'economistic' conception of development; they are also beginning to wonder whether social, and above all political, factors ought not to be restored to their former positions of pre-eminence. It is becoming clear that development has not been exclusively an economic issue, but also one that has impacted on socio-political questions. Attempts are being made to persuade 'partners' that, by democratising the State - by making it responsible before its citizens - it is possible to establish conditions of a new order favourable to market efficiency, the development of world capitalism and the promotion of world peace.

It is in this international context that the fierce struggles waged by social forces, particularly the trade unions, against poverty and the decline of the social structure in Africa have identified the need for political change. It will be recalled that one of the routes used in Benin to achieve this change was the celebrated National Conference of the country's activists (les forces vives du pays),[1] and it was here that a number of observers first glimpsed a once-and-for-all recipe for peaceful political change in Africa.

These events brought fresh inspiration and encouraged a new start; moreover, the National Conference found symbolic support in the fall of the Berlin Wall and verbal[2] backing from the French Head of State at the La Baule Summit in 1990. The whole of Benin, now gripped by euphoria, at once began to entertain lavish hopes of freedom - of a freedom that would, as if by magic, bring development and social peace.

Although Benin's human rights record is improving, it says much for the current situation that voices are constantly calling for the 'SMIC démocratique' ('democratic official minimum wage') to be replaced by two qualities now rapidly losing their resonance: transparency and participation.

The example of Athens in Ancient Greece tells us that the essence of democracy consists of transparency, responsibility and participation. However, when a chasm opens up between the enjoyment of formal liberties and citizens' involvement in public affairs, clearly 'the foundations of democracy are undermined in the eyes of all who no longer see it as the way of making themselves heard, or even of ensuring that they are acknowledged as protagonists in a common destiny' (Cassen, 1991: 22).

Surely the form of democracy envisaged in Benin and elsewhere in Africa involved people truly participating in the decision-making that affected their lives, and enabled citizens to make their aspirations known to their leaders and ensure that they were taken into account? Could democracy have done better than shout slogans or utter incantations (Kâ Mana, 1991) if it had not still been struggling to break out of the isolation in which social forces and civil society had become ensnared? Six years after the National Conference, and the advent of an era of 'Democratic Renewal' that ushered in the Structural Adjustment Programme (SAP), players in the Beninese trade union movement are increasingly pondering these matters. After their experience of the compromising, paralysing participation that marked the earlier 'Marxist' government, what the unions should now be concentrating on is determining the best way of participating in decisions on socio-economic matters - and without losing their independence from the public authorities in the process.

In dealing with these questions, our approach will initially focus on the incoherence between the concept of democracy and the 'liberalist' anti-social SAP project; we shall then examine the possible reasons for the half-way victory that participative democracy represents for the Beninese trade union movement.

## The spearhead of civil society in Africa

The conditions for direct participative democracy may already have been present in small populations such as Athens, but a problem is posed by the demographic density and size of modern States in the West and in Africa.

That is the reason for the representative structure of present-day democracies in which citizens give their elected representatives extended terms of office. However, we know from bitter experience how dangerous it is in politics when cleavages emerge between elected representatives and the electorate, and between representatives and constituents. That is why democracy is monitored by a counter-power exercised in turn by autonomous networks, namely civil society. By civil society, we mean institutions that protect public freedoms, associations and pressure groups, political parties and trade unions - all of which, through their daily interventions in social life, ensure that decisions taken by elected representatives are implemented and democracy is consolidated.

However, the two main components of civil society in Africa are political parties and the trade unions. As Michalon has remarked, 'Unlike Europe in the 19th century, Africa had no industrial revolution that broke up the characteristic community bonds of rural life based on family relationships and clannish disciplines, and replaced them in the towns and cities with completely new forms of solidarity founded on common sociological interests' (1993: 26). As a result, political parties still have a long way to go before they free themselves from an approach based on ethnicity. The main manifestations of solidarity are still strongly marked by ethnic factors, and they are unable to engender a true 'social movement', in the sense used by the French sociologist, Alain Touraine - that is to say a movement containing a truly national political project.

There is therefore good reason for turning to the trade union movement: its mission is to defend socio-professional and well-defined class interests, and today it is the spearhead of civil society in Africa. Moreover, among social forces, African trade unions are clearly the best structured and, since independence, they have accumulated substantial experience in the political arena. They also know better than anyone that, unless citizens take a clear role in the running of the economy, they 'will find themselves reduced to the level of simple puppets of the government that they themselves have elected, and buffeted by economic forces that treat them as no more than producers and consumers' (Julien, 1991: 17).

Nonetheless, with African and Beninese trade unions manifestly under the control of the IMF and the World Bank, how much room do they have for manoeuvre? It may simply be that an SAP's economic programmes and its celebrated 'conditionalities' on the one hand - and the aspirations of workers and African peoples on the other - are quite simply incompatible.

In fact, there seems to be a fundamental contradiction between true, participative democracy as defined above and the absence of autonomy and the renunciation of sovereignty that have characterised SAPs in Benin. To put it mildly, the country's rulers are little more than 'yes-men'.

Participation is a trade union campaigning strategy that embraces the kind of dialogue and concertation on decisions with which both partners (public authorities and unions, employers and unions) identify. However, anti-social SAP projects are utterly dependent on authoritarian, repressive régimes if they are to be successful (Asante, 1994); they also rely on the annihilation of social forces, including the trade union movement, through a range of strategies that range from oppression to political manipulation. Clearly, the most legitimate of these strategies is the 'democratic SMIC', which is paraded in Benin as a form of democracy.[3] This is what we shall attempt to demonstrate in the next section; it focuses exclusively on the situation of trade unions in the Republic of Benin during the period of the revival.

## Trade union pluralism: strength or weakness?

One question is exercising the minds of all union leaders at the present time; it is whether trade union pluralism, a feature of the new era of multi-party politics introduced by the National Conference, really benefits the trade union movement. To answer this question, we need to examine the past history of the Beninese union movement, the situation immediately prior to the changes that recently swept the country, and the contribution that unions made to the advent of democratic revival.

First, however, let us explain the approach we adopted in this section of our study. It is mainly based on a survey of senior officials in trade union centres, union activists and a number of resource-persons. The conclusions of the study reflect this, and we supplement them with the results of an exhaustive questionnaire survey of 141 civil servants in five different Ministries.[4] For historical and professional reasons, the civil servants were likely to be sympathetic to trade unionism; they were from the following Ministries: Public Sector and Administrative Reform; Labour, Employment and Social Affairs; Public Works and Transport; Environment, Housing and Town Planning; and Mines and Water. Our method involved an element of random sampling, but most socio-professional categories were nonetheless well represented.

In former Dahomey, now Benin, and elsewhere in Africa, the first trade unions were formed at the time of political struggles for independence. Indeed, many, if not all, of Africa's old political guard made their political bows in the trade union movement; the most successful were Sékou Touré and Félix Houphouët-Boigny, both of whom served as Head of State in their own countries, respectively Guinea and Côte d'Ivoire, until their deaths.

*Political destabilisation*

There has always been a pronounced link between trade unions and politics in Benin. For example, from independence in 1960 until 1972, during which time Benin was ruled by a long succession of governments, there was a persistent rumour, which may or may not have been true, that the unions were behind moves to destabilise the government.[5] Heads of State and government, some of whom had originally come from the trade union 'inner circle' themselves, gave further credibility to this notion through their morbid hatred of unions and the unremitting war they waged on them; they sometimes went to the lengths of imprisoning union leaders and even outlawing the organisations altogether.

This was the position taken by the military-Marxist régime that came to power in 1972, and which promptly rode roughshod over this particular section of the working population; the régime also created a single party and imposed a single trade union, the Union Nationale des Syndicats des Travailleurs du Bénin (UNSTB - National Union of Beninese Trade Unions). The UNSTB was seen as a 'mass organisation' of the party, and supported a régime that claimed to be the party of 'proletarians' and workers doing battle with the common enemy: international imperialism and the 'local bourgeoisie'.

The political conjuncture of the period divided States into purveyors of oppression and capitalist exploitation on the one hand, and anti-imperialist forces (i.e. Socialist States) on the other; it also crystallised these expressions of inflexibility. It was therefore impossible to make much sense of trade union activity in Benin outside the strict framework of what was termed 'responsible participation'. However, the ulterior motives underpinning an approach of this type, together with the implications they had for an effective defence of workers' interests, are well documented and do not merit extensive treatment here. In short, it came down to little more than dogmatism, and the indoctrination and incorporation of the trade union movement, and the only people to benefit were a small élite that occupied positions of power. An UNSTB Head Office acknowledgement that 'With us, the situation of trade unions under the former one-party system was far from perfect' effectively identified two of the national centre's leading officials.

*Self-reliance*

Nonetheless, on a political plane, the government did continue to foster a highly dubious kind of participation. Since coming to power in 1974, the régime had banned all young people's associations and politically oriented societies; the only ones to be tolerated were associations that could scarcely be ignored, such as the Red Cross and Red Crescent, the scouts and a number of charitable and religious bodies. However, the two years leading up to the old régime's demise saw a nationwide proliferation of regional, ethnically-based organisations called 'Development Associations'.

These continued to evolve amidst much ambiguity: as forums, they were sometimes noted for a degree of freedom of expression that compared favourably with government dogmatism; on the other hand, through their highly publicised objective of contributing to the development of a region in collaboration with political and administrative commissions of the Party and the Beninese State, they were also associated with the political slogan 'Rely on your own strength'. In practice, they were often no more than springboards to help disgraced former barons of the régime 're-position themselves'.[6]

*Crisis*

Throughout 1989, following serious delays in the payment of salaries and financial failures of banks - this had the effect of preventing workers from getting hold of their meagre savings - people grew weary of the sweet talk peddled by trade union leaders, and even began to make light of the soldiers' guns. Widespread discontent linked to persistent economic stagnation, itself exacerbated by the rigours of the first SAP, then triggered events that prompted the 'new democratic winds'.

These mainly took the form of wildcat strikes led by organisations that were (not surprisingly) unrecognised, and by duplications of workers' structures in the form of 'Workers' Action Committees' (abbreviated to 'Action Committees'); there were also acts of intimidation perpetrated on workers who were afraid or unwilling to take part in industrial action. It should be noted that these movements only affected civil servants; they were the only people to receive their salaries from the State, which in turn was the largest employer to become insolvent.

Pay demands quickly turned into political demands, and the Syndicat National de l'Enseignement Supérieur (SNES - National Higher Education Union) was the first to make its intentions clear when its General Secretary announced, 'Even if the government paid our salaries today, it would not be enough to get us back to work...' Other unions had no difficulty in understanding what this threat implied, and moved quickly to follow his lead. The unions' political thrust therefore led to the collapse of the old régime. In the event, as so often happens, it would have faded away in time anyway through a process of erosion: it had abandoned all pretensions to 'Socialism' and, in response to the enthusiastic urgings of international finance institutions, had resigned itself to a market economy.

Trade unions had previously played a corporatist role, and the union project at the time was in every way a truly social movement with collective, 'societal' and national aims. However, the new Beninese trade union movement emerged as a new, unmistakable social force capable of demonstrating strength and patriotism when confronting the total disintegration that threatened the country. This capacity was acknowledged by the National Conference whose delegates elected two influential union leaders as members of the Conference Committee, one of them as Vice-President.

## Changes

When the new government came to power, the design of representative institutions underwent radical change. As a result of the political pluralism that had been introduced into the Constitution and everyday life, there was no longer a place for political dogmatism. However, the autocratic tendencies of the old régime were briefly resurrected through a crude distortion of the democratic system; this took the form of an interplay of highly opportunistic political alliances and the addition of an (albeit brief) government parliamentary majority. President Soglo had the wind in his sails, and any critical acumen was swiftly discredited. This development encountered widespread acceptance, which may explain the non-legitimacy of the famous strikes of September 1991 and also why they were greeted with such hostility by the public at large (*Forum*, N 74, 18-24 September 1991).

However, the Beninese people did have something to be pleased about: the restoration of human rights, and particularly freedom of association, freedom of the press and freedom of opinion. This was followed by the setting up of a large number and wide range of associations (e.g. trade unions, socio-professional organisations and human rights groups), nearly all of which adopted the neologism 'NGO' (non-governmental organisation). These diverse groups expressed their freedom without restraint, sometimes even anarchically, and particularly so during the transitional period between March 1990 and April 1991; these months were marked by a wave of strikes, protest marches and sit-ins. However, as soon as the transition was over, the new government, now supported by a new interplay of political alliances, once more grabbed the reins of power.

Nearly all requests to hold marches were turned down for the same reason, namely the need to maintain security, and the government had no hesitation in sending in the state security police to break up demonstrations with excessive brutality. The public authorities were also happy to slide back into the paternalistic ways that had characterised the previous régime, and they even asked religious organisations to assist in educational work; to this end, they were given air time on television and radio. In short, the newly established government believed that an association was only acceptable if it was charitable - or edifying. Trade unions, too, began to lose their former strength, and were at a loss to explain how these developments could have occurred under a democratic, pluralistic government. How had it all come about?

## The trade union movement disintegrates

After the success of the National Conference, the trade unions felt confident of the effectiveness of their work, and decided to join forces in a single movement. However, now jealous of their independence and convinced of the virtues of multi-trade unionism (69% of those questioned in the survey were in favour), they set up the Confédération des Syndicats Autonomes du Bénin (CSA - Confederation of Beninese Autonomous Trade Unions), but declined to go any further. This concertation platform was designed to coordinate claims presented to the government and, if necessary, bring back replies to its proposals.

At the same time, unions that still had not done so were urged to conform to new trade union and political realities: these included issuing new Rules and Constitutions, fixing statutory meetings, and organising elections when committees completed their terms of office. The Deputy General Secretary of the UNSTB also drew attention to government intrusion into trade union affairs in a Ministerial circular, which called for the wholesale regeneration of trade unions and encouraged the setting up of concurrent workplace unions.

However, there were also top-down actions designed to disseminate information and establish local branches. All these activities during the 'transitional' period led to increased union membership.

The trade union situation in Benin began to crystallise from 1991 onwards. The CSA Constituent Congress (8-10 February), which the CSA itself organised, noted the departure of a number of affiliated unions which went on to form a new grouping: the Coordination des Syndicats de l'Administration Publique (CSAP - Coordination Committee of Public Sector Unions). Subsequently, the CSAP became the Fédération Nationale des Syndicats de l'Administration Publique (FENSAP - National Federation of Public Sector Unions), and later on the Centrale Générale des Travailleurs du Bénin (CGTB - General Trade Union Centre of Beninese Workers).

At the present time, Beninese trade unions are grouped as follows:
1) the three main centres:
   - UNSTB
   - CSA
   - CGTB;

2) three influential, but small, organisations:
- Fédération Nationale des Syndicats des Personnels de la Santé et de la Médecine Vétérinaire (FENSAMEV - National Federation of Health and Veterinary Medicine Workers)
- Fédération des Syndicats du Développement Rural (FESYNDER - Federation of Rural Development Unions)
- Centrale des Syndicats des Travailleurs du Bénin (CSTB - Trade Union Centre of Beninese Workers);
3) organisations affiliated to neither of the above, and whose membership may lie outside the constituencies of some of the trade union centres; one such example is the Syndicat National des Travailleurs des Travaux Publics (SYNUTRAP-TP - National Union of Public Works Employees), which organises staff in three key Ministries.

Over time, trade union pluralism was predictably revealed for what it was: a large number of national centres strongly influenced by the personalities of its leaders and by political and ethnic links. Political ambitions (73%) and regionalism (17%) were key reasons given by our interviewees for the weakness of trade unions and their lack of credibility. Furthermore, as if they stood to benefit from division, unions even attempted to form themselves into autonomous centres that were almost identical philosophically and strategically. Sadly, this move did not prevent them from launching into highly damaging altercations.[7]

*Divide and rule*

With so much divisiveness, unity of action was initially difficult to achieve; for example, it was not easy to organise broad-based action designed to ensure a hearing for workers' views on common problems. This division among the trade union centres was a weakness that the government had no qualms about exploiting as it sought to undermine strike calls.

As far as the public authorities were concerned, these strike calls sounded more like sabre-rattling than genuine threats, and the government did not shirk from using intimidatory methods in its dealings with workers. Over time, these methods persuaded workers to respond passively to union calls for strike action, and consolidated the State's strategy of 'divide and rule'. Significantly, after several years' experience of trade unionism, 31% of those interviewed now doubt the ability of multi-trade unionism to improve the situation of workers. Interviewees placed this high on the list of their basic demands.

At UNSTB headquarters, trade union pluralism attracts criticism for 'weakening the trade union movement and causing participation to fall away'. On a less radical note, the General Secretary of CSA-Benin has underlined the negative impact that this situation has on the 'cohesiveness of the struggle against the public authorities', and wonders if pluralism might not sometimes 'disadvantage workers'. Our interviewees expressed themselves in similar terms:

> 'Pluralism ought to be a source of enrichment for the trade union movement, but it is none of the sort.'
> 'Trade union pluralism should not be encouraged.'
> 'Ideally, there should be only two trade union centres ... on the grounds that pluralism leads to a dispersion of forces.'
> 'The various centres should be brought together ... and make common cause with a view to fighting the battle more effectively.'

It should not be forgotten that the government is aware of the low level of trade union organisation (9% of interviewees referred to this expressly, 30% in passing), and has taken to using delaying tactics such as:
-   extending government/union negotiations indefinitely when an immutable decision has already been taken following agreement with funders (e.g. the devaluation of the CFA franc);
-   setting groups of workers against one another by giving concessions to some and not to others (e.g. returning 10% levies to private sector employees, and temporarily refusing to treat civil servants in the same way);
-   refusing to honour promises (e.g. an agreement signed with CSA-Benin but not implemented);
-   setting peasants and civil servants against one another by describing the latter as an 'oligarchy'.[8]

The ease with which a trade union can set itself up as a national centre is obviously a problem. Thanks to a degree of complicity on the part of the Ministry of Labour (the result of inaction on the Ministry's part or just plain incompetence?), the trade union movement is pervaded by an anarchy that allows centres to be established and the existence of sectoral Federations to be ignored.[9]

By and large, the activity of most trade unions is concentrated at the level of the single centre, and ignores the invaluable intermediate stages between grass roots and leadership that Federations can provide for thought and analysis. Federations alone have the job of examining problems specific to their type of employment, identifying employers' policies and practices and proposing more judicious alternatives.

To conclude, multi-trade unionism has had little success at national level in tackling serious problems at the workplace; workers are still waiting to see if it has the capacity to force the State to address their main concerns. However, for a better explanation of the hiatus between the public authorities and trade union participation, we need to analyze the economic context in which post-revival Benin evolved under the constraints imposed by the Bretton Woods Institutions.

**A hiatus between economics and democracy: a step back from participation**

Mention of the international context is a reminder of the route that Benin, like most of its neighbours, took to escape from economic stagnation. This was the Structural Adjustment Programme. Indeed, the need to cooperate with the IMF and the World Bank was so clear in people's minds during the National Conference that it seemed quite natural to choose a Prime Minister from their ranks.

In fact, when Benin finally, and after much procrastination, opted for its first SAP in 1989, it was difficult to believe that there could possibly be an alternative. Beninese workers were fully aware of the disastrous condition of the country's economy, and broadly understood that they had to make sacrifices and resign themselves to some kind of economic and financial adjustment. As a result, they enthusiastically followed the negotiations that culminated in the signing of the first SAP; for Beninese people, it carried their hopes of solutions not only to the problems of the 'illiquidity' of the banks, but also to the backlog of civil servants' salaries, increased household consumption and social issues of unemployment. Somewhat naïvely, most of them fantasised about a benevolent SAP, one containing a plan that would (financially) re-establish the major macro-economic balances and put the whole of the country's socio-economic situation to rights. In other words, they imagined it would be a proper development programme. The SAP introduced into Benin certainly had some positive aspects: these included welcome measures designed to regularise the payment of civil servants' salaries, improvements to community infrastructures, higher productivity in the agricultural sector (particularly cotton), and a large inflow of foreign investment capital into the expanding Gross National Product.

However, disenchantment soon set in; indeed, the unions were articulating fears and reservations about the SAP almost from the outset. For example, in his 1994 annual report, the SYNUTRAP-TP General Secretary reminded members of their earlier 'anxieties about the way the political authorities viewed austerity, and that for the government it meant only one thing - the Structural Adjustment Programme'. Like the three trade union centres, the UNSTB, CSA and CGTB, SYNUTRAP-TP was

quick to realise that the SAP was not a true development programme because it so patently contained totally unsatisfactory measures. These included:
- a fall in workers' real income, and an exacerbation in the poverty level of low-income sections of the population caused by the withdrawal of subsidies on staple products;
- a block on public investment and ordinary operating expenditures;
- the use of a substantial part of export revenue to pay off external debts.

The decisive elements of Benin's economic reforms were the privatisation of public enterprises, devaluation of the national currency (the CFA franc), liberalisation of trade through the introduction of stiff competition (the Beninese business community now had to compete with certain products coming in from abroad, but were unable to stay the course), and reform of employment legislation leading to reduced protection for workers (see Law 90-004 of 15 April 1990 on conditions for recruitment and on terminating contracts of employment).

The key word here was the State's 'disengagement' from certain activities in the public service domain; this disengagement was immensely damaging in a number of ways. For example, in public works and town planning, the decision taken on the World Bank's recommendation to exclude the Ministry's own technical services from doing work that was well within their competence - and hand it all over to foreign and Beninese private sector agencies (e.g. research consultancies and public works contractors) of doubtful probity - was, to say the least, debatable. Not only did this push a large number of white- and blue-collar workers into unrecorded unemployment but, as the Head Office of the public works union explained to us, no fewer than 300 employees were actually sacked. In town planning, it has been common practice for some time now to force competent State employees into unemployment, and to hand the drafting of national regulations and town planning policies over to private sector consultancies.

*Social subjugation*

For these reasons, participants at a CGTB seminar in Cotonou in April 1994 on 'The SAP and social justice' agreed unanimously that 'the acceptance of the SAP by Beninese political leaders constituted a serious threat to socio-economic development in general, and to workers in particular' (CGTB, 1994: 21). While government and much of the political class persist in describing the programme as 'inescapable', trade unionists see unmistakeable signs of 'social constraint' and a 'new form of colonisation'. For the present, they see no likelihood of being able to change the direction in which things are moving because the Beninese government has committed itself to a rigorous application of the Programme so as to become the IMF/World Bank's 'model pupil'.

The phrase 'model pupil' is often used by senior politicians in Benin, and it accurately expresses the country's current state of alienation. According to General Secretary Todjinou of the CGTB, 'a kind of parallel government not accountable to civil society has been set up by international financial institutions working on behalf of powerful interests ... subordinating peoples and governments to the anonymous interplay and resolute manipulations of foreign forces' (p 77). There is no longer any economic sovereignty, and national sovereignty has therefore evaporated as well.

Blatant infringement of democracy and participation rights has reduced the legitimate influence that social players, such as trade unions and members of the business community, have long wished to exert on Benin's economic policy. The economic policy that the country implements under the IMF's tutelage brings the government into conflict with both the trade unions and the Committee of Benin's Chamber of Commerce and Industry (the body representing business people operating in the formal sector). Both 'note, under the Jeune Afrique formula, that the best news they hear relates to macro-economic data rather than to their day-to-day lives';[10] both share the same frustration at exercising no control over the management of their economic environment, and at having to put up with the famous 'conditionalities'. Political parties, NGOs, trade unions and business people also want the government to organise a (sovereign) National Economic Conference to re-draft the country's economic and social policy.

However, there is no point in trying to delude ourselves; a SAP is bound to produce constraints. Indeed, one of the IMF's aims is to force 'under-developed' members to accept the dogmas of the major liberal macro-economic equilibria. The Fund's Statutes also insist on borrowers' economic policies guaranteeing that they intend to reach certain 'liberalist' economic objectives. We need to be very clear that this means nothing less than opening up Benin's frontiers so that the country can integrate better onto the world market, substituting the private market for the State in order to make the national economy more competitive, reducing the State's budgetary deficit, and cutting internal demand. The latter is deemed to be too high, and responsible for inflation and the balance of payments deficit (Elie, 1994: A7). It is easy to understand why currency is frequently devalued in order to reduce national purchasing power and cut imports; it is also easy to imagine the consequences that these policies have on workers and the trade union movement generally. No one in Benin is lingering under illusions any more.

Since it is their job to defend workers' material and moral interests, trade unions predictably become the natural enemy of governments more preoccupied with getting high marks from the IMF. They are tolerated simply as pieces in the game of democracy, but in principle their strength and influence represent a considerable threat, and that is why there is opposition to their independent participation in big economic, social and cultural decision-making. It is also based on a paradox: in cultural terms, we are in the country of open democracy (palabre - palaver) and participation (Adegbidi, 1993, 1994), and nearly all workers (i.e. all socio-professional categories) think that the government has a duty to consult trade unions and take their views into account when negotiating with the Bretton Woods Institutions (93% of interviewees against 7% of executives employed in responsibility posts).

In Benin and elsewhere, workers find evidence of this exclusion of the trade union movement (unions are also seen as an 'encumbrance') in their daily lives; they are also urged to capitulate to what the government presents as the Bretton Woods Institutions position (i.e. the famous agreements) on the country's problems. When the government tries to defend these *absurd*, cavalier privatisation programmes of companies in key sectors of the national economy (e.g. energy and town planning), it rarely offers an convincing justification apart from a reference to these 'agreements'; privatisations are, of course, highly attractive to foreign investors. Quite clearly, most Beninese people, and trade unions in particular, do not understand these decisions and protest accordingly but, to quote UNSTB Head Office, the government refuses to shift its ground because 'it is more important to be in the IMF's good books than to satisfy citizens' needs.' In this way, one begins to see how giving trade unions a position of influence through some coherent form of participation would effectively block decisions that were unacceptable to workers.[11]

It was therefore in the name of extreme liberalism, and with strong backing from by the IMF, that the Minister of Commerce of Benin, a country not self-sufficient in food, announced the unrestricted export of food products mainly to central Africa; this has resulted in over-bidding and an abnormal rise in inflation on the Beninese market.[12] One wonders whether it would have been possible to get away with such nonsensical behaviour - it benefits only a few peasants and merchants, and provides the State with tiny amounts of tax revenue - if civil society were not so weak and the trade union movement not marginalised within Benin's 'young democracy'. What is not in doubt, however, is that the purchasing power of Beninese workers dropped so alarmingly as a result of this exceptional jump in inflation that even World Bank officials were quick to acknowledge it,[13] and the government equally keen to mitigate it.

'This is a good moment,' insists the SYNUTRAP-TP General Secretary, 'to recall that civil servants' salaries are frozen at the 1990 index. After the National Conference, the State already owed civil servants two pay rises (1988 and 1990); it now owes them three more - for 1992, 1994 and 1996.' Calculations by SYNUTRAP-TP experts show that every civil servant is losing a sum of money every month representing 40-50% of salary owed. This was corroborated in a statement on national television by the Minister of Finance who said that, if he had to pay the salaries in accordance with the real index, civil servants would be paid for only six months in 1994. Clearly, no other group makes such a contribution to the functioning of the State or accepts such sacrifices; if these problems were resolved, everyone would have to agree to a fairer distribution of deductions for the State to function properly. In this context, as Gaston Bio comments in *Forum*, it is surprising how accommodating IMF experts are towards ways of substantially raising political salaries which do little to reduce the State's overall lifestyle (1993, N 114). Exclusive salary increases were being authorised by a government refusing to tighten its own belt during a period of financial austerity; such decisions might well have been blocked through trade union involvement.

The circumstances surrounding the devaluation of the CFA franc reflect the servile relationship that African countries saddled with SAPs currently have with the Bretton Woods Institutions. Even more disturbing, during the 'Battle of the Budget' crisis in Benin in 1994, was the way the government saw fit to publish a letter from an 'ordinary' IMF official in support of its decision to limit pay rises to 10%, instead of the 15% agreed by parliament following concertation with the unions.[14] On this occasion, those who chose to treat the letter as irrelevant soon discovered the harsh realities of life. As many of our interviewees pointed out with some bitterness, our governments are obliged to obtain the agreement of funders for their draft national budgets even before parliaments get to hear of the contents. In 35 years of independence, the World Bank and the IMF have never had so much influence over life in the 'Quartier Latin' (Dahomey was sometimes known as the 'Latin Quarter' in colonial times) as they do now. The slightest suggestion of trade union activity has the government bending over backwards to apologise, and offering explanations that are, to say the least, disturbing. Here is an example from the then Public Sector Minister:[15] 'In addition to the limitations of which the unions are only too aware [sic], the funders who have come to our assistance are threatening to freeze their contribution to vital projects ... These are the constraints that have prevented us in the Budget from ...' The government ignored recommendations that it should consult members of parliament, trade unions and civil society before signing agreements committing Benin; by so doing, it created conditions that encouraged a repeat of the January 1996 scenario, with new warnings from the World Bank, this time signed by T Ahlers and M Azefor.

Workers may feel frustrated and cheated, but they do not have much choice, and they continue to place their hopes in trade unions (75%). However, the trade union movement will have to resolve its own shortcomings if it is ever to regain its former strength. The main shortcoming relates to the paradox that trade unionism is all about the democratisation of decision-taking at all levels it ultimately mobilises the efforts and total commitment of all members - although trade unions, too, are woefully short of democracy themselves.

## Promoting internal democratisation

Trade unions undoubtedly have their failings, but in their defence we cannot ignore the indifference, and sometimes hostility, of the workers they try to defend. Too many of them think that trade union activity is to do with de-stabilising a government they sometimes support for ethnic or 'clientelist' reasons. This is particularly true of certain directors and departmental heads who are only interested in hanging on to their jobs.

Just the same, we cannot turn a blind eye to the sociological problem posed by an evaporating sense of responsibility and a refusal to make a contribution to the life of the nation. For Beninese trade unionists, this takes the form of not paying union dues, refusing to take part in union demonstrations, and rejecting all idea of committing themselves to the country's political life. For most workers, participation in the life of the nation is confined to members of the political class having discussions in corridors and after radio and television debates. The following, somewhat caricatured, description of what a trade union leader has to put up with illustrates the problem well. The trade union leader, explains the SYNUTRAP-TP General Secretary, must expect to:
- receive inadequate union dues;
- pay for urgent expenses out of his/her own pocket;
- put up with the rantings and ravings of his/her superiors;
- be the whipping boy in a branch that does not pay its dues but expects everything to be done for it;
- see Executive Council initiatives blocked by certain branch members.

In these circumstances, there is nothing to be gained by refusing to acknowledge the truth. What trade union activity comes down to is finding the external funding to organise seminars - which continue to have little impact. Given that trade union centres have no difficulty in finding foreign partners to provide financial support for their programmes, one gains the impression that trade union life consists of little more than demonstrations organised by the CGTB, CSA and UNSTB, and that these organisations are fairly unimaginative when it comes to spending the money that their partners give them.

## Under-representation of women and young people

Union activists direct plenty of grievances at their leaders. They claim, for instance, that the main reason why workers do not get involved in trade union activity is its lack of credibility;[16] reasons for this include the fact that many use their union positions as a political springboard, and the lack of internal democracy. Many interviewees expressed themselves in terms such as:

'Union representatives do not involve the grass roots sufficiently when taking the big decisions that affect everyone.'
'Workers are ill informed about the steps taken by their trade union leaders.'
'Decisions are not thought through, and they are taken without any consultation with the grass roots.'

No fewer than 40% of interviewees see the lack of internal democracy as the main weakness of trade unionism, and the main obstacle to the development of participation. In this context, 30% of interviewees also pointed out that two important categories of workers, young people and women, were under-represented. They could certainly revitalise the trade union movement with a new kind of dynamism and spirit. This is not a reference to the seductiveness that women might employ across the negotiating table, but rather to the seriousness and sense of responsibility they bring any claim-making movement to which they make a sincere commitment. We know from experience that women are better at resisting corruption than men; moreover, their active presence in the trade union movement can only reassure all those interviewees who believe that, 'Trade union leaders are corrupt! End of story!'

As for the marginalisation of women in the trade union movement, the national seminar held in Porto Novo in July 1994 on the participation of women in the democratisation process called for vigorous action to foster women's involvement; this is still limited mainly because trade union 'machismo' does not provide them with 'the necessary reverberations and the right sort of climate' in which to express their specific needs (M Dahoun, 1995: 5). Women attending the seminar argued that a new list of women's issues should be drawn up with a view to establishing a platform of demands and mobilisations. Clearly, as women now make up a substantial proportion of the workforce in Benin, the trade union movement is not going to walk off with any prizes for democracy if it does not win them over. This also reflects current interest in a new form of trade unionism that is equally removed from the 'trade unionism of irresponsible demands' and the 'trade unionism of "responsible participation"' that have marked the country's history since independence.

## The routes to autonomous participation

Following the experiences of 'responsible participation' and the faltering trade union pluralism of the present period, there is another question that now occupies the minds of Beninese trade unionists: What is the best way for the trade union movement to participate in taking decisions on socio-economic matters without losing its autonomy from the government? The embarrassment that trade unionists exhibit when answering this question gives some idea of the complexity of the problem. Many of our interviewees mentioned trade union training as an antidote to the errors that unions make: 4% deplored 'the absence of training sessions dealing with mobilisation and awareness', and said that it 'was the main obstacle to effective trade union action'. In fact, trade union leaders themselves are unanimous in placing this at the top of their own lists of problems they face at work; however, when they start to look for solutions, they get terribly confused. They first of all forget that the people they have denounced are themselves trade unionists (there are at least three of them) who are currently members of the government; what is more, these individuals are using their past experience to thwart the strategies of trade union campaigns, and even threaten trade unionists with dismissal (in violation of labour law). These union leaders then go on to suggest 'encouraging trade unionists to involve themselves politically and fill posts of high responsibility in the State apparatus to ensure that the voices of workers are heard.'

It is particularly hard to make any sense of such proposals (and not to rail at the fecklessness of it all) when one recalls the egocentricity that has so often marked the exercise of power by Beninese officials, both trade unionists and others. One is tempted to fall back on the classic of excessive demands - the sort that new democracies absorb so well when trying to take credit for their tolerance and re-discovered freedoms. There may be real freedom to put in demands (that in itself is something to be proud of) and government and trade unions may periodically negotiate, but the leaders of the trade union centres are now rebelling against these *ersatz* consultations in which the unions are simply required to make concessions and take on board the demands of the 'development partners' (i.e. the IMF and the World Bank). What the unions want is not ordinary consultations, but real concertation involving concessions on both sides.

The fact that 93% of interviewees see concertation as an absolute right for Beninese workers is good reason for demanding a form of democratic participation. This would be based, firstly, on a society-wide political project aimed at democratising decisions at all levels; and secondly, on the mobilisation of the creative energies of all citizens in national integration (otherwise known as promoting 'active citizenship' (Robin, 1991)) by strengthening civil society so that it can replace the current oligarchy and 'élitocracy'. In this context, it is worth recalling that, unlike politicians, African trade union activists are 'socially and economically linked to peasants, manual workers, the unemployed and the poor; they feel a responsibility for them, and they share with them (from near or afar) their pay, their resources, their lives, their worries, their day-to-day problems - and therefore their future' (Diallo et al, 1992: 108).

Given that participation involves dialogue and an exchange of information between trade unionists and the public authorities, it is necessary to come to terms with the State's responsibility to promote such a work structure in the interest of the whole nation through patriotism. By way of responding to union struggles and aspirations, Social Democratic governments in Sweden have developed a system of social administration of the economy; within it, questions of economic and social policy are widely discussed by all the major social groups through a process of concertation (Rolland, 1992: 64).

Rolland describes it as follows: 'In Sweden, the committee charged with proposing a new labour market policy was made up of members of all parties, together with trade union and employers' representatives ... The State invites interests groups to participate in drafting and applying the policies, as this gives the committee the expertise that groups have in various fields and, through their participation and support, confers the legitimacy that government policies require' (pp 67-68). Things are not so far advanced in Benin, despite the democratic revival, and it is sad to note the repeal[17] of laws institutionalising the participation of workers' representatives on the Boards of Directors of companies and the Management Committees of public administrations; it is important to remember that workers' representatives on these committees have not always played passive or symbolic roles. There should have been wide-ranging consultation when the National Assembly Committee drew up the new Labour Code; in the event, it was carried out exclusively by a handful of civil servants in the Ministry of Labour; their only guiding light was a requirement that Beninese law should conform to the liberalist prescriptions laid down by the IMF.

To make matters worse, they were influenced by the Labour Codes that the Fund had already agreed to elsewhere in Africa.

Addressing the concerns of the social forces in economic, social and political matters has not always been an item on the agenda of 'Beninese democracy'; in fact, the government has consistently restricted itself to the minimum - the celebrated 'democratic SMIC'. The former single trade union centre, the UNSTB, argues that trade union participation has fallen back during the period of the revival. Without wishing to side with that position, one has to agree that the gains made by the 'new democratic winds' stop at multi-trade unionism, and that the latter does nothing more than submit joint demands. The trade union movement needs to find new strength through training and action; it also has to find an effective formula of unity in action if the legitimacy of trade unions is to be consolidated and the State forced to take them seriously. More than at any time in the past, the future of the Beninese trade union movement is on a knife edge.

## Notes

1  The Sovereign National Conference - Benin is held to have pioneered this kind of meeting in Africa - took place in Cotonou from 19 to 28 February 1990.

2  The backing can only be described as verbal because France's attitude to subsequent events, particularly in Cameroon and Togo, cast some doubt on the sincerity of President Mitterrand's proposals.

3  After the legislative elections of 1995, after which the State behaved in a manner that recalled the practices of the former government, there were justifiable reservations about exactly how democratic the 'democratic SMIC' really was. Trade unionists were often banned from organising demonstrations, and particularly in the period following the devaluation of the CFA franc; for some time, they had been able to savour their hard-won freedoms for what they really were.

4  The survey was carried out in February 1994; it focused on the following issues:

- Do you rely more now (post-revival) or before (pre-revival) on the effectiveness of the trade union movement in defending workers' interests?

- Do you believe that trade union pluralism offers more advantages or disadvantages in an effective campaign to ensure victory for workers' demands?

- Why do you think the trade union movement is weak?

- Do you think the government has a duty to consult trade unions and take their concerns into account when negotiating with the IMF and the World Bank?

5   As the Editor of *Forum de la semaine* has hinted, that when trade union demonstrations took place, the public authorities usually unearthed political manoeuvrings aimed at destabilisation (S Dodji, *Forum* N 77, 9-15 October 1991: 5).

6   The full story is set out in an article entitled *La participation populaire en question* (Popular participation in doubt) by Jean Sourou Agossou (*Ehuzu*, 10 August 1988).

7   See G Bio, 'La querelle des centrales syndicales profite-t-elle aux travailleurs béninois?' (Does the argument between the trade union centres benefit Beninese workers?), *Forum*, N 114, 1993: 9.

8   These proposals came from the former Beninese Head of State, Nicéphore Soglo.

9   See Article 60 of the Labour Code, which defines the conditions governing trade union representativeness.

10  L-M Gnacadja, 1995, in a speech by the Chair of the newly formed Chamber in a New Year's message to the Head of State in 1995.

11  These privatisation exercises, which often take place against a background of political crisis, sometimes attract allegations of incorrect procedures and violations of Article 139 of the Benin Constitution; this states that all economic and social projects must be submitted to the Economic and Social Council. Trade unionists have seats on the Economic and Social Council.

12  Significantly, in the light of the resulting destabilisation, this decision was at one point challenged by the Beninese government. However, the Bretton Woods institutions were quick to remind the Beninese authorities that, when in signing the SAP, they had given an undertaking to observe the principles of liberalism to the letter.

13  Broadcast statement by regional representative of the World Bank while passing through Cotonou in May 1995.

14  This small rise was discussed by Deputies under social measures accompanying the 50% devaluation of the CFA franc. In fact, the IMF official opposed a decision that the Beninese parliament had passed by a very large majority of Presidential and opposition votes (54 for, 4 abstentions, 5 against). In a letter to Minister Dossou, the IMF's E Sacerdotti wrote that the Fund had been informed of discussions that had taken place in the National Assembly during the 1994 Budget debate. The IMF did not wish to go into the detail of these discussions, but noted with some anxiety the risks associated with the measures relating to pay. In so far as they diverged significantly from the agreed economic programme, the IMF felt they could compromise the outcome of the mid-term review of the programme with the Fund. Sacerdotti concluded by saying that the Beninese government needed to have the matters drawn to its attention so that the forthcoming discussions were based on the full facts (Letter in 'La Nation', 2 August 1994: 8).

15 See statements made by Minister Gbégan reported by F Agbanglanon in
*Forum*, N 145, 10-16 February 1993.

16 Some express lack of credibility in terms of the bleakest pessimism. 12% of
our interviewees doubted whether any kind of trade unionism could fight
effectively for better conditions for workers.

17 The move to repeal laws promoting workers' participation at the workplace
began during the time of the last government; it followed the promulgation
of Law 88-005 of 26 April 1988 on the setting up, organisation and operation
of public and semi-public enterprises. The trend continued after the democratic
revival.

# 7 Burkina Faso
# The Land of Incorruptible Men

GUILLAUME SILGA

*Burkina Faso has not been spared the 'new winds' that have been blowing across the African continent - sweeping a dictatorship out of the way here, sowing the seeds of IMF and World Bank Structural Adjustment Programmes there. Multi-trade unionism has been in existence here for many years, and it continues to evolve in a climate of relative social tranquillity. However, it may be that this apparent calm, of which Burkinabe leaders are so intensely proud, conceals social turmoil which trade unions, because of their lack of effectiveness, will have the greatest of difficulty in quelling.*

Burkina Faso made the transition from state of emergency to rule of law without any great damage done; there were no stories, for example, of civil servants failing to get their pay packets at the end of the month. However, as the Structural Adjustment Programme (SAP) has tightened its grip, so the crisis has deepened. The devaluation of the CFA franc in January 1994 was a major body-blow, and the poverty base has broadened substantially as a result. As little as 20 or so years ago, the very idea of anyone in Burkina Faso rummaging through dustbins was unheard of; today, however, it is by no means uncommon to see hungry people doing just that - and, what is more, within a stone's throw of some of the country's more affluent villas. In the countryside, too, peasants nowadays make do with one meal a day, often consisting of no more than calabash of 'dolo'.[1]

Burkina Faso, or 'the country of incorruptible men', was known as Upper Volta before it received its new name from the August Revolutionaries; this landlocked enclave in the heart of West Africa is surrounded by Côte d'Ivoire, Mali, Niger, Benin, Togo and Ghana. According to 1994 estimates, the country has a population of 10,171,000 inhabitants distributed among some 60 ethnic groups, and covers an area of 274,000km. The main languages are French, the language of administration, and the vernacular tongues of Mooré, Dyula and Fulfuldé; the main towns are Ouagadougou, the political capital, Bobo-Dioulasso, the former business capital, Koudougou, Ouahigouya and Banfora.

Burkina Faso is immensely poor economically, but it does have one outstanding asset, its men and women, and to them we should add their courage, industriousness and keen sense of justice, all of them qualities that need to be carefully nurtured and preserved as the foundation for sustainable democracy. Burkinabe trade unionists have long acted as custodians of these qualities.

For an understanding and appreciation of the country's economic, political and social situation, it is important, not to say essential, to re-examine the past, and to assess the roles that the main players have assumed in the life of the nation, and what their contributions have been.


## Trade unions and democracy

Trade unionism is a major legacy from the period of colonial rule, a system that the unions and political parties joined forces to eradicate. Taking its lead from trade unions in other African countries, the Burkina Faso movement was the spearhead of the struggle for independence, and is now seen as one of the best organised forces in the land. The history of the country's trade union movement is in two parts, and these two periods serve to analyze its actions in the trade union and political arenas.

### The period from 1960 to 1980

This was the golden age of Upper Volta trade union history. At least one commentator has described it as little short of a trade union epic characterised essentially by difficult relations with political régimes, and later by victories over them (Sandwidi, forthcoming). At this time, the trade union movement was noted for its pluralism and its combativeness.

Trade union pluralism exists both organisationally and doctrinally; it has also been a tradition since the earliest days of the country's trade union movement when 'metropolitan' (i.e. French) unions established themselves in Upper Volta with such success that there were eventually as many as three national trade union centres altogether: the Union Syndicale des Travailleurs Voltaïques (USTV - Trade Union of Upper Volta Workers), founded in 1948, the Confédération Nationale des Travailleurs Voltaïques (CNTV - National Confederation of Upper Volta Workers (1950)) and the Organisation Voltaïque des Syndicats Libres (OVSL - Upper Volta Organisation of Free Trade Unions (1960)).

A number of autonomous unions sprang up alongside these centres, and in 1974 they came together to form a fourth centre, the Confédération Syndicale Voltaïque (CSV - Voltaic Trade Union Confederation). A split in the OVSL in 1978 led to the formation of the Union Générale des Travailleurs Voltaïques (UGTV - General Union of Upper Volta Workers), although this centre turned out to be of little importance.

At the time, the trade union movement was dominated by two doctrinal currents, reformism and revolutionary politics, each with its 'reformist' and 'revolutionary' centres.

The 'reformist' unions were not opposed to the power of the State as such. Rather they campaigned for reforms that would immediately meet the aspirations of employed workers and the mass of workers; they described themselves as apolitical. The national centres that supported this current were the CNTV, OVSL and UGTV.

Revolutionary trade unionism was based on the theory of class struggle, and sought to overthrow the established order in favour of the working class. The conquest of political power by individuals who argued this position inevitably attracted support from this school of trade unionism. The two centres defending this current were the USTV and the CSV. Unions in both currents made no secret of their wish for independence from the régimes that ruled the country.

## The combativeness of Upper Volta's trade unions

Trade union pluralism provided Upper Volta's unions with the broad base and strength they needed to resist government assaults on democracy. The First Republic's Constitution made no mention of the right to organise or freedom of association; nor did it say anything of organised labour. This omission was underlined by the fact that no reference appeared in President Maurice Yameogo's proclamation of independence of 5 August 1960: 'I express my gratitude to all the architects of our national independence, to France, to General de Gaulle who deserves a special place in history for his courage and outstanding lucidity, to all the nations that assist us, to the clergy who send us their finest men and women, to the French teachers who have patiently trained our country's leaders, to our traditional chiefs who have protected the integrity of our State against intruders, to former warriors and soldiers who remained honourable to the end, to all members of parliament, to political activists at all levels, to the brave fighters who died to give us freedom. In the name of the government, I give this token of my profound gratitude.'

So the trade unions, which had been in existence and active in Upper Volta since 1947, and had formed the vanguard of the struggle for independence, were passed over in silence. And that was not all. The President of the Republic even instructed the Minister of Labour and Social Affairs to take all appropriate measures to unite the country's unions and bring them into line with the ruling party. In time, the Union Nationale des Syndicats de Haute-Volta (National Union of Upper Volta Trade Unions) was founded as the single trade union centre, and all other centres were ordered to affiliate. However, the reaction of existing unions was one of immediate and outright opposition, and the government was obliged to look for other ways of bringing them to heel.

In 1962, the ruling party's Congress passed a resolution on trade unions which stated that, 'as a new trade union spirit is now of paramount importance, Congress urges trade unions, now that national unity has been achieved, to coordinate their actions with those of the party with the intention of re-launching the economy.'

Then, in 1964, the National Assembly passed Law N 1-64/AN of 24 April which banned unions from affiliating to international trade union bodies, thereby cutting off the support that the latter gave to Upper Volta's unions. The law came in for trenchant criticism from all trade unions and, as Muasa Kabeya put it, the political stage was thereafter marked by fierce antagonism between government and unions (1989: 69). To all intents and purposes, trade union activity was outlawed during the first few years of independence. In his 'Évolution de l'Histoire du Mouvement Syndical Burkinabé' (forthcoming), Sandwidi has said that, despite these repressive measures, the trade union movement managed to preserve its organisational autonomy, and even developed the rank-and-file unity of action which later proved to be the First Republic's downfall. As Sandwidi wrote, the death knell of the First Republic rang out on 3 January 1966; it was the trade union movement's first victory over the government.

As we remarked earlier on, the First Republic was marked by two factors:
- firstly, the government's desire to crush citizens' basic rights and freedoms; the previous opposition party had been dissolved in January 1960, and a one-party system immediately enforced. This was in breach of a Constitution which prided itself on its basic liberal principles, and Article 7 of which guaranteed political pluralism;
- secondly, government attempts to harmonise social and political issues; these initially took the form of a brutal elimination of political opposition, and later the imposition of a single trade union structure. Although this policy failed, the trade union movement was put 'on probation' under the Law of 31 August 1959, and effectively went into voluntary hibernation.

When the First Republic fell, it was replaced by a military government and there was no return to normal constitutional ways until 1970. The new rulers remembered the collapse of the First Republic and realised that trade unions were a force to be reckoned with; the opposition, too, was no less aware that the unions were a springboard from which to settle old scores. That was why the Preamble to the Second Republic's Constitution gave such prominence to individual and collective freedoms, including freedom of association, and provided that any violation of these freedoms would come before a Constitutional Judge. However, the Second Republic's good intentions quickly turned into threats to, and attacks on, freedom of association, and when teachers later took industrial action, the government adopted methods that recalled the days of the First Republic. These included threats to dismiss the strikers, and the setting up of a yellow union to block actions that were taken by other unions by way of support. Even Joseph Ouedraogo, a former trade unionist who was now National Assembly President under the Second Republic, opposed the government's treatment of trade union members. The crisis brought institutions to a standstill and led to a Constitutional coup d'état on 8 February 1974. This was the second time that the unions tasted victory over the government.

President Sangoulé Lamizana, in power since January 1966, then brought in a Government of National Revival (Gouvernement de Renouveau National (GRN)), but he failed to learn the lessons of the demise of the Second Republic. In 1975, General Lamizana formed a single party, the Mouvement National pour le Renouveau (National Movement for Revival), but the unions rejected his one-party system; instead, they called a General Strike for 17-18 December in support of their corporate claims and a return to constitutional rule. There was an excellent response to the strike call and the country was totally paralysed for two days. The President backed down, but he never forgot the snub that the unions had administered, and from 19 to 28 January 1976 he carried out a lengthy consultation exercise with the country's active citizens (les forces vives de la nation), but excluded the trade unions. The Constitution of the Third Republic was adopted on 27 November 1977 and, like its predecessor, it guaranteed the right to organise and freedom of association.

General Lamizana won the 1978 elections, but only on the second round; these elections placed Upper Volta in the league of democratic nations, but shortly afterwards he set the tone for his Presidency in an interview for Jeune Afrique. Lamizana had previously been thought of as weak, but he now made his new tactics clear saying he was not prepared to let the country be torn apart by a minority of protesters; trade unions, in particular, were in his sights. The threat came closer to reality in a speech he gave commemorating the 18th anniversary of the proclamation of independence on 5 August 1978: 'Clearly the time has come for a return to firm government. It is also time for all behaviour that claims to be in the name of freedom - but is in fact nothing but a negation and caricature of freedom - to be contained and suppressed. Accordingly, the authority of the State will be firmly restored in all areas and at all levels through the resuscitation of the State Security Court; this will put an end to the persistent climate of unrest that stems from certain activities against the State's internal security' (Sandwidi, op cit: 15). This aggressive posture on the General's part did not augur well for relations between the government and the social partners; in fact, relations got steadily worse until 25 November 1980 when the Third Republic fell to a military coup d'état. That was the third time that the trade unions won a victory over the government.

The military government that succeeded the Third Republic carried the hopes of many, and received support from large sections of the population. However, it was also responsible for the most serious attacks on the right to organise and freedom of association. These included:

- a ban on popular demonstrations and trade union meetings;
- a refusal to grant recognition to a newly established union;
- sanctions against strikers in May 1981;
- suppression of the right to strike under Ordonnance N 81-004/CMRPN/ PRES of 1 November 1981;
- dissolution by Ordonnance of a national trade union centre (the CSV) and legal proceedings taken against its General Secretary.

This brutal clampdown on trade unions led to a coup d'état in 7 November 1982, and that signalled the end of the Colonels' régime. It was the trade unions' fourth victory. Between 1960 and 1980, constitutional and emergency governments alike had had one aim in common: to get rid of the trade unions.

These governments were never interested in applying the principles of democracy; they sought to rule the country through dictatorial means and, in so doing, attracted the implacable opposition of the unions. From 1960 to 1980, Upper Volta was never once governed by a President truly committed to the cause of democracy, and the same went for the politicians who gravitated to the various régimes that held power at different times. In fact, all the coups d'état were welcomed by the majority of the population, but they had learned to judge the behaviour of their leaders by the fervour of their anti-union denunciations.

For 20 years, then, Upper Volta's trade unions fought for real democracy in their homeland, but their actions were forever being sidetracked by shady, unscrupulous politicians and others. The period was also marked by a yearning shared by all citizens for a climate of social justice and peace.

By the end of these two bellicose decades, the cutting edge of the Upper Volta trade unionism had been well and truly blunted. Indeed, when these bitter struggles finally came to an end, the country's trade unions put one in mind of King Sisyphus who once tried to roll a heavy stone up a hill, but as soon as he reached the top, it rolled straight back to the bottom again.

## The 1980s: a transitional period

Even 20 years after independence, Upper Volta's economy had not yet properly taken off and, despite a period of timid upturn between 1974 and 1976, the country slid back into economic stagnation. In political terms, however, the 1978 elections propelled Upper Volta into the ranks of democratic countries: General Sangoulé Lamizana, who had now been in power since 1966, put himself up for election and won through, albeit in the second round. All in all, the 1980s were a period of transition in the country's political, economic and social development.

During the 1980s, life in Upper Volta was marked by poverty and economic and cultural backwardness. After 20 years of independence, Upper Volta was still an undeveloped agricultural nation whose rural sector, which employed over 90% of the economically active population, accounted for no more than 45% of GDP and provided 95% of the country's total exports. By comparison with other countries where 5% of the population working in agriculture provide for the needs of the entire country, and where large quantities of agricultural products are exported, over 90% of the Upper Volta population worked exceptionally hard, yet were forced to endure famines and food shortages. The country frequently had to import agricultural products and seek international aid. The considerable imbalance between exports and imports made the country totally dependent on foreign nations; Upper Volta imported more than it exported, exports representing only 25% of imports.

In education, illiteracy stood at around 92%, and in health, morbidity and mortality rates were the highest in the sub-region due to under-nourishing and the proliferation of transmittable diseases. To make matters worse, Upper Volta had only 1 hospital bed for every 1200 inhabitants, and 1 doctor for every 48,000, and the great majority of the people had no access to drinking water. In terms of culture, each of the country's 60 or so ethnic groups had its own culture which it guarded jealously, and there was no racial intermixing to promote the emergence of a truly Upper Volta culture. Lastly, certain persistent cultural practices such as female circumcision and forced marriages were retrogressive and dangerous for social equilibrium.

Economically, the situation verged on the catastrophic, while in the political arena, the protest current called louder and louder for an end to the chaos, corruption and neo-colonial and pro-imperialist rule for which the government was held responsible. There were also rumblings of revolution, such ideas even gaining a foothold among progressive officers. In 1983, the country experienced its most acute economic and political crisis yet, two coups d'état followed in quick succession. This time, however, the revolution was bloody, and the country stood on the threshold of an era of violence.

*The revolutionary government*

On 4 August 1983, Captain Thomas Sankara and friends took power and installed the Révolution Démocratique et Populaire (RDP - Democratic and Popular Revolution), an anti-imperialist, democratic revolution based on the tenets of Marxist-Leninism. Their aim was to break with neo-colonial Upper Volta and build a national economy that was independent, self-sufficient and planned. And so Upper Volta became Burkina Faso. The President's 'Discourse of political guidance' (Discours d'orientation politique) ran as follows: 'The August Revolution does not seek to install just another government in Upper Volta. It hereby breaks with all previous governments that have ruled the country. Its overriding objective is to build a new Upper Volta society in which citizens, spurred by revolutionary awareness, shall be the artisans of their own well-being ... To this end, the Revolution shall be a ... total and fundamental upheaval sparing no field of endeavour, and no sector of economic, social or cultural activity.'[2]

The upheavals led to reforms in the following areas:
- the civil service;
- agriculture;
- education;
- production and distribution;
- women's policy;
- health;
- housing;
- the army.

The Conseil National de la Révolution (CNR - National Revolutionary Council) pursued its policy of transforming the economy through popular participation, and the country's administration was sanitised by the arraignment of dignitaries of previous régimes before Tribunaux Populaires de la Révolution (TPRs - Popular Revolutionary Courts). All officials found guilty of embezzlement of public funds, fraud, active or passive corruption and waste were dismissed.

The Programme Populaire de Développement (PPD - Popular Development Programme) was launched in October 1984; it 'comprises a series of sectoral investment programmes to be carried out at provincial and national level. Completion of the programme will enable people to improve their material living conditions with regard to such matters as food, water, housing, health, education and sport. The PPD is a challenge that the people of Burkina Faso must themselves accept ... they know there can be no true national development without popular participation' (Capt Thomas Sankara, 'Burkina Faso: CNR AN II, Programme Populaire du

Développement' (Burkina Faso: CNR AN II, Popular Development Programme), October 1984-December 1985).

To achieve this, the people were asked to make an 'Effort Populaire d'Investissement' (EPI - people's investment), which took the form of contributions of any size, although employees' deductions were mandatory. It paid for 30 hospitals in the 30 provinces, each equipped with two mobile clinics. A Caisse de Solidarité Révolutionnaire (CSR - Revolutionary Solidarity Fund) was also set up; this, too, accepted contributions from any source, including the diaspora in Côte d'Ivoire, Gabon and elsewhere.

The PPD laid the ground for the five-year popular development plan; scheduled for 1986-1990, this was premised on the organised participation of all social players in the development of a productive and prosperous national market. It also brought about a record 82% rise in GDP, marking a 12-month increase over the previous 15 years.

During the four years of CNR rule, there were major changes in economic and social affairs. Reforms announced in official policy documentation affected all sectors; interestingly, building work made use of ordinary people through projects of public importance such as the construction of schools, clinics, housing and roads.

Work of this sort needed financial contributions from the people, and particularly from employees in the public and private sectors. 'However, the harshness and austerity of the measures introduced by the CNR, the attacks on individual and collective freedoms, the repression of political and trade union opponents, the bitterness felt towards the traditional chiefs (still well established in the country), the spectre of Communism and its various manifestations, and a lack of courtesy in international relations - all of these things somewhat eclipsed the economic gains that the revolutionaries undeniably achieved. After Sankara's tragic death, the economy was soon thrown into turmoil and, after a period of 'rectification', Burkina Faso was sucked into a spiral of IMF and World Bank SAPs' (Nazi Kaboré, forthcoming).

## The Popular Front government

After Sankara's death, a pseudo-revolutionary régime took control with the objective of salvaging a revolution accused of right-wing deviationism, and putting it back on course. In fact, what it did was to terminate the process while preserving the outward form. The directions adopted by the new government were also influenced by the fall of the Berlin Wall and the break-up of the Socialist bloc. The new administration even began to extol the virtues of a political opening, and urged citizens to form parties and join the Front Populaire (Popular Front).

At this time, many African countries living under emergency and/or dictatorial governments responded to pressure from western democracies, particularly France (e.g. President Mitterand's speech at La Baule, 1990) and the United States, and Burkina Faso, too, found itself obliged to opt for democratic government and organise a General Election. The year 1990 marked the beginning of the country's transition to becoming a democratic State under the rule of law; further democratic institutions were organised as follows:

- adoption of the Constitution of the Fourth Republic by a referendum (2 June 1991);
- Presidential elections (1 December 1991);
- legislative elections (24 May 1992);
- local Council elections (12 January 1995);
- establishment of a Chamber of Representatives (January 1996).

## From revolution to democratic transition

From 1983 onwards, the country was run by a new group of politicians; they were extremely young and followed the teachings of Marxist-Leninism. During this revolutionary period, the country's trade union movement had two currents:
- one that was marginalised and suppressed;
- another that rebuilt the movement or sought a trade union revival.

Given its revolutionary credentials, one might have expected the new government to take its cue from eastern European countries and promote trade unions in all fields of activity. However, in their enthusiasm to make a success of running the country, the revolutionaries threw their minds back to the role that unions had played on the political stage between independence and 1982, and relied instead on new mass organisations which they themselves built up from scratch. These were the Comités de Défense de la Révolution (CDRs - Committees for the Defence of the Revolution). By contrast, most trade unions were characterised as small petit bourgeois organisations in the hands of reactionaries and populists; in the eyes of the revolutionaries, they were enemies of the people[3] and had to be rooted out and destroyed. At first, they were marginalised; later, they came under more direct attack.

Two important factors accelerated the marginalisation of trade unions and dealt a lethal blow to their unity of action: these were a division of views among trade unions about the revolutionaries' coup d'état, and the work of the CDRs.

The trade union movement was dominated by two doctrinal currents which survived until just before the August 1983 coup d'état that brought the revolutionaries to power. These currents had consistently given direction to united action on defending workers' interests and protecting democracy, but in fact they were fundamentally at odds with one another; in fact, they were in such conflict that, by the time of the coup d'état, trade unions were in total doctrinal disarray.

The trade union movement contained two currents, but it boasted no fewer than three positions on the August 1983 coup d'état:

- the reformist current, which adopted a passive position and warned the revolutionaries against a review of trade union freedoms (this was what had always happened previously after coups d'état);
- the revolutionary current, which welcomed the revolution enthusiastically and urged its militants to support revolutionaries against reactionaries of all kinds (particularly reformist trade unions whose centres they said should be closed down);
- a third current, that emerged from autonomous unions, and particularly the Syndicat National des Enseignants Africains de Haute-Volta (SNEAVH - National Union of African Teachers in Upper Volta) whose Congress happened to be in session at the time of the coup d'état; they passed a motion condemning what had happened and distancing themselves from the coup and its perpetrators.

## Defending the revolution

The revolutionary government's Discourse of political guidance stated as follows: 'Committees for the Defence of the Revolution (CDRs) constitute the authentic organisation of the people in the exercise of revolutionary power. They are the instrument that the people have themselves forged to secure sovereign sway over their destinies, and thereby extend their control into all areas of society.' In fact, CDRs already had a wide-ranging role that encompassed the unions; what is more, they were everywhere - from Burkina Faso's cities and towns down to the smallest village. It was mainly the Service CDRs that took on the trade unions; between 1983 and 1988, the latter were stripped of nearly all of their powers and activities were, to all intents and purposes, banned. However, on 28 January 1985, a trade union front made up of some ten autonomous organisations once again picked up the banner of trade union struggle, and issued a statement denouncing CDR measures that ran counter to workers' interests and freedom of expression.

Suppression of the trade union movement included the following measures:

- wage cuts as part of the people's investment (EPI) strategy;
- non-recognition of trade union activities;
- failure to observe traditions associated with 1 May;
- refusal to examine the workers' traditional list of grievances.

The CNR government undeniably made a positive contribution to the country's development, and particularly to the raising of moral standards in public life, but there was another side to the coin that involved human rights violations; these included the dismissal of large numbers of strikers and the arrest and torturing of political opponents. As time passed, this climate of fear forced the trade unions to withdraw from the fray altogether.

The trade union revival was given impetus by two major events: the foundation of the trade union front in January 1985, and the fall of the CNR government.

Despite the clampdown on its leaders and activists, the trade union front had continued to give battle throughout the reign of the CDRs until the President, Thomas Sankara, died and the CNR government fell. To win popular support, the new political leaders had no alternative but to right the wrongs that they had committed under the previous CNR government.

The establishment of the Popular Front government on 15 October 1987 marked the beginning of a new era. The unions gradually re-discovered their 'freedom of action' and, at a Congress in October 1988, the trade union front became a trade union centre, the Confédération générale du travail du Burkina Faso (CGTB - General Confederation of Burkina Faso Labour). There were now six trade union centres and about ten autonomous unions.

Reconciliation took place between the unions and the new rulers through:
- the re-instatement of all workers previously dismissed or laid off for various reasons;
- the freeing of all political prisoners;
- wage rises;
- the restoration of May Day celebrations.

The unions were invited by the Popular Front to take part in the following activities:
- a review of four years of revolution (1988);
- a review of a year of 'rectification' (1989);
- the framing of a draft Constitution (1990);
- the abortive Forum of National Reconciliation (1992).

**The social and economic situation**

So far in this study, we have focused on trade unions and democracy; this has enabled us to assess what trade unions have done to establish and defend democratic institutions. In the following sections, we shall examine

Burkina Faso's economic and social situation in the period preceding the economic reforms.
- What were the justifications for these reforms?
- What were the outcomes of these reforms?
- How did the trade unions react to these reforms?

The economy of Upper Volta (later Burkina Faso) went into structural decline during the 1980s despite an exceptional upturn between 1984 and 1987. The decline, the underlying problems, and the serious constraints hampering the country's economy were predominantly structural, institutional, macro-economic and sectoral.

The structural constraints derived from water shortages, infertile land, persistent droughts, rapid degradation of the environment, demographic problems and the fact that the country is landlocked. The institutional and macro-economic constraints were the result of a low level of productive investment, poor marginal productivity on these (mostly public) investments, incompetent management of public resources, and the application of inappropriate economic policies generally. The sectoral constraints on the Burkinabe economy reflected extensive, but backward, agriculture and cattle breeding, a poorly developed and fragile industrial base, a commercial sector that was unorganised and easy prey to fraud and smuggling, and a public transport system that was extremely expensive, yet vital in a country with no outlet to the sea.

*Justifying the reforms*

By and large, the ongoing economic, financial and structural problems faced by the Burkina Faso economy amply justified the government's reforms. The problems included:
- sluggish growth of GDP (3% annually);
- substantial debt accumulation;
- a current account deficit (14.7% of GDP between 1986 and 1990);
- low reserves.

Given the economy's current plight, some development partners made the adoption of an SAP a condition to giving Burkina Faso aid. The reforms sought to restructure the economy and reduce the major financial imbalances, and the overall aim was to make the country's productivity more competitive and lay the foundation for sustainable economic and social development. Following the devaluation of the CFA franc, the promised positive results are taking some time to filter through; negative outcomes are much more in evidence for the time being.

*The outcomes of the reforms*

The privatisation of some 20 State-owned enterprises failed to whet the appetite of Burkina Faso's own economic operators. The reason for this may have been that their assets came nowhere near the 9bn francs (8992bn francs to be precise, according to 'Le Pays', N 552, Monday 20 December 1993) needed to purchase State and parapublic shares. Then, when the market was totally liberalised, these enterprises were unable to compete with transnational companies because of constraints linked to the country's landlocked situation and high energy costs.

Given that the objective of privatisation was to promote the private sector, it is difficult to understand the urgency that surrounded the sell-off of strategically important enterprises such as the Société des chemins de fer du Burkina Faso (SFCB - Burkina Faso Railway Company), the Régie nationale des transports en commun (RNTC-X9 - National Public Transport System - X9) or the Société nationale d'approvisionnement pharamaceutique (Sonapharm - National Pharmaceutical Supply Company). The same might be said for others, such as the Société nationale d'assurance et de réassurance (Sonar - National Insurance and Reinsurance Society), the breweries or Zama Publicité, that were profitable and therefore made no call on the State Budget. This is all the more remarkable in a country where the private sector controls the most productive sectors such as agriculture, commerce, construction and public works, is responsible for 81% of Burkinabe production and employs 90% of the economically active population - and yet is insufficiently competitive and says it requires further support. The only possible explanation can be that privatisation and the State's disengagement (the phenomenon may also be observed in health and education) are part and parcel of a 'decisive step away from State collectivism and centralised planning' ('L'Observateur Paalga', 1993). In short, although privatisation leads to a reduction in State subsidies (and therefore the release of credits to pay off debts), it apparently only benefits international company rescuers - and a few from Burkina Faso itself.

Liberalisation and free competition not only pose a threat to industrial enterprises. For example, if the cornflour, sorghum and American soya we are given free in times of famine were to be scattered hither and thither onto our markets, the sufferers would presumably be small farmers. There again, European and Argentinian meat coming in via the main cities along the Gulf of Guinea has already cut livestock exports from countries of the Sahel to such an extent that, on 2 December 1993, our cattle breeders took the unusual step of staging a demonstration outside the European Union headquarters in Brussels. Their action eloquently highlighted the cynicism of setting up competition between, on the one hand, peasants from Kiembara who work the unforgiving climate and terrain of the Sahel armed only with a hoe and, on the other, American farmers who work hand in glove with laboratories and have combine harvesters to help them at harvest time - not to mention even Chinese or Thai peasants with their long traditions of growing rice.

For the most part, liberalisation has meant that even more foreign finished products have flooded onto the Burkinabe market; in the long term, this could easily destroy the country's embryonic economy, or restrict it to the production of raw materials (e.g. cotton) and minerals (e.g. manganese from the Tambao area and zinc from Perkoa). As for minerals, at a meeting in January 1993 with representatives of Burkinabe trade union centres at a top Ouagadougou hotel, the Political Counsellor from one of the Chancellories intimated that his country was interested in our mineral deposits - except that our currency was too strong!

It is becoming increasingly clear from the foregoing that the real objective of SAPs is not to develop a national economy so that it can operate as a true partner in international trade, but rather:
- to enable transnational enterprises - or else companies that are already local subsidiaries or will be acquired as the State disengages - to domesticate the manufactured products market, and make it profitable;
- to reduce production costs, particularly payroll costs, on agricultural and mineral raw materials;
- to establish a national budget capable of servicing the debt.

In many ways, these objectives are a reminder of the old colonial system.

According to a study by Salifou Konaté (Konaté, 1994), the short-term impact that devaluation had on enterprises may be summarised as follows:
- the change of parity had a wholly negative effect on company finances; positive results were restricted to the few enterprises that had an eye on the export market;
- increased production costs linked mainly to a rise in intermediary consumer prices;
- enterprises passing on some of these increases in rises mostly above 20% in services;
- continued under-use of production capacity aggravated by insufficient demand and financial difficulties.

The CFA franc was devalued during the time of economic liberalisation; as a result, many enterprises had to close down, or else restructure; knock-on effects included widespread job losses and a steep rise in unemployment.

*The social impact of devaluation*

The social impact of devaluation is examined in the light of its effect on household purchasing power.

After devaluation, purchasing power fell in the wake of sharp rises in the price of goods and services, despite the fact that the government had set up a system of nationwide price monitoring. The consumer price index for the first ten months of 1994 is set out in the table below:

**Table 1:    Consumer price index 1994 (January - October)**

| Month | Jan. | Feb. | Mar. | Apr. | May | June | July | Aug. | Sept. | Oct. |
|---|---|---|---|---|---|---|---|---|---|---|
| Index | 133,6 | 143,4 | 145,4 | 154,1 | 155,4 | 160,9 | 156,6 | 158,8 | 162,3 | 161,4 |
| Inflation compared with 1993 (%) (average over 12 months) | 6,2 | 14 | 15,6 | 22,5 | 23,5 | 27,9 | 24,5 | 26,2 | 29 | 28,3 |
| Monthly inflation (%) | 6,2 | 7,3 | 1,4 | 6 | 0,8 | 3,5 | 2,7 | 1,4 | 2,2 | -0,6 |
| Inflation slide (%) | 10,5 | 17,8 | 18,3 | 25,8 | 26,9 | 28,1 | 24,1 | 28,2 | 29,3 | 28,3 |

*Source*: Institut national de la statistique et de la démographie (INSD - National Statistics and Demography Institute)

Inflation rose from 6.2% in January 1994 to 28.3% in October, but price rises hit urban consumers more sharply. This was partly because of their consumer habits; it was also because they purchase their supplies differently from people in rural areas, where there is a much longer tradition of consuming one's own production. Households in the towns and cities found that, to cope with the deterioration of purchasing power, they had to manage the family budget quite differently and reduce expenditure on recreation, clothes, and facilities and amenities, and in favour of items seen as priority such as transport, medical costs and food. These households settled for a survival policy.

All in all, devaluation has clearly had negative social effects, but these have been mitigated by moderate price rises and by a series of social measures which the government took immediately after devaluation.

The trade union movement did not feel that these measures went far enough towards defending the jobs and purchasing power of public and private sector workers, and the government kept dialogue with the social partners alive in the hope of finding concrete solutions to workers' problems.

According to 'Ajustement structurel et pauvreté au Burkina Faso' (Structural adjustment and poverty in Burkina Faso) in 'Tradition et modernité' (N 00, January 1996), the poverty threshold has been assessed at CFAF 41,099 per adult per year. If that is so, 44.5% of the population of Burkina Faso live below the threshold and are therefore deemed poor. The poorest of all have previously included food-producing peasant farmers, wage-earning farmers, the unemployed, and polygamous families; they have now been joined by people impoverished by the recent economic reforms. Typically, the 'new poor' are low-income employees who have lost their jobs as a result of the SAP, and cannot break back into the labour market because they lack vocational skills.

*Trade union reaction to the economic reforms*

Although it was widely accepted that SAPs were a failure, in that they further impoverished already vulnerable social categories, Burkinabe trade unions reacted in a variety of ways when the government announced that an SAP was to be put in place.

The CGTB, ONSL and some of the autonomous unions rejected the SAP out of hand, but the CNTB, CSB, USTB and UGTB (together with the autonomous unions they lined up with) said that it was a system of coherent measures designed to knock the country's economic system into shape. In 1990, the latter grouping took part in a national meeting on the SAP, with only the CGTB, ONSL and some of the autonomous unions staying away; they argued that the SAP was bound to add to economic difficulties, and that workers would suffer. Insurrection in the ONSL ranks in July 1990 resulted in the removal of its General Secretary and some Executive members, and the new Executive moved behind the CNTB, CSB and USTB in giving approval to the SAP. As a group, they opposed the CGTB's overall assessment of the government's economic and political policies.

However, on examining the country's economic problems, and following the government's anguished appeal to the Bretton Woods Institutions, all the national centres (with the exception of the UGTB) and autonomous unions joined forces calling a Joint Conference of the Burkina Faso Trade Union Movement for 15-17 November 1991. The Conference looked at how trade unionism had shifted, it offered a candid evaluation of Burkina Faso's economic, political and social situation, and enumerated workers' concerns and aspirations. It decided that trade unions should not enter the political arena and take up positions vis-à-vis political parties, and also resolved that trade union activity should concentrate on finding a solution to workers' problems, particularly those that stemmed from the enforcement of the SAP.

Lastly, the Union Conference presented the government with a minimum platform of urgent demands. Negotiations concluded with the signing of a draft agreement on 12 December 1991, but the government dragged its feet over implementing the provisions; trade union distrust of government promises was thereby intensified.

Then, in 1993, when the dust had settled on the draft agreement and the government's less-than-universally-trusted word, the unions brought the public authorities abruptly to the negotiating table through the offices of a Comité Tripartite de Concertation (CTC - Tripartite Concertation Committee). The talks produced the following outcomes:

- a review of relations between unions and the government;
- a review of relations between unions and employers;
- a review of relations between the government and employers;
- the framing of a draft Social Charter;
- acceptance of certain demands.

While the CTC demonstrated the virtues of dialogue, it also widened the gulf between trade unions and government, with the former accusing the latter of not keeping its word. It should be noted in this context that the CGTB and some of the autonomous unions were not party to the CTC negotiations.

This division within the trade union movement persisted, and since 1993 the two groups of unions have celebrated May Day independently and have submitted separate lists of grievances to the government. This situation very much plays into the government's hands as it is able to capitalise on the lack of unity when responding to the claims.

Interestingly, the two sets of claims presented to the government have been very similar despite the division; for example, both lists submitted on both 1 May 1994 and 1 May 1995 called for the SAP to be withdrawn. The government's answer was to challenge the unions to come up with an alternative. In practice, no union alternative to Structural Adjustment Programmes has any chance of being adopted, given that the SAP philosophy is quite alien and takes no account of the country's realities. The 'soft SAP' that the government subsequently announced has turned out to be a very bitter pill indeed.

Only through combined efforts and joint action will the two collectives of trade unions achieve most of their demands. Negotiations between the government and the collective of twelve trade unions commenced on 1 July 1996 and concluded on Friday 12 July in almost complete disagreement. The collective had asked for increases in salaries and pensions, a reduction in the price of the major consumer goods, a halt to privatisations, cutbacks and lay-offs, a health policy that responds to people's needs, and an end to pedagogical innovations in education. The government pleaded the economic difficulties of the time, and granted a rise of 3-5% on salaries and pensions rather than the collective's demand for 8-12%. The reaction of the collective's spokesperson summed up the disappointment that this rejection caused: 'The government's position falls well short of workers' expectations and there is total disagreement between ourselves and the government. The government needs to take a serious look at our problems.'

The salary increase took effect on 1 October 1996 at the same time as a 3% rise in VAT; this now stood at 18% on consumer prices. The effects of the salary rise did not in any way counterbalance the increase in VAT. In other words, what the government had given with one hand it had taken away with the other.

The second collective of seven unions boycotted the negotiations as the previous talks had come to nothing. It is waiting for the government to respond to its list of grievances of 1 May 1996; this included a 15% rise in salaries and pensions, a rapid and complete resolution of all human rights violations, the immediate publication of the results of surveys carried out by the Inspection Générale de l'État (General State Inspectorate), a halt to the sell-off of national heritage, cutbacks and collective lay-offs of workers, and punishment for anyone found guilty of embezzlement, corruption and misuse of public goods. In the view of this second collective, 'so far, all that the government of the 2nd Republic has done as far as negotiations and concertation are concerned is deceive us and fob us off. The government thinks that workers and people have no capacity for analysis and understanding ... [it] cannot go on like this for ever.'

## Institutionalising democracy

Democracy made little headway between 1960 and 1990, and the advances that were in fact made were remarkable for their rarity; in only 30 years, for example, Burkina Faso has had four constitutional governments and seven military or emergency governments. The explanation for this may be that the country has no democratic culture. This absence of a democratic culture takes the following forms:
- a failure to abide by democratic rules;
- a refusal to accept alternation of political parties in power;
- no real separation of executive, legislative and judicial powers;
- limited support for individual and collective freedoms.

An earlier section devoted to trade unions and democracy demonstrated how the Burkinabe trade union movement has played a key role in the people's day-to-day struggle to exercise real democracy. The struggle has been instructive, even if results have fallen short of expectations, but the unions have never had an opportunity to exercise State power and intimate the kind of democracy they would like the country to have. Just the same, politicians, trade unions and civil society still need to join forces and institutionalise Burkina Faso's nascent democracy; moreover, this institutionalisation can, and should, involve a reinforcement of existing support structures of democracy and the implanting of a democratic culture at all levels.

## Support structures of democracy

Democracy's legal support structures consist of the laws and amendments that determine the functioning of the State and the life of the nation. The most important is undoubtedly the Constitution, but it is not enough on its own. The Preamble to our Constitution guarantees fundamental rights including civil, political, trade union, economic and cultural rights, but there are other laws that specifically affect trade unions, notably the general statute on the public sector, the Labour Code and collective agreements. All of these documents recognise and guarantee the right to organise and freedom of association, and contain provisions for setting up structures[4] that enable workers to participate directly and indirectly in decision-making at national and local level. They include the Commission Consultative du Travail (Consultative Labour Commission) in the private and public sectors, the Convention Nationale du Travail (CNT - National Labour Agreement) which provides the basis for social dialogue, and company-level Health and Safety Committees which contribute to the smooth running of enterprises. Workers are on the Boards of Directors of some State-owned firms and, as such, are able to have an influence on decision-making.

Other documentation over and above the Constitution includes:
- the Information Code;
- the Electoral Code;
- laws on decentralisation.

These decentralisation laws comprise a remarkable institutional reference point and democratic tool. By affirming the principle that the country was divided into regions, and that these regions were to be administered by elected bodies, the Constitution of 2 June 1991 clearly sowed the seeds of decentralisation. This policy forms part of the process of democratisation now under way in Burkina Faso; indeed, the Constitutional Referendum and the Presidential, legislative and municipal elections were all organised on a decentralised basis.

Institutional support structures include the following bodies and institutions:

- Assemblée des députés du peuple (Assembly of People's Deputies): elected by universal suffrage to represent the people in the exercise of legislative power; controls actions of the government;
- Chamber of Representatives: members elected by indirect suffrage; has a consultative role on all matters relating to the competence of the Assembly of People's Deputies; workers and civil society both represented;
- Economic and Social Council: members appointed by Decree; deals with economic and social questions, and includes workers' representatives;
- Constitutional Court: checks the constitutionality of laws;
- human rights defence organisations and other bodies (particularly trade unions) with similar objectives;
- free, privately owned press: provides people (mainly in the towns and cities) with information and raises their awareness.

Both legal and institutional support structures are essential if a State living under the rule of law wishes to move towards sustainable democracy. However, experience has shown that there is nothing definitive about a democratic State living under the rule of law; in fact, the State constructs itself slowly but surely, and the individual and collective rights and freedoms that provide the foundation of democracy broaden and consolidate through the people's ongoing actions and struggles. In Burkina Faso, the enforcement of laws frequently leads to dissent between the government and the governed, as represented by civil society.

There have been a number of examples of this dissent: a participant in student demonstrations by the name of Boukary Dabo questioned by the police in 1989 but not heard of since; in 1990, the turn of Guillaume Sessouma, a teacher at the University of Ouagadougou: disappeared without trace; then, in May 1995, two high school students from Garango (le Boulgou Province) beaten up by the police following a school pupils' demonstration. More recently, on 12 May 1996, a policeman shot a citizen in Réo (la Sissili Province) in cold blood for driving at night without lights and not answering a summons. This murder triggered widespread anger among the population of Réo, and led to serious riots in which public buildings were destroyed and policemen, their families and property were attacked. This was only one of many cases brought to the government's attention in a declaration of 5 October 1995 issued by the Comité de suivi pour le juste règlement des affaires contentieuses et pendantes en matière des droits de l'homme (CRADH - Monitoring committee for ensuring the just resolution of current and pending human rights cases). Paradoxically, for a State living under the rule of law, not one human rights violation has yet been satisfactorily resolved.

*Trade unions and the institutionalisation of democracy*

The section above on trade unions and democracy described how the trade union movement had played a major role in establishing democracy, but that victories over non-democratic governments have been annulled to such an extent that progress towards democratisation has been only minimal. The trade union movement as a whole is disintegrating, but individual unions can still play key roles in the institutionalisation of democracy; to this end, they need to establish and nurture a permanent democratic culture within their own organisations. In fact, signs of the absence of trade union democracy have long been self-evident, and they were at the root of the 1987 uprisings. Autocracy and the absence of alternation among the leaders have also led to 'trade union coups d'état' and splits.

It is too early to say how much the unions have contributed nationally to the establishment of sustainable democracy. However, factors like a major reduction in the number of general strikes - frequently responsible for bringing governments down in the past - and the philosophy of participative, constructive dialogue fostered by certain trade union centres may be seen positively as passive contributions. In this context, the fact that workers' representatives have seats on national institutions considered to be support structures of democracy reflects a desire among trade unions to see the democratic process in our country to a successful conclusion.

Locally, workers have been elected municipal Councillors; by taking responsibility for administering their areas in this way, they too have contributed to laying the foundations for sustainable democracy. By contrast, at company level, economic difficulties (and the dismissals that they bring about) and the phenomenon of de-regulation (which further strengthens the factory manager's authority) are among the factors that weaken workers' unity, and therefore prevent them from sharing in economic prosperity.


**For sustainable democracy**

Democracy formally returned to our country with the adoption by referendum of the Constitution on 2 June 1991, and later by the Presidential elections on 1 December of the same year and the establishment of all institutions of the rule of law. However, they have not been enough on their own to make Burkina Faso a democratic State. In our country, as elsewhere in Africa, the democratic process has been imposed from outside. Moreover, democracy is not just a matter of holding elections; a democratic culture is firstly required at all levels, together with a real yearning for democracy shared by those who govern and those who are governed.

It is not possible to acquire democratic values in the absence of a democratic culture and a grounding in human rights. This grounding is essential in any society, and specifically so in a democratic society: the need for freedom may be innate, but we are not born with an understanding of what social and political institutions can do to make freedom possible and sustainable.

This education process should be democratic; in other words, it should be founded on participation, and conceived in such a way as to enable individuals and society to improve the quality of life. There is nothing natural or spontaneous about the fundamental human rights (sometimes referred to as 'natural rights') that appear in various statements and charters; we have to learn them and teach them.

The crisis currently gripping our education system is making it difficult to teach human rights in schools; the main reasons are an already overloaded curriculum, a shortage of classroom materials, and poor teacher training. We believe that reform of our school system and the introduction of human rights teaching would help to make more sense of, and inject more interest into, a classical education system that is wholly inappropriate.

## Women and democracy

Devoting a whole section to women is justified by the role that women must play in the establishment of a democratic culture in Burkina Faso. Women are usually given responsibility for bringing up children; it is therefore vital to educate them in matters of human rights so that they have a democratic culture and can introduce their children (i.e. the citizens-to-be) to democracy. The family may be seen as the most elementary school where the mother is the first teacher. Democratic culture is also vital if women are to play their rightful role in the democratisation process currently evolving in Burkina Faso. Their numerical importance (they account for approximately 52% of the population) gives them a chance - even the right - to have a say in decisions. However, they rarely figure in the struggle for the establishment of democracy, and in trade unions they play only the most humble of roles, if they are involved at all.

Reasons for this include a very high rate of illiteracy among women, restrictive traditions and family constraints; statistics also show that only one in four public sector employees are women. Burkinabe society is male-dominated and relegates women to domestic duties and child rearing, but economic hardship is increasingly making women come together to do gainful work. Men have no choice but to accept this revolution, as husbands no longer earn enough to feed their families. Women are making great strides in the political and trade union arenas, but much remains to be done on behalf of the great majority of women who have no voice at all.

For example, the fact that there is currently a movement towards democratisation does not mean that the government will automatically address women's concerns. As long as women receive no grounding in human rights, they will not be able to play a broader role - for all their numerical weight - in making progress towards democracy by raising the moral tone of politics.

If Burkinabe women are to have roles in trade union and political life, initiatives will have to be taken by social partners in the private and public sectors to give them more economic and decision-making influence. A combination of these factors will help women to occupy their rightful place in a proper democratic system.

## The trade unions

Democratic culture relies on trade union and workers' education to instil the great principles of democracy. Respect by a union's leaders for rules and internal regulations is the prime criterion for measuring how far democracy is actually practised within the organisation itself. At the level of the State, the opportunity for different parties to take power measures the level of democracy that the country has achieved; in trade unions run according to democratic principles, much progress would be made if there could be alternation among the leadership. Trade union autocracy and the cult of the individual are killing off trade unionism in the same way that dictatorship has destroyed democracy and the State. In Burkina Faso, trade union autocracy and the perpetual sniping at trade union democracy have produced revolts and splits: between 1987 and 1995, there were six trade union putsches in three national centres, and other minor splits also had a further debilitating effect. Even if one detects the hand of outsiders in these disaffections, the main responsibility lies with the leaders themselves. From the point of view of credibility and effectiveness, one of the big dangers facing Burkina Faso's trade union movement today is excessive pluralism; there are no fewer than seven centres and fifteen autonomous unions, yet they represent a working class that is contracting fast as a result of the SAP. There is also the issue of the lack of united action, a problem aggravated by political divisions within the unions. At least rank-and-file activists still call for unity when their interests are under threat. As one militant said during a trade union training session, 'What will become of this country if the unions become over-politicised and disintegrate like the political parties?'

This cry from the heart pinpoints exactly how important the trade union movement is to our country. As custodians of uninterrupted democratic practice going back over half a century, Burkina Faso's trade unions have never allowed themselves to be incarcerated in a monolithic structure; on the contrary, they have always fostered the pluralistic expression of political ideas and fought to preserve the economy and democracy.

To conclude, the democratic transition that started in 1990 is not yet complete; much remains to be done. If the shortcomings raised in this chapter are systematically dealt with by players on the democratic stage, and as long as the unions do not lower their guard, sustainable democracy could still come to 'the land of incorruptible men'. For the time being, the road to democracy in Burkina Faso relies heavily on the trade unions.

## Notes

1   A local, millet-based alcoholic drink.
2   Discourse of political guidance, October 1983.
3   Discourse of political guidance, 2 October 1983: 25 et seqq.
4   -   Kiti N AN VII/FP/PRESS/TRAV dealing with the composition, role and operation of the Convention nationale du travail (National Labour Agreement).
    -   Decree N 92-0016/ETSS/SG/DT dealing with the composition and operation of the Commission consultative du travail (Consultative Labour Commission).
    -   Raabo N 511/TSS.FP dealing with the setting up, composition and operation of Health and Safety Committees.

# 8 Cape Verde Concertation

Niki Best

*The democratisation of Cape Verde took place against a background of exemplary political alternation with one democratically elected government following another. On Cape Verde, multipartyism and multi-trade unionism go hand in hand and aim to achieve a more egalitarian society. The recent history of the trade union movement might suggest that such exemplary progress is no more than superficial. As we shall see, it is going to be hard work.*

It is a widely accepted dictum these days that 'the more progress that is made along the road to democratisation and the restructuring of society, the more likely it is that donors will get out their cheque books'. This is a key issue for a small, dependent country like Cape Verde. The archipelago State of Cape Verde off the west coast of Africa is heavily dependent on development aid and on the inflow of remittances from citizens who have emigrated. However, leaving the country's basic, short-term survival needs to one side for a moment, if there is to be any long-term economic future, Cape Verde needs to revive its economy and introduce structural adjustments. A similar outlook faces the trade unions, for which draconian cuts in State expenditure pose the most serious problem. Budgetary cuts of this sort have a debilitating effect on people in general, but particularly on workers because it is frequently they who suffer even more grievously than the expenditure itself.

It is essential for people to participate in matters that concern them; this factor is intimately bound up with the process of democratisation. However, in practice, economic adjustment programmes are often introduced without any consultation with the unions, which therefore react in a variety of different ways: sometimes, they are unable to put up effective resistance at all; sometimes, they embrace the changes completely and wholeheartedly. Predictably, the role played by trade unions in the process of democratisation, and the introduction of economic measures is closely linked to the extent that they have been able to be independent of government.

In the most recent wave of democratisation that has swept across Africa, Cape Verde was one of the first countries to organise multi-party elections. The first free elections took place in January 1991, and the MPD

(Movimento Para a Democracia - Movement for Democracy) came to power after 15 years of one-party rule under the Socialist PAICV (Partido Africano de Independência de Cabo Verde - Cape Verdean African Independence Party). The MPD immediately introduced a series of restrictive measures, sought to bring the economy under control, and called new elections in December 1995. Democratisation is proceeding slowly, and this is a source of considerable satisfaction to western donors.

However, what is the real democratic position in Cape Verde? What is the nature of this form of democracy which involves the participation of major civil organisations such as trade unions? Indeed, is there any democracy at all? This report is the result of research conducted in Cape Verde between May and July 1995, and is based on interviews and archival study; additional interviews and a bibliographical search were subsequently carried out in the Netherlands. We shall seek to provide answers to the following questions:

- how has the process of democratisation moved forward?
- what effect have measures of economic adjustment had?
- is the trade union movement democratic and independent?
- what are the implications of democratisation for trade unions?

We shall first deal with the country's political and economic development; this has been characterised by two major phenomena: drought and population migrations. We shall then consider political and economic events from independence in 1975 to the advent to democracy in 1991. Finally, we shall look at the recent history of the trade union movement, and the consequences for trade unions of political and economic developments.

Cape Verde is a dry, arid country with no natural resources except for bananas and tuna fish. The move towards independence began during one of the longest droughts in the country's history between 1968 and 1984; this period was also marked by the failure of infrastructures that were inherited from the Portuguese are were designed to cope with such disasters. It is estimated that, between 1747 and 1960, hunger accounted for the deaths of 250,000 people, more than the total population of the islands in 1960. One result of this has been a strong tradition of people emigrating in search of work: in the 19th century, for instance, many found work with American whalers, and a large number of Cape Verdeans eventually settled in New England, still home to a substantial community of some 400,000 expatriates.

The United States began to tighten up its immigration policy in the early years of the 20th century, and Cape Verdeans were forced to opt for Brazil and other Portuguese colonies in Africa; the poorest of them ended up on plantations in São Tomé and Príncipe and had to endure working conditions marked by the utmost brutality. Since the end of the Second World War, most people wishing to emigrate have looked towards Europe. One of the consequences of this emigration is that there are probably twice as many Cape Verdeans living abroad as there are living on the archipelago itself. Annual emigration has rarely fallen below 2000; in the 1970s it topped 10,000. The country has had to rely heavily for its survival on development and on money sent back home by emigrants; between 1989 and 1992, remittances contributed an average of 12% to Gross National Product (GNP), and 60-70% of families are estimated to benefit from transfers from overseas. In proportion to the number of inhabitants, Cape Verde receives more foreign aid than any other country. There was an estimated population of 417,000 in 1995 (Economic Intelligence Unit (EIU), Country Profile 1995-1996: 95); aid accounts for 70% of the country's total budget.

## A centralised economy

500 years of Portuguese rule ended when Cape Verde won independence in 1975; in the years that immediately followed, the country was run by a single party, the PAICV. It was known as the PAIGC until 1981, when the coup d'état in Guinea-Bissau brought the curtain down on attempts to form a closer relationship between the two countries.

PAICV policy typified a centralised economy: fusion of the State and the single party, suppression of autonomy, and substantial expansion of investment in the country's capital city. The party's economic policy was also marked by a preference for grand projects which were frequently State-owned; however, in practice, the private sector - and particularly, the foreign private sector - enjoyed considerable latitude. Numerous public enterprises were established with the help of international aid, and State control over the essential sectors of production grew rapidly.

The number of employees in commerce and the public sector increased dramatically after independence when the tertiary and State sectors underwent development. During the period of the First National Development Plan of 1982-1985 and the Second National Development Plan of 1986-1990, the agriculture budget fell substantially and composition of the GNP underwent many changes: between 1980 and 1984, for example, the tertiary sector proportion rose from 60% to 68%, mainly in transport; the share of the primary sector declined from 20% to 13%; and the contribution made by agriculture, then employing 60% of the population, fell from 19% to 15% (Cahen, 1991: 351).

Despite the radical positions that the PAICV frequently espoused, and the friendly relations that it maintained with the Soviet Union and Cuba, centralised State control was not reflected in a drift towards Socialism. Indeed, factors crucial to the PAICV's survival included the excellent relations it enjoyed with the West (particularly development aid from the United States), the European Community and Portugal, and accession to the Lomé Convention (1977-1978). During the terrible drought of 1968-1984, most food aid was provided by western countries. Cape Verde also established links with Brazil, the Gulf States, Senegal and the ACP countries in 1978, re-established relations with Portugal, sent observers to meetings of the francophone African Summit, and even allowed South African Airways (SAA) to keep its landing rights in the face of an international boycott.

The political climate has always been somewhat liberal, despite the single-party structure's limited tolerance of criticism emanating from civil society. It should be noted in passing that there was no shortage of criticism, most of it appearing in the columns of 'Terra Nova', a religious periodical that published numerous condemnatory articles during the 1980s. The leading opposition party, the UCID (União Caboverdiana de Independência e Democracia - Cape Verdean Union of Independence and Democracy) was outlawed, but it flourished in Boston and Rotterdam.

## The political opening

The PAICV's third Congress in 1988 marked a turning point in Cape Verde's post-colonial history, for it was there that the decision was taken to move towards economic and political liberalisation. Major constitutional reforms were announced, and the Congress also decided that the free market should henceforth play an important role in the national economy (EIU Country Profile 1995-1996: 93).

State control over all economic sectors, save for the central bank, was suppressed, and the country opened up to national and foreign private investment. The government also sought to attract foreign capital in order to help develop the export of services; the ultimate aim was to turn Cape Verde into an Atlantic 'service station' with an airport, shipyards, and clearing and off-shore banking facilities. The party was keen to take advantage of Cape Verde's low wages and unique geographical position between Europe, Africa and Latin America. There were also plans to develop the tourism and fisheries sectors.

Following a meeting of the leadership in February 1991, the PAICV finally decided to set up a multi-party democracy. The Constitution was amended, and Article 4, which referred to PAICV supremacy, was deleted. The party went on to lose the legislative elections in January 1991 and the Presidential election one month later.

This came as a surprise, despite the gradual transition towards multipartyism that had been taking place since the late 1980s. The decision to hold free elections was probably influenced by international events;

moreover, to ensure the uninterrupted flow of aid, the PAICV had been obliged to preserve the high level of credibility that it had painstakingly developed with international funders.

Despite Cape Verde's exceptionally harsh natural conditions, economic growth was relatively stable thanks largely to international aid and migrants' currency remittances. President Pereira's pragmatic management, or 'management of dependency' (Meyns, 1993), also ensured that international aid continued to flow in after independence; according to the World Bank, average growth was approximately 4.3% between 1986 and 1991, well above the birth rate. It was also widely expected that the PAICV would win the multi-party elections and remain in power.

The PAICV, or the PAIGC as it was then known, had given support to the popular resistance, and non-property-owning peasants in particular, during the struggle for independence; this enabled the party to rally enough forces against both the Portuguese régime and the merchant class and landowners who had not supported the struggle for freedom. The PAICV held on to power for 15 years without interruption or challenge, and this period under Prime Minister Pedro Pires and President Aristide Pereira was notable for great political stability. In the event, there was too much stability as the old freedom fighters hung onto the reins of power to the bitter end. The PAICV had committed the sin of vanity and assumed that the people's support was a foregone conclusion.

The PAICV established a base in civil society with help from three mass organisations: the organisation of women and youth, the trade unions and the neighbourhood committees; however, their support was no longer as unconditional as it had once been. In 1987, for example, the women's organisation, which had always been more independent and better structured, made the mistake of ratifying the law on abortion too quickly; this inevitably triggered fierce criticism from the country's powerful Catholic Church; 90% of the Cape Verdean population is Catholic, and large demonstrations were organised against the law, the PAICV and the government. Under PAICV rule, Cape Verde was never really a repressive State, and it continued to remain open to the outside world because of its long-established links with emigrants living overseas.

*Time for change*

The UCID had been formed at the time of independence and was the oldest political grouping in Cape Verde. It seemed to represent the only serious threat to the PAICV, despite the fact that most of its members lived abroad, mainly in the United States. However, the party was heavily defeated in the first free elections because of a law preventing foreigners from taking part; in the event, it failed to field any candidates in time. Between February 1990 and January 1991, the PAICV did not expect to encounter any real competition.

However, shortly after the announcement of free elections, the MPD was formed in Praia, the capital; its leader was Carlos Veiga, a highly popular lawyer and former adviser to the Prime Minister, Pedro Lopes. With his experience of Cape Verdean politics, Veiga was soon able to build the party up on São Tiago and other islands of the archipelago, and recruit groups and individuals that had turned against the PAICV.

When land reforms were introduced following independence, the PAICV had come under frequent attack from landowners. This was largely because some of the large estates, most of them banana plantations, were nationalised, and land was then redistributed under a new law passed in 1981. Private entrepreneurs and activists in grass-roots organisations supported the MPD. Carlos Veiga was thus able to form a broad anti-PAICV coalition, and the MPD ultimately became the rallying point for everyone seeking an end to one-party rule. No other party was able to organise itself sufficiently to take part in the elections, and it also received strong support from the Church. The MPD inveighed against what it called the global failure of single-party governments, demanded an effective separation of executive, legislative and juridical power, and called for the decentralisation of politics (still dominated by the capital, Praia), free trade unions and the right to strike. Using the theme of 'change' (mudança), the party had a simple message that appealed to a large number of voters: with 66.5% of the votes, the MPD carried off 56 of the 79 seats in the Parliament. The PAICV won only 23 and went into opposition.

A key element in the MPD victory in Cape Verde's first free elections was that it reflected a popular desire to do away with an arrogant and paternalistic single party, and a yearning for pluralism and democracy. The MPD symbolised these aspirations, although its programme did not propose anything that was inherently original. However, it still managed to attract the generation that came after the earlier freedom-fighting generation, and whom the PAICV had been unable to win over. The MPD also took advantage of the shortcomings of the all-embracing State, and emerged as an ardent defender of private initiative and free market competition. The picture was completed by the presence of popular personalities like Carlos Veiga, the head of a large private law firm and Cape Verde's only independent Deputy since 1985.

In September 1992, the MPD adopted a new Constitution which focused on democratic rights and freedoms. Parliament, henceforward known as the 'Assembleia Nacional', also became more effective: for instance, it now provided a setting for open debate in which Ministers could be cross-questioned, and its sessions became longer and more frequent. Then, in

January 1993, Carlos Veiga announced a fundamental restructuring of the economy and termination of the adjustment programme in 1997. The MPD also repealed the law on agrarian reform in the same year; this ensured them much popular support, as many peasants had seen this legislation as an attempt by the PAICV government to subject them to further State authority.

With the MPD in power, Cape Verde preserved the political stability it had previously enjoyed, despite the difficulties inherent in the process of democratisation and the introduction of economic reforms. It even proved possible to turn the economy around and honour electoral promises. However, the party was unable to avoid criticism emanating from the opposition concerning its failure to reduce unemployment of around 30% and combat extreme poverty. Reform projects were making laborious progress, and the government was also coming under pressure from people increasingly impatient with poor economic results.

The MPD itself was racked with internal dissent and increasing discord. For the radicals, keen to introduce market forces and privatise speedily and at any cost, the process was too slow and did not go far enough. In March 1993, this caused three Ministers to resign; they felt that the government was lukewarm about cutting the number of civil servants and carrying out dismissals in public sector enterprises, and that the reason for this was that it wanted to preserve the good will of donors and attract potential investors. More moderate critics voiced fears about the feasibility of the adjustment programme, and were tempted to seek an accommodation with the opposition.

All of these developments led to a redistribution of Ministerial portfolios and the removal from government of its most vociferous critics; indeed, during the government's term of office, there were no fewer than nine Ministerial changes. Political collaboration and an openness to divergent opinions were not among the MPD's strong points, and the party did not really see any great need for them. There were of little importance in tactical terms, as the MPD had an absolute majority in the Parliament and could do whatever it liked. However, Cape Verdeans were now beginning to wonder how it might be possible for formal democracy and a range of political convictions to live side by side.

The party was now regularly, and with increasing frequency, being accused of not tolerating criticism and of not allowing the opposition to perform its rightful role. Germano Almeida, a writer and judge as well as an MPD representative, has referred to the party's regrettable tendency to follow the PAICV's example and brook no criticism (EIU Country Report 1993 4th quarter). Similarly, Onesimo Silveira, the Mayor of Mindelo, who had originally backed the MPD's economic programme, later said the party's attempts to eliminate all opposition reminded him of the days of the PAICV. He ultimately left the MPD and founded Espaço Democratico (Democratic Space), which he described as a forum rather than a political party. The need to create alternative spaces in order to facilitate discussion was itself an indication of the way democratisation was developing in Cape Verde; according to the EIU, the game of ministerial musical chairs was in fact a smokescreen for innumerable personal rivalries (Country Report 1994 1st quarter).

The PAICV even accused the MPD of behaving as if Cape Verde were a one-party State. In its enthusiasm to restructure the country, the MPD had upset many people by getting rid of the national flag and changing the national anthem, and had even considered renaming street names that recalled the (PAICV) struggle for independence.

The problem for the main opposition party was the difficulty it was experiencing in getting used to its new role: in fact, the PAICV had recovered better and more quickly from its 1991 defeat and was more united; by contrast, the MPD was weaker than it appeared on the surface, although it still had an absolute majority in Parliament.

Many people felt that the announced changes did not match expectations. The fact that many senior party officials had no time for the MPD's political polarisation and internal rivalries underlined its inability to function properly as a political party. What is more, rumours of corruption multiplied as division in the key anti-PAICV coalition deepened. Then, moderate MPD dissidents founded a new party, the PCD (Partido de Convergência Democrática - Party of Democratic Convergence), headed by Eurico Monteiro, a former MPD Minister of Justice. This brought the number of political parties fighting for seats in the National Assembly to five: the two smallest were the PS (Socialist Party) and the UCID; the three largest were the MPD, PAICV and PCD. Each of the latter three said they were confident of winning a majority at the legislative elections scheduled for December 1995.

*A new climate*

The government's efforts to attract investment, privatise public enterprises and acquire the necessary infrastructures began to bear fruit in 1995 when the economy at long last had the foreign capital it needed to create jobs. That year, the first signs of success were reflected in renewed support for the MPD, and the party was soon restored to health and able to escape from the impasse in which it had become trapped (EIU Country Report 4th quarter 1995).

The decision to extend electoral rights to members of Espaço Democratico led by the popular Mayor of Mindelo, Onesimo Silveira, unquestionably contributed to the MPD's renewed popularity. Espaço

Democratico was an enthusiastic supporter of decentralisation, and regularly called for more local autonomy in economic and social matters; it also enjoyed considerable popularity throughout the country. As a result of this move, the government gave more priority to decentralisation, and at a stroke was able to rid itself of one of the main criticisms of its policies.

In foreign policy, the MPD followed broadly in the footsteps of its predecessor, the PAICV. Although it had initially announced its intention of joining an African anti-Marxist alliance, the MPD maintained a policy of non-alignment; in fact, Cape Verde is still active in the group of five African Portuguese-speaking countries. It is also a member of the Organisation of African Unity (OAU), the Economic Community of West African States (ECOWAS) and the Permanent Inter-State Committee on Drought Control in the Sahel. Furthermore, the country has partly reorganised its armed forces; they comprise some 1100 men including about 1000 in the army and fewer than 100 in the air force engaged on transport duties. There is no navy. Members of the armed forces are involved in development projects, although a number of conscripts have been demobilised. The popular militia has been stood down, although there were still 15 Cape Verdean observers working in Mozambique with Onumoz in 1994.

The PCD is still unable to put its ideas on democratic convergence into practice; this is because the MPD won yet another crushing victory in the December 1995 legislative elections, capturing 59% of the votes compared with 28% for the PAICV and 6% for the PCD. A 70-80% turnout of the registered electorate of 190,000 was higher than in the first free elections in 1991. The MPD won a majority of votes in Praia, the other towns of São Tiago, and the districts of Santo Antão where the main agrarian reforms had taken place; it also carried off eight of the eleven seats on São Vicente. The party even managed to gain a footing in the former PAICV strongholds of Fogo and Boa Vista.

The result came as a surprise to many observers as the MPD had been expected to lose votes because of its unpopular economic policy. A coalition involving a centrist party such as the PCD had been widely canvassed and, if that had come about, economic adjustment measures would have been put in place, albeit more slowly as a result of the PCD's more prudent approach. In reality, even under PAICV leadership, the economic opening would probably have been less precipitate as the reforms continued to be linked to economic support and loans from the World Bank (EIU Country Report 4th quarter 1995).

The privatisation of Cabo Verde Telecom (CVT) in October 1995 was fiercely debated in the course of the electoral campaign. The opposition was against selling off State property to foreigners, but in the event a 40%

stake of CVT was sold to Portuguese company, Portugal Telecom Internacional (PTI). The MPD stoutly defended its policy on the grounds that the sale would bring in USD 20m in foreign currency, that PTI would invest USD 90m on improving and extending services, and that this would represent a considerable saving for the government. Shortly afterwards, CVT was linked to Afrikanet, a consortium of African, Brazilian and Portuguese telecommunications enterprises.

The election result put an end to any thoughts of the widely predicted coalition government. The MPD won 50 of the 72 (previously 79) seats in Parliament, the PAICV 21 seats and the PCD just 1. The PCD's disappointing result was totally unexpected as they had rapidly become the third largest party, and had expected to win.

During the election campaign, Carlos Veiga announced that he would retire if his party did not gain an absolute majority; he also dismissed the possibility of a coalition government on the grounds that it would lead to instability and that the country would be caught in an unending electoral spiral. The electorate gave Veiga what he wanted: the absolute majority without which he could not have governed. Veiga argued that voting for the PAICV would make life on Cape Verde even tougher, and that the other parties were too small to run the country efficiently for the forthcoming five years.

The MPD's other electoral themes were employment, infrastructures, better access to drinking water and a more optimistic future; these were issues that brought the party close to the programmes of the other parties. Not even the PAICV opposed the MPD programme; in fact, in the words of former President Pereira: 'Everyone acknowledges that the MPD has succeeded in consolidating democracy. If any differences remain, they do not appear to have been reflected at the ballot box' (*Jeune Afrique*, 18 January 1996: 42).

## Beholden to the Church

The UCID claimed that the elections had been rigged and that the MPD had bought votes. In fact, even before the elections took place, the Comissão Nacional de Eleicoes (CNE - National Elections Committee) had received complaints from various parties accusing one another of fraud. Despite repeated demands by the PAICV for international observers to be called in, the CNE concluded that the accusations were ill-founded, and it subsequently declared itself satisfied with the overall conduct of the elections.

The Church plays a key role in Cape Verde's political life and, during the election campaign, it gave the MPD mute - some would say explicit - support. In fact, it issued strong recommendations to vote for the MPD, even in places of worship. The abortion issue continued to dog the PAICV and, by endorsing the law in 1987, the party had attracted the all-powerful Church's disapproval. When Parliament voted against repealing the abortion law in 1993, the PAICV was delighted, seeing this rejection both as a victory and as a snub for the clientelist relationship between the Church and the MPD. The Church considered the law immoral, but was opposed to the MPD's suggestion of a referendum on the question.

## Carlos Veiga's recipe

The Presidential election of February 1996 was won by the MPD candidate, Antonio Mascarenhas; he was the only man to stand, and was thus able to serve for a second term. The low turnout of 30% may be explained not only by the fact that there was no choice of candidates, but by the limited power at the President's disposal. Under the new Constitution of September 1992, he could do little more than delay the ratification of laws, propose amendments, and dissolve Parliament in the event of a motion of censure. In other words, the President was quite ineffectual and unable to oppose the political parties in any practical way (EIU Country Report 4th quarter 1995).

The MPD also won the municipal elections held in January 1996. Carlos Veiga's recipe for the electors was that politics and cooking were one and the same thing: You need three stones to support the cooking pot, he said: an MPD Parliament, MPD municipal councils and an MPD President.

According to the UNDP's Human Development Indices of per capita GNP, educational level and life expectancy, Cape Verde is the eighth most developed country in SSA Africa after Mauritius, the Seychelles, South Africa, Botswana, Gabon, Zimbabwe and the Congo. Poverty and unemployment nonetheless loom large in the country's socio-economic life with 30% of the population designated poor and 14% very poor.

There is a high correlation between poverty, unemployment and the plight of women. 44% of households whose family head is unemployed are poor, and 34% of them are lone-parent families headed by a women; what is more, over a quarter (26%) of the working population are unemployed, and disguised structural unemployment is widespread. In 1990, it was estimated that there was a potential active population of 122,000; in percentage terms, this represents a much smaller proportion of the population than in most African countries, and reflects the fact that emigration is still high among young men. The labour force was expected to rise by 3% per year and reach a total of 135,000 actively employed persons by the end of the Third Development Plan (1992-1995) (EIU Country Profile 1995-1996: 100).

In 1980, 31% of the labour force were employed on permanent contracts, and half of them worked in agriculture. In 1990, women accounted for

37% of the entire workforce; three quarters of workers in the formal sector were men and 55% of unemployed people were women. The tertiary sector, which mainly comprises public services, provided 42% of full-time jobs, the primary sector 47% and the secondary sector 11%.

At 66%, the level of literacy in Cape Verde is relatively high; on average, it is 11% better than in other African countries. However, there is still a low level of education among the working population in general: 51% are thought to have completed only primary education, 6% reach the first level of secondary education, and 2% the second level; only 1% of the population go on to university. These figures explain how difficult it is to sustain employment and productivity.

Moreover, the employment situation is likely to deteriorate as a result of rapid demographic growth and obstacles to emigration. Annual demographic growth is currently running at about 2.5%, and the World Bank estimates that the Cape Verdean population will reach 777,000 in the year 2030; 70% are under the age of 30. People are increasingly moving into the towns and cities, with the capital Praia and the harbour town of Mindelo on the island of São Vicente being the most popular destinations. Almost half of the population lives on the island of São Tiago. In 1986, there was an estimated (semi-)urban population of 180,000 and a rural population of 160,000. In response to this, the government undertook to make a substantial increase in the social budget; in 1992 and 1993, this came to 30% of the country's total expenditure (EIU Country Profile 1995-1996: 96).

*Key sectors of the economy*

The Cape Verdean economy has been described by the World Bank as a 'low-middle income country'. Agriculture and fishing continue to be important sectors, but most GNP derives from the services sector, which accounts for 70% of GNP and 55.5% of exports. Most export receipts come from international sea and air transport. The services sector employs a quarter of the active population and makes a key contribution to permanent employment; it is therefore crucial to the Cape Verdean economy. About 12,000 people work in the public sector, and commerce and the informal sector are also particularly important sources of employment; it is estimated that 8.5% of the informal sector is involved in the importing of goods. Programmes run by FAIMO (Frentes de Alta Intensidade de Mão de Obra - Labour-Intensive Manpower Fronts) play a major role in the creation of temporary jobs. They were set up by the government in 1979 and provide work for the great majority of unskilled and low-skilled workers; most of these jobs are linked to the construction of roads, schools and hospitals, or are in the reforestation sector. For reasons of productivity, the government intends to cut these Programmes back despite the fact that, like the informal sector, they are of considerable socio-economic importance to the lives of many Cape Verdeans.

The industrial sector, which accounts for about 15% of GNP and employs 5% of the working population, is still quite small. The government would like to change this state of affairs and, by focusing on certain attractions such as the country's geographical position and the existence of a skilled labour force and low wages, the MPD has high hopes for light industry (EIU Country Profile 1995-1996: 105). The major State-owned industries are being, or have already been, privatised and the government is confident of attracting Spanish and Portuguese investment with a view to moving into the competitive European market. These industries are mainly in fishery processing, textiles, shoe manufacture, rum distilling and bottling.

The Third Development Plan has focused on fishing, and the MPD has privatised the State-owned Pescave de Mindelo and the deep-sea fishing fleet. Thanks to the excellent location of its harbour and its refrigeration facilities and modern shipyard, Mindelo on the island of São Vicente has the country's greatest capacity. Most artisan fishing is carried out in small boats using traditional equipment, and the industry accounts for no more than 4% of GNP. However, production in the fishing industry altogether accounts for over half of all exported goods, and is an important source of currency. A considerable amount of currency also comes from the renting of maritime facilities to foreign countries, mainly those in the European Union.

Agriculture accounts for 13% of GNP. Conditions for farming are so bad that the country is almost entirely dependent on food imports, which are themselves largely provided by food aid. Local production of maize, rice and corn is insufficient, and the islands provide no more than 15% of food needed for domestic consumption. Following a succession of droughts, only 10% of the land is cultivable and a maximum of 6% can be used for cattle breeding. Despite these unfavourable conditions, agriculture continues to provide employment for about half the economically active population.

*Commerce and international aid*

Cape Verde's main exports are bananas, canned tuna, frozen fish, lobster, salt and pozzolana; the principal purchasers are Portugal, Spain and the United Kingdom. On average, exports cover no more than 5% of imports, and the balance of trade is therefore in almost constant deficit. In 1993, foreign debt came to USD 158m, the great majority of which (USD 149m) was long-term. However, a rise in exports is forecast over the next few years when the country will begin to sell light industry products to West Africa. Cape Verde is totally dependent on imports of food, energy and industrial products; the main suppliers are Portugal, France, the Netherlands and Côte d'Ivoire.

In 1992, the development aid that Cape Verde received officially reached a new high of USD 124m; this was mainly due to multilateral aid from the European Union, with Portugal far and away the largest bilateral donor. In 1992, aid accounted for 86% of donations, but development aid fell to USD 115m in 1993.

The MPD has committed itself to the continued and accelerated introduction of market forces, and the private sector will henceforth be the motor of the economy. The Third Development Plan is characterised by a decision to provide the agricultural sector with new opportunities, foster more balanced regional development and promote the private sector. GNP is forecast to rise by 4%, and it has been estimated that the Plan will require investment to the tune of 48bn escudos (USD 730m); 81% of this will come from foreign aid and private investment. In 1992, growth of the GNP slowed to 3.4% and per capita GNP also rose insignificantly. However, the situation has improved since then with an estimated growth rate of 4% for 1993 and 4.5% for 1994. Annual growth for the period 1995-1997 is expected to be 5.5% (EIU Country Profile 1995-1996: 99).

State control has declined sharply over the last few years, and the public sector has been completely restructured; a special commission has even been established to help reform public enterprises. Since 1993, 13 of the 44 State enterprises have been privatised, 6 have been sold off, 11 are in the process of restructuring, and the rest are looking for a private buyer. Those already privatised include the Arcaverde shipyard, the Júlio Lopes agricultural company and a number of hotels. The MPD has also privatised the national bank, the Banco de Cabo Verde (BCV), and the new Banco Comercial do Atlantico (BCA) was due to go the same way during 1996. The air company TACV and several hotels are also on the list of companies to be transferred to the private sector.

In January 1993, Carlos Veiga announced a 50% reduction in the number of civil servants, a total of 122,000 jobs, but without any compulsory lay-offs. He stressed that the economic adjustment programme had nothing to do with the Structural Adjustment Programme (SAP) devised by the IMF, and that it formed part of the government's own unilateral Development Plan. Nonetheless, according to the EIU, the programme for reforming the public sector and improving the management of public enterprises is financed by the World Bank (Country Profile 1995-1996: 97).

A Centre for the Promotion of Investment and Export (PROMEX) was set up in 1991. Like its predecessor in power, the PAICV, the MPD is making great efforts to ensure that the capital accumulated by the numerous Cape Verdean emigrés, the richest of whom live in the United States, is invested in the country's economic development. To this end, an investment fund has been established together with an attractive taxation package for those who return home. The inflow of remittances from emigrant Cape Verdeans covers much of the commercial deficit, and the MPD government has passed a law aimed at encouraging all types of foreign investment. It has also had considerable success in attracting Portuguese capital into light industry (shoe manufacture and fishery processing) and tourism.

The MPD's impressive victory at the last election greatly encouraged the party to pursue its economic and social policy; one outcome will undoubtedly be an acceleration in the programme of World Bank-sponsored economic reform.

However, a policy of this type aimed at reform, the privatisation of enterprises and entry into the world economy can actually increase poverty and unemployment if the developing private sector does not create new jobs for workers laid off by the public sector. For the moment, the Cape Verdean labour market is marked by a structural imbalance between supply and demand, and unemployment continues to be one of the country's greatest economic headaches; with 3000-6000 new workers coming onto the labour market each year, joblessness has a particular impact on the young (ILO, 1994).

Current trends suggest that the number of new jobs will have to double each year in order to absorb these new arrivals. The government estimates that 15,000 new jobs will be created during the life of the Third Development Plan, but that will not be enough to compensate for the rise in the working population or reduce the high unemployment rate. Much reliance is being placed on increased public investment in infrastructures and on private investment in export activities, but it difficult to see how enough jobs will be generated given the heavy pressure that the labour market is under. In these circumstances, effective and representative participation by employers' associations and trade unions is vital.

When the PAICV was in power, retail prices of the main consumer products were directly controlled by the party, and food aid supplied by international donors was also placed on the market through the intermediary of the State-owned enterprise EMPA (Empresa Pública de Abastecimentos - Public Supplies Enterprise). The new government has abolished price regulation in certain areas, but not all; there is also still a mechanism for distributing food aid, and the State continues to have a measure of control over staple products.

In 1987, inflation was below 4%, and in 1988 it was still under 5%, but it rose considerably in 1990 and 1991 by about 11% before falling back to 2.7% in 1992 and 6.2% in 1993. In 1994 and 1995, inflation is estimated to have settled at an average of 4.5%.

*The trade union movement*

Cape Verde has had two national trade union centres since the formation of the CCSL (Confederação Caboverdiana dos Sindicatos Livres - Cape Verdean Confederation of Free Trade Unions) in November 1992. Prior to that, there had been only one centre: the UNTC-CS (União Nacional dos Trabalhadores de Cabo Verde-Central Sindical - National Union of Workers of Cape Verde-Trade Union Centre), which was set up by the PAIGC after independence and during the short-lived relationship with Guinea-Bissau.

Unions existed in colonial times, but they focused on professional issues and played a negligible role during the period of Portuguese Fascist rule. After independence, they were turned into more effective and democratic organisations, and aligned themselves with the PAIGC programme that called for 'trade-union freedom and guarantees for their effective operation' (Foy, 1988: 99).

Trade unions were established at enterprise and sector (industry, commerce, transport and private construction) level, and received financial aid and organisational support from the government. When the PAICV was in power, they claimed they had the advantage of a sympathetic, understanding government, and membership rose steadily; in 1978, they affiliated to the UNTC-CS. At the time of the UNTC-CS's first Congress in 1987, there were only 10,000 members out of a working population of 67,000, but trade unions still played an important political and symbolic role, keeping close to the party line of revolutionary class struggle.

When the PAICV's position was strengthened after independence as the 'leading political force in the State and society', it became necessary to set up a trade union structure that acknowledged the principle of mass participation; at the same time, there was no question of the trade union movement becoming an organisation that appealed to opponents of the party and the political régime. It was not until the PAICV's second Congress in 1983 that serious thought was given to establishing a system of trade unionism that conformed to the party line; at that time, the unions had no internal democratic structure. Alfonso Carlos Gomes was re-appointed UNTC-CS General Secretary at the PAICV Congress. Gomes was not only a trade unionist of many years' standing; he was also a faithful PAICV activist, and this ensured personal links between the party and the UNTC-CS (Foy, 1988: 99).

One Congress resolution related to the tasks of trade unions. It was clear that their activities overlapped with those of the government and the party and, in addition to a guarantee of better working conditions for workers, there was also the matter of finding mechanisms to ensure that the UNTC-CS had the maximum power to intervene more effectively in government policy on employment, pay, labour law and social security (Foy, 1988: 100). The UNTC-CS needed to bring all workers' organisations together and extend the scope of unions into sectors as yet unorganised; the latter included the public sector, public enterprises, agriculture, fishing and cooperatives. This led to great changes in the trade union movement; all union members had hitherto been employees of small private enterprises, as these constituted the only area where unions could operate within the law.

The situation changed in 1985 when a national organisation was established with local and sectoral structures for workers in all sectors; a network of UNTC-CS regional structures - each group was known as a USR (União Sindical Regional - Regional Union) - was set up at the same time. Autonomous unions operating at company level also gave way to sections reporting to the national body; these were comparable to local groups and committees of the party and other mass organisations.

For José Manuel Vaz, the CCSL General Secretary, these changes reflecting the party line spelled the end of trade unions. The regional sections had neither the power nor the autonomy necessary to negotiate independently, and everything now hinged on the UNTC-CS. The UNTC-CS itself argued that these reforms flowed from a desire to adapt to Cape Verde's specific geographical features, and that was why each important island was allocated a representative. Following a meeting of union leaders that looked afresh at the rapidly changing scenario, it was decided to bring the trade unions closer together. The aim was to enable local sections to have a better understanding of the specific problems facing all nine islands; the result was a structure at national level that was horizontal rather than vertical.

## Participation in change

The transition was not easy. Foy (ibid: 101) stresses how many workers felt wronged and dispossessed by their unions, and some of them, who had been active trade unionists under the Portuguese régime, criticised the intervention of the party and saw it as a return to the old Fascist ways.

Alfonso Gomes deplored these reactions, concluding that some older workers were unable to understand the changes that had taken place in employee-employer relations between independence and the PAICV's accession to power. He felt that one of the leaders' tasks was to convince members, and workers in general, that it was in their interest to be involved in these changes. At the opening of the UNTC-CS's first Congress in 1987, the President of the National People's Assembly, Abilio Duarte, emphasised that the party, the State and the UNTC-CS shared the same objectives, and therefore could and should work together to develop, carry out and evaluate workers' education. The UNTC-CS was part and parcel of the political structure and 'the way was now open for the UNTC-CS to assume its place in the vanguard ... alongside the party and the state, participating in the remodelling of Cape Verdean society' (Foy, 1988: 101). This interpretation of trade unionism was based on collaboration with the State and the authorities, and ruled out the possibility of workers having much independence. Under Gomes, the UNTC-CS had no time for members' 'autonomous' and ill-considered activities. The accent was on support for the party and its programme, and on collaboration with employers in all sectors. In public enterprises, the UNTC-CS took part in meetings on company plans and was a member of organisational committees where it defended workers. The UNTC-CS also attempted both to represent workers at all possible levels and to head off any problems that might arise. This meant that managers had to take trade union ideas seriously. Abilio Duarte words were as much a warning to employers as they were to any hotheads there may have been among the membership (ibid: 102).

The UNTC-CS had long been involved in managing enterprises but, as Gomes admitted, this had not always been a success. At the UNTC-CS Congress in 1987, he explained that there was danger of Boards of Directors losing their way when managers' views prevailed. Even more dangerous, he felt, was the fact that some trade union leaders had turned enterprises into private companies. In his opinion, the solution was to give trade union representatives a special status on the Boards of Directors of public enterprises.

Not everyone in the UNTC-CS shared this view and, in his Congress report, Gomes had to argue with 'some elements within the trade-union organization who seek the way of confrontation in preference to negotiation'. These individuals, he went on, laid themselves open to criticism as they ignored 'the principles of the party and its project for Cape Verde and the still fragile and limited Cape Verdean productive structure'. The UNTC-CS had to combat such subversive activities that were 'against the national interest' (Foy, 1988: 102).

Other mass organisations encountered the same problems as the UNTC-CS. They were all offshoots of the party and, although they enjoyed relative autonomy, they remained under its control. The credibility of these organisations was in doubt once it became obvious that they were serving the party's interests - that is to say interests that were different from those of their members. Trade unions can easily find themselves facing such conflicts of interest, particularly when the country is unable to meet the needs of the majority of the working population because of under-development.

The PAICV faced a dilemma that was typical for a progressive single-party government. The party gave the working class, which it sought to represent, autonomy and opportunities for self-expression; however, at the same time it risked open conflict between the trade union movement and the

State on matters relating to sectoral interests (i.e. interests narrower than the national interest). In Cape Verde, the system was put to the test by the introduction of the Second National Development Plan which the Assembly adopted in 1986; it provided for increased productivity accompanied by a cut in expenditure. As an integral component of the State and the party apparatus, the UNTC-CS was obliged to play a part in implementing the Plan and urge workers to agree to sacrifices to ensure its success. In a situation where interests diverge, workers have to demonstrate unusually keen awareness, as in the time of war, when accepting sacrifices for the national good. According to Foy (1988: 103-104), the PAICV was still ruled by the logic of the struggle for independence going back to the period 1974-1975; in other words, it was a search for genuine freedom and political and economic independence. However, although most Cape Verdeans had accepted this argument without demur for over ten years, popular support was no longer guaranteed, particularly as it entailed a significant financial loss for those whom the Revolution was supposed to profit most, that is to say the working class. They could well be forgiven for wondering if the formation of the UNTC-CS as a national, democratic organisation of all workers was a cynical manoeuvre by the PAICV and the government, rather than a genuine attempt to provide them with more effective representation.

*Autonomy*

In the view of the UNTC-CS's current General Secretary, Júlio Ascenção Silva, the organisation's first Congress in late April-early May 1987 coincided with a rapid shift by the Cape Verdean trade union movement to achieve greater autonomy and keep the party at arm's length. The tone adopted by trade union leaders was now more aggressive, the most important UNTC-CS posts having hitherto been occupied by PAICV activists: 'We cannot deny the relationship between the PAICV and the UNTC-CS. Our union is almost as old as the country is independent. Those days have now gone; we cannot ignore history' (Silva in an interview in *Vozdipovo*, 4 February 1992).

Members of the Central Council (CC), the union's supreme body between Congresses, were democratically elected at the Congress by the 226 delegates, themselves elected representatives (Movimento Sindical em Cabo Verde, 1993). It was by secret ballot, and each island was represented, and the appointment to each post in the organisation was the result of a democratic vote in which workers at all levels had participated.

Many CC members had started their careers on the bottom rung as workplace representatives. There was no co-opting or use of outsiders; it consisted solely of PAICV activists. Starting with these elections, however, the UNTC-CS leadership comprised both party members and individuals who had no connection of any sort (Júlio Silva in an interview in *Vozdipovo*, 7 March 1991).

After Alfonso Gomes died in November 1987, the new General Secretary, who already sat on the CC, was elected by the same Council. José Luis Livramento, who was also a CC member at the time, stated in an interview in the magazine *Vozdipovo* (27 February 1988) that the way in which the election of the UNTC-CS General Secretary had been conducted reflected the trade union movement's maturity and sense of democracy. 'This process,' he said, 'has once again demonstrated that there is a desire for a strong, decisive organisation and a means of representing workers' aspirations.' Domingos Monteiro also felt the UNTC-CS was taking an important step towards autonomy from PAICV (*Vozdipovo*, 8 August 1991). In an interview with *Vozdipovo* on 7 March 1987, Júlio Silva said that the USRs, which held elections every two years, already had a broad range of representatives including PAICV, MPD and UCID members. This, according to Silva, was quite normal and positive for an organisation aspiring to greater opening, strength, pluralism and unity: 'The current diversity of the UNTC-CS demonstrates that it has always been an open, pluralist and democratic organisation.' He also stressed that the UNTC-CS was united despite this breadth of views: 'There is one thing that unites us now and will unite us for ever, and that is the struggle for the rights and interests of Cape Verdean workers, whether they are Faimo workers, civil servants or private or public enterprise employees.'

After the first Congress, the trade unions stood firm as labour relations deteriorated against a backdrop that included an absence of dialogue with the employers and the dysfunctioning of bodies dealing with labour law (APADEP-Mali, 1993: 19). During the Congress, delegates had for the first time called openly for legislation defending the right to strike; their aim was to fight the injustice and arbitrary behaviour that prevailed in numerous enterprises, and public enterprises in particular. There was therefore a need to open the public sector up to trade unions, and this involved working closely with the government to repeal the agreement barring civil servants from trade union activities (*Vozdipovo*, 9 May 1987).

It also meant a radical change in attitude on the part of UNTC-CS leaders (Silva, *Vozdipovo*, 4 February 1992). Strikes had not previously been unlawful, but they had not been covered by legislation either. There are those who say that Cape Verdean workers have Júlio Silva to thank for the right to strike. As an Assembly member of the Standing Commission for Health, Labour and Social Affairs, he regularly urged Parliament to adopt the law on the right to strike; this, together with other legislation banning lock-outs, was eventually passed in September 1990 (*Boletim Official*, (Official Bulletin), 10 September 1990: 8-10).

*Negotiations*

In December 1987, open warfare broke out between the UNTC-CS and the government over labour law, and this prompted fresh negotiations. A start had been already made earlier in the year when the government attempted to introduce a number of amendments, but in June it pushed the bill through without taking the UNTC-CS proposals into account. Trade union leaders who also sat in the Assembly called for the original law to be ratified and improved and, to avoid a confrontation in the Assembly, the government accepted a compromise in the form of talks on the decree with the UNTC-CS. Negotiations concluded with an agreement in May 1989 and the passing shortly afterwards of a new law incorporating the changes demanded by the unions (Movimento Sindical em Cabo Verde 1993; Official Bulletin, 26 June 1989).

At the UNTC-CS's request, government and trade unions met again in August 1989 to discuss the situation of Faimo workers; this group was on the receiving end of exceptional injustice, arbitrary behaviour and abuse of power, and also suffered pay discrimination between men and women. Improvements were made in respect of pay inequality. In an interview with *Vozdipovo* (7 March 1991), Júlio Silva admitted that the situation was not ideal but that things were now a lot better, particularly as far as labour relations were concerned. All parties agreed that Faimo workers should enjoy minimum social protection and higher wages. In the same interview, Silva also made it clear that the Comissões de Litígios de Trabalho (Employment Disputes Commission) had been able to function more effectively thanks to the UNTC-CS, and that dock workers had obtained social protection, health insurance and a pension scheme. 'And these are struggles fought out at national level. Let us not forget actions carried out by trade unions on the various islands of the archipelago and at company level.'

*The UNTC-CS and mudança*

When the UNTC-CS published a discussion document on trade union strategy entitled 'Reflexão sobre a estratégia de actuação dos Sindicatos' (Thoughts on the action strategy of trade unions) in February 1990, the PAICV organised a meeting to discuss its contents. In particular, the UNTC-CS proposed that Article 10 of the Constitution, which stated that the PAICV was recognised as the 'leading political force in the State and society', should be amended. Workers' conditions of employment were also criticised and the right to strike fiercely defended. The meeting took place in March 1990, and the Article was declared null and void by the union's leadership in the same month (Movimento Sindical em Cabo Verde, 1993).

The CC in turn took up this decision, recommending to the next Congress that the Article relating to the Statutes should be deleted and, at the second Congress in February 1992, the UNTC-CS declared itself independent of political parties, the State, employers, religious bodies and all other non-union organisations (Article 3). Articles 4, 5 and 6 set out the principles of democracy and free trade unions (Movimento Sindical em Cabo Verde, 1993). As Silva commented, 'There was a declaration of a state of political liberalisation and, by the same token, of multipartyism. The UNTC-CS therefore had to adopt a different position from the time when there had been a one-party State, hence the need to declare Article 10 null and void. From that moment onwards, the union's relations with political parties were based on equality' (Silva, *Vozdipovo*, 4 February 1992).

In June 1990, the UNTC-CS published a platform for the forthcoming legislative elections, and a review of the Statutes in which it set out its demands. The union defended trade union autonomy and independence from political parties, the State and religious bodies; it also defended workers' unity, demanding recognition of the right to strike as a means of struggle, and also the right of everyone, particularly civil servants, to join a trade union (Plataforma sindical (Trade union platform) published in *Vozdipovo*, 14 August 1990). This platform was addressed to all parties and was discussed with the two most important ones, the PAICV and the MPD. The UNTC-CS was certainly not going to support any single political party during the campaign or the elections, but officers and members were free to do as they saw fit on an individual basis. On a number of occasions, the UNTC-CS announced that it would remain independent from the political parties, but that it was prepared to enter into serious negotiations with each of them (see inter alia *Vozdipovo*, 13 March 1990 and 29 January 1991).

*The first strikes*

On 24 September 1990, the workforce at the Cabnave Shipyard (Estaleiros Navais de Cabo Verde) came out on strike. They had been demanding better pay and conditions for some time, but management had refused to listen. In April, negotiations between the São Vicente USR and Cabnave reached an impasse, and a month later the Director rejected out of hand a fresh UNTC-CS attempt to hold talks. Despite renewed contact between the government and the UNTC-CS, the Director stuck to his guns and, seeing no prospect of negotiations, the union called on the government to intervene as a matter of urgency. A number of claims were then met, but the key question of a retrospective pay rise was left in abeyance. During the campaign, Cabnave came to be seen as the country's most troubled enterprise where workers' rights were systematically ignored and dialogue was non-existent. Comparisons were also made with Portuguese colonial days on São Tomé where Cape Verdean slaves had endured appalling conditions on the sugar plantations. On the day that the strike started, the government had launched a powerful attack on the UNTC-CS with a statement that the union 'had no good reason for justifying recourse to action as radical as a strike' (Movimento Sindical em Cabo Verde, 1993).

The UNTC-CS has continued to campaign in defence of workers' rights in other workplaces; these include the CTT (a Cape Verdean telecommunications company in the process of being partly privatised), several hotels (including the Praia Mar and the Atlantico), the Justino Lopes State-owned agricultural enterprise (due to be privatised), the Ceris brewery, the Transcor transport company, Faimo, the Empa warehouses and large State-owned company with a workforce of 850, the Mindelo customs, civil servants employed by the Caixa Economica (Savings Fund) in Praia, and the Electra electricity company. Defensive actions continued after the MPD came to power, particularly on the archipelago's largest island of São Tiago where the capital Praia is located.

## The UNTC-CS splits in two

When the UNTC-CS Central Council met in Praia in November 1990, several members unexpectedly announced that they no longer supported the union leadership. In their view, the UNTC-CS was not an independent organisation, and they criticised it for maintaining links with the PAICV. It was well known that most of these members were not PAICV activists and that they had always approved the union's activities, including the new 'horizontal' structure, but they had given no hint of any disagreement. One of them was a PAICV member by the name of José Manuel Vaz who had much to thank the party for, and was also indebted to the PAICV for his education; he was the head of the São Tiago USR. After the Congress, his friend José Luis Livramento, who was not a PAICV activist, praised the auspiciously democratic path followed by the UNTC-CS. This lively meeting left many people very confused (interview, 12 July 1995). The São Tiago USR, the bastion of the union's 'dissidents', demanded that an extraordinary UNTC-CS Congress be called to remove Article 10 from the Statutes and discuss the impact of political change on the union. The leaders of the São Tiago wanted to resolve the problem as soon as possible, and referred to 'the need for radical changes within the organisation and among leaders of the union's bodies' (*Vozdipovo*, 20 June 1991).

Bringing the date of the Congress forward was not so easy: not only did union representatives from all over the country have to make themselves available, but money for their journeys to Praia also had to be found. All of these factors enabled the São Tiago representatives to have a disproportionate influence on the Congress, and therefore on the election of a new CC. Moreover, everybody was obsessed by mudança and probably more easily influenced as a result. At the May 1991 meeting, the CC decided not to accede to the São Tiago request, and opted to hold the second Congress in April 1992 as planned. The Council justified this move on the grounds that it was necessary to make suitable preparations for a Congress that was expected to determine the course of the UNTC-CS for years to come. The CC also wanted an in-depth discussion both on the proposal to change the structure of regional sections by economic sector at national level and on the change in the Statutes. Another important issue for the CC was the participation of civil servants who had had the right to belong to a trade union since 1990; they could not therefore be ignored.

In his interview with *Vozdipovo* of 4 February 1992, Júlio Silva felt there was no point in holding an extraordinary Congress simply to strike out an Article from the Statutes; in the opinion of the CC, it was already meaningless. In Silva's view, the forthcoming Congress was an excuse for the São Tiago USR leadership to stir up ill-feeling among the members. The vague 'dissident' feelings within the UNTC-CS came exclusively from the São Tiago USR, a view borne out by José Manuel Vaz. The General Secretaries of the other unions made it clear that they would not be over-concerned by that sort of upset in their own ranks; Silva also pointed out that the São Tiago USR could not lay down the law for others, and he was also concerned about 'the problems that this episode and the São Tiago USR's eccentric involvement could cause them' ( *Vozdipovo*, 20 June 1991). José Manuel Vaz believed that the UNTC-CS should have come to terms with the new situation in the country back in January of that year at the time of the meeting of the São Tiago union leaders. They had then referred to the need to set up independent unions at national level 'because regional structures diluted the aspirations of workers whose demands only had the same impact when unions were organised by economic sector' ( *Vozdipovo*, 20 June 1991).

In the event, the 'dissident' São Tiago group did not succeed in bringing forward the date of the Congress, at which support from over half the members was needed, and July 1991 saw the formation of the GSI (Grupo de Dinamização de Sindicatos - Trade Union Pressure Group). This 'group, dedicated to the establishment of independent, democratic trade unions', attracted many sympathisers, and the first 'independent' unions were set up in late 1991. The first to do so was the STCT (Sindicato dos Transportes, Comércio e Turismo - Union of Transport, Commerce and Tourism Workers); it was supported by the São Tiago USR, and declared itself an independent union in Praia in November 1991. This was seen as a historic event at the time, and reference was made to 'the freedom of workers to set up their own unions and organisations, a fundamental right recognised by democratic countries all over the world'. Several UNTC-CS affiliates followed suit and formed themselves into independent organisations; later on, other unions were founded and, in November 1992, they came together under the banner of the CCSL (Confederação Caboverdiana dos Sindicatos Livres - Cape Verdean Confederation of Free Trade Unions).

Júlio Silva held the view that the activities of the São Tiago USR and subsequent events concealed a strategy by the new government to divide and rule the trade union movement ( *Vozdipovo*, 4 February 1992). In March 1991, two months after the MPD came to power, the government had announced that it was withdrawing the UNTC-CS monthly subvention of 1000 contos; this tactic immediately made the union heavily dependent on contributions from members and international trade union organisations.

Moreover, only a short time before, in a talk on Rádio Nacional De Cabo Verde, the Minister of Justice, Public Sector and Labour, Eurico Monteiro, had accused the UNTC-CS of having 'passively collaborated' with the previous PAICV government ( *Vozdipovo*, 16 March 1991). Then, after the subvention was withdrawn, a senior civil servant travelled abroad to attend a meeting of the ICFTU (International Confederation of Free Trade Unions); there, he stated that the UNTC-CS no longer existed as it had been totally dependent on a subvention now withdrawn. He also announced that a new organisation was to be founded, and that he himself was a member of the group charged with setting it up ( *Vozdipovo*, 4 February 1992).

*Certain victory*

However, this did not prevent the ICFTU from taking the UNTC-CS into full membership on 22 November 1991; the Brussels-based ICFTU is the world's largest international organisation of trade unions, with 143 confederations and over 100m members. Júlio Silva described ICFTU membership as 'a victory for all involved in the fight to keep trade unions in Cape Verde alive, and a defeat for all who took part in the campaign to sully the image of the UNTC-CS and its leaders'. He also pointed out that affiliation provided many opportunities for collaboration at international level: 'The unions that will emerge from the reorganisation of the UNTC-CS's current sections will also be able to establish relations with the ICFTU's international sections' ( *Vozdipovo*, 26 November 1991).

José Manuel Vaz of the UNTC-CS describes how the union's property also suffered in the course of the conflict, particularly its training and congress centre, the Centro Social 1 Mayo (1 May Social Centre). The FNV (Dutch Confederation of Trade Unions), which had been involved in originally setting it up, argued that it had been a solidarity project with the UNTC-CS which was therefore the rightful owner, despite changes that had taken place on the political stage. After the São Tiago USR refused to pay the UNTC-CS rent for the area they occupied at the centre, the UNTC-CS changed the locks. The São Tiago USR then claimed it had been thrown onto the street by the UNTC-CS which, in turn, retorted that it had driven nobody away and that the centre was at the disposal of all workers, but that the facilities had to be paid for. São Tiago USR members recalled having been among the first to applaud when the UNTC-CS subvention was withdrawn; they thought that the UNTC-CS ought to pay for its own facilities (*Vozdipovo*, 19 December 1992). It should be noted that the centre was one of the UNTC-CS's main sources of revenue.

At this point, the police surrounded the building, confiscated part of the social centre and handed it over to the São Tiago USR. The FNV was greatly exercised about this and reacted angrily, describing the measure as illegal and a violation of the UNTC-CS's rights. It also called on the Prime Minister to condemn the action and to authorise no further interference in the internal affairs of trade unions: 'The UNTC-CS is incontestably the legal owner of the social centre. If other groups in Cape Verdean society wish to have access to the centre, it totally contradicts the processes of the rule of law' (J Stekelenburg in a letter of 7 January 1992 to Prime Minister Carlos Veiga). The affair then came before a judge, who decided to turn the dissident group out of the centre, and close the building down until a final decision was taken. At the time of writing, no final decision has been taken, and the building is in the same dilapidated state as the two jeeps that were also seized on the judge's orders (Report of the ICFTU Mission to Cape Verde, 1995).

The Prime Minister denied any government involvement in what he described as a private dispute, and announced that an independent judge would make a finding on events so far; he also said he was not 'amused' by a letter that he had received from the FNV (Report of ICFTU Mission to Cape Verde, 1995). As a result, the UNTC-CS once again found itself on the list of organisations that had had moveable property and real estate confiscated (*Vozdipovo*, 8 August 1991).

In 1991, the government declared the UNTC-CS an illegal organisation, a GSI spokesperson announcing that, 'it's all over with the UNTC-CS - it's no longer legal; union support has arrived too late because no trade union can affiliate to a centre that has been declared illegal' (*A Semana*, 17 January 1992). In an interview with *Vozdipovo* on 31 December 1991, José Manuel Vaz claimed that the UNTC-CS had not been in existence for some time; however, in an interview with the same newspaper on 4 February 1992, Júlio Silva replied that, as far as he was concerned, the UNTC-CS was alive and well and ready to fight on. The union had already contacted the President and the Minister of Justice and Labour, informed them of the difficulties it found itself in, and drawn attention to the danger facing it and its leaders. Actions undertaken by an illegal organisation could themselves been deemed illegal, with all the consequences that that implied, and Silva, expecting that things would quickly come to head, signalled that he would make an appeal to international bodies. The President, Antonio Mascarenhas Monteiro, then announced that he would do everything within his power to resolve the problem, that in his view it was an irregular practice, and that in all the circumstances the UNTC-CS could not have its legal status taken away. The Minister of Justice and Labour told Silva and his colleagues that there had never been any question of the government withdrawing the UNTC-CS's legal status, and that the matter would soon be placed in the hands of the head of the government.

The low regard in which the head of government, the lawyer Carlos Veiga, held legal status soon became clear when, in 1992, he sent a delegation to the annual international conference of the ILO in Geneva. Every year, the government appointed three delegates, one from the trade unions, one from employers' associations and one from the government and, in both 1992 and 1993, the government chose the union representative from the ranks of the CCSL. According to José Manuel Vaz, the UNTC-CS refused to take part in talks on the choice of delegates (they believed they were orchestrated by the government) as it did not recognise the existence of the CCSL in the first place. The CCSL, which had been set up in November 1992, was then declared legal in March 1993; in July of the previous year, it had still been acting as Conselho Coordenador de Sindicatos Livres (Coordinating Council of Free Trade Unions), a body set up in the previous January. Since 1994, there has been a rotating system whereby the UNTC-CS and the CCSL take it in turns to go to Geneva. The UNTC-CS has protested about this two-yearly arrangement.

The ILO asks for participation from the most representative organisations, and although the UNTC-CS has often asked the government to carry out an independent survey on the representativeness of trade union centres in Cape Verde, this has not been done. On the contrary, when, after the mudança, the government made proposals to privatise the Justino Lopes agricultural enterprise, it recognised the CCSL as the representative union despite the fact that most Justino Lopes employees were UNTC-CS members. The workforce has since succeeded in taking the company over (Report of ICFTU Mission to Cape Verde, 1995).

Marktest, a market research consultancy eventually called in by the UNTC-CS, found that 85% of trade unionists were UNTC-CS members and that 15% were in the CCSL (Marktest, March 1995). At the time of writing, the government has not reacted to the results of this survey. José

Manuel Vaz claims the government would have preferred to ignore the whole business on the grounds that it was a 'put-up job' by Marktest and the UNTC-CS (interview, 26 July); they also hoped to be able to spread counter-information about CCSL membership figures, and could not understand why the UNTC-CS was making such a fuss.

*Attempts to discredit the UNTC-CS*

The year 1991 was surely the most catastrophic in the UNTC-CS's short existence. On the union's radio programme, *A vos do trabalhador* (Worker's Voice), a speaker had spoken up for the UNTC-CS and criticised government actions; as a result, the programme was taken off and UNTC-CS's air time on national radio was reduced. The matter has since been resolved: the UNTC-CS has its air time back again and can express its views freely. However, the attack continued in the press, with innumerable articles accusing the UNTC-CS of never having been independent, of being incapable of adapting to the new political situation, of being anti-democratic and opposed to freedom of association, of having always been slow to carry out actions in support of workers, of shamelessly calling strikes without first negotiating, of being 'some strange, callous monster', of harbouring parasites, and of being in the midst of a major crisis - even of no longer being in existence. All of these articles deplored the fact that there had ever been a real trade union in Cape Verde; the 'discussion' was led by a government adviser, Antonio Pascoal Silva dos Santos ( *Vozdipovo*, 8 August 1991).

In an interview with the magazine 'A Semana', the Minister of Justice stated that the principles espoused by the government were different from those of the UNTC-CS, and explained that he was in favour of a large number of trade unions whereas the UNTC-CS only wanted one. He again appealed to workers to join independent unions. Carlos Veiga, for his part, went to São Vicente where he urged dockers to form their own union, arguing that the UNTC-CS provided no guarantees and there were no trade unions at all in Cape Verde ( *Vozdipovo*, 4 February 1992).

In a letter sent to the ICFTU in November 1991, Carlos Veiga explained his government's position on the trade union situation in Cape Verde and the legal registration of the UNTC-CS. He said that the UNTC-CS had always been opposed in principle to any attempt to introduce freedom of association and trade union pluralism into Cape Verdean society; he added that the UNTC-CS had always been 'an instrument of destabilisation attached to the old single party, and had sunk to appalling depths in an attempt to destabilise the first democratically elected government'. The Prime Minister also wrote that workers had neither respect for, nor confidence in, the UNTC-CS as it did not represent any of its affiliates (*Vozdipovo*, 21 November 1991).

Júlio Silva believed that the São Tiago USR demands were an attempt at manipulation; in his view, they were designed to distract workers from the real problems - privatisations, the reorganisation of Faimo and workers' social security. In fact, as far as social security was concerned, the UNTC-CS had presented the government with a number of proposals, particularly relating to low and obsolete allowances that had not been reviewed since their introduction eight years earlier. The UNTC-CS also proposed reducing the working hours of shipyard workers; they were putting in as many as 48 hours a week, while the average in other parts of Cape Verde was 44 hours (*Vozdipovo*, 5 March 1991). Following this proposal, the Prime Minister replied that he would immediately contact the union with a view to getting talks off the ground. One year later, nothing had really happened.

'As a result of the confusion currently reigning in the trade union movement, the government avoids meeting us, and the UNTC-CS finds itself diverted from its main tasks. It is my belief that, since the beginning of the inter-union "struggle" - it ought to be a dispute between the trade unions on one side, and the employers and the government on the other - the workers' interests have received less and less attention' (*Vozdipovo*, 4 February 1992). 'How can it be that, at a time when the UNTC-CS is fighting for its very life and workers are under threat from privatisation, people are more concerned with bringing forward the date of a Congress?' (Silva in *Vozdipovo*, 20 June 1991).

José Manuel Vaz told those who doubted the authenticity of his claims that 'it was not a question of political manoeuvring but of a legitimate demand by workers trying indefatigably to make their unions stronger' (*Vozdipovo*, 20 June 1991).

In August 1991, workers in the Empa public warehouses in Praia took action to improve their working conditions, and the security staff went on strike for improved working hours. The Empa management announced in a statement that 'recourse to strike action, something that has never previously been advocated by the São Tiago USR, encourages workers to put in illogical claims of doubtful legality, and incites them to violence' (*Vozdipovo*, 27 August 1991). During the same week, there was a fire in the warehouses and the strikers were accused of having started it. The Minister of Labour, Eurico Monteiro, claimed that the workers had used force, threats and violence to exert pressure on the employers, and considered it 'regrettable that the main aim of the country's first strike, which had been encouraged and supported by the UNTC-CS, had been to create a climate of confrontation, rebellion and social instability'. He also added that 'it had not escaped the government's notice that those who defended the strike were the very people who had stifled workers' opinions for 15 years in a desperate attempt to prop up the single-party government'. Mario Montero of the São Tiago USR sensed that 'that the government was protecting the Empa', and argued that 'a democratic government should not intimidate strikers' (*Vozdipovo*, 29 August 1991). Júlio Silva categorically dismissed the accusations directed at the UNTC-CS, pointing out to the Minister of Labour that it was not the UNTC-CS that had called the strike, 'but the São Tiago USR, an intermediary body of the UNTC-CS'. He added that the UNTC-CS supported the strike because it considered it to be justified and legal: 'We are in solidarity with the strikers and have asked the government to resolve the dispute, but sadly nothing has come of our request' (*Vozdipovo*, 31 August 1991).

## The implications of democratisation for the trade union movement

While the CCSL is busy counting its members, the UNTC-CS has to spend time distinguishing between registered members and paying members - that is to say between unemployed (registered) members temporarily unable to pay their dues, and active members. There are approximately 5000 paying members out of a total of 15,000; paying members have to pay 1% of their wages. Like the CCSL, the UNTC-CS operates a check-off system. The UNTC-CS has also accused the government of trying to divide workers to make it easier for them to get their economic adjustment programme and privatisation policy through. The UNTC-CS accepts in principle that the Cape Verdean economy has to be reformed, but it is opposed to the rigour with which the government applies the reforms. The unions have also protested against the plan to cut public sector jobs by half (from 12,000 down to 6000), and argue that the voluntary severance formula promised by Carlos Veiga is not workable in a country with such high unemployment. The government also encountered difficulties when the unions demanded a 20% pay rise for public sector workers at the end of 1993 (EIU Country Report 1993 4th quarter). Privatisation of the greater part of the public sector in the space of four years is a delicate operation in a country where the State provides most of the jobs and over a quarter of the working population is unemployed. For example, the TACV employs some 750 people, although it has to be said that it could be just as efficient with 200; however, one can understand why any government might hesitate to exacerbate the labour relations situation any further by putting 550 people out of work and, in so doing, attract the wrath of the trade unions.

The UNTC-CS claims that the government is using the former leaders of the São Tiago USR to neutralise the UNTC-CS's activities and destroy the Cape Verdean trade union movement's influence on economic and social policy. Indeed, current developments do appear to reflect the government's official policy of promising an 'independent' trade movement in Cape Verde. In its proposals to party members on party strategy and the 1993 statutes, the ruling MPD refers to '... [a]ctive participation of party members in the establishment of a new kind of trade union movement, and in the formation, promotion and actions of free, democratic unions which they are encouraged to join' (Moção de estratégia e estatutos de MPD 1993 - Motion on MPD Strategy and Statutes, 1993: 13).

The question is how far the government is prepared to go. For example, during the strikes at Electra on 5 May 1995, the CCSL played only a minimal role because most of the workforce were in the UNTC-CS. Then, back in 1993, the government was very keen to set up a central consultative body known as the Conselho de Concertação Social (CCS - Social Consultative Council) incorporating the social partners (i.e. employers, trade unions and government). The UNTC-CS does not expect anything to emerge from it; the union reports that meetings have taken place, but that they rarely come up with anything useful. The UNTC-CS has even threatened to pull out, but this would give no little satisfaction to the CCSL, for whom the CCS is an important body on which (in the CCS's view) the UNTC-CS does nothing but create problems (interview with José Manuel Vaz, 26 July 1995).

Fear, in the opinion of Júlio Silva, is the main effect that mudança is having on workers - fear of taking part in strike action, fear of being involved in activities and finding themselves cast in the role of opponents of the government, and fear of losing their jobs. In Cape Verde, as in many Third World countries, the labour market is extremely limited and demand is great, and for that reason the UNTC-CS has always been an advocate of workers' unity.

At all events, the UNTC-CS expects that there will be even more strikes against the current economic measures, despite the fact that there is no money to organise them. It is true that wages have gone up in the last few years, but this increase has fallen a long way short of the rise in the cost of living. Referring to the demonstration by civil servants protesting against the 'scandalous' 5% pay rise offered by the government, the 'Novo Jornal' of 14 February 1995 pointed out that bread went up by over 16% in the same year.

*Internal conflicts*

In Cape Verde, as in many single-party States, political opening and democratisation have been accompanied by an economic opening. International donors such as the European Union, the United States and the World Bank wield great influence over the management of the country's political and economic affairs. For their part, trade unions, preoccupied with internal moves for increased autonomy and democracy, have not greatly influenced the democratising process; by contrast, democratisation has had a major impact on the trade union movement as it grapples with conflict and division. It is difficult to ignore the conclusion that the present government has tried to restrict the main trade union centre's autonomy by encouraging the formation of a second national centre more sympathetic to its adjustment policy. Since the late 1980s, the older and more important centre, the UNTC-CS, has become more and more independent and has adopted an increasingly uncompromising stance. When it was linked to the single party, and was thereby limited in its actions, the UNTC-CS refused to stray from the road to independence and the defence of workers' rights; the present government appears to have understood the UNTC-CS's intentions well enough. The union's behaviour forced the MPD, like the PAICV before it, to be on its guard: the PAICV because the union focused on interests other than the national interest, and the MPD because it was afraid that, with support from their unions, workers would demand the fulfilment of promises made during the election campaign.

Since it came to power in 1991, the MPD has thrown all its energy into economic reforms, liberalisation, privatisation and measures to attract foreign investment. The success of the new Development Plan depends on the accuracy of the assumption that economic liberalism increases foreign private investment and creates a class of local entrepreneurs willing and able to invest. Measures aimed at economic restructuring do not in any way improve the already appalling living conditions that workers have to endure. In the framework of a democratic political apparatus, a consultative structure exists in which various organisations in Cape Verdean society have an opportunity for effective participation; trade unions therefore ought to claim a strong position in it. However, this depends on whether workers have the ability to belie their small numbers and exert influence on the government via consultative bodies, or through the use of an equally democratic tool - the right to strike. Most workers are employed in strategic urban sectors such as the ports, electricity companies and the public sector, but this potential influence is not always easy to mobilise.

## Limited democracy

Cape Verde is an example of the 'limited democracy' seen in other African countries; little room is made in the country's economy for the effective participation of well-trained, organised workers in decision-making processes. Under Cape Verde's 'democratic' government, there is little emancipation and certain practices of manipulation and intimidation may be observed.

The government does virtually nothing to encourage effective participation by workers. Instead, it believes that the political participation of, and consultation with, workers is a threat to MPD leaders and their policy; it also sees this as a trend to be curbed rather than an elementary right of workers in a democratic system. Popular dissatisfaction, together with the risk of destabilisation that it can engender, has to be contained, and the government has not recoiled from incorporating workers' organisations into structures of the State. Nor has it stopped short of smear campaigns against the UNTC-CS.

Communications are very difficult, and they very much depend on who has access to them - that is to say, highly placed individuals in the State apparatus. What is more, the government does little to emancipate its citizens and provide them with the information that is essential for a democracy to function well. The people have no knowledge of their rights and opportunities, and the democratic system does not let Cape Verdeans into numerous secrets like the whys and wherefores of a Structural Adjustment Programme. Indeed, the government denies the very existence of an SAP in Cape Verde, and explains union objections to SAPs as an attempt by the opposition to destabilise the ruling MPD. All that Cape Verdeans know is that they depend on the government in Praia for everything, and that it is best to dance to their leaders' tune.

Things were no different under the previous government, but the PAICV had no democratic pretensions. In those days, there was no place in politics for discussion or dissident voices, and divergent opinions had no illusions about the government's lack of enthusiasm for democratic debate. This time round, despite its comfortable majority in Parliament, the MPD is no more sympathetic.

Some African countries have already reverted to authoritarian forms of government. Such a scenario is unlikely in Cape Verde because the country is too dependent on international aid, and on donors who demand peace and stability in exchange for continued financial support.

If democracy is seen as an essential condition for real economic development, such economic development in Cape Verde is, for the time being, completely dependent on international donors and investors. This dependence is all that Cape Verdeans can be sure about. Funders have the task of promoting the private sector development project as the basis of the Cape Verdean economy; they also decide the conditions of this economic development, and in practice determine the new face of Cape Verdean democracy. Once again, Cape Verdeans will have to wait their turn.

# 9 Ghana
## Going Beyond Politics

KWASI ADU-AMANKWAH AND KWADWO TUTU

*The World Bank would have us believe that Ghana is the model pupil of structural adjustment. Wrong. Since the setting up of a democratic constitutional framework, Ghanaian trade unions have not been prepared to acquiesce in government policy, and have instead attempted to reaffirm their right to promote workers' interests. They also propose an alternate framework for the economy; this is an option that transcends political infighting, as the phrase is normally understood.*

The process of democratisation in Ghana was given a boost in 1992 with the resurgence of party political organisation and activity, the conduct of elections to choose a president and constitute parliament, and the establishment of other nascent independent and democratic institutions like the Commission on Human Rights and Administrative Justice (CHRAJ), the National Media Commission (NMC) and the National Commission for Civic Education (NCCE).

The recent democratisation was preceded by ten years of military authoritarian rule clothed in revolutionary garbs under the Provisional National Defence Council (PNDC) regime. Before then, in the first two decades of independence from colonial rule, Ghana experienced varying regime types, predominantly military, but also with brief periods of constitutional civilian rule. Economic policies that were pursued over the period have had different implications for labour and have contributed to shape labour relations and the relationship between governments and the trade unions.

The period of PNDC anti-democratic rule, the longest for any single government in Ghana's history, coincided from 1983 onwards with the implementation of an International Monetary Fund (IMF) and World Bank-sponsored Structural Adjustment Programme (SAP), otherwise known as the Economic Recovery Programme (ERP) in Ghana. The implementation of SAP has continued into the 1990s in spite of the advent of democratisation. Indeed, the most active forces in the Ghanaian political arena and contest for political power consider that Ghana needs SAP, but merely differ on the manner of its implementation. There are, of course, those who believe that there can be an alternative to SAP but their voice remains a relatively weak one today.

207

The implementation of SAP has had consequences for the economy and society as a whole, and has impacted heavily on labour and the trade unions. In the following pages, we discuss the economic reforms since 1983 and their effect on economic performance in Ghana and impact on labour and the trade unions. We examine the objectives and measures of SAP and their implications for labour's access to resources as well as the responses of the trade unions. We also look at the political democratisation that has taken place and the role of the trade unions.

## Economic reforms and macroeconomic impacts

### Background to SAP

The structure of Ghana's economy has always weighed heavily in favour of the primary sector even though the first government of Kwame Nkrumah planned to change this. In the first decade after Independence in 1957, the primary sector's share of GDP dropped from 57% to 40%. The government put a high premium on industrialisation and modernisation by establishing many import-substituting industries. Manufacturing grew rapidly, increasing its share of GDP from 2% to 9% within the same period. Manufacturing also became an important contributor to exports with a 14% share in 1969, plus another 11% from the processing of cocoa and timber for exports (Sowa, et. al., 1992).

The modernisation also involved extensive expansion of the social sector such as communication, education and health. The manufacturing sector was not based on agriculture and needed substantial imports. With the main price of the main foreign exchange earner, cocoa, falling drastically in the early 1960s, severe balance of payments difficulties were encountered; this led to the institution of a controlled regime such as control on exchange rate, prices of outputs, inputs, etc. These controls continued into the 1970s and early 1980s.

The controls resulted in several bottlenecks, the most important being shortages of goods and services for consumption and for industry. Scarcities and other policies such as huge budget deficits financed by currency printing led to hyper-inflation rates which averaged 50% between 1972 and 1983 reaching 116% in 1977 and 1981 and 123% in 1983. These high inflation rates were fuelled by drought and bush fires in the late 1970s and early 1980. There were also balance of payments problems, a lack of incentives to producers, a breakdown of significant infrastructural facilities, and low (in most cases negative) growth rates of the economy.

By 1983, the economy was at rock-bottom and drastic measures had to be undertaken. In 1982, the PNDC, which was chanting socialist rhetoric, tried to get assistance from the then socialist block, but failed. They then turned to the Breton Woods Institutions (i.e. the World Bank and IMF) for support.

*Objectives and policies of SAP*

From 1983 onwards, the Provisional National Defence Council pursued a Structural Adjustment Program (SAP). This was divided into two phases: the initial three-year stabilisation phase which ended in 1986, and the subsequent years of adjustment and growth. The broad aim was to reverse he decline in the economy. Specifically, it was meant to provide incentives to producers, rehabilitate infrastructure and industry, curb inflation and promote sustained economic growth.

The main policies that have been pursued include exchange rate and financial reform, budgetary restraint, withdrawal of subsidies and removal of controls, retrenchment of labour, divestiture of state enterprises and trade liberalisation.

On foreign exchange and financial reform, there has been a complete liberalisation of the foreign exchange market with the operation of foreign exchange bureaux and banks. The result is a constantly depreciating local currency from a rate of ¢2/75 to US$1.00 in 1983 to ¢1600 to US$1.00 in April, 1996. There is also a decontrol of interest and lending rates, and a discontinuation of selective credit guidelines to bank for presumed important sectors of the economy, such as agriculture and manufacturing.

Until 1992, government maintained strict budgetary discipline with the ultimate objective of obtaining budget surpluses. This was achieved by cutting down government expenditures even in productive areas such as education, health, agriculture and employment. Specifically, subsidies on all items including those on agricultural inputs were withdrawn, beneficiaries of education and health were made to contribute towards cost recovery, state enterprises were divested, and some liquidated and significant labour was retrenched.

Massive trade liberalisation was undertaken by abolishing quantitative and qualitative trade barriers. Tariffs were significantly reduced and narrowed.

*Performance under SAP*

We analyse the impact of the ERP on the economy in terms of output, infrastructural improvements, structure of the economy, agriculture, balance of payments, trade and payments liberalisation, industry and investment, inflation and debt. In a separate section, we examine the impact of the reform on labour.

The ERP has contributed to a reversal of the negative growth rate in GDP. Between 1984 and 1995, GDP recorded an average growth rate of about 4% per annum (QDS, 1992; Budget Statements). This is significant considering the fact that, between 1970 and 1983, the economy grew at a negative rate in most years.

SAP has helped in the rehabilitation of roads, health and educational facilities, water and electricity. While these facilities have been improved, the policy of cost recovery and cost cutting has made it impossible for most of the rural and urban poor to utilise them (Sowa, 1991). Despite these laudable achievements, the economy seemed to have been stuck at the stabilisation level. There has not been any fundamental structural change in the economy. Besides, a greater part of the expenditures on these facilities are from loans and grants, and this gives rise for concern for debt and economic independence.

The structure of the economy has not changed from what it was some two decades ago. Preliminary figures for 1990 put the composition of Gross Domestic Product (GDP) at 48% for agriculture, 16% for industry and 36% for services (World Bank, 1991) compared with 48%, 21% and 31% respectively for agriculture, industry and services in 1975 (Economic Survey, 1977-80). However, the share of agriculture has fallen since the 1990s, and has been taken over by services. An examination of the sectoral sources of growth shows that total aggregate growth rates for industry, services and agriculture was 48%, 30% and 14% respectively during 1984-1987 (QDS, 1989). However, between 1988 and 1990, the growth rate in agriculture and industry averaged 1.8% and 5.3% respectively while services averaged 7.4%. Manufacturing saw a reduction from its high annual average growth rate of about 13% during 1984-87 to about 3.6% during 1988-90. In the 1990s, manufacturing has been growing at an annual average of 2%.

The problem is that while it is apparently thought that agriculture has benefited from the ERP, it should be noted that it is cocoa whose output has doubled over the ERP period. The food-crop and livestock sector which make up at least 33% of the GDP still suffers from problems of marketing, credit, low productivity and technology. Whenever there is bad weather, the growth rate in agriculture worsens, affecting overall GDP growth. This happened in 1990 and 1992 when agriculture experienced negative growth rates.

A close examination of the Balance of Payments (BOP) shows that it has even worsened under SAP. The trade balance was negative for only 3 years between 1970 and 1982 while for the 7 years of the SAP period, it was negative for 6 years. While current account was positive for 6 years during 1970-1982, it has been negative throughout the ERP period. The average trade balance for 1967-82 was $25m, while that for 1983-89 was -$62m. Furthermore, the current account average for the 1967-82 period was -$116m as against -$215m for 1983-92 (Economic Surveys, QDS; Budget, 1993).

Table 1:    Annual growth rates and division of GDP
            (at constant 1975 prices)

| Sector | Percentage 1975 | Percentage 1990 | Annual Growth Rate |
|---|---|---|---|
| Agriculture | 48 | 48 | 1,8 |
| Industry | 21 | 16 | 5,3 |
| Services | 31 | 36 | 7,4 |

*Source*: World Bank 1991

Table 2:    Average trade balance and current accounts
            (millions of current US dollars)

| | 1967-1982 | 1983-1992 |
|---|---|---|
| Commercial balance | 25 | -62 |
| Current account balance | -116 | -215 |

*Source*: Economic Surveys, Quarterly Digest of Statistics, 1990, 1994

As a proportion of export earnings, BOP deficits in the 1970s were under 20%. It reached its highest point ever in 1981, recording 71%, but dropped to 25% in 1982. It increased again to 52% in 1983 before falling to 27% in 1987. The poor performance resumed again in the middle of the SAP and hit a high of 62% in 1992.

On nominal levels, it is only in 1994 and 1995 that export earnings have exceeded the highest in 1980 of $1104 million over the period 1970-1975. Even this was due to an increased level of extraction and exports of gold, and was not a result of higher world price increases or of a higher level of processing. The only saving grace is that the significant inflow of foreign loans and grants has enabled Ghana to pursue the ERP, service its debts and build some external reserves. But this has also led to significant external debt, which in 1993 was estimated to be about $4.5 billion.

Trade and payments regime has seen a major overhaul. During the ERP period, quantitative controls were scrapped while tariff rates were drastically reduced (Jebuni, et al., ibid). This liberalised trade regime and exchange rate system have led to increased availability of imported goods and services. These manufactured and agricultural imports have resulted in stiff competition, with local production causing some firms to die.

On the one hand, the exchange rate reform has led to the availability of goods and services and inputs for businesses. There has also been a significant inflow of private transfers improving the availability of foreign exchange. On the other hand, the continuous depreciation of the cedi has meant increasing expenditures for consumers and for producers who use imported products, making it difficult for the latter to compete in the liberalised environment. Besides, it is expensive for manufacturers to borrow money at the high average interest rate of over 30% to finance ever-increasing operating expenditures.

*Industry and Investment*

Despite the improved macroeconomic environment coupled with an attractive investment code, local and direct foreign investment has been poor under the ERP period. In current dollar terms, it averaged about $6.8m a year between 1983 and 1990 compared with an average of $21m a year between 1967 and 1982. It is only recently that this has averaged $30m a year.

There has been significant rehabilitation in infrastructure and industry. In spite of this, the level of capacity utilisation in the manufacturing sector remains low. Even though the level of capacity utilisation increased substantially, it still remained at a low level of 37% in 1990. From a low of 18% in 1984, capacity utilisation on the basis of a single shift increased to 40% in 1988 but dropped to 37% by 1990 (World Bank, 1991).

This could be a result either of trade liberalisation, which is making it difficult for local manufacturers to sell their output and hence expand capacity, or of their inability to find sufficient foreign exchange and hence inputs to expand capacity. It could also be a result of a low level of investment from local and foreign entrepreneurs.

The rate of inflation has been reduced from double and sometimes triple digits (116% in 1977 and 1981 and 123% in 1983) to a yearly average rate of 30% for 1984-90. One significant point is that the rate of inflation fell from 123% in 1983 to 40% in 1984 and to the lowest rate of 10% in 1985 before increasing again to the average rate of 30% for the 1984-90 period. Of late, however, inflation has become a problem with the rate reaching 25% and 59% in 1994 and 1995 respectively. The remarkable performance of the inflation rate in 1984 and 1985 could be explained by the bumper harvest of food crops as a result of exceptionally good weather. This highlights the significance of the contribution that the food crop sector makes to inflation in Ghana.

Recent research has shown that the main causes of inflation during the ERP period could be attributed principally to increased food prices and, to a lesser extent, to increased production costs resulting from a depreciation of the cedi and removal of subsidies from all items including agricultural inputs (Sowa, et. al., 1992).

*Debt*

Ghana's total external debt increased from $550 million in 1970 to an estimated $4.5 billion in 1993. Total debt as a proportion of GNP increased from 26% in 1970 to a peak of 59% in 1987 and declined to 55% in 1988. The total debt to exports ratio increased from 108% in 1980 to 312% in 1988. The debt service ratio which remained above 60% during most part of the SAP period (except 1986) is expected to decline with the introduction of the IMF's ESAF and the elimination of external arrears (World Bank, 1990: 226). Thus, while some progress has been made, it has been at the expense of increased debt. What is significant is whether, without increased industrial capacity, Ghana can even service its debts with traditional exports alone.

The sectors that have been growing fast are services and the mining sub-sector of the industrial sector. In the agricultural sector, it is only the cocoa sub-sector which has experienced high growth rates. Even so, this sector is populated by a large number of small farmers who hardly produce a tonne of cocoa a year. Considering that the world price for cocoa has been fluctuating, most of these small farmers have not fared well at a time when the cost of living has been increasing.

On the other hand, the informal sector, where a large number of the labour force can be found, has expanded but it is also characterised by lower earnings than in the formal sector. Workers in the informal sector can therefore be added to those wage earners who, as we have seen, have experienced a lower standard of living under structural adjustment.

The service and construction sectors have been growing, and this is where the benefits of the reform can be found. The benefits here go the few contractors and the big operators in the service sector.

The mining sector has grown with a reduction of formal workers due to increased capital intensity. The remaining workers have had relatively increased incomes, but those who have really benefited are a few owners of mining firms.

Table 3:    Debt indicators

|  | 1970 | 1980 | 1988 | 1993 |
|---|---|---|---|---|
| Total Debt (TDE, M$) | 550 | 1 398 | 3 076 | 4 590 |
| External Debt | - | 115 | 319 | 378 |
| Total Debt /GNP | 26 | 32 | 61 | 77 |

*Source*: World Bank, World Debt Tables, 1994-1995, p. 182

## Impact of SAP on labour and the trade unions

Trade unions in Ghana cover mainly labour employed in the wage-earning formal sector of the economy. This category of labour constitutes about 16% of Ghana's labour force.

The economic effects of SAP have had direct and indirect effects on trade unions in Ghana. The direct effects have been discussed below; the indirect effects involve the negative effect on the economy, which have been discussed above, and their effects on unions.

The effects have been particularly powerful on declining, stagnant or fluctuating real incomes, the increasing inaccessibility of social services, and growing insecurity of employment for large numbers of workers.

### Employment, retrenchment and divestiture

In Ghana, only about 16.1% of the labour force are in waged employment, where earnings are relatively higher. The rest of the labour force is in self-employment, including 66% in agriculture. There is significant under-employment in the informal sector, and during the ten years beginning in 1974, the average productivity of workers and their real earnings declined sharply (Ghana: Structural Adjustment for Growth, 1989: 176).

Between 1985 and 1990, 90,000 workers in the public and civil service were laid off. With a low gross capital formation of an average of 9% between 1984 and 1989, and at least 100,000 graduates from the educational system entering the labour market each year, the unemployment situation has become serious (PAMSCAD). These figures do not include workers who were laid off in the private sector in response to certain Structural Adjustment measures. From 1990 to date, retrenchment of labour continues to be a significant feature of economic measures, with over 15,000 workers retrenched from the public sector.

A number of factors account for the massive lay-offs. In the public sector, these include restructuring and the privatisation of certain enterprises, and in some cases the introduction of new technology. The withdrawal of subsidies to state-subsidised organisations and the liquidation of SOEs have also contributed to labour retrenchment. They have indirectly weakened the power of the trade unions.

Two main reasons have accounted for job losses in the private sector: the first relates to severe liquidity problems resulting from the inability of businesses to borrow from the banking system due to the high interest rates; the second is the inability of business to compete with the influx of indiscriminately imported goods onto the local market through trade liberalisation.

For trade unions, the consequences of retrenchment have been very severe. Table 4 demonstrates the membership loss of a sample of trade unions affiliated to the Trade Union Congress of Ghana (GTUC).

Table 4:     Membership of some industrial unions
             affiliated to the GTUC

| Unions | 1987 | 1991 | % Decrease in Membership |
|---|---|---|---|
| General Agricultural Workers Union (GAWU) | 101 000 | 95 900 | 5,1 |
| Industrial & Commercial Workers Union (ICU) | 130 000 | 100 000 | 23 |
| Local Government Workers Union (LGWU) | 35 000 | 25 000 | 28,5 |
| Maritime Dockworkers Union (MUD) | 31 085 | 28 292 | 9 |
| National Union of Seamen (NUS) | 4 999 | 1 523 | 69,5 |
| Public Utility Workers Union (PUWU) | 20 000 | 10 036 | 49,8 |
| Railway Workers Union (RWU) | 8 955 | 5 907 | 34 |
| Teachers & Educational Workers Union (TEWU) | 40 300 | 30 674 | 23,8 |
| TOTAL | 371 339 | 297 332 | 25,6 |

*Source*: GTUC, Accra, 1993

Unions suffered membership losses of an average of 26% between 1987 and 1992. These heavy membership losses have affected workers' confidence in unionism and have also meant that trade unions have lost income since dues are the main source of funding. Limited finances constrain trade union organisation, the provision of services to members, capacity building, and the effectiveness of the unions as a whole.

## Increased expenditure of social services, income losses and poverty

The removal of subsidies and price controls has meant increased prices for social services such as education, health services and utilities. This has resulted in increased expenditure and with controlled incomes, the standard of living of the average person has been relatively reduced. The minimum daily wage, the average monthly income and per capita income are used to illustrate a stagnant real income.

The minimum daily wage has increased from 65 pesewas in 1963 to ¢1,700 in 1996. This, however, does not represent an improvement in the standard of living when the real income is taken into consideration. Table 5 indicates that, with the exception of the major increases of wage rates in 1991 and 1994 which were higher than the rate of inflation, all other wage increases since 1988 have lagged behind the rate of inflation. The real minimum wage in 1986 was only 29% that of the real wage in 1975 while that of 1990 was 50% of the 1975 real wage (Tutu, 1995). The rate of inflation has always undermined the rate of increase of the minimum wage and has thus contributed to a continuing erosion in real incomes for wage earners.

Table 5:    Rate of inflation, minimum wage

|  | Rate of Inflation % | | Minimum Wage | |
|---|---|---|---|---|
|  | Actual | Projected | Actual in Cedis | Increase % |
| 1987 | 40 | 15 | 112,5 | - |
| 1988 | 31 | 20 | 146,25 | 30 |
| 1989 | 25 | 15 | 170 | 16 |
| 1990 | 37 | 15 | 218 | 28 |
| 1991 | 18 | 10 | 460 | 111 |
| 1992 | 10 | 5 | 460 | 0 |
| 1993 | 25 | 20 | 460 | 0 |
| 1994 | 25 | 15 | 790 | 72 |
| 1995 | 59 | 18 | 1 200 | 52 |
| 1996 | - | - | 1 700 | 42 |

*Source*: GTUC, Accra and Budget Statements

Using the average monthly earnings, we find from Table 6 that although earnings increased from ¢33 in 1960 to ¢24,257 in 1989 real earnings (using 1977 as a base year) fell from ¢554 in 1960 to the lowest level of ¢47 before bouncing back to ¢232 in 1989. Based on income increases which are at best equal to the rate of inflation since 1988, the real average income in 1995 will not exceed ¢252 (Tutu, ibid).

Table 6:     Average monthly earnings:
             nominal and real wages for all sectors

| Year | Nominal Wages | W/CPI |
|---|---|---|
| 1960 | 33 | 553 |
| 1961 | 36,17 | 566 |
| 1962 | 37,7 | 545 |
| 1963 | 38,6 | 533 |
| 1964 | 38,69 | 477 |
| 1965 | 38,97 | 382 |
| 1966 | 42,25 | 394 |
| 1967 | 45,64 | 453 |
| 1968 | 49,67 | 448 |
| 1969 | 52,87 | 455 |
| 1970 | 54,99 | 403 |
| 1971 | 60,73 | 407 |
| 1972 | 67,01 | 408 |
| 1973 | 69,71 | 361 |
| 1974 | 95,24 | 417 |
| 1975 | 102,69 | 347 |
| 1976 | 115,23 | 249 |
| 1977 | 217,37 | 217 |
| 1978 | 235,95 | 136 |
| 1979 | 294,47 | 110 |
| 1980 | 460,22 | 114 |
| 1982 | 645 | 60 |
| 1983 | 1 110 | 46 |
| 1984 | 2 287 | 69 |
| 1985 | 3 633 | 99 |
| 1986 | 7 433 | 163 |
| 1987 | 10 524 | 165 |
| 1988 | 13 805 | 165 |
| 1989 | 24 257 | 232 |

Where W/CPI is the consumption wage, i.e. earnings deflated by the consumer price index (CPI). The base year for the CPI is 1977.

*Source*: Statistical Services Quarterly Digest of Statistics, various issues, Accra

Furthermore, on average the real per capita income for 1990 was less than that for 1980. The income in 1960 constant cedis increased from 540 in 1960 to 619 in 1972, and dropped to 373 in 1984 before increasing gradually to 445 in 1990. Real income losses are even heavier for the large number of unprotected workers, particularly employees in small-scale enterprises who lie outside the ambit of union organisation and activity and are subject to the ravages of plain market forces.

These show that although there have been some increases in real earnings during the ERP era, these are very marginal and that in 1989 it was one-third the 1960 level. The overall objective of the ERP was to raise the standard of living of the average Ghanaian. Considering the huge inflow of foreign resources, which is unprecedented in the history of this country, what has so far been achieved (it is below the 1960s and most of the 1970s) represents a failure of the programme.

The contraction in trading activity as a result of the erosion of the real incomes of urban and rural wage employees has also contributed to low incomes for the labour force engaged in that sector.

The analyses imply a reduction in the standard of living for the average person during the SAP period because of increased unemployment, reduced real earnings and increased expenditures in the social sectors, especially health and education.

An IFAD report estimated that the proportion of rural poor increased from 43% in 1970 to 54% in 1986. Green (1988) also showed an increase in poverty: he estimated that the number of urban people below the poverty line increased from an average of between 30% and 35% in the late 1970s to a range of 45-50% in the mid-1980s. For rural people, there was also an increase in poverty from a range of 60% to 65% in late 1970s to between 67% and 72% in mid 1980s. The Ghana Living Standard Survey partly supports this assertion (GLSS, 1987).

Furthermore, on average, the real per capita income for 1990 is less than that of 1980. The income in 1960 constant cedis increased from ¢540 in 1960 to ¢619 in 1972 and dropped to ¢373 in 1984 before increasing gradually to ¢445 in 1990. This shows that despite the improvement in the standard of living of the average Ghanaian, it is only above the standard for 1983, the lowest level ever of economic activity (Jebuni, Oduro, Tutu, 1992).

## Coercion and manipulation in labour relations

Under Structural Adjustment, labour relations have been characterised by disregard for Collective Bargaining Agreements and laid-down procedures, the use of force or the threat of it to settle industrial disputes, and the application of intrigue and subterfuge in government's dealings with trade unions and other labour organisations.

Violations of collective bargaining have occurred most significantly with regard to methods of implementing retrenchment and of reducing or freezing wages.

Government's initial implementation of labour retrenchment was based largely on force and coercion. In December 1984, over one hundred Posts and Telecommunications Corporation employees were dismissed by radio announcements without any stated reason. Union protests had no effect. In November 1985, the government passed a decree, the COCOBOD RETRENCHMENT AND INDEMNITY LAW, PNDC L 125(1985) to facilitate the retrenchment of about 20,000 workers from the Cocoa Industry. Union Leaders were arrested, harassed and threatened by state security police, while mass meetings of workers were prevented by armed police personnel. The establishment of the Manpower Utilisation and Redeployment Committee (MURC) achieved little because of the absence of any genuine commitment on the part of government to devote resources to retrain and actually re-deploy labour. There was little commitment on the part of the trade unions to the work of the MURC because they did not want to be compromised as willing parties to the Structural Adjustment policy of retrenchment. After the initial use of force, government established the practice of laying off workers without full payment of redundancy awards. Redundancy awards and gratuities have been allocated in a haphazard fashion; moreover, these have been paid out in meagre instalments, which have tended to undermine the value of the money, given the persistent inflationary situation in the economy. In some cases, as in the Ghana Education Service, for example, full redundancy awards have not been paid to retrenched workers since 1986.

The pattern of payment of redundancy awards that the government has established in the public sector has also influenced the pattern in the private sector. After weak resistance in the initial stages, the trade unions have largely succumbed to this pattern.

With regard to income cutback or freeze, the government has employed arbitrariness, intrigue, manipulation, or the threat of force in achieving its ends. The main assault has been on allowances and terminal benefits of workers. This has sometimes met resistance and struggle from the trade unions on a national scale.

Allowances have been the means of supplementing workers' incomes. In the decades preceding reform, the trade unions fought for the introduction of certain allowances as part of the pay packet, subject to negotiation and agreement between trade unions and employers: for instance, in 1984, the minimum wage was 25 cedis while the daily cost of living computed by the

Central Bureau of Statistics was 218 cedis. The gap was partly made up by certain allowances for such items as lunch, transport and rent. For the government and employers, the addition to workers' income through allowances, rather than through outright increases in wages and salaries, enabled them to avoid the responsibility of paying higher sums in respect of employers' contribution to workers' social security and for their end-of-service and retirement benefits. The principal allowances gained by workers and their trade unions which were not subject to tax included rent allowance (20% of basic wage/salary), canteen and transport allowance (5-10%), leave allowance (5-10%) and end-of-year bonus (often supposed to be based on productivity). Overtime earnings, which were largely untaxed in order to encourage overtime work in some sectors of the economy, particularly the export sector, were also considered to be an allowance.

In June 1986, in a move that appeared to be a desperate attempt to make up for a shortfall in expected revenue, the government attempted unilaterally to cancel leave allowance for employees in the civil service and public sector. Labour resentment and trade union opposition compelled a temporary withdrawal of the measure. In August of the same year, government imposed a tax on canteen, transport and leave allowances. In May 1987, government issued a decree, PNDC L 177 to legalise taxation of these allowances. At the beginning of 1991, the government again unilaterally announced a policy of consolidation of wages and allowances. These measures provoked responses from the trade unions who were able, to a very limited extent, to affect the way the policies were implemented.

*Trade union protest*

Between 1983 and 1988, the government paid scant regard to the existence of the Tripartite Committee; this consisted of representatives from trade unions, employers and government as the body responsible for determining the national minimum wage. Throughout this period, the government fixed the minimum wage without necessary consultation with the trade unions or employers. These measures received written and verbal protests from the trade unions until 1989 when government began to consult the trade unions when determining the minimum wage. Even so, the actual increases in the minimum wage - compared with the rate of inflation, and therefore with the erosion in real income as demonstrated above - show that the government largely succeeded in getting the trade unions to accept the harsh effects of Structural Adjustment on incomes.

The erratic manner of the Tripartite Committee's operations finally provoked the threat of a general strike by the country's main trade union centre, the TUC, in January 1995. It was only after this that the government finally agreed to institutionalise the operations of the Tripartite Committee.

Coercion and manipulation by government was also evident in the government's handling of Terminal Awards; these form part of many negotiated Collective Bargaining Agreements in Ghana. The government's attempts since the end of 1986 to abolish End-of-Service Benefits (ESB) have met with considerable trade union resistance. By the end of 1990, the government finally managed through subterfuge and intrigue to secure the acquiescence of the trade unions in a freeze of End-of-Service Benefits. After reneging on its promise to pay the frozen ESB for almost two years, it was only at the end of 1992, that the trade unions managed to secure agreement with the government on clear ways in which they could be paid. Even this concession was won only as a result of widespread discontent among the rank and file, and an apparent readiness of the trade union leadership to lead a struggle on this issue. The payment was spread from 1992 to 1994.

*Grievance handling and dispute settlement*

In the period of Structural Adjustment, the government's hard-line attitude when dealing with the trade unions has also sometimes overlapped into dispute settlement. The police have sometimes been used to intervene directly against workers in the private sector, for example at Pioneer Food Cannery Limited in Tema in 1984 and Assene Household and Enamelware Limited in Accra in 1986.

In the public sector, the government has on occasion reacted to workers' agitation by carrying out mass dismissals. In 1988, the government dismissed thirty-six union leaders and activists from the Ghana Broadcasting Corporation (GBC), dissolved the local union and banned officers of the relevant national industrial union, the Public Services Workers Union, from entering GBC premises. The ban on union activities lasted from 1988 to 1992. The same kind of arbitrariness was displayed in the dismissal of over thirty union leaders and activists representing mine workers at the State Gold Mining Corporation (SGMC) in 1988 over agitations during negotiations for a collective agreement. Also in 1990, government carried out a mass dismissal of over two hundred workers at the Ghana Italian Petroleum Company over an alleged illegal strike of workers against management malpractice. The inability of the TUC to secure reinstatement of the dismissed workers contributed to a growing loss of the influence of the unions among workers.

The above demonstrates that, under Ghana's Structural Adjustment, the government has employed considerable political muscle to implement its harsh socio-economic measures.

## Democratisation and the trade unions

After the military coup d'etat which brought the PNDC to power at the end of 1981, severe restrictions were imposed on freedom of political organisation and association as well as on free expression and assembly within the framework of revolutionary rhetoric. Between 1983 and 1985, trade union struggles were focused mainly on issues of workers' economic rights. From 1985, the struggle by the trade unions began to take on political dimensions, albeit, in a limited manner. The Trades Union Congress (TUC) expressed the need for working people to be consulted by government on the formulation of socio-economic policy.

In 1986, the TUC began to move away from being limited to economic issues and called for the establishment of a democratically constituted 'People's Assembly' to serve as the institution for national policy formulation and legislation. This was followed in 1987 by a statement on the need for district and national elections to be held within the framework of a democratically-drawn national constitution.

However, these calls for political liberalisation by the TUC were not followed by any mobilisation aimed at pressing home the demands. Indeed, overall, the trade unions could not be said to be committed in practice to the positions expressed by the TUC.

By 1990, international developments - particularly the collapse of state socialism in the Soviet Union and Eastern Europe as well as the political liberalisation there - and growing concern and agitation by some local political groupings for democratisation at home compelled the government of Ghana to start taking some hesitant steps towards democratisation. The trade unions submitted memoranda that called for political liberalisation and constitutional rule to a body that was set up by government to collate views wide on democracy on a nationwide basis.

The trade unions did not join forces with the nascent mass movement that sought to mount pressure for the re-introduction of multipartyism into national political life. The nascent mass movement took organisational form in the Movement for Freedom and Justice (MFJ); this tried to mobilise support for a democratic programme of transition to multipartyism and the rule of law. Without the active involvement of organised labour, the pro-democracy movement failed to develop sufficient political muscle to guarantee an open and fair process of democratic transition.

The transitional process to constitutional rule was criticised by the opposition to the government as a subterfuge to perpetuate the rule of the then Chairman of the PNDC, Flt-Lt. J.J. Rawlings. This caused much resentment, and certain recognised opposition leaders took some aspects of the political party decree to court. This pressure by the opposition to ensure an environment which would not bias the future elections was not sustained. In the rush for constitutional rule, the opposition accepted the timetable for a return to civilian rule, including the fact that it was to be overseen by the PNDC, even though they had expressed serious reservations on some aspects of it and doubted the fairness of the impending elections. The TUC did not make any public pronouncements on the transitional process.

The presidential elections were conducted under conditions that were proclaimed to be unfair by all the groups opposed to the government. And amidst allegations of fraud during the Presidential elections which returned Rawlings to office as President, the major opposition political parties boycotted the parliamentary elections.

The result has been a de-facto one-party state in which all the seats in parliament are occupied by three parties, all of which were sponsored by avowed loyalists of the PNDC regime and supported the election of Mr. Rawlings. Rawlings' own party, the National Democratic Congress (NDC), occupies 189 out of the 200 seats in parliament, with the Speaker of Parliament being a former member of the previous ruling council, the Provisional National Defence Council (PNDC).

Workers and their trade unions have sought a voice in decision-making and in securing access to resources through collective bargaining and other forms of representation and initiatives.

With the establishment of a political framework of constitutional democracy in Ghana since 1992, the trade unions have tried to re-assert their right to  promote the interests of workers through the pursuit of collective bargaining and other ways of representing workers.

In the period since 1992, the trade unions have struggled vigorously to defend collective bargaining rights from being violated by the National Democratic Congress (NDC) Government, which was born out of the authoritarian PNDC regime of the past decade, and the hostile labour relations atmosphere that it spawns. The TUC filed a complaint against the Government at the International Labour Organisation (ILO) for interference in collective bargaining in 1993. Again in 1993, the TUC went to court in an attempt to overturn an arbitrator's award that was considered to be biased and ill-founded and also to be an abuse of process. At the beginning of 1995, the TUC threatened a general strike over demands to get the national Tripartite Committee to negotiate a national minimum wage and for the Committee to be recognised as an institutional framework for articulating trade union concerns on the economy. The TUC also went to court in 1996 to compel the government to accede to the right of unionisation by senior staff of a foreign controlled bank, Stanchart Ltd. Trade unions organised within the framework of the TUC have undertaken various forms of struggle ranging from demonstrations to strikes to press home their concerns for better incomes, severance awards, better conditions of service and respect for due process.

Other organisations of labour and professional bodies have also engaged in struggles that have been aimed largely at securing better compensation for services rendered and for the clear establishment of due process for negotiating incomes and conditions of service. Teachers, lecturers, civil servants, nurses and doctors, have all registered struggles of varying organisation and intensity.

## *Other forms of representation and participation*

Trade unions have persistently commented on the economic direction of the country, particularly as represented by annual government budget statements over the period.

In responding to IMF and World Bank-sponsored structural adjustment policies, which continue to be implemented under the new democratic dispensation, the unions have called for a serious review of economic policies and the framework for economic decision-making. They have proposed a review of unbridled trade liberalisation, the free-floating foreign exchange system, the wholesale removal of subsidies on everything, retrenchment of labour and doctrinaire privatisation.

Alternatively, the trade unions have posed a vision of the economy where every individual has access to education and health, and contributes to the growth of the economy by means of employment. With arable land, industries and people as major national resources, such an economy is to be based on agriculture, and it must be supported to become the engine of growth and sustainable development. Trade union interventions have played an important part in mitigating the harsh effects of SAP policies on workers and other sections of the population.

The trade unions have also made representations to Parliament on issues that have been considered vital. In 1993, the TUC presented a memorandum to Parliament that expressed concern over aspects of a Serious Fraud Office Bill that were considered to be anti-democratic and unconstitutional. Also in 1994 and 1995, the TUC made representations to Parliament concerning aspects of a Value Added Tax (VAT) Bill and an Export Processing Zones (EPZ) Bill. As part of these interventions, the TUC organised mass meetings and sometimes demonstrations to show its mass base.

Other representation has been through the National Advisory Committee on Labour, and by applying for administrative justice in respect of the right to mass demonstration and accountable conduct by public officials.

The trade unions have also undertaken important initiatives towards promoting workers' participation in decision-making and workers'

enterprise ownership. The TUC is currently implementing a programme
of education and research on workers' participation and how to make it
effective. It is also acting as the promoter for the establishment of a labour-
owned enterprises trust as the main vehicle for getting into economic
ventures to promote employment and higher incomes as well as to improve
the financial base of unions.

## Making democracy survive in Ghana

In spite of the difficulties that attend the nascent constitutional democracy
in Ghana because of the way the transition to democracy has gone, the
national constitution of 1992 embodies important elements that make viable
the pursuit of democracy. These include:
-   principle of limitation of the power of government - provision of rule of
    law and separation of powers;
-   entrenched amendment process such that the Constitution cannot simply
    be changed by Parliament;
-   entrenched Bill of Rights;
-   for judicial independence and power of review;
-   for important state institutions that are independent of the executive
    and legislature - Commission on Human Rights and Administrative
    Justice (CHRAJ), National Commission on Civic Education (NCCE),
    National Electoral Commission (NEC),National Media Commission
    (NMC);
-   for a Council of State to advise the President.

Against a background of these elements, the trade unions have identified
factors that militate against democratisation in the country, and have
consequently set out what they consider needs to be done to consolidate
democracy in Ghana. They include:
-   ensuring free and fair elections;
-   promoting freedom of expression;
-   encouraging a respect for, and strengthening of, fragile democratic
    institutions;
-   promoting respect for law and order;
-   encouraging the independence of the judiciary;
-   promoting economic development, stability and poverty alleviation;
-   promoting tolerance of divergent views as part of the political culture;
-   keeping chiefs out of active politics;
-   promoting unity of action among the organisations of civil society (TUC,
    1996).

## Challenges facing the trade unions

The experience of the past decade - economic reform, the impact of SAP on workers and their trade unions, recent developments in democratisation, and existing possibilities for further progress in Ghana - raise important challenges for the trade union movement. These relate to the internal development and dynamics of the trade unions themselves as well as to trade union activity and intervention in the policy process and in accessing resources. The key challenges are the need to strengthen organisation and internal democracy and the demand to provide more effective representation and participation for workers.

### Strengthening organisation and internal democracy

Retaining current union members' interests is important if organisation and internal democracy are to be strengthened. In this regard, more membership involvement has to be generated in trade union affairs through consciously improving communications inside the organisation. Furthermore, efforts that have been initiated towards promoting more participation by women trade union members should be intensified to ensure that the unions benefit fully from the important contribution of this segment of membership.

The provision and expansion of services to membership is also an important demand that the trade unions have to meet to retain membership interest. The demands that arise from the needs of the times include vocational training and retraining that helps workers to prepare for redeployment and to meet the uncertainties associated with loss of employment. With the trade unions as the driving force for this, they can demand the support and cooperation of government and employers.

The provision of counselling and other welfare services are other means by which the trade unions can hope to retain the interest of their membership.

To further expand membership of their organisation, the trade unions have to undertake conscious recruitment of new members into their ranks. This involves intensifying efforts at unionising senior staff in the formal sector into unions as well as extending unionisation into hitherto uncovered areas, particularly the fast-expanding informal sector of the Ghanaian economy. Since the end of the 1980s, a number of trade unions in Ghana have already begun organising in the informal sector. This must be given a further boost by more conscious planning so that the appropriate organisational forms can be developed for bringing operators in the informal sector into the framework of union organisation.

Other initiatives to strengthen organisation have to do with the need to improve trade union finances that have been adversely affected by the heavy losses in membership as a result of SAP. The unions have to develop more sources of funding and also improve the management of their resources.

*More effective representation and participation*

The trade unions also face the challenge of working to become more effective in the representation of membership interests. Their research activities have to be deepened and expanded to improve the trade union bases for collective bargaining. This has to be complemented by well designed education and training programmes with clear target groups at local, branch, district, regional and national levels, and including elected officers and staff, youth and women. In particular, attention must be paid to the training of negotiators who will sit across the table with government and employer representatives.

But beyond more effective collective bargaining, the trade unions also face the challenge of making democracy relevant to workers at all levels of the policy process, from the workplace through to national level. In pursuit of this, unions have to increase their capacity for collaborating in the policy process and for providing policy initiatives where necessary. On the one hand, this means that, at the political level, they must struggle to ensure the rule of law and respect for fundamental human rights; on the other hand, research and education to support workers' participation must be carried out in such a manner that trade union collaboration in the policy process does not become simply cosmetic. The practice whereby trade union acquiescence is secured for hostile policies and measures will not find a place in a well educated union. Rather trade union intervention must become the means by which workers participate in deciding matters that affect their lives and that of their companies.

An important initiative has been taken by the TUC in Ghana to promote the establishment of worker-owned enterprises. This initiative is an attempt to contribute to employment generation and to expand the base for union membership, as well as improve and broaden the main source of union finances. But it also has the potential to assist in creating the conditions for workers' participation to gain legitimacy and acceptability in Ghana.

Conclusion

The implementation of a Structural Adjustment Programme in Ghana since 1983 has had severe consequence for labour. Government has been able to implement the programme essentially on the basis of political repression and within the framework of an effective military dictatorship. In spite of the difficult political conditions, trade unions struggled modestly to defend the interests of their membership.

Events worldwide and also locally have pushed for a degree of political liberalisation in Ghana. These offer some opportunities for the development of democratisation in Ghana and for the trade unions to better defend and promote trade union rights and contribute to the shaping of socio-economic policy. Whether the trade unions are able to achieve this or not depends on the extent to which they develop their resources and build their capacity for struggle, bearing in mind that for a mass organisation like the trade union movement, their development of internal strength and democracy is a prerequisite for their ability to contribute to the development of democracy in the larger society.

# 10 Mali
## Evolution: an Unlikely Outcome

Ousmane Oumarou Sidibé
with Sékéné Moussa Sissoko and Massa Coulibaly

*March 1991: With bloody repression at an end, and the government of Moussa Traoré no more, could the country at long last make a move towards democracy? At the time, political neutrality enabled the National Union of Malian Workers (UNTM) to stand out as a body that could bring together organisations opposing the government. Today, it no longer confines its activities to the needs of workers, but also concerns itself with the problems of all social groups affected by the crisis. However, the UNTM still has plenty to do if it is to turn itself into a democratic organisation. It also may lose its hegemony.*

Since the early 1990s, African countries have been engaged in a major democratisation process that has involved a large number of social players. This chapter presents an analysis of the political, economic and social changes and events that have taken place in Mali during that period.[1] In particular, we shall seek to throw light on the role of the trade unions.

A short period of multi-party government during the dying years of colonial rule was followed by independence in 1960. This ushered in a de facto one-party system of government when, in line with the ideology of national unity that held so much sway in African countries in those days, the Sudanese Progressive Party (SPP) was subsumed into the US-RDA (Union pour le Rassemblement Démocratique Africain - Union for African Democratic Assembly).

Eight years after independence - on 19 November 1968, to be precise - a military coup d'état put an end to the single-party State and brought to power a military junta under the Comité Militaire de Libération Nationale (CMLN - Military Committee for National Liberation). In time, following pressure both from democratic forces inside and outside the country and from the international community, the CMLN felt the need to give the military régime a more presentable face, and set up a constitutional single party, the Union Démocratique du Peuple Malien (UDPM - Democratic Union of Malian People).

However, activists in the democracy movement - they came from all walks of life, particularly trade unions - were not fooled by this democratic façade, and they set about organising a wide range of actions designed to bring democracy to their country. Their efforts came to fruition on 26 March 1991 when a comprehensive multi-party system of government came into being, and effective recognition was given to individual and collective freedoms. Their movement had a national and international perspective in which peoples entertained a powerful yearning for freedom and democracy.

The year 1990 was notable for events of an extraordinarily decisive nature; indeed, it was an exceptional year in every way. When it was over, the political map of Africa had to be redrawn. What have come to be known as the 'winds from the east' had already brought the Socialist bloc tumbling down; they now turned into the catalyst of an enormous movement that crushed virtually all one-party governments and Socialist and Socialist-leaning governments all over the world. Then, taking advantage of the end of the Cold War, the major bilateral and multilateral donors began to insist on respect for human rights and democracy as a condition for aid; at a meeting of French and African Heads of State and Government at La Baule in June 1990, for example, President Mitterrand of France clearly articulated the principle that development aid was conditional on democratisation in the countries concerned. Some Heads of State such as Houphouët-Boigny and Oumar Bongo fell in with the democratisation movement to a greater or lesser degree; others, including Hissène Habré and Moussa Traoré, expanded their governments' military base, turned their back on France and refused to have any dealings with their former colonial power.

Mali's refusal to have anything to do with the democratic opening created considerable political tensions; these came to a head between December 1990 and March 1991. The democratic movement consisted of political associations, school and college students, trade unions and youth movements, and of people who had fallen victim of structural adjustment; during this period, the movement organised a large number of marches and meetings, and wrote numerous articles in newspapers denouncing the rigorous demands laid down by the State and calling for multipartyism. Sensing that nothing could be done to halt the democratic movement's onward march, General Moussa Traoré, who was both UDPM General Secretary and President of the Republic, chose to gain time by introducing the concept of 'democracy within the party'.

To celebrate its 11th anniversary, the UDPM organised conferences up and down the country focusing on the 'exercise of democracy within the Party', but Malians simply used them as an the opportunity to reject the idea of democracy within a single party, and demanded full-blown multipartyism instead. This was the backdrop to the 9th Session of the UDPM's National Council held on 27-30 June 1990. People now fully expected to embrace the democratic opening, so their disappointment was all the more acute when, in his closing speech, the President of the Republic said he was deferring any decision on it. This had the effect of radicalising the democratic movement. However, the government response was one of further entrenchment and, in a Ministerial shake-up, the Justice and Internal Affairs portfolios went to men seen as loyal to the President. The result was explosive, and the bloody repression that descended upon Bamako claimed many victims. The bloodbath and the General Strike that ensued were only brought to an end by army intervention on 26 March 1991.

## Economic instability

The economic situation in Mali has been exceptionally unstable since the early 1990s. Every sector has been forced to contemplate total ruin: poorly managed State-owned companies have been left empty, or closed down, or else they have been sold off cheaply leaving thousands of workers without a job; meanwhile, peasants who had to endure the invidious marketing policy are now saddled with unfair taxes.

Mali is classified as one of the world's five poorest nations and, while the SAPs are in force, it is effectively under the control of the IMF and World Bank. The country reported a persistent trade deficit throughout the period 1980-1990.

Table 1: Balance of foreign trade (CFAF billions)

| | 1980 | 1981 | 1982 | 19836 | 1984 | 1985 | 1986 | 1987 | 1988 | 1989 | 1990 | 1991 |
|---|---|---|---|---|---|---|---|---|---|---|---|---|
| Current account (source-applications) | -31 | -37 | -41 | -51 | -21 | -53 | -73 | -46 | -46 | -48 | -50 | -24 |
| Net financial flows (transfers received/net purchases) | 8 | 9 | 11 | 14 | 17 | 24 | 19 | 19 | 24 | 20 | 19 | 22 |
| Self-financing capacity | 23 | 28 | 30 | 37 | 4 | 29 | 54 | 27 | 22 | 28 | 31 | 2 |

*Source*: DNSI, Mali Economic Accounts Office (Comptes Économiques du Mali), Bamako, October 1993

The main macro-economic indicators suggest that extremely sluggish economy; this is particularly true of mining, textiles and commerce. GDP rose by 3% per annum between 1985 and 1995, but the population grew at an identical rate during the same period.

Table 2:    Movements in GDP and its components (CFAF billions)

|  | 1985 | 1986 | 1987 | 1988 | 1989 | 1990 | 1991 | Growth rate % |
|---|---|---|---|---|---|---|---|---|
| Agriculture | 110 | 136 | 141 | 131 | 156 | 161 | 164 | 7 |
| Cattle-rearing | 66 | 63 | 73 | 76 | 78 | 79 | 78 | 3 |
| Mining/Quarrying | 14 | 15 | 14 | 12 | 7 | 10 | 11 | -4 |
| Industry | 39 | 41 | 41 | 43 | 46 | 49 | 59 | 7 |
| Construction | 24 | 28 | 26 | 25 | 28 | 28 | 28 | 2,6 |
| Commerce | 109 | 106 | 92 | 93 | 104 | 116 | 102 | -1 |
| VAT (1+...6+) | 527 | 560 | 559 | 558 | 607 | 628 | 633 | 3 |
| Duties, Import-export taxes | 31 | 33 | 31 | 31 | 35 | 38 | 38 | 3 |
| GDP | 558 | 593 | 590 | 589 | 642 | 666 | 671 | 3 |

*Source*: DNSI, Mali Economic Accounts Office, Bamako, October 1993

Table 3:    Movements in the national budget (CFAF billions)

|  | 1981 | 1982 | 1983 | 1984 | 1985 | 1986 | 1987 | 1988 | 1989 | 1990 | 1991 | Growth rate % |
|---|---|---|---|---|---|---|---|---|---|---|---|---|
| Revenue of which | 73 | 78,4 | 85,6 | 47,2 | 53,7 | 59,8 | 57,9 | 57 | 75,3 | 76,3 | 96,1 | 2,8 |
| % direct taxes | 20 | 20 | 15 | 15 | 13 | 13 | 11 | 11 | - | 13 | 10 | |
| % custom duty | 36 | 35 | 37 | 44 | 39 | 38 | 38 | 35 | 36 | 38 | 46 | |
| % indirect taxes | 12 | 13 | 18 | 18 | 18 | 19 | 20 | 20 | 4 | 18 | 17 | |
| Expenses of which | - | 88,3 | 95,1 | 53,2 | 58,3 | 63,9 | 63,6 | 65,5 | 71,6 | 73,6 | 99,4 | 1,2 |
| % Wages salaries | - | 65 | 66 | 65 | 64 | 64 | 64 | 56 | 53 | 52 | 47 | |
| % Materials equipment | - | 21 | 20 | 21 | 21 | 21 | 17 | 20 | 23 | 23 | 20 | |
| Balance | - | -9,9 | -9,5 | -6 | -4,6 | -4,1 | -5,7 | -8,5 | 3,7 | 2,7 | -3,3 | -10,4 |

*Source*: DNSI

This period has also been marked by large budget deficits. The implementation of economic reform programmes in 1982 brought these deficits down gradually by about 10% until 1987, but the deficit rose again in 1987 and 1988 from CFAF 5.7bn to CFAF 8.5bn. Production of export crops (cotton and groundnuts) is growing significantly, although food production is rising less quickly. Production fell across the board in 1989 and 1990.

Table 4: The fall in food production (1,000s tonnes)

| | 1989 | 1990 | 1991 | Variation | |
|---|---|---|---|---|---|
| | | | | total | % annual |
| Soghum | 1 505 | 1 415 | 1 142 | -363 | -13 |
| Maize | 222 | 207 | 181 | -41 | -10 |
| Paddy rice | 259 | 304 | 254 | -5 | -1 |

*Source*: DNSI

During the same period, consumer prices rose as follows:
- 1 kilo of soghum: from 70F to 140F between August 1989 and August 1991;
- 1 kilo of maize: from 70F to 125F;
- 1 kilo of riz brisure (unsorted, poor quality rice): from 160F to 200F between December 1989 and December 1991.

## The social climate

People's standard of living is determined by economic performance. The social climate is a product of the economic situation, and the collapse of the Malian economy has had major social repercussions. An increasing number of people are condemned to living in poverty, the overall standard of health leaves much to be desired (the quality of health cover is very poor), and educational levels are also low. Using gross national disposable income as a measurement, the standard of living in Mali has risen only very slightly during the period under examination.

Most of the people living in penury constitute an underclass. The result has been an erosion of social values. Any means of survival, however degrading, is acceptable. The number of SAP 'victims' (e.g. workers sacked from their jobs in State-owned companies, former public sector employees who took voluntary severance, and young graduates) grows annually, while the affluent minority (not necessarily members of the State hierarchy) arrogantly drive around in expensive cars. The social situation had become unstable, and the democratic movement received the boost it needed from by the revolt of small traders. Social tension had reached a new high, and people were prepared to make the final sacrifice and challenge the government to a show-down.


## The role of the UNTM in the introduction of democracy

Of the many groups that fought for democracy, the Union National des Travailleurs du Mali (UNTM) played a role of the highest importance. It has been the country's sole trade union federation since its foundation, and for many years - virtually the whole time that the UDPM was in power - workers consistently claimed it was beholden to the régime through its involvement in the latter's 'responsible participation' policy. However, to everyone's surprise, it then gave a decisive nudge to the democratic process and quite suddenly changed the course of history.

At an Extraordinary Central Council meeting on 28-29 May 1990, the UNTM wrote its name in Mali's new history books by calling for the deconstitutionalisation of the UDPM and the introduction of multipartyism. The implementation of this decision inevitably brought the government into conflict with the UNTM, and the union called a 48-hour strike in support of the following demands:
- a review of Article 44 of the Labour Code;
- the organisation of special vocational examinations;
- a review of the parliamentary institutions;
- alternating chairmanship of the governing bodies of the INPS (Institut National de Prévoyance Sociale - National Social Welfare Institute) and OMOE (Office National de la Main-d'Oeuvre et de l'Emploi - National Manpower and Employment Office);
- a 50% pay rise across the board;
- backdating promotions;
- payment of salaries on the basis of updated indices (1987-1990) at the end of January 1991;
- a review of the price structure of crude oil, natural gas etc;
- consultation with trade union officials before any decision is taken to close down, restructure or dispose of a State-owned company.

When negotiations failed to meet the UNTM's aspirations, the union called a nationwide General Strike for 8-9 January 1991. It was successful on all counts, and enabled the UNTM both to measure its capacity for organising actions and to find its niche in the democratic movement. After the violence that took place that month, the UNTM Executive Committee wrote a protest letter to the UDPM General Secretary who, of course, was also President of the Republic. The letter was backed up by a General Strike that was originally intended to last an indefinite period, but was called off when the government fell on 26 March.

The UNTM's radicalisation over pay demands, which it knew were outside government control, was the outcome of a strategy for struggle. The UNTM leadership now knew that, without true democracy - without fundamental change in the way the affairs of State were handled - there was no prospect of any improvement in workers' purchasing power in the medium or long term. Other members of the democratic movement acknowledged that only the trade unions could deliver the final coup de grâce through indefinite strike action, and they reminded the union of its historic responsibilities; then, following the carnage of 24 March, the UNTM decided to throw its full weight behind the campaign to bring the régime down once and for all. At that point, the trade union centre took over coordination of the organisations opposing the government.

In this context, it is important to recall the important roles that various associations and organised groups played alongside the UNTM. They included political associations (ADEMA) (Alliance pour la Démocratie au Mali - Alliance for Democracy in Mali)) and CNID (Congrès National d'Initiative Démocratique - National Congress for Democratic Initiative)), both of which were set up shortly after 7 August 1990 when an open letter was sent to the President of the Republic on the eve of the 7th Extraordinary Session of the UDPM Central Council. There were also three other youth associations: ADIDE (Association des Initiateurs et Demandeurs d'Emploi - Association of Job Providers and Job Seekers), AJDP (Association des Jeunes pour le Développement et le Progrès - Youth Association for Development and Progress) and JLD (Jeunesse Libre et Démocratique - Free Democratic Youth); all were particularly active in the struggle for democracy.

Other important partners in the democratic movement were the Catholic Church and the Malian Bar; they demonstrated their support through their unequivocal position in favour of change. However, the majority of those who fought for democracy under the leadership and moral authority of the trade union movement were school and college students in the Association des Élèves et Étudiants du Mali (AEEM - Association of Malian School and College Students), women who came spontaneously onto the streets, and members of other associations. Many meetings attended by all of these groupings were held on union premises. Lastly, we should also mention a fringe group in the army made up of young officer intellectuals; they had a strong sense of the torment that the people of Mali were enduring, and on the night of 26 March 1991, brought the President-General's government down. Theirs was a last-minute contribution, but a salutary contribution nonetheless since it saved human lives.

The UNTM was not a founder member of a democratic movement that originated in political opposition inside and outside the country. However, it can reasonably claim the credit for uniting the forces for change, by reason of its neutrality on upcoming political issues and the important place it occupied in society.

Since the establishment of democracy in March 1991, the UNTM has been heavily involved in the country's political life; it has even been represented on the highest political body responsible for transition, the Comité de Transition pour le Salut du Peuple (CTSP - Transitional Committee for People's Welfare). The union has taken a particular interest in resolving the following issues:
- the crisis in education;
- the injection of morality into public life;
- the problem in the north of Mali.

*UNTM involvement in managing the country through the medium of the CTSP*

After Moussa Traoré's government was brought down, the CTSP was set up by the Comité de Réconciliation Nationale (CRN - Committee for National Reconciliation); the latter consisted of 15 officers and a 21-strong coordinating committee of democratic associations and organisations. The CTSP itself had 25 members, 10 of whom were representatives from the CRN and 15 were from the democratic associations; the latter included two representatives from rebel movements operating in the north of the country, and three UNTM representatives.

The CTSP, which was given the powers of Mali's supreme political and legislative body, repealed the 2 June 1974 Constitution, and replaced it with a basic law that ruled the country during the nine-month transitional period set for the establishment of new democratic institutions. According to this basic law, the CTSP President had to appoint a Prime Minister; the incumbent was to be the recipient of wide-ranging powers, some of which, under the country's previous Constitutions, had traditionally been devolved to the President of the Republic.

It is remarkable that the UNTM accepted a co-managerial role at all during the period of transition; in fact, it not only sat on the CTSP, but even held the Vice-Presidency in the person of its General Secretary, Bakary Karambé. The union's justification was its fear that the various political associations might, after collaborating with the UNTM for democratic change, start tearing one another to pieces when they came to power, and thereby undermine the institutions.

It was against this backdrop that the UNTM, as an apolitical force, came to play a stabilising role within the CTSP. Subsequent events confirmed the union's worst fears when the political associations (i.e. ADEMA and CNID), which had now turned into political parties, squared up to one another in a bid for power. However, these newly formed political parties then threw themselves into electioneering, and were not prepared to devote time to resolving the country's fundamental problems (e.g. the infusion of moral values into public life) during the period of transition. In the opinion of many workers, UNTM involvement in managing the transitional period served to moderate workers' demands that had previously harmed the trade union movement.

*The injection of moral values into public life*

Contrary to the view taken by recent studies, people who involved themselves in the struggle for change that finally came on 26 March 1991 did not do so because they were supporters of multipartyism. The great majority of those who came onto the streets did so simply because they had reached the end of their tether with poor management, nepotism and the embezzlement of public funds. In short, they had been fighting for the introduction of moral values into public life. That is why even though individuals who held positions of authority during the transition did not make this one of their main objectives, popular pressure ensured it was one of the key issues of government action in the early months. The main criterion that the average Malian used when judging the government's performance was the speed and seriousness with which moral values were introduced.

Moral values constituted one of the government's most problematic issues, partly because the problem was so deep-seated and partly because significant social groups were implicated. In fact, despite enormous grass roots pressure, the government did not even attempt to come to grips with the question because of the danger of slippage caused by well-organised groupings that had done well out of the newly emerging state of law.

The government meant well but, apart from a few brave outbursts, it remained timid when it came to action. In fact, one of the few weaknesses of the transition was that the government was not more active, and did not take advantage of the new climate to radically change the old habits and mentality. Perhaps it was asking too much of an administration that had only 14 months in which to deal with a mountain of problems. On the other hand, it was surprising that the union soft-pedalled on such an issue that had long been one of its hobby-horses. One might have expected the UNTM to give it high priority, particularly as it had been a key player during the period of transition. The reasons emerged at the time of the UNTM crisis of 1995.

They were contained in a statement dated 5 August 1995, and addressed to members of the Extraordinary Council called for 8 August to deal with the suspension of Secretary General Issé, known as Issa Doucouré; in it, the Executive Committee levelled serious accusations relating to the falsification of documents, forgery and the use of forgeries, fraud and double invoicing. This is not the time and place to comment on the accuracy or otherwise of these accusations, but they certainly tell us something of the way the union was being managed. If a trade union cannot give an unambiguous demonstration of transparency and sound management, it is hardly in a position to tell the government to introduce moral values into public life.

The whole affair raised the issue of credibility with regard to the UNTM's statements and its choice of leaders. According to case studies that APADEP has carried out in Mali, workers have little confidence in the leadership; they claim that union leaders are incapable of defending workers' interests because they have become bogged down in administrative problems.

## Restoring the authority of the State

People throughout the country were profoundly shocked by the violence of 26 March 1991. The repressive methods that marked that horrendous time had a traumatic effect not only on ordinary people, but also on the forces of law and order. The authority of the State declined sharply as a result.

In workplaces, employees now bombarded management with pay and conditions claims and resorted to all-out stoppages; in most cases, they also called for their bosses to be dismissed. Demands of this sort that were made in nearly all companies in Bamako, and in many others in the interior of the country, were backed up by violence. Workers sustained these wildcat strikes for several weeks until their demands were met. The demands included the sacking of managers, their own involvement in the selection of new bosses, improved working and living conditions and, in a few cases, the disbanding of the company Works Council (Sonatam and Somapil).

The decision to meet the more deserving claims helped to restore calm. From the workers' point of view, it also gave credibility to the new teams of stand-in managers who had been brought in following the dismissal of the former bosses, and when the posts of (excessively high-spending and ineffective) Chairmen of Boards of Directors were abolished. At a time when people were beginning to fear the worst, the role played by the national centre was decisive in helping to restore calm.

As a result of these crises, companies had been at a standstill for so long that it was necessary to set up four-sided committees to examine workers' demands; these committees consisted of representatives of the

Ministère de tutelle (Ministry of Administrative Supervision), the national trade union centre, company management and the company Works Council). Their work proceeded in an orderly manner and amid an atmosphere of mutual respect, and they eventually reached solutions that were acceptable to the workers' side.

## The impact of democratisation on the trade union movement

Workers were critical of the fact that the UNTM sat on the CTSP, as the latter was seen as an obstacle to their demands. The union was therefore in a double bind: on the one hand, it had to see transition through to a satisfactory conclusion; on the other, it was obliged to meet workers' demands, the most important of which was a 50% pay rise.

The UNTM gave notice of a strike in support of its pay claim on 22 April 1992, but on 7 May, the transitional government and the union signed an important agreement known as the 'Social Pact'. Under Article 2 of the Pact, both parties committed themselves to a multi-annual review of civil servants' pay, and the agreement has turned out to be a regular focus of the UNTM's activities ever since. For example, at the opening of the UNTM's 8th Congress, the President of the Republic, Alpha Oumar Konaré, gave a 'solemn assurance that the 3rd Republic was wholeheartedly committed to all undertakings that have been given to workers on behalf of the State, and the provisions of the Social Pact in particular'. He also stated that the 'government will honour them according to a timetable and implementation plan that will be agreed with you (the unions) quite openly, in an atmosphere of total honesty and uncompromising candour'.

The UNTM had a mandate to apply the Social Pact diligently and comprehensively, and initiated talks with the government as soon as its new Executive Committee was installed; concrete gains were required to appease a rank and file rapidly running out of patience. After lengthy talks about talks, negotiations finally commenced; they lasted from 22 June until 27 July 1993. The government was represented by the Minister of Labour, Ousmane Oumarou Sidibé, flanked by Budget Minister Bakari Konimba Traoré, and Employment Minister Fatou Haidara; the UNTM representatives were Assistant General Secretary, Hamadoun Amion Guindo, and two Executive Council members, Chaka Diakité and Tibou Telly.

Hard-nosed talks finally produced a draft protocol agreement covering ten issues. The main points were as follows:
- statement of civil servants' promotions for 1990, 1991 and 1992;
- payment of salaries as from 1 January 1994 on the basis of indexation applied from 1 January 1993;

- payment of CFAF 2.2bn in January 1994 to cover backdated promotions due on 1 January 1990;
- discussions to open during 1994 with a view to signing a protocol agreement on settling outstanding arrears agreed under the Social Pact, and backpayments due for 1990, 1991 and 1992;
- discussions to open during 1994 with a view to increasing workers' purchasing power.

However, the proposals were thrown out by the UNTM Executive Council. What the union wanted was an announcement, however symbolic, of pay rises in order to keep the rank and file quiet.

The government, for its part, was trapped by a wage sum ceiling imposed by the SAP, and was unable to accede to the pay demand; in response, the union called a nationwide General Strike for 17 August 1993. The action was well supported, but the Syndicat National des Banques et Assurances (SYNCAB - National Bank and Insurance Union) took no part, and came within a hair's breadth of leaving the UNTM altogether. The General Secretary of SYNCAB was also the UNTM Assistant General Secretary; in other words, he was the man who had led the negotiations with the government, and had won a protocol agreement which, given the country's financial crisis, he felt was acceptable to workers in all the circumstances. At all events, SYNCAB did not join the strike, and this led to the suspension of its General Secretary. SYNCAB threatened to leave the UNTM if the Executive Committee did not reverse the decision to suspend, and the breakaway was avoided in eleventh-hour talks. After three months of statutory suspension, the SYNCAB General Secretary resumed his position in the UNTM.

In the end, thanks to the devaluation of the CFA franc, the government was able to honour certain provisions of the Social Pact; these included the backdating of promotions, and offering 10% and 5% pay rises for 1994 and 1995 respectively. Then, in November 1995, the UNTM presented the government with a fresh list of demands.

*Active groups of workers*

As a result of the various SAPs that Mali had concluded with international financial institutions, other groups of workers found themselves in precarious employment situations; this was due to difficulty in finding jobs at all (e.g. young graduates), or because they had left their previous employment either voluntarily (voluntary retirement) or involuntarily (dismissal from State-owned companies).

During the period of transition, and as a result of the democratic opening, these groups of workers formed themselves into associations and became extremely active[2] and, thanks to a wide variety of actions, these associations successfully negotiated some of their demands both during and after the transition. Their successes included the setting up of a fund for re-training civil servants who had gone on voluntary retirement, and providing work for young unemployed workers. Following heavy pressure on the government of the 3rd Republic, workers taking voluntary retirement were also won unsecured bank loans underwritten for just under 100%. However, many of the projects that expected to get funding were unsuccessful because of banking constraints and problems that the State had in exercising drawing rights; at least it indicated a degree of political will to confront the problem.

To back up their actions, the various associations that had suffered from the effects of the SAP then set up a coordinating committee. Following a meeting with the Prime Minister, Abdoulaye Sékou Sow sent a written demand (letter N 513/PRM-CAB of 16 November 1993) to the Ministerial committee responsible for monitoring the Enhanced Structural Adjustment Facility (ESAF), with a view to meeting the coordinating committee and discussing its demands. After a number of meetings,[3] agreement was reached on certain issues. These are set out in an agreement dated 6 January 1994, and jointly signed by the Minister of Finance and the president of the coordinating committee. They were as follows:

*in respect of ADIDE:*
- the organisation of two civil service entrance examinations during 1994 to make up for the failure to hold examination at all during 1993;
- the possible establishment of a National Employment Council on condition that it was a consultative body and made no financial calls on the national budget;

*in respect of workers who had gone on voluntary retirement:*
- monthly transfer of CFAF 100,000,000 into four banks as guarantee funds; this sum will only continue to be transferred at this frequency if the repayment rate reaches 80%;
- setting up a body charged with recouping unpaid salaries owed by employers who had gone into liquidation;

*in respect of workers dismissed by State-owned companies:*
payments due to dismissed workers to be handled as follows:
- CFAF 80m per week by 31 January 1994;
- CFAF 100m per week between 1 February and 31 March.

## The debate on trade union pluralism

The subject of trade union pluralism was first raised at the Central Council in May 1990 when the UNTM made a brave decision to argue for multipartyism and political pluralism. However, after further consideration, the union said that workers were in favour of a single structure because political pluralism did not necessarily involve trade union pluralism; nonetheless, it would not oppose the setting up of other unions if that was what workers wanted. However, as far as the UNTM was concerned, it was equally clear that the imposition of any policy in this connection would be a violation of trade union freedoms. At all events, the UNTM continued to be on the look-out for any attempts by political parties to sow seeds of division and undermine the position of workers.

The leadership believed that, because the UNTM had taken an active part in the democratic movement, the union was now seen as a threat by certain political parties, and these were now trying to destabilise it by setting up rival unions. It was also the UNTM view that the press had poured oil on the flames by running an insidious campaign aimed at discrediting the union in the eyes of working people. Quarrels going back many years between union leaders, particularly in the SNEC (Syndicat National de l'Éducation et de la Culture - National Education and Culture Union), were also believed to be behind the breakaway; it resulted in the establishment of four autonomous education unions covering the three layers of education and Catholic education;[4] these four unions later formed themselves into the Fédération de l'Éducation Nationale (FEN - National Education Federation). Some people even encouraged the split as a way of moving into responsibility posts.

While not wishing to comment on any government attempt at destabilisation, it has to be said that the union failed to give its activists any explanation of what responsible participation really meant, and its objectives in particular. In fact, many activists believed that, by adopting this form of participation, the UNTM had become incorporated into the single party. Similarly, the failure to meet workers' main demands, the social impact of SAPs, the selling-off of State-owned companies and job insecurity led many workers to distrust the UNTM; these were the very arguments that FEN leaders used to justify the setting up of new unions.

In many cases, the setting up of independent unions in health and education was the result of long-standing personal feuds, but it was also encouraged by the existence of unacknowledged corporatist interests. For example, teachers in secondary and higher education felt they were poorly represented by the SNEC, most of whose members were elementary school teachers; and health sector executives argued that their problems were inadequately addressed by the health service union which was dominated by nursing and lower-grade staff.

The debate on trade union pluralism, which began in the wake of the events of 26 March 1991, was conducted by the population at large and also by the union internally. Public opinion seemed to be divided but, following conferences organised by the 12 national unions, a clear consensus within the UNTM emerged in favour of a single structure. The UNTM still believed that trade union pluralism divided and weakened the workers' movement, but such a view cut little ice with those who no longer identified with UNTM affiliates, particularly people employed in teaching and the magistrature.

Although much discussion has taken place among retired trade unionists, no rapprochement has proved possible between the UNTM-affiliated Snec and the FEN, the autonomous federation consisting of five independent unions[5] founded during the period of transition. Veiled hostilities could also be observed developing between the two federations as they sought a leadership role among teachers. For example, on 3 August 1992, SYLDEF issued a communiqué criticising the SNEC for organising a training session 'as a way of trying to blackmail elementary teachers to stay in the SNEC'. The SNEC appears to have better international trade union connections and, unlike the FEN, it boasts a network of contacts which enable it to organise a large number of seminars specifically aimed at teachers.

Apart from the rivalries that one might expect to find between concurrent unions, trade union pluralism raised the question of how unions were to be represented on consultative bodies such as the Economic and Cultural Council, the Upper Public Sector Council and the Upper Labour Council. The main reason for the delay in setting up the Economic, Social and Cultural Council was the difficulty in applying representation criteria in a country with no relevant case law.

It remains to be seen whether the closer working arrangement between the Syndicat Libre des Cadres (SYLCAD - Free Union of Managers), which was set up in 1993, and the UNTM - particularly over the issue of administrative premises - will spread to the FEN and the autonomous union representing magistrates.

*Trade union policy*

Following the success of the democratisation process, the responsible participation policy that the UNTM had adopted at its Congress back in 1974 now attracted fierce criticism from workers. For that reason, the Extraordinary Congress held on 30-31 January and 1 February 1992 introduced participation at grass roots level, that is to say in the workplace, and took steps to ensure that it was made more effective. It was also why

Article 11 of the UNTM's new Rules banned anyone from holding trade union and political positions concurrently. On the one hand, this provision sought to guarantee the union's independence from political parties and the government; on the other hand, it was this very independence that enabled the UNTM to make its voice heard on the major matters of State, and help solve the main problems, particularly education. In fact, responsible participation had no significant impact while the single party was in power; it has, however, been used in a manipulative manner in that the government has used it to introduce anti-worker legislation.

The most striking new feature of trade union policy since the advent of democracy has been the fact that unions no longer deal exclusively with employment issues, but have broadened their horizons to include all social groups affected by the crisis. For example, the UNTM has taken up the problems of such groups as workers dismissed from their jobs in State-owned companies, civil servants who have taken voluntary retirement, and young, unemployed graduates.

Further evidence of this shift comes from a list of demands that the UNTM Executive Committee presented to the government in November 1995. The 12 points, many of which, strictly speaking, have anything to do with the situation of workers, are as follows:
- pay rises for 1996;
- conditions surrounding the privatisation of State enterprises;
- security and development in the north of Mali;
- the situation of Malians living abroad;
- the Malian education system;
- the problem of public, administrative establishments;
- the problem of workers who have been dismissed or have taken voluntary retirement;
- the situation of women workers;
- youth employment;
- the management of mining resources;
- a review of the Electoral Code;
- sub-regional economic integration.

Before finalising the list of demands, the UNTM commissioned a study from a private sector consultancy to make sure that the claims were feasible and technically defensible. The claims focus not only on strictly trade union matters like pay rises and privatisations, but also on broader questions such as the management of mining resources and sub-regional economic integration, and even political issues like a review of the Electoral Code. In other words, the union broadened its field of competence by addressing the country's socio-economic and political problems.

*Trade union democracy*

Prior to the democratic change that took place in March 1991, not even the UNTM, particularly the upper échelons, had operated in a truly democratic manner. Local branch elections were conducted democratically because the issues were not of critical importance, but the same could not be said of elections to senior committees such as national unions, much less the Executive Council. The government also made a habit of influencing the make-up of the Executive Council elections at UNTM Congresses.

Nor was the quality of democracy at Executive Council level beyond reproach. In this respect, political democracy has had a positive effect on the way the UNTM operates, and the union is now running a major internal debate on the subject. In all probability, the threat posed by the independent unions contributed to this positive move towards internal democracy, but much remains to be done if the union is to be fully democratised. Old habits die hard. The crisis that rocked the UNTM has opened people's eyes to how the union really functioned.

Internal democracy also led to the suspension of the Assistant General Secretary, Hamadoun Amion Guindo, in 1993, and of General Secretary Issé, known as Issa Doucouré, in 1994; the crisis also laid bare the extent to which money, personal favouritism and clientelism influenced the way the union was run.

True, the UNTM has been on a learning curve as far as democracy is concerned, but there is plenty still to be done. The union may have found a temporary solution to the leadership crisis through a mediation that resulted in the General Secretary's suspension being lifted in August 1996; it has even enabled the union to approach government with a semblance of unity. Just the same, much remains to be done if mechanisms are to be put in place to prevent the institutional stagnation that paralysed the organisation for a whole year.

## The UNTM and the programme of economic reforms

With a per capita GNP of USD 270 in 1990, Mali is one of the world's least developed countries. UNDP Human Development Indicators describe a highly precarious socio-economic situation with life expectancy at birth of 45 years, health care for no more than 15% of the population, access to drinking water for 17%, and primary education available to only 14% of girls and 23% of boys.

The dramatic consequences of almost endemic drought since 1973, a deterioration in exchange rates and totally inappropriate economic policies have been precipitating the Malian economy into major crisis since the late 1970s. This crisis has taken the form of serious macro-economic imbalances, an acute crisis of public finances, a sharply increased balance of payments deficit, an accelerated rise in the public debt, and - it goes without saying - an ever-expanding gap between domestic saving and investment.

In its attempts to correct these now intolerable economic and financial imbalances, the Malian government was forced into a series of Structural Adjustment Programmes with the IMF, World Bank and other development partners; they began in 1982. Between 1982 and 1987, the Malian government signed three agreements with the IMF and one programme of economic reforms with USAID, and since 1988, further SAPs have been concluded with the IMF and World Bank. The programme agreed with the IMF for the period 1988-1991 was designed to achieve a gradual easing of structural constraints and a reduction of financial imbalances. By contrast, provisions of the World Bank programme had macro-economic objectives:
- adjustment in the agricultural sector;
- reform of rural development operations;
- adjustment in the public enterprise sector;
- restructuring in education, water and electricity, post and telecommunications, and health.

In May 1991, the transitional government agreed a micro-economic framework with the IMF and World Bank; it was designed to mitigate the effect that a shattered economy was having on economic growth, public finances and balance of payments following the violence of 22 and 24 March. Then, in August 1992, the government signed a three-year agreement with the IMF on an Enhanced Structural Adjustment Facility (ESAF); its aim was to consolidate the impact of structural reforms, with the ultimate intention of improving incentives for the private sector (particularly through the adoption of a new Commercial Code and Labour Code) and raising the standard of management of public resources.

Probably the most delicate aspect of the SAP for the trade unions was the Public Enterprise Structural Adjustment Programme (PESAP); this had the following objectives:

*reduce the burden represented by the public enterprise sector by:*
- rationalising the public enterprise sector through the sale of non-viable enterprises, State disengagement from non-strategic enterprises, and keeping those with strategic role;
- subjecting all new investment to systematic review and ensuring that it is justified on economic and financial grounds;

*improve the economic and financial performance of viable enterprises by:*
- reforming the institutional framework of public enterprises;
- rationalising key sectors (mainly energy, water, and post office and telecommunications);
- reforming the financial sector, particularly by restructuring the Banque de Développement du Mali (Mali Development Bank) and improving the system of post office cheques.

The PESAP tried, albeit indirectly, to promote a dynamic private sector but, although more than 15 enterprises were sold off, about 10 were privatised, and several more were restructured, the Programme was still beset with difficulties. The most important of these were the restricted financial base of the Malian private sector and limited managerial skills among the country's economic operators.

The social consequences of the PESAP were very considerable, and expected results were unable to compensate in terms of job creation. Approximately 6300 people lost their jobs between 1985 and 1989, and this resulted in CFAF 4826bn being spent on dismissal and job integration compensation. Furthermore, although 2786 jobs were created in 1488 projects, only 2214 workers dismissed by State-owned companies had found new employment by the end of November 1990; these projects cost CFAF 1908.5m.[6]

From 1990 to 1992, the PESAP included an voluntary retirement scheme that affected about 2700 employees, in addition to the 3700 voluntary retirements that had taken place under the earlier USAID programme. The attempt to find new jobs for these people who had taken voluntary retirement was a complete failure, and the government accordingly brought the programme to a close. The impact of these voluntary retirement programmes was all the more embarrassing as they affected employees in key sectors, such as health and education, which were theoretically supposed to be excluded.

*What did the SAP achieve?*

The overall objectives of the SAP were a reduction in public deficits and imbalances and the creation of the conditions for sustainable economic growth. With regard to growth, the SAP has achieved limited results. As for the reduction of macro-economic imbalances, there have been some successes:
- monetary aggregates developed as provided for in the Programmes;
- objectives linked to inflation have been achieved;
- the budget position has improved, although gains have been irregular and have not always been attributable to the internal dynamic of the economy;

- the State's disengagement from the public enterprise sector has meant that this sector has been greatly sanitised, but at the cost of colossal job losses; all the partners acknowledge that attempts to find new employment for these workers have failed.

Economic growth has continued to be sluggish and very irregular because of its dependence on the amount of rainfall; moreover, despite devaluation, and apart from improved exports in a few sectors such as livestock, gold and cotton, there has been no reflation of the economy. Ten years after the reforms were first introduced, and despite a satisfactory report from funders on macro-economic balances, there has been no sustainable reflation of the economy likely to improve employment prospects or provide any alleviation of poverty. Implementation of these programmes ran into a number of difficulties:

- the harmonisation and coherent application of the government's economic policy was undermined by the termination of these programmes and the existence of several other action frameworks and programmes that were being run in parallel; these included the government action programme for 1994-1997, the cancellation of regional concertation processes, documents relating to the economic and financial policy framework for 1994-1996, documents from discussions that the government and funders had in Geneva in 1995, and guidelines and/or sectoral action plans;
- the lack of broad-based concertation in preparation for the reform programmes impeded a consensual view of the country's economic policy, particularly as a large number of political, economic and social players in Mali were involved.

The unions not only represented workers but also acted as a mouthpiece for the informal sector; however, they were not party to drawing up the programmes. This may explain their mistrust of the SAP, given that its success depended on the collaboration of all citizens actively participating in the development of the country (les forces vives du pays). By contrast, all social groups were most certainly consulted when, after a meeting of the Extraordinary Council of Ministers on 14 September 1993, Abdoulaye Sékou Sow's government adopted measures for breaking free from the crisis; the same was also true when measures were agreed following the devaluation of the CFA franc.

Many observers take the view that the concertation that took place around the time of devaluation, and the many apposite proposals that were forthcoming - particularly from the trade unions - helped Mali to contain inflation to a certain extent. This concertation procedure now needs to be systematised, not to say institutionalised. The social partners have provided so much evidence of their maturity when the country has been in trouble that the government has no excuse for not involving them in framing economic policy, or at the very least in drawing up the broad outlines.

## The institutionalisation of democracy

Democracy is not simply a matter of going to the polling-station every five years. It is a day-to-day living experience. Mali is a land of dialogue. Indeed, concertation and dialogue have an almost dogmatic quality that all governments have rigorously enforced since independence - but sadly only at times of major crisis. Malians have been able to avoid catastrophe when things have looked bleak by organising concertation exercises involving all socio-professional categories. In fact, the 3rd Republic administration elevated this concertation policy almost to the status of system of government as it attempted to see off the challenges threatening Mali's burgeoning democracy. An illustration of this occurred in August 1994 when the government organised regional concertations and a 'coming together' (synthèse nationale) on certain major problems facing the whole country. These included:
- the problem in the north of Mali;
- education;
- lack of security;
- structural adjustment and the impact of devaluation;
- democracy, rights, freedoms and national reconciliation;
- decentralisation;
- foreign policy and regional integration;
- employment.

These regional concertations were attended by 2786 people from all walks of life: political parties, civil service departments, traditional and religious VIPs, grass roots associations, trade unions and professional organisations. In the session that brought the synthèse nationale to a close, Prime Minister Ibrahim Boubacar Keita spoke as follows: 'The regional concertations have given a clear indication that all sections of our people want our active citizens (les forces vives) to be fully involved in seeking and implementing constructive, effective solutions to the major problems facing our country. They wish to do this through free, open and serious dialogue underpinned by a genuine wish for conciliation, tolerance, participation - and even consensus - based on a responsible understanding both of our realities and needs and of the limited means at our disposal and opportunities open to us.'

Notwithstanding the opposition's reservations regarding the government's true intentions in setting up these forums, all players, both economic and social, played a full part; as a result, a start could be made on finding solutions, particularly to the crisis in education and to the problems of a demoralised army.

Outside the regional concertations, each time the government has brought political and social forces together to discuss the main issues facing the nation, they have participated fully. It happened over the preparatory work that preceded the crisis measures adopted by the Abdoulaye Sékou Sow government in 1993, and the measures that followed the devaluation of the CFA franc in January 1994. On each occasion, the UNTM and the autonomous unions played a positive, constructive role.

Today, Mali is in the process of constructing a truly participative democracy. When Alpha Oumar Konaré took over as Head of State on 8 June 1992, he said that concertation was going to be the 'master-word' (maître-mot) that informed his policy. His method has not always been fully understood at the time of major social crises, but dialogue and concertation have still enabled the country to emerge from difficult periods precisely because the various players, including opposition parties, have played their parts.

It now remains for this process to be institutionalised. If participation is used exclusively as a way of dealing with crises, it will lose its effectiveness and become discredited. It needs to be codified as a basic component in the day-to-day practice of democracy at local, regional and national level. To this end, there is an especial need to revive the Economic, Social and Cultural Council; this is the institution best suited to discussing the nation's major problems and giving the government objective advice. The fact that the trade union movement has significant representation - 12 seats in all - ensures that the Council will focus on problems affecting workers. One of biggest challenges facing the institutionalisation of participative democracy may be the problem of finding competent, honourable, serious-minded citizens to direct the destiny of a trade union movement that continues to be a key player in the life of the nation.

In the view of Bakary Karambé, the UNTM's long-serving former General Secretary, 'the UNTM needs to make a fresh start if trade union action is to contribute to the consolidation of democracy. If we are to succeed, the union needs to be restructured and competent staff will have to be recruited. Competent managers will have to come into the union to give it a new vision and come up with a constructive alternative to the government. The days of amateur trade unionism are over. Although trade union work is determined by elections and votes, we must ensure that trade union representation is based on objective criteria'.

# Notes

1  The research tools used in this study comprise interviews and documentary analysis.
   Statistical data have been mainly extracted from documents published by the Direction nationale de la statistique et de l'information (DNSI - National Statistics and Information Directorate): Statistical Yearbook, Economic Accounts, Agricultural Economic Survey, Consumer Budget Survey, Informal Sector Survey, Population and Housing Census, and Economic and Financial Information Bulletin ('Tableau de bord').

2  ADIDE was formed before Moussa Traoré's government was brought down.

3  These were held on 18 November 1993, 10 December 1993 and 3 January 1994.

4  Syndicat National de l'Enseignement Catholique (SYNTEC - National Union of Catholic Education).
   Syndicat National de l'Enseignement Supérieur (SNESUP - National Higher Education Union).
   Syndicat Libre de l'Enseignement Fondamental (SYLDEF - Free Union for Elementary Education).
   Syndicat National des Travailleurs de l'Enseignement Secondaire (SYNTES - National Union for Employees in Secondary Education).

5  SYLDEF, SNESUP, SYNTES, SYNTEC AND SYNET (Syndicat National de l'Enseignement Technique - National Technical Education Union).

6  Source: Conference on the social dimensions of structural adjustment in Mali, ICFTU, UNTM and Friedrich Ebert Foundation, 26-28 April 1993, Bamako, pp 18-19.

# 11 Mozambique
## Organise or Disappear

PERSONAL TESTIMONIES
COMPILED BY KEN HANSEN

*In Mozambique, a country marked by civil war, the history of the trade union movement has long overlapped with that of Frelimo, the ruling party. Production councils masquerading as trade union bodies are in fact powerful Soviet-style political organisations. The country's first strikes in the early 1990s forced the government to take part in concertation. The trade unions now face an uphill struggle.*

### Introduction

Trade unionism embracing significant numbers of black workers, dates from 1976 in Mozambique. This is to say that there were no trade unions involved in the anti-colonial struggle, and that rather than being previously-independent organisations with relations (as equals or as subordinates) with the ruling post-independence party, in the Mozambican case they were in fact a direct creation of this party (the Mozambique Liberation Front — FRELIMO).

The model adopted for this post-independence union structure owes much to the Soviet experience, in which unions are seen as a transmission belt from the vanguard to the masses. The vast majority of the current (and past) leadership of the Mozambican unions, were factory workers at the time of independence, recruited by FRELIMO and sent for trade union training in the former Soviet bloc.

This model for worker representation ceased to be effective in the late 1980s, as a result of internal and external political developments, as well as the social pressures of structural adjustment. The crisis in the model has been evident since a sudden strike wave in early 1990, and in particular since the withdrawal of three national unions from the trade union central, the OTM, in 1992. (These three unions later formed themselves into a coordinating body known as SLIM — the 'Free and Independent Unions of Mozambique'. To date they have remained non-competitive with the OTM in the sense of continuing to operate only in their original industrial sectors.)

This chapter traces the history as outlined above, from the viewpoint of four veteran participants in the Mozambican trade union movement. All four come from the generation that created the first Production Councils in 1976, and the OTM in 1983. They came of age in the 1960s and 1970s, and thus their worklife experiences embrace both the pre- and post-independence periods.

In May of 1995, these four took part in a two-day oral history session — a 'collective interview' animated by the author of this chapter (a Canadian trade unionist working in Mozambique). They have somewhat different positions — two being OTM staff, one being a national union and OTM leader, and the other being the Secretary-General of one of the independent unions. Nonetheless, they speak essentially in one voice. This is reflected in the layout of the chapter, which maintains the original question-and-answer format, but without distinguishing the responses as being from one or another of the four.

The full text was published in Portuguese in Mozambique, by the APADEP-Mozambique program in cooperation with the Eduardo Mondlane Foundation.[1] While the history of Mozambican trade unionism is highly political, the only political party mentioned is FRELIMO, which has been in power since independence, and which won the first multi-party elections in October of 1994. FRELIMO's main rival in those elections was RENAMO, which had been the government's adversary during fifteen years of civil war. Although the 'mass democratic organisations' formed by FRELIMO after independence (including the unions as well as women's and youth organisations) were a point of contention between the two parties, the nature of the conflict (armed and rural, at least until the peace agreement in 1992 and elections in 1994), helps explain why RENAMO has not been a force within the trade union structures, and why this political party is not dealt with by the interviewees.

*Workers and the liberation struggle*

The participants began by telling their stories as Africans and as workers during the colonial period. The questions then moved in the direction of asking whether real worker trade unionism was possible during the colonial regime:

It seems to me that the division was perhaps racial or national — one could say that it was between the Mozambicans and the colonial population (colons). At any rate, that is the picture which is emerging. When you say that the unions didn't defend the workers, this for me raises two aspects. One is that the great majority of the workers were without any kind of representation, as they had no right to join those structures. But the other point that is raised is that the colonial unions, didn't perform a trade union role as such, even for the white workers, but rather a political role of defence of the colonial system.

*Given the fact that the unions that existed in the colonial era were unions more of privileges for the whites than anything else, integrated into the colonial structure and defending that system, and the well-known fact of repression by the colonial political police, which made it impossible to create unions that were really representative of the majority of the workers... in this context, if there had been any possibility of developing structures that were representative of the majority, what for you would have been the most important demands of such a union movement in that period?*

The colonialists had a system of repressing any kind of demonstration, taking men and putting them in a sack and throwing them into the sea, or digging a hole and throwing people in alive... You could have ideas, but you kept those ideas to yourself, inside your head... In those days, in order for you to be a trade union member, it was at the discretion of the boss to send a letter to the union saying that you could become a member.

Any and all kind of demonstration along trade union lines, the colons immediately interpreted as pro-independence. The first question was that of independence, and that's exactly what they wanted to avoid... As well, we here in Mozambique were closed off from the rest of the world and from any kind of interchange. For that reason, we had no concept of trade unionism at that time...

What was possible, was what happened: some people left the country in the name of the whole people — not as representatives of the working class but in the name of the whole oppressed people. They left and organised themselves abroad. That is to say that the voice of the worker was only able to be heard from abroad.. FRELIMO didn't only undertake a liberation struggle for political independence, but as well there was union work that was done; there was contact with other countries.

At that time the question was that of independence, and the union movement was organised through those comrades who were there abroad and who participated in various meetings, to spread the word. But at that time we had little possibility of understanding what a union is, as the primary question was that of independence...

It wasn't possible to speak of other tasks as long as we were colonised. It wasn't possible — the idea was to explain the objectives of FRELIMO's struggle, amongst the workers... The workers had hope, following independence, of being able to undertake other tasks of an organisational or trade union character... So FRELIMO set up its structure within the enterprises, to educate the workers to be vigilant — above all, the first task was that of vigilance — because when the struggle got tough, the colons went about destroying the factories. The slogan at that time was to defend the factories... When FRELIMO arrived here, it was received with open arms by the entire population — but their hope, the first question, was that of independence. No one could speak about unions, because the only union that we had known was that of the colons...

*What was the process by which each of you got involved in setting up the Dynamising Groups, and in implanting FRELIMO — as a Liberation Front, one could say — here in the city, specifically in the enterprises, and in the whole process leading to the creation of the Production Councils in 1976?*

At Facobol we set up the Dynamising Group at the end of October, under the direction of a group of FRELIMO militants that were going around the enterprises promoting such ideas... In the meetings, the bosses weren't present but all the curious white workers went. That is where they clarified what FRELIMO was. On that basis we created our Dynamising Group (GD). That is when I was elected as Secretary of the GD. One of the tasks that the GD had was to undertake Adult Literacy in the workplace. We did that, and as well distributed tasks amongst all of the members. There were people placed in charge of the tasks of Secretary, Assistant Secretary, Person in Charge of Organisation, Women's Organisation, Youth organisation, and other tasks like Education and Culture — doing up songs and dances, etc...

From that point on we joined into the life of FRELIMO, as FRELIMO's presence was by then a fact. In 1974-75, I passed through all those places where we did political studies under the aegis of FRELIMO... In October of 1976 I was selected to be involved in training for the Production Councils. At that time a Production Council Implementation Committee was set up... The process kicked off on October 13, with President Samora Machel's speech...

It was the head of state who announced the necessity for the workers to be organised along collective lines, and given that, one can imagine the huge numbers of workers who joined... So this force wasn't just a trade union force — it was a political force, of implantation of FRELIMO...

I was selected in 1976 to participate in the first course for Secretaries of Dynamising Groups, at the FRELIMO School in Matola. The course lasted 60 days, in which FRELIMO gave the first lessons on the creation of the Production Councils, since that course took place following the Eighth Session of the Central Committee of FRELIMO. That session decided to unleash the Generalised Political Offensive on the Production Front, directed by President Samora Machel, in the enterprises where he noted that there were large problems with disorganisation and indiscipline. It was following this that it was decided, upon analysing the work of the offensive, that a structure ought to be created that would be dedicated to organising workers to better carry out the work in the enterprise — these were the Production Councils. So it was there that I benefited from the classes given at that time by Mario Machungo, the Minister of Industry and Commerce. He gave classes on how the Production Councils were to arise, their structure, tasks, objectives and relationship with the employer...

So as I was saying, during the days of the liberation struggle, there were Trade Union Departments, and FRELIMO leaders who were designated to represent FRELIMO in trade union meetings in relation to national and international organisations. So following independence, these were the people who ended up being placed in the sectors dealing with workers — like in the case of Mariano Matsinhe, who during the armed struggle headed up the Department linked to the trade unions. In ILO meetings, or any national or international or trade union conference to which FRELIMO was invited, it was he who participated, along with some others... That is why he was appointed Minister of Labour.

Because of this experience, he continued to be the one who passed on all of that experience of Mozambicans in the international forums, discussing trade union matters, and it was he who ended up being placed in the National Production Councils Implementation Committee, on behalf of the government...

(During the phase of nationalisations starting in 1975), many firms ended up being put into trusteeship, and during that phase the bosses started to abandon the enterprises and create serious problems for the future life of the workers. They sabotaged the economy or gave wage increases that couldn't be supported... These were increases made on purpose to weaken the firms...

At the time of the Generalised Offensive, the enterprises noted that there was great disorganisation, sabotage, lack of discipline, uncontrolled theft, and generalised anarchy in the firms. Accordingly, this put into danger the proper functioning of the production process, and didn't contribute at all to increasing production and productivity. Therefore it was decided to create the Production Councils. Happily, we were lucky enough to be selected to make up part of the first teams... We had no office — our headquarters for meetings was the then Ministry of Industry and Commerce, because the persons heading up the commission were Mario Machungo, Mariano Matsinhe and Augusto Macamo... and other comrades who came from the Party...

The specifically trade union tasks were left out. FRELIMO was directing all of this. No one at that time thought that we were doing wrong — firstly because we didn't have a trade union culture. This was the first appearance of an organisation more or less dedicated in the few activities that it carried out, to the welfare of the workers. This was quite a lot for the workers, as it had never before existed...

We were the executive arm of the Party at the time. Therefore FRELIMO had to send its cadres abroad to get trained, to be able to direct the workers of the country...

*What advantages were there in this for the individual worker — combating indiscipline, theft, fighting the enemy, etc.? What reason did he or she have for joining in on these campaigns? They may or may not have had a developed political consciousness, but they continued to be individuals with their concerns and problems, as workers. Concretely, when you people arrived to set up the Production Councils, what advantage was there for them to join in?... In other words, if everyone was in favour of independence and of FRELIMO, why was there so much theft and indiscipline — why was it necessary to have a campaign?*

There was no possibility of the worker thinking about what the advantage was, because he arrived at the meetings with a full belly. We used to explain that now is not the time to demand wage increases — only later.

The content of the mobilisation was for everyone to join in the movement as their organising structure, a structure that was dedicated exclusively to defending the workers' interests. It was not for anything else, that was what it was to do — but we did everything on the basis of the slogans of the single Party, on the basis of a socialist economy, Marxism-Leninism, scientific socialism...

On that basis, the criticisms weren't directed straight at the government... In the firms that were under trusteeship or nationalised, the struggle was not directed in the same way as in a private firm, because there we had our Director, who was our comrade...

The Production Councils constituted a strong political organ. Any worker who had a problem could count on their presence, even in the Ministry of Labour, and elsewhere...

As well, the workers were told that we were to go on to struggle for defence, protection, hygiene and safety at work — we were to demand from the employers that they take care of medical and pharmaceutical coverage — and this came to pass in fact. Health posts began to be set up in the enterprises, first-aid attendants were trained by us in cooperation with the Red Cross. We signed an agreement with the Ministry of Health to supply the health posts in the enterprises with medication, and this was a concrete result of our work. We motivated the workers. During the colonial period, the worker was simply a tool of production — he or she left home, went to work, and didn't know what the product was for. Now he or she would participate in the planning of production of their department, coming to know exactly what the firm was going to produce each day. They came to follow the economic life of the firms through the meetings and structures they belonged to... Socialist emulation emerged as a way to stimulate those who met the plan...

The Production Councils struggled for the firms to take care of transport for the workers, to build creches for the workers' children, to build Social Centres, to fit out the canteens, to ensure meals in some cases — these were concrete cases, struggles that were waged, in which we won some advances.

In 1981 I participated in the first seminar in which people involved in the Production Councils went abroad. There were 25 of us who went for a five-week seminar in the Soviet Union. It was a trade union seminar with subjects that included political economy and scientific socialism. It was a good experience, in which we learned about the Soviet trade unions, as well as the international trade union movement, after which I spent four months in the GDR for a course for union leaders, from January to April of 1982.

As I said in my introduction, I am a product of FRELIMO in terms of placement in the political arena, and the transition from politics to trade unionism, as I entered the Dynamising Groups in 1974, carrying out FRELIMO policies. In 1976 I was integrated into the Production Councils, with the designation of what we can call trade unionism — but in the final analysis exercising a political function. On that basis I benefited from a lot of training, perhaps of an ideological nature, studying FRELIMO's ideology...

The material that we studied was international trade unionism, unionism in the socialist countries, which was then contrasted with the system in the capitalist countries. It was necessary to make a differentiation leading to a demonstration that the socialist system was superior in relation to the capitalist system... Those who were behind these seminars also needed to have people be clear that the best is what I'm offering; I'm better, I'm superior in relation to the other system. Accordingly this had many reflections on people's daily life. But it's clear that today we are faced with another reality, which is that of a trade unionism that isn't from the socialist system, and that we now must develop trade unionism within the framework of the market economy.

*Was this in fact trade unionism?*

... To be a trade union leader you had to be from FRELIMO. Here what came first was the political struggle leading the country to independence, and the Front that led this struggle, created the workers' structure. So it's only now, with multi-party democracy, that we're beginning to see that in the final analysis, we were saying "viva FRELIMO", "viva Samora" (Machel), instead of saying "viva workers" — we spent a lot of time saying a lot of "vivas" to FRELIMO and not our own "viva". We couldn't carry out strikes, we couldn't directly criticise the government no matter how wrong we saw that they were — because it was our government...

We were against the West and capitalism; we defended the socialist economy and not the capitalist one — at that time the market economy was considered a backward phase in relation to the working class, but later when multi-party democracy arose, we threw Marxism-Leninism into the rubbish bin. Today everyone's for the market economy — we're all happy; we speak badly of the past, but we were all promoters of that phase — all of us were mobilisers of that whole phase. It's the problem of changes between phases.

Everything we did starting from the creation of the Production Councils — all those tasks, the way we arose, the political regime that we followed, which was that of scientific socialism — all that had no other name than trade unionism. The trade unionism which was carried out here, was also practiced in the USSR, Bulgaria, the GDR, Czechoslovakia, Yugoslavia. In China and Korea they continue to do everything that we used to do here... Here we didn't have strikes, we didn't criticise the government (since it was our government), because we defended the Party, we were guided by the Party's orientations, we defended the Party's program in our trade union activities. So each and every trade unionist defended the Party, the Government; it was very rare that we opposed a decision — the times can be counted, since they are very few. In a socialist society, this is the trade unionism ... a trade unionism with all of its omissions, but trade unionism nonetheless...

The trade unionism which is found in a country under a market economy isn't the same as in a socialist country, since in a socialist country the struggle is for the benefit of the majority, and the fruits of the national economy are distributed to the whole people.

But that's not what happens in the countries that aren't for the benefit of the majority, but rather for the benefit of the boss. He contributes to the state only through taxes and nothing else — the rest of the profits are his. In a socialist country for example, in which there are state enterprises, in which the state budget comes from those enterprises, how is the trade union working in that enterprise going to criticise the government, how is it going to go on strike against the government, if everything is negotiable...? These are phases of different processes, but it's all trade unionism. We weren't just doing political work, we were doing trade unionism in general, under the conditions of socialism. Now we are doing trade unionism as well, in market economy conditions...

We didn't have a real trade union tradition. We arose from a single Party in power, but the changes that we are experiencing here in the country, are due to the government itself having opted for the privatisation of the enterprises, selling them to the capitalists, which means that we have to be well-organised in trade union terms, in defence of the workers in true trade union tasks, in accordance with the current situation...

Following independence there were no errors — the errors committed were as a function of the concrete reality at that time, since almost none of us knew anything. For example, in my case, I took on the direction of the Production Councils having studied only to Third Grade. First of all, I didn't know what the trade union movement was, and as well I had only Third Grade. I heard people talking about trade unionism and then with the little bit of observation that I undertook, I heard that a trade union leader had to be an Engineer, and so how was I, who lacked that level of education, going to perform this job? But there was no one else, as you couldn't import people from outside to direct the trade union movement — it had to be done by us...

*Was it possible for FRELIMO itself to have thought of setting up something different?*

During five hundred years of colonial domination, we knew only suffering. So when FRELIMO arrived it was the saviour, and when within FRELIMO, cadres, militants or leaders tried to go against FRELIMO ideas, they were considered reactionaries. We can take the example of the National Liberation Struggle. The policy that people like Gwenjere tried to implement was considered reactionary, the work of an infiltrated enemy agent. So no one was interested in going against FRELIMO's ideas in order to create something different, as they could be branded with these names. So there was no possibility of any other structure emerging, even if some top FRELIMO leaders had ideas...

We're the ones who educated, we gave classes, so we were seen as important people who were educating the workers... There was no chance of a worker rising up against us, since that worker also had no other experience, he only knew that which arrived with FRELIMO...

The workers aren't interested in names and definitions — they are interested in an institution that is good at defending their interests. If that institution is called OTM, that's a question of names...

This is so as well in the case of a trade unionism from the socialist system being the one that best serves the workers, if we ourselves adapt ourselves to best serve the workers, then we're on the right track. If that's not the case, because the (political) system implicitly pushes people to adopt another kind of structure to better serve the workers, then so be it...

We have to adapt ourselves to the reality of the local problems of the workers here in Mozambique, in order to be able to identify why we should exist...

We're saying that on the basis of the socio-economic system in effect at the time in the country, it is necessary to conform to that reality. If we don't, we're condemned to failure — we'll have problems that it will be difficult to solve. In the previous phase, we conformed ourselves to socialism — the stage is different now...

In a firm owned by a private owner, this owner is not going to accept a Party, OMM or OJM.[2] He'll only accept a trade union, in line with the international conventions. So now we're obliged to change the angle of our struggle...

History evolved, and with this evolution FRELIMO itself began to change, in response to reality. That is why today there are options...

We are a sub-system within the general overall system of governance. We are a trade union, we are a workers' union organisation; we have to make a correlation between the management of government and trade union management...

The possible errors are those of a process; errors are inevitable, whether with this model or with the other. Even if the model hadn't been that of socialism, if we had adopted a capitalist model, errors would have been identified. So the question is to see if the errors of a capitalist system are more prejudicial in relation to those of a socialist system — it all depends.

*I admit that the errors were those of a historical process, but for example Operation Production[3] did not constitute an essential and inevitable component of socialism; the imprisonment and execution of those political prisoners, Gwenjere and the others, isn't an inevitable fact arising from the socialist option... Saying that there were no errors or that all of the errors that existed were those of a political option is hard to accept. Does this mean that it was only with political-economic change that the need arose to change one's way of seeing things?*

FRELIMO had no previous experience of governing. They were Mozambicans who organised themselves on the basis of the exploitation of the Portuguese colonialists; they had no experience. It was the first time for us to govern, and so we were subject to various errors. On the error that you highlighted concerning Operation Production: in all these areas the government had to seek ways of disciplining society, and it was inevitable that they made mistakes...

I don't want to say that there were no errors — it would be a lie, as there were errors — but they were the errors of a process, since we had never had experience in governing...

## Changes in the Mozambican trade union movement

In 1990 the OTM decided that the Union Central should be composed of its affiliates, the national unions. Formerly the workers were members of the OTM directly, it was the OTM that collected the dues, that directed the whole process inside the unions. I will say that that was an error, but not one of procedure, but an historical error...

We arose in a very complicated way, and the change will take a long time. When the Production Councils arose, they organised all of the workers... From today's perspective it was an error, because all of the workers elected the Union Committee in the enterprise, when it should have been elected only by the members of that organisation...

*When you raise the question of the involvement of both members and non-members of the union equally in meetings, it makes me think of another aspect that you didn't raise, which is the insertion within the trade union process, not only of manual workers, office workers and technical staff, but of the management of the firms. Until very recently what one found was that any and all salaried worker(s) could be a member of the union. If the unions at present are now not including the Directors of the firms in their membership, why did they include them in the past?*

In a state enterprise the means of production belong to all of the workers of the firm, and the decision-makers are all of the workers. In a private firm the means of production belong to the boss. In the state enterprise the Director can never decide alone. In order to take a decision there would have to be a meeting for development of a position to be approved by the workers. But unfortunately those Directors started to analyse the question, they began to see that it's hard that way... that the management's power wasn't being felt, and that they had to have collaborators within the management, workers' representatives. That's when those "rubber stamps" that I mentioned arose — management collaborators for taking decisions, in order to avoid having meetings constantly...

In Czechoslovakia there were Workers' Councils that arose in 1968, as well as in Hungary and in Poland, where there were many experiences of independent worker organisation in a socialist society. So it's not so simple as to say that in a socialist society everyone's together, while in a capitalist society the unions and government are separate...

*The Secretary of the Union Committee was part of the management group, and even today no worker can be fired without the approval of the Union Committee. In practice, it was more or less a question of the Secretary of the Union Committee rubber-stamping the Management decision to fire workers... In principle this Secretary answered to the OTM and FRELIMO... What was the conflict which did nor did not exist, between dependence on the Party, and a possible dependence on the Management of the firm...*

The errors that appeared in the Union Committees, constitute a process that will take many years to work through; it's a question of incompatibility, and it won't be overcome from one day to the next...

We have to change rapidly, but it's hard; it's an ideological struggle that will take some time. When people raise issues, we're constrained in our answers because we were the ones who did those things, and so to break free or point out the truth is hard. But the errors that were made, we're the ones who made them...

At that time we were quite sure, but now we see that something wasn't quite right — I couldn't criticise the government; it wasn't possible. But now through those legal measures, I can criticise, and the government gave way and accepts dialogue. In the past there was no tripartite forum, no Social Concertation.[4] Why is there a Concertation now? It's because the government is feeling the pinch of the problems and the only way forward is through dialogue...

(The independent unions) were identified with the West, then with the new political parties, and called all sorts of names... But I was sure of myself (as Secretary-General of one of the three breakaway unions), because I have in my union sociologists, engineers, economists and lawyers as members. I met with all of those people, and asked them what would happen. On the basis of the law, they said that no one could do anything (as a result of our declaring ourselves independent of the OTM)... Nothing did happen, because there exists the Union Freedom Law No. 23/91...

*What has the process been, of change from a situation where the Union Committee didn't have the workers' confidence, especially in those moments of crisis, revolt, strikes...? Concretely, the change from that situation to one in which the Union Committee could act as an intermediary or negotiator...*

During the strike wave (in early 1990), the workers didn't have success because the laws of this country legitimate the Union Committees. They are the representative of the workers. So the ad hoc committees didn't have success, because the managements of the firms during that wave of agitation, didn't know what to do. They received demands through an ad hoc committee, in workplaces where a Union Committee was in existence, which shouldn't occur in terms of the law...

I remember that I was called in by the government at the time of the Maputo city transport strike. The strike wasn't being led by the Union Committee, but rather by an ad hoc committee... I told them that I had nothing to say (as Secretary-General of the union), because the people presenting the demands were an ad hoc committee, and in terms of the law that's not permitted , since there's a Union Committee there that is the representative of the workers of that firm. We were thrown out by the workers and so I couldn't say anything...

We later had to meet with the management in the firm, not with the government. We told the workers: "Look, you've seen that the entity that represents the workers in the Production Unit is the Union Committee. Now you're seeing that your strike is a wildcat strike — we can even say that it's anti-union, since they wanted to 'necklace' the Director. So this is a wildcat anti-union strike and you sent me away. You saw that you didn't have success with the government, you've seen that the Union Committee has its value. It's true that your strike is just, but it didn't follow the formulas set out in the law. You're going to have problems."

The Director had taken the position of firing all of the workers, but we reconciled with him... so that these problems didn't repeat. The strikes ought to be led by the Union Committee in the enterprise. This ad hoc committee could have presented the issues to the union, to oblige the union to lead the strike...

From what I saw, the ad hoc committees appeared precisely because the Union Committees, when they received the problems of the workers, took the workers' demands and handed them over to the Management, and the workers were called in by the Management instead of being heard by the Union Committee itself... I don't know if you can see the incompatibility here, because if I go to the Union Committee and hand over demands to it as my representative, and then it goes and complains to the boss and the boss calls me in to his office, saying that he got the list of demands and you have to explain why... The boss called people in like it was some kind of trial, in the presence of the Secretary of the Union Committee, for the worker to explain his behaviour to the Management...

## Economic forces leading to change

The economic and social reality of the country has its effects on the workers. The Economic Recovery Program,[5] to speak concretely, has its effects on the workers... The trade union organisation has to come to grips with the fact that the loaf of bread that used to cost 500 meticais, is now at 1500 meticais...

Prices went up, since the currency was devaluing almost monthly. There was also the problem of the increase in fuel prices, and an attempt to increase house rents — that is to say, all of this arrived and was felt at the same time. It was necessary to tighten one's belt. The belts were tightened to a position that still left three holes to tighten more. Those holes were used up and now it's necessary to punch more holes, but the belt itself just can't tighten any more...

That's when the demonstrations started — already in 1989 and 1990, the strikes were happening. To my mind, the strikes played a very important role, a determinant role in trying to discipline and call to attention the government itself — because from the time of independence up to that date, the word "strike" constituted a crime. The word in and of itself was prohibited — it couldn't be pronounced in any meeting or other circumstance. So when the workers suddenly rose up against any and all directions, and any and all prohibition against strikes/demonstrations, that scared the government...

On the one hand the strikes produced positive effects, and following that uprising, it was possible to have an opening-up to a new phase, which is to say, we tried to put more meat on the trade union struggle from the time of those strikes, leading to all of the efforts made to approve a strike law, which was a victory that was won from the initiative of the workers themselves... Today, we're free to organise strikes...

The government felt itself in trouble to the point of accepting direct negotiation — the so-called Social Concertation — thanks to the strikes. In order for there to be dialogue with the government, for the government to know the workers' problems up-close... The government analysed and saw that the union itself had nearly lost its power. So when strikes are led by the workers without union direction, difficult problems are bound to arise. When for example in the transport sector, they burnt cars, broke store windows and all those things — it was then that the government accepted the recognition of the unions' value, through the Social Concertation.

In January 1987, when the introduction of the PRE was announced, at first I thought that we would all be happy, from the way in which the program was announced and the measures that accompanied the announcement — an increase of 50% in salaries, which motivated the workers a lot. The sale of the majority of products was liberalised, and thus the possibility opened up to anyone who wanted to be able, for example, to buy a truckload of rice in a warehouse, and set up sales on a street-corner, whether or not they had a commercial licence... (Those who bought in South Africa or Swaziland) sought to sell at prices below those found in the shops, and often the shops didn't have the quality of articles that these people did. And as I had just received my wage increase, it was a good thing as far as I was concerned — which is to say, at first it had this impact, which reflected our limited capacity to analyse the reach of the PRE, in what it represented for the workers and for the population as a whole. But with the passage of time, the currency was devalued step by step, in line with the IMF and World Bank. Thus the belt-tightening policies began to be introduced, and those prices started to rise...

The strikes that broke out in February 1990 were provoked by economic effects of the PRE... These economic effects directly touched people's lives. The PRE aimed to reactivate the process of the economy in the country and halt inflation, to reverse the negative growth in production and productivity. It had to halt all of these counter-productive trends, but at the same time it provoked great disadvantages in people's social and financial lives...

Before, there was a situation on shop shelves of there being no products, but a certain buying power. When products appeared people had the money from their wages, but in fact there was nothing... Buying power was in fact nearly nil.

It's true that some adjustments and reforms were made, but those entities like the World Bank and the IMF, have a universal pattern for their procedures, and they weren't about to make exceptions for Mozambique... But there are specific characteristics of this Mozambique, which they ought to take into account — first, as a country in the state that it's in, severely weakened, and as well with its economic and social specificities and characteristics, etc. etc. But the PRE doesn't have this flexibility; it is carried out rigidly.

In fact when the wildcat strikes broke out, with the worker having tightened his belt down to the bone, the workers looked on the Union Committee as something that held them back, because it "mobilised" us to accept our conditions while we were in fact dying. That's when ad hoc committees arose in places that had Union Committees, because the worker was saying that the Union Committee wasn't defending him... The workers communicated amongst themselves, and started losing faith. The Union Committee was seen as ensuring that there would be no strikes to resolve their problems. So we know the history of the PRE.

The workers also question these matters — the fact that there is a group that tightens its belt and another that does not. They knew that some folks eat like it's going out of style, while others are going hungry. And the former arrive to mobilise those that are starving, to put up with their starvation, while they carry on with their eating. That's when we saw that the PRE wasn't what we thought it would be.

Those in charge of the IMF are rigid — the programme have to be carried out, whether or not people die, they have to be carried out... The strikes ought to be run in accordance with the laws of the country, but the workers' hunger knows no laws. The word "strike" doesn't follow all these formalities. The Strike Law No. 33/90 came about, but it wasn't being followed, because the logic of the PRE was otherwise. So it's obvious that the Union Committee or union got discredited...

In the conditions in which the PRE was introduced, the country was in a weakened economic situation, and the PRE allowed the country to rise out of that situation, in economic, social and political terms. But with the PRE being introduced at a time of war, all attention was turned to feeding the war in the country, to the detriment of the most vulnerable. The government introduced the PRE without there being minimal prior conditions created for it. This situation is felt up to the present day, in this period of market economy...

## Internal changes

*The changes within the OTM during a number of months following the departure of the three that formed SLIM, culminating in the OTM's Third Congress — did this process resolve the problems? Have the bases been created for trade union unity? ... Has at least part of what motivated the three to leave, been resolved? If not, what's still missing, or how are these matters going to be dealt with?*

One of the problems that was raised at that time, was the decentralisation of the dues collection system.

Everything was concentrated in the OTM — the collection of dues from the province and district level, all of which converged in the OTM, with the OTM distributing an equal share to each union... What was requested was that each union be able to collect dues from the OTM members in their sector, after which it would be up to the union to channel a percentage that would be defined, to the Central, with the union keeping the remainder to carry out its work...

The second point was to hand over the membership of the OTM to the unions in each sector, so that they would stop being direct members of the OTM and become members of each of its unions, in such a way that the union would collect the dues money itself, and with the workers as its members, would affiliate to the OTM.

The time that it took to understand this problem and deal with it, constituted a long process, and a slow one. This slowness ate away at the willingness of the union leaders to see the problem resolved — which is to say, the willingness to stay within the OTM got eaten away. The reason and need to split, grew.

Following the departure of the three unions, the decision taken was to alter the Constitution in some of its articles... The unions as such came to have financial and administrative autonomy — they came to have their own constitutions... With the relevant articles suspended, each union came to enjoy such autonomy. The members came to be members of the national unions and not of the central. With the unions now being the members of the OTM, a percentage of 25% was established for the part of the dues collected from the member, to be handed over to the OTM...

As far as I'm concerned, it's a process. The changes that are being introduced are still incomplete. Better put, we can say that we still need to introduce more changes, real changes, changes that correspond to the current phase of agitation within the union movement — changes that don't need to satisfy the independents, nor those that are in the OTM; they don't need to satisfy the President, nor anyone else. They need to satisfy and defend the objectives of the organisation!

## Challenges for the Mozambican trade union structures

The current Mozambican trade union structures share most of the challenges faced by trade unionism elsewhere in the continent, as regards representation of workers in an unfriendly economic environment and in the face of the neo-liberal onslaught. However, they also face additional challenges that arise from their particular history. Unlike elsewhere in Africa (with the partial exception of the other former Portuguese colonies), the current unions were neither a force in the liberation struggle (black unions did not exist), nor have they been a factor as such in the recent democratisation process. They were the creation of the party in power, to mobilise and discipline workers and deliver social services; they were a 'transmission belt' built for this purpose, not 'domesticated' to do so on the basis of a previous history. And in the current period, they have been in a position of reacting as one of the structures of the establishment, to spontaneous revolts amongst the workers and urban poor. The OTM declared itself independent of the Party-state, only following the decision of this Party-state (at the same time as the other 'mass democratic organisations of that party did so). The three unions that left the OTM and provoked organisational changes within it, did so once a law had been passed saying that they could (in December 1991). 'Democratisation' is essentially an external element that has acted upon the unions, and not the reverse.

The unions were not semi-autonomous bodies seeking a 'margin of manoeuvre' allowing them to maintain a minimum of credibility amongst the workers; the credibility that they had, was precisely equivalent to the credibility that the ruling party had. With the loss of that credibility by the ruling party, and its radical change in programmatic style, the trade unions are left with a major problem if they wish to be representative of the workers. They need to pose in very concrete terms, the question of when and how they organised the workers in whose name they speak. And regardless of the answer that they provide, they need to go back to those workers, workplace by workplace, seeking a (continued) mandate. To the extent that they assume that tradition and law guarantee that they are the representatives of the workers, they will be incapable of really acting as such.

The question here can be posed in other terms. Elsewhere in Africa, even in the period of closest control of the trade unions by the party-state, the "base" maintained some autonomy, and was a permanent force to question the incorporation of the unions into the state. In Mozambique this pressure as such has not been felt — ie, as pressure from a base within an organisation. What has been felt more, is the unorganised pressure of the mass of workers, whether members or not of the unions. All of the questions of organising, representing and negotiating on behalf of specific groups of workers, remain as future challenges for the unions — not as an obligation that arises from government-initiated change in the laws (regarding collective bargaining, union freedom and strikes, in 1990-91), but as a fundamental element of their existence.

The Mozambican trade unions have been struggling since 1990 to come to grips with what are essentially internal questions. These are in part exemplified by the issues that led to the three ('SLIM') leaving the OTM. But other issues remain, having to do with division of powers within the structures, and with the heavy load of functionaries that continues to be carried. A large part of this load continues to be paid for by a state subsidy. The challenge faced in this area, is that if the unions don't soon direct their attentions to the real external challenges, they could suddenly find themselves irrelevant and/or non-existent. In other words, organise or die.

*So far, the emphasis in worker representation and negotiation has been at the national, tripartite level, through the Social Concertation. What is the real bargaining power that the unions bring to this forum? Is it enough to say that the government has provided a means for worker input, if the workers' representatives go there with no prior basis of serious local- or sector-level bargaining?*

In the cases where local collective bargaining does take place, it usually provides little more than what is already in the law; most workers continue to earn the state-determined minimum wage of 19 USD per month. When strikes happen, they are, almost without exception, seen as a route which is alternative to that of collective bargaining (once the latter has 'failed'), rather than as an inherent part of the process. They continue to be led in most cases, by 'ad hoc committees' which are able to organise the anger of the workers, but lack experience in negotiating agreements.

It is very questionable if we can consider the structures that were mounted by the ruling party after independence, to be worker unions. My own view is that they were rather instruments of corporatist representation. Given the history of the country, this was perhaps inevitable.

After more than 20 years of independence, including over 15 years of civil war and other disasters, Mozambique is now enjoying a relatively stable period, with an elected government and the beginnings of democracy and the rule of law in various areas. At the same time, its economy is virtually non-existent, it is still hugely dependent on the foreign aid industry, and it is open to all sorts of 'free market' projects. Starting from the nationalist sentiment of Mozambican workers with their specific sufferings under colonialism, and passing through the political struggle for independence and a self-declared socialist project following independence, trade unionism in Mozambique is now in a position — perhaps for the first time in history — of being obliged to address itself to direct representation of workers. If it succeeds, this may be in itself a significant and lasting contribution to democracy in this country.

## Notes

1   Very little has been written on the modern trade union situation in Mozambique. This situation, combined with a desire to allow Mozambican trade unionists to speak in the first person, led to the format of the present chapter being the transcription of a collective interview, rather than an analysis based on written sources and statistics. On the trade unions in Mozambique prior to the Portuguese New State, see Jose Capela, "O Movimento Operario em Lourenco Marques, 1898-1927" (Porto, 1981). On labour conditions under colonialism, including migrant labour in South African mines, plantation labour and forced labour, see various articles in the journal of the Centro de Estudos Africanos ("Estudos Mocambicanos") published in the 1980s, including by Jeanne Penvenne, as well as her book "African Workers and Colonial Racism" (Portsmouth, Heinemann, 1995). The FRELIMO project is reviewed critically but supportively by various works in English, including "Mozambique: the Revolution Under Fire" by Joe Hanlon (London, Zed Books, 1984) and "Mozambique: a Dream Undone" by Bertil Egero (Uppsala, Scandinavian Institute of African Studies, 1987). For the creation of

FRELIMO's trade union structures, see published speeches and directives of the period, including "Discurso do Camarada Presidente Samora Moises Machel Dirigido a Classe Operaria do Pais, em 13 de Outubro de 1976", and the observations of Peter Sketchley, including in "Casting New Molds. First Steps Toward Worker Control in a Mozambique Steel Factory" (San Francisco, IFDP, 1980; with Frances Moore Lappe). A more analytical approach is taken by Michel Cahen; in relation to FRELIMO's project, see "Mozambique - La Revolution Implosee" (Paris, L'Harmattan, 1987), where he argues that social relations in production were not significantly changed by independence. His treatment of Portuguese corporatism in Mozambique, through the example of SNECI (first and largest corporatist structure for white and 'assimilated' workers), and brief reference to the post-independence structures, is a useful point of departure for applying the corporatist problematic to Mozambique. See "Corporatisme et colonialisme - Approche du cas mozambicain, 1933-1979", in Cahiers d'Etudes africaines, 92, XXIII-4, 1983, pp. 383-417, and 93, XXIV-1, 1984, pp. 5-24.

2    Women's organisation and youth organisation, originally created as 'mass democratic organisations' by FRELIMO.

3    Arbitrary forced removal of so-called "unproductive elements", including unemployed people and single women, from the cities to the remote province of Niassa in 1983.

4    A national-level tripartite forum which has concentrated on the minimum wage, the prices of staple consumer items, and other economic questions.

5    PRE: Mozambique's structural adjustment program, initiated in 1986.

# 12 Sudan
# What Future?

EL-KHIDER ALI MUSA

*As far as democratisation is concerned, Sudan and the rest of Africa are moving in opposite directions. Between 1985 and 1989, the trade union movement contributed much to democratic life, but now it is having to adapt - ironically - to one-party government. These days, traditional political parties and trade unions have to go into exile to work for the re-establishment of a pluralist democracy. Inside the country, the trade union movement is in ruins and fighting for its very survival.*

## Background

Generally speaking, the trade union movement has played a significant role in the social, political and economic development of Africa (Michael, 1988). Colonialism, with its racial discrimination, the expropriation of peasants' land and the introduction of forced labour, compelled workers and peasants to come together and demand their land, fair wages and subsequently political independence. Historically, therefore, trade unions in Africa came into existence during the colonial era, and they were stimulated by campaigns for political independence, spontaneous labour conflicts and the actions of colonial administrations. In Sudan, for instance, trade unions have played a key role in the struggle for political independence (Musa and Khaliel, 1989, Malik, 1988).

Following independence, national governments expected trade unions to play a dual role that involved helping with overall economic development and representing the interests of their membership (Michael, 1988). Trade unions in Africa lived up to these expectations to a greater or lesser extent, and have continued to play this important role since independence. During the mid 1980s and early 1990s, however, many African countries, including Sudan, underwent many changes, which were predominantly imposed from outside, on the political and economic fronts. African politics have been characterised by the shift from one-party rule to multi-partyism. On the economic front, many African countries have implemented structural adjustment programmes (SAPs), which were also imposed by the

273

international aid donors and financial institutions such as the World Bank and the International Monetary Fund (IMF).

These political and economic changes have far-reaching implications for trade unionism in Africa. Because of their key role in the political and economic development of many African countries, trade unions have responded in different ways, and to varying degrees, to the challenges posed by these changes.

In all these respects, trade unionism in Sudan is no exception. The trade union movement was hard hit by the effects of SAP, protracted drought and civil war and, together with the political parties, had no alternative but to take to the streets and go on strike; this culminated in the overthrow of the Nimeiri regime in April 1985. In the ensuing four years, the trade unions and political parties made concentrated efforts, with little success, to rebuild the economy and sustain both political and industrial democracy. In June 1989, a military coup halted the multi-party democratic process and stepped up the structural adjustment policies. (For more details see following Sections).

During the 1990s, the trade unions in Sudan have been involved in these changes to a limited extent. They strove to come to terms with the new realities and a new era of 'accommodation' commenced, and they took a large number of political and economic initiatives to mitigate the impact of these changes. The nature of these changes and challenges, the involvement of trade unions therein and the response of the trade unions thereto is the focus of this chapter. Additional emphasis is placed on more recent events in the 1990s.

To this end, the chapter uses two sources of information. The first comprises direct interviews with former and incumbent senior officials of the trade union movement; the second is document analysis. Accordingly, a number of documents, including newspapers and other publications, will be investigated and critically analyzed. This will be supplemented by the author's personal opinions and comments.

## Trade unions and democracy

The trade union movement in Sudan, led by the Sudan Workers' Trade Unions Federation (SWTUF), has played a generally active role in the political life of Sudan. Back in the 1940s, led by political elites, the SWTUF became one of the main forces for Sudan liberation as it opposed colonialism until independence was achieved in January 1956. Thereafter, the SWTUF continued its role in political life during the time of the military and civilian governments. Government-trade union relations after independence were characterised by significant state interventionism (Musa, 1992). All governments made continuous attempts to control the trade unions either through detailed Labour Laws or even by incorporating them as part of the sole legal party. Another characteristic feature of government-trade union relations was the unions' 'accommodation and conformation' policies with the various civilian and military governments. During the first military government, the SWTUF played a key role in the overthrow of the Abboud government through civil disobedience in October 1964. Since then, the SWTUF has continued to play a pivotal role in the restoration of democracy. For practical reasons we will discuss the role of the SWTUF in Sudan's political life during the mid-1980s.

The SWTUF's efforts to restore and sustain multi-party democracy in Sudan continued when a new military government seized power in May 1969. Although it did not try to incorporate trade unions into a comprehensive political structure, the regime which came to power through a pro-communist military coup established an alliance with the trade union movement, which was itself dominated by communists (El-Jack and Leggett, 1980). During the first two years of the government-labour alliance, preparations were made to recognise trade union structures and for labour legislation which considerably differed from British-style legislation. However, the government-trade union alliance did not last for long, and the failure of another communist military coup in July 1971 brought the alliance to an end and resulted in a purge of labour and other pro-communist leaders.

During the period 1978-85, during which Sudan implemented a SAP for the first time, there was high inflation and workers' standards of living deteriorated rapidly. There was also continuous conflict between the government and the trade unions. The government tried to appease the trade union movement by enabling workers to have more participation at the national and enterprise levels. At the national level, workers were represented in one ruling party, the Sudanese Socialist Union, and in the legislature - the People's Assembly. At enterprise level, under the terms of the Public Corporations Act of 1976, workers were for the first time represented by a member of the board of directors of their public enterprises (PEs); this law was later abolished. Workers' representation continued, but the trade union movement joined the pro-multi-party democracy movement and took part in a general strike; this resulted in the overthrow of the Nimeiri regime in April 1985.

Following the popular uprising in April 1985, a conservative government of traditional parties assumed power during the period 1986-1989. The trade unions' demand for wage increases was the main source of conflict with the government. The period saw increasing industrial unrest and 'going on strike' was quite fashionable. At a later stage during this period, the government directed its efforts towards involving trade unions in national decision-making through a social contract. The proposed arrangements of this social contract required trade unions to restrain their industrial power, industrial actions and wage demands in exchange for a greater role in public policy-making, guarantees of a measure of protection and the adoption of sound public policies that benefited working people in general. Employers, on the other hand, gained a respite from union wage pressures as well as the expectation of increased productivity. The government as policy-maker hoped to create more employment opportunities, optimise the utilisation of employees, adopt sound economic policies with a view to controlling prices and make essential commodities available. Before this social contract was put into effect, the government was overthrown by a military coup in June 1989. Although the trade union movement continued to be autonomous and free during this period, political parties still tried to control its activities. In some cases, political parties attempted to penetrate the SWTUF and politicise its position on certain political and economic issues.

Unlike the situation in many African countries, which moved from a one-party system to multi-party democracy in the 1990s, the situation in Sudan is quite the reverse. A military coup in June 1989 brought in a new government which was very much in favour of the one-party system. When the new government assumed power, trade unions were very active and 'going on strike' was once again fashionable. It was no wonder, therefore, that the new government made serious attempts to control the trade union movement. Immediately after the military coup, the new government suspended political parties and trade unions. Trade union committees of officials, professionals and teachers were dissolved and, pending the enactment of new trade union laws, later replaced by government-appointed steering committees. A few weeks later, the SWTUF, the biggest and most powerful federation, was allowed to resume its normal business. The SWTUF's elected trade union committees were allowed to continue as preparatory committees, pending formation of new trade unions.

The government's efforts to regulate the trade union activities continued. In July 1990, the political committee of the Revolutionary Command Council, the military body then governing the country, organised a Trade Union Dialogue Conference in which trade unions, the employers' association and the government took part. The conference ended up with significant recommendations which later shaped the structure, objectives and participation of trade unions in Sudan. The most important of these was the unification of the trade union movement (Trade Union Dialogue Conference, 1990). The four trade union federations were amalgamated in one national centre, the Sudan Workers' Trade Unions Federation (SWTUF). Whether this unification was internally inspired or externally imposed by the government is still a controversial matter. Proponents of unification argue that unification was a trade union demand for a long time. Critics of the unification, on the other hand, contend that while unification is an old trade union demand, it was imposed by the government to facilitate control of trade unions. They argue it is only workers at the grassroots level, and not the conferees or the government-appointed steering committees, who can decide on the unification of the trade union movement or otherwise.

Following this, the then Political Committee of the Revolution Command Council, which used to supervise trade unions, formed a Higher Council for the Trade Union Federations to implement the recommendation of the Trade Union Dialogue Conference. The Trade Union Act 1992 was then passed to guide the formation of trade unions in their new structure. The Act emphasised the freedom of association and the formation of trade unions through fair and free elections, outlined the election procedure and guaranteed protection for trade unionists (Bakhiet, 1992). In practical terms, however, trade union committees were chosen by consensus. This procedure involves nomination of candidates by existing government-appointed steering committees and ratification through signatures by workers at grassroots (i.e. workplace) level. There were neither clear criteria nor manifesto for the selection process. The procedure was justified on the basis of creating harmony and stabilizing the trade union movement to help the country achieve overall political stability. Critics of the procedure argue that there were neither free nor fair elections. Internationally, Sudan is seen as an African country that 'does not allow for the full development of trade unions and where trade unions formed under the 1992 Act are no more than "Puppet Unions"' (Free Labour World, 1993).

Once the trade union committees at the sub-sectional, trade union and general trade union levels were formed, the Revolutionary Command Council issued a decree dissolving the SWTUF's Preparatory Committees (including the three main officers), and the General Congress was held to elect the unified SWTUF's executive committee for the term 1993-97 (SWTUF's documents, 1993). The meeting was attended by representatives of the Organisation of African Trade Union Unity (OATUU), the International Confederation of Arab Trade Unions (ICATU), the Arab Labour Organisation (ALO) and a number of national centres from Arab and friendly countries. In the General Congress, the three officers, that is to say the Chairman, General Secretary and Treasurer, as well as the SWTUF's Executive Committee, were chosen by consensus.

Judged by the industrial stability which the country has enjoyed since June 1989, it can be argued that the national centre, the SWTUF, is on good terms with the government. Although the right to go on strike was secured under the Industrial Relations Act 1976, it has never been exercised despite the hardships caused by the government's structural adjustment policies. The reasons for this are two-fold: firstly, the recommendations of the Trade Union Dialogue Conference considered the 'right to strike' to be sabotage, and this discouraged workers from going on strike; secondly, a senior SWTUF official justified it on the grounds they fully supported the government's national goals. This sacrifice is seen as essential to the realisation of political stability, economic development and social justice. The official emphasised the SWTUF's autonomy and described its relationship with the government as 'independent and participatory'. In other words, the relationship amounted to an alliance. Critics, however, argued that internal trade union democracy was undermined and that the SWTUF was 'reduced to a government tool which was imposed on workers' (El-Soudani International, 1994). Whatever government-trade union relations may have been, the political changes of the 1990s had far-reaching implications for trade unions and participation in Sudan. This is the focus of the next section.

On the other hand, the political changes of the 1990s had significant implications for trade unions. For example, the Nimeiri military regime had taken pragmatic steps to involve workers in the decision-making process both at the national and enterprise levels. It seems that the move was designed to serve two purposes: firstly, to appease trade unions, and secondly, to recognise the important role which trade unions have played, and are still playing, in the country's economic, social and political development. Thus at national level, trade unions have participated in all the conferences organised by the government to tackle various political, social and economic issues, and trade unions have been represented in the legislature, the Transitional National Assembly (TNA). The SWTUF is also a permanent member of certain national bodies. These include:
- National Council for Wages;
- The Governing Body of the National Fund for Social Insurance;
- The Governing Body of the Public Corporation for Workers' Education;
- National Fund for Pensions;
- The Engineering Council;
- National Committee for Labour Standards;
- The Higher Committee for the Divestiture (Privatisation) of Public Enterprises.

At the enterprise level, the government has been enthusiastic about having workers represented on the board of directors of public enterprises and corporations. One of the recommendations of the Trade Union Dialogue Conference emphasised this new role for workers, as they are perceived as active partners in the production process. The SWTUF and its affiliates are members of a number of boards of directors of public corporations and enterprises (SWTUF documents, 1993).

Whether workers' participation at enterprise and national levels has been effective or not is questionable. At national level, it is very difficult to see how workers actually participate in the decision-making process. Workers as representatives are always in the minority in all the above-mentioned national bodies. Moreover, most of the resolutions of these conferences and national bodies are no more than recommendations which can be accepted or rejected by the Executive. Their role is therefore only advisory. Likewise, workers' representation on board of directors has suffered serious limitations at enterprise level. Firstly, workers are represented by only one member; furthermore, it is up to the management of the public enterprise, rather than the workers, to select the workers' representative. Secondly, there is no legal backing for this representation; it has only been introduced in the public sector in light of recommendation of the Trade Union Dialogue Conference, and many public enterprises are under no legal obligation to give workers representation on their boards. Thirdly, workers' representation in the boards of PEs has been undermined by the privatisation process currently sweeping the country. Legally, once PEs are privatised, workers have neither the right to be represented on the board of directors nor access to information. The Company Ordinance of 1925 (currently being amended) provides that only shareholders have the right to sit on the board and access to information in the private sector. According to a senior SWTUF official, the SWTUF is now endeavouring to change these provisions in the new Company's Act (currently being drafted) to facilitate workers' representation.

A positive development in the development of workers' participation in Sudan was the convening of the first national policy workshop on workers' participation in October 1990. During this workshop, the SWTUF for the first time debated ways and means of fostering effective and meaningful workers' participation. The workshop made concrete recommendations on the objectives, structure and modalities of workers' participation in Sudan (SWTUF, October 1990). The planned follow-up including a vast programme of education and research did not take place, as external financial support was withheld in view of the changed trade union situation.

Finally, to conclude this section on trade unions and democracy, a few words on the role of the trade union movement in the democratisation process in Sudan in the 1990s. In this context, one has to reiterate the unique position of Sudan, which has experienced a complete cycle of military and democratic governments. Since June 30 1989, political parties in Sudan have been officially banned indefinitely and the one-party system, now called the National Congress, has been adopted. It is therefore not possible to talk about an official democratic process at present. It would be wrong, however, to conclude that the traditional political parties and forces have abandoned their efforts to restore multi-party democracy. The traditional political parties and an underground trade union movement are active in exile to restore multi-party democracy in the country. They have now regrouped under the umbrella of the National Democratic Alliance (NDA). In June 1995, the NDA convened a conference in Asmara, Eritrea entitled 'Conference on the Fundamental Issues of the Nation'. The return to multi-party democracy and an end to civil war in the South were high on the agenda and the final communique of the NDA conference (Eritrea Profile, July 1995).

## Trade unions and the institutionalisation of democracy

As has already been mentioned, the present government's official policy is opposed to the Western type of multi-party democracy. Apart from the role of the underground trade union movement in the restoration of democracy, it is therefore not possible to speak of the role of the trade unions in the institutionalisation of the multi-party democracy in the country. However, this does not mean that the trade unions have made no attempt to sustain multi-party democracy in the country in the past. Following their active role in the overthrow of the Nimeiri regime and the restoration of multi-party democracy in April 1985, trade unions and political parties have tried hard to sustain the fragile democracy. For example, in 1987, political parties and trade unions agreed and signed the 'Charter for the Defence of Democracy'. The SWTUF was one of the signatories to this Charter. One of the Charter's provisions stipulates that all the signatories will automatically go on indefinite strike once a military coup takes place, and until democracy is restored. On the basis of experience, trade unions and political parties see strikes as the most effective weapon to bring down military governments. This threat, however, was not carried out on June 30 1989 when a military coup toppled the democratically elected government. Nor has it been carried out more recently because of government control over trade unions.

And so, although the democratisation process swept across many African countries in the late 1980s and the early 1990s, Sudan seems to have swum against the current. This is illustrated in the country's political history and development. Back in the 1940s, and at the time of independence in January 1956, Sudan adopted multi-party democracy as a system of governance. Unfortunately, that fragile democracy lasted for only two years. In 1958, the first military coup took place and ruled the country for another six years. In October 1964, the alliance of trade unions and traditional political parties restored multi-party democracy in a popular revolution. Again, that experience proved to be short-lived. Another military coup seized power in May 1969 and ruled the country for another sixteen years. Once again, it was a popular uprising that brought down the military regime in April 1985. Multi-party democracy was once more established in the country but again, this experience did not last long. A military coup took over and ended the three-year fragile democracy of the traditional parties.

This historical background to the political development of Sudan suggests one thing: that Sudan, unlike most other African countries, started the democratisation process only recently and has been caught in a vicious circle for over half a century. Many factors have contributed to this long history of political instability, and the most important have been the long civil war in the South and the deteriorating economic conditions. In my opinion, the necessary conditions for sustainable multi-party democracy in Sudan are the creation of democratic institutions (such as a permanent constitution and an independent judiciary), democratisation of the traditional political parties themselves (some of them are established on an ethnic basis and lack democracy), a peaceful solution to the civil war in the South, and reformation of the military establishment (always seen as a threat for democracy).

As for the promotion and institutionalisation of industrial democracy (i.e. workers' participation), the trade union movement has made concerted efforts during the 1990s with help from the government. At national level, the SWTUF leadership is represented on many national councils that have been established to tackle various political, social and economic issues. The SWTUF is also represented in the government-appointed parliament (the Transitional National Assembly). At enterprise level, the SWTUF has campaigned hard to institutionalise workers' participation in the public sector and has made sure it had legal status in the private sector in the wake of the current privatisation wave. Despite these efforts, plenty remains to be done by the trade union movement to make workers' participation more effective, meaningful and sustainable. Nonetheless, much has been achieved given the fact that the trade union movement has to fight on another front, the economic front, to enhance the national interest and its members' interests. This is the focus of the next section.

## Trade unions and the economy

Various Sudanese governments have followed the SAP strategy recommended by the World Bank very closely since 1978. Structural Adjustment Policies have been continued more aggressively under the present government within the framework of Sudan's Structural Adjustment and the Three-Year Economic Salvation Programme (1990-93) - ironically, this time without consultation with, or pressure from, the IMF or World Bank (Sudanow, 1992). However, they were certainly designed to appease the international donor community and financial institutions. The two main ingredients of SAPs are price liberalisation and privatisation. In the following paragraphs we will discuss the implications of each for workers, workers' participation and the response of the trade union movement. Because of the poor performance of the economy, the protracted civil war in the South and the IMF's declaration of Sudan as a non-cooperative country, the present government had no alternative but to adjust. The adjustment policies were adopted by the then Economic Committee of the Revolutionary Command Council, and they were later supported by a national conference at which workers were represented.

Price liberalisation meant abolition of price controls on almost all locally produced and imported commodities. These policies were misunderstood to mean a free hand to charge higher prices. In fact, they resulted in what can only be called price anarchy (El-Soudan El-Hadieth, February 1996). Prices sky-rocketed as a result. This brought much hardship to workers. Because of low salaries, workers could not make ends meet, their standard of living fell sharply and minimum wages were not enough to pay for 25% of the monthly cost of living (El-Soudani International, 1994). Although the National Council for Wages, on which workers are represented, reviews salaries every six months, salary increases do not match inflation, which continues to rise, and the gap between the cost of living and salaries is widening day by day.

Despite these hardships, the SWTUF did not oppose the price liberalisation policies; some critics argue that this is because it is government-appointed (El-Soudan El-Hadieth, February 1996). Instead, the SWTUF Chairman called on the government to review the effects of SAP on the working class, and to subsidise workers through basic commodities. This initiative, however, was not successful because the government was unable, according to the SWTUF Chairman, to raise the necessary finance (El-Soudan El-Hadieth, February 1996). Yet another response to these hardships is the establishment of more workers' economic institutions. The SWTUF has now established the Workers' National Bank, the Workers' Central Cooperative Corporation, and the Workers' Economic Corporation. The SWTUF has also decided, with very limited success, to buy public enterprises that were on sale. While these economic institutions have eased these hardships somewhat, the working class is yet hard hit by the price liberalisation policies.

The second element of SAP, which has far-reaching effects on workers and workers' participation, is privatisation. The debate on privatisation and measures adopted in Sudan were fuelled by the same factors as in other developing countries (Musa, 1995). The government started the privatisation programme in the early 1980s against a background of an acute public finance crisis, but very few PEs were in fact privatised. The privatisation plan was slowed down for several reasons including the fact that the trade unions, which were then very strong, publicly opposed the government privatisation plans for fear of the job losses that would follow a takeover by the private sector.

The present government pursued the privatisation policy as a major feature of the Three-Year Economic Salvation Programme (1990-1993) and the Ten-Year National Strategy (1992-2002). The Programme's major objective is to attach high importance to the role of the private sector (whether domestic or foreign) as 'an engine of growth'. To implement this programme, the government created the necessary institutional and legal frameworks, and in August 1990 published the Divestiture of Public Enterprises Act. The Act established the High Committee for the Divestiture of Public Enterprises, which was chaired by the Federal Minister of Finance himself. The committee consists of representatives of the various government ministries, the employers' association and the trade unions. The committee is empowered to privatise target enterprises through the transfer of all or some of shares to the private sector (domestic or foreign), by leasing or even by final liquidation (Musa, 1992). All in all, about 140 PEs have been earmarked for privatisation. Of these, only 13 have been privatised to date, either through full/partial sale or lease. The slow progress of the privatisation operations in the 1990s is attributable to many problems other than the opposition of the trade union movement (Musa, 1995). Opposition by the trade unions to privatisation during this period is weak due to the regulation of the trade unions in the 1990s. However, the privatisation process in Sudan, though slow, has far-reaching implications for workers' participation and the social impact is also negative.

In short, if the existing privatisation trend in Sudan continues during the 1990s, however slowly, PEs may become dinosaurs and workers' participation may suffer the same fate. This discussion has shown how workers' participation is mainly introduced in the public enterprise sector. It follows that the disappearance of PEs means the disappearance of workers' participation. As Kester (1994) concludes, the future of workers' participation in Sudan, as in many other African countries, is therefore very bleak. This is because 'Structural adjustment makes for an overhaul of ownership structures in Africa. Where workers' participation is not legalised, it is defenceless'.

The trade union movement is Sudan, however, is endeavouring to ease this impact. As has already been already mentioned, the SWTUF is trying hard to formalise workers' participation, legalise it and introduce it in the private sector.

Moreover, the SWTUF has tried, though unsuccessfully, to take advantage of the privatisation policy and introduce workers' participation into the ownership of privatised public enterprises. The reasons for this are twofold: firstly, workers either do not have the money to invest, or else they are reluctant to take risks and invest their meagre resources in the mostly loss-making public enterprises (Musa, 1994); secondly, against a backdrop of an acute public finance crisis and the need for sale proceeds to finance the budget deficit, the sale of public enterprises to the management or the workforce is not seen as a means of promoting privatisation in Sudan.

Besides, privatisation has resulted in mass retrenchment among the workers of public enterprises. Though there is no statistics on the exact number of lay-offs, it is certain that thousand of workers have been retrenched as a consequence of the privatisation activities (El-Soudani International, 1994). The Chairman of the SWTUF has acknowledged recently that privatisation has made the unemployment problem in Sudan worse (El-Soudan El-Hadieth, February 1996). The problem is further complicated by the lack of training for the retrenched workers and the lack of prospects for redeployment.

In conclusion, the SWTUF has come to realise the negative effects that economic changes (i.e. the SAP) of the 1990s have had on workers. Though it stopped short of opposing these policies, the SWTUF leadership has called for their review and for the involvement of workers in these decisions. In this respect, the recommendations of the SWTUF's General Congress of 1993 called for an 'easing [of] the negative side-effects of Structural Adjustment Programmes and involving workers' trade unions and the SWTUF in decisions on the future of public enterprises and protecting workers against lay-offs and promoting self-management in some public enterprises' (SWTUF document, 1993).

## Summary

This chapter discusses the involvement of the trade union movement in the political and economic developments of the 1990s. The chapter also discusses the response of trade unions to political and economic changes in Sudan in the late 1980s and the 1990s. In the political arena, the trade union movement has adopted tactics of 'accommodation and confrontation' according to the circumstances. On the economic front, trade unions have been hard hit by the SAP: a rising cost of living, mass retrenchment, disappearance of participatory structures, and loss of membership, dues and hence power base. In view of this, it is likely that trade unions will spend most of their resources on the struggle for survival.

# 13 Tanzania
## A People in Distress

Samuel Chambua

*Tanzanian trade unions were under political tutelage during three decades of centralisation and political control. Despite the process of democratisation that got under way they are still weak but on the move to gain momentum and autonomy. The country is in the grip of a major economic crisis that various Structural Adjustment Programmes have been unable to resolve. Economic performance has improved slightly, but it is the ordinary Tanzanian people who have had to pay.*

## Introduction

Trade unions in Tanzania played a positive role in the struggle against the colonial system. They were also active in the struggle not only for better working conditions but also for the promotion of industrial democracy through various forms of workers' participation. However, soon after gaining political independence, the new post-colonial state used a variety of various pretexts to remove the autonomy of trade unions, and as a result they fell under the control of the state or the ruling political party or both. Indeed, as was the case with many African countries, many previously autonomous organisations in the country were compelled to lose their autonomy and were placed under the direct control of the state and/or the (sole) ruling party.However, from the mid-1980s onwards, many governments in Africa were compelled both by internal and by external forces to adopt political pluralism; this implied, *inter alia*, adoption of the multi-party political system, the separation of Party and State and freedom for Trade unions from control by the ruling and /or any other political party. The focus of this chapter, therefore, is on the following: the new socio-political and economic situation; the interaction of trade unions with the political and economic environment; and participatory reality in Tanzania.[1]

The chapter is divided into four major themes: i) The Social, Political and Economic Context; ii) Trade Unions and Democracy; iii) Trade Unions, Democracy and Economy; iv) Institutionalisation of Democracy.

## The social, political and economic context

'...... no people will ever release its creative capacity for productivity and development without real participation in the democratic process designed to promote development and self-reliance.' (Chambua, 1991: 195)

Tanzania (then Tanganyika) attained political independence from Britain on 9 December 1961. The Tanzanian trade union movement, which took an active role in the struggle against colonialism, started to lose its autonomy as early as 1962. In that year an Act of Parliament was passed which, among other things, authorised the Minister for Labour to declare any federation a 'designated federation' to which all labour unions in the country had to affiliate.[2] Against strong opposition, the Tanganyika Federation of Labour (TFL) was designated the sole federation which every trade union had to affiliate to and consult before taking any industrial action. The General Secretary of the TFL was brought into the Cabinet as Minister for Labour and the TFL itself had to act in accordance with the directives of the Minister for Labour and of the Registrar of Trade Unions (Coulson, 1982: 39 - 40).

The final blow to the autonomy of the trade union movement came in 1964 when a sense of mistrust developed between the TFL and the government following the army mutiny of January 1964. In February of that year, the Government enacted the National Union of Tanganyika Workers (Establishment) Act (No. 18 of 1964) which disbanded and outlawed all labour unions, dissolved the TFL, and established in its place a single union, the National Union of Tanganyika Workers (NUTA) (Rutinwa, 1995: 6-7). The union was compelled to affiliate to, and promote, the activities of the ruling party (the Tanganyika African National Union - TANU). Its top executives: the General Secretary and Deputy General Secretary were to become Presidential Appointees; in turn, the General Secretary (who was also the Minister for Labour) appointed all other key officers: nine Assistant General Secretaries of the industrial divisions; the Financial Secretary; and Directors of Organisation, Research and Economics. The NUTA was denied the powers to dissolve itself. 'This power was reserved for the President of Tanzania who could, at any time, dissolve NUTA and establish another body which would be deemed to be a trade union (ibid: 7).

NUTA was therefore a creature of the TANU government and one of its objectives was "to promote the policies of TANU and to encourage its members to join TANU (Pratt, 1976: 189).

Similarly in Zanzibar (which united with Tanganyika to form the United Republic of Tanzania on 26 April 1964), the Zanzibar and Pemba Federation of Labour was replaced by the Federation of Revolutionary Trade Unions

(FRTU); this was formed soon after the January 1964 revolution which brought the Afro-Shiraz Party (ASP) to power. FRTU was formed and controlled by ASP, the sole political/ruling party in Zanzibar. FRT was dissolved in 1966 and its activities were taken over by the Workers' Department of the ASP.

In 1965 Tanzania was officially declared a one-party state, but there were two political parties: TANU (for the Mainland/Tanganyika) and ASP for Zanzibar. Early in 1967, Tanzania adopted the policy of socialism and self-reliance which implied, *inter alia*, state control of the major means of production. On the political scene, constitutional amendments in the 1970s led to the merger of TANU and Afro- Shiraz to form one political party (Chama cha Mapinduzi - CCM) for the United Republic of Tanzania in 1977.

The CCM came with the policy of Party Supremacy, meaning that the Party was above the government and the latter had to receive orders/directives from the former. Thus, the Party became very powerful and all leaders of public institutions (village governments, schools, hospitals, public enterprises, etc.) had to be CCM members. As for the armed forces, all of its employees had to be members of the CCM as from 1964 following the army mutiny. Even applications to higher learning institutions had to be channelled through the applicants' local CCM branch for comments before they were sent to the particular higher institution for consideration. In short, the Party and its government abhorred any opposition. Thus, in the same year (1977) people's mass organisations were brought under the CCM's control and leadership; in other words, they were made the CCM's mass organisations and had no separate constitution of their own except that of the CCM. These included: NUTA, Union of Women in Tanzania (UWT), Cooperative Union of Tanzania (USHIRIKA), Tanzania Parents Association (WAZAZI) and VIJANA (National Youth Association) (Fashoyin, 1986: 174).

The above political changes prompted the need for a trade union which would cater for the entire republic. So in 1979, an Act of Parliament was passed to repeal the NUTA Act and replace it with the Jumuiya ya Wafanyakazi wa Tanzania (JUWATA) Act. The Act disestablished NUTA and established JUWATA as the sole trade union for the entire republic. JUWATA also became one of the CCM's mass organisations which dealt with workers. The objectives of JUWATA were similar to those of NUTA. The only differences were that JUWATA extended to cover Zanzibar, which was initially not covered by NUTA and NUTA had its own constitution while JUWATA operated under the CCM's constitution. The General Secretary of JUWATA and his/her two Deputies (one for the Mainland and the second for Zanzibar) were appointees of the Party President (who was also the President of Tanzania) while all of its chief regional and district executives had to be screened and appointed by the National Executive

Committee of the CCM. The tradition of appointing the Minister for Labour to be the General Secretary of the trade union as well continued. Thus, the first General Secretary of JUWATA was also the Minister for Labour. The so-called workers union was therefore more or less a department of the ruling party. This tactic might have been borrowed from Zanzibar where the workers' union was dissolved in 1966 and its activities placed under the Workers' Department of the ruling party there, the ASP.

As a result of the above developments, by the end of the 1970s the country's economy was highly state-controlled and characterised by monopolistic and heavily regulated production structures in all sectors. Political monopoly had engendered economic monopolies and therefore an inflexible economic system.

Thus, at the end of 1980s the trade union movement in Tanzania was under the control of the ruling and sole political party, the CCM. But the country was in a deep socio-economic crisis which started at the end of 1970s and became very severe from 1980 to 1985 (Table 1). This included economic stagnation, a decline in per capita income which lasted for almost a decade, a balance of payments crisis, shortages of food and manufactured products due to poor performance of both the industrial and agricultural sectors leading to scarcity of foreign currency. There was also corruption, a rise in the crime rate, silent and open opposition to some government/party policies (e.g. the single-party political system, state control of the economy and party supremacy over the Government) although it was difficult at that time to separate the two, i.e. 'state' and 'party'. Some people even started to question the official ideology of socialism. This was a period of empty shops and long queues for virtually everything, as the Government threw its efforts into fighting a war against what it called economic saboteurs; these were mainly people hoarding/hiding things to sell to those who needed them (and many people needed them anyway) secretly and over and above the official/fixed price.

Perhaps as a result of these developments and of the economic crisis, Local Governments/District Councils which were abolished in 1972 were revived in 1982, and Cooperative Unions which were nationalised in 1976 and replaced by state owned Crop Authorities were also revived in 1982, although the Crop Authorities were left intact (Chambua, 1991: 194). In the same year, JUWATA Congress passed a resolution to distance itself from the party. This resolution requested the Government permission to elect its own General Secretary and Deputy General Secretaries, formulate its own constitution, end political affiliation to the CCM, and hold free elections without interference from the CCM. This request was rejected by the National Executive Committee of the CCM. The Party and its government was still afraid of potential opposition from outside, especially from an organised group.

Coming back to the economic situation, we note that, in an attempt to resolve the economic crisis, the Government formulated and adopted various adjustment programmes between 1981 and 1985. These included the National Economic Survival Programme (NESP) of 1981/82-1982/83 and the Structural Adjustment Programme (SAP) of 1982/83-1984/85 (Skarstein et al, 1998: 90 - 104). These measures did not significantly improve economic performance, partly because of lack of foreign exchange and partly as a result of the lack of donor support because of what they called failure of the Government to develop adequate adjustment measures.

Table 1:    GDP, GDP annual growth rates and GDP per capita
(at constant 1976 prices)

| Year | GDP in million Ths | Annual Growth rate % | GDP per capita | Per Capita Index (1976=100) |
|------|------|------|------|------|
| 1976 | 21 652 | - | 1 328 | 100 |
| 1978 | 22 142 | 1,1 | 1 303 | 98 |
| 1979 | 22 943 | 3,6 | 1 306 | 98 |
| 1980 | 23 888 | 4,1 | 1 295 | 98 |
| 1981 | 23 666 | -0,9 | 1 249 | 94 |
| 1982 | 23 439 | -1 | 1 217 | 92 |
| 1983 | 22 886 | -2,4 | 1 152 | 87 |
| 1984 | 23 656 | 3,4 | 1 154 | 87 |
| 1985 | 24 278 | 2,6 | 1 172 | 88 |
| 1986 | 25 070 | 3,3 | 1 181 | 89 |
| 1987 | 26 345 | 5,1 | 1 189 | 90 |
| 1988 | 27 460 | 4,2 | 1 203 | 91 |
| 1989 | 28 558 | 4 | 1 223 | 92 |
| 1990 | 29 904 | 4,7 | 1 262 | 95 |
| 1991 | 31 609 | 5,7 | 1 295 | 98 |
| 1992 | 32 724 | 3,5 | 1 304 | 98 |
| 1993 | 34 088 | 4,2 | 1 321 | 99 |
| 1994 | 35 125 | 3 | 1 287 | 97 |

*Source*: Economic Surveys: 1986,1992 and 1994 and Statistical Abstracts, various
        issues
Note:   Growth Rates and Index calculated by the author.

Perhaps because of the persistence of the economic crisis and his opposition to the World Bank/International Monetary Fund (IMF) aid conditionalities, the first President of Tanzania (J. K. Nyerere) resigned in 1985. A new President (Ali Hasani Mwinyi) was elected in his place. He completed negotiations with the IMF and in July 1986 the country adopted a three year (1986-1989) World Bank/IMF sponsored Structural Adjustment Programme known as the Economic Recovery Programme (ERP). Most of the conditionalities rejected by Nyerere were accepted by Mwinyi's government. These included trade liberalisation, massive devaluation of the Tanzanian currency, privatisation, removal and/or reduction of government subsidies, price decontrol, reducing the size of employment within the public/state sector, and promotion of the private sector. The accommodation of many of the demands presented by the World Bank/IMF was necessary if extra foreign aid was to be obtained not only from the Bank but from other donors as well. Actually, the Bank praised the ERP as an important step towards solving the country's economic problems (ibid: 105).

As a result of this, many donors came forward to aid the economic reforms, and economic performance started to improve as a result. But the reforms had a negative impact on the social services, especially health and education. At the same time, the measures led to an intensification of income inequalities between and within urban and rural areas, increased regional inequalities, a widening of the gap between rich and poor, and the abandonment by relatives of invalids or disabled people who were thus forced to resort to begging (Tungaraza, 1991). But local shops became flooded with large quantities of imported products though the prices for most of them were too high for many people. Local industries were also faced with stiff competition from these imports, and the hardest hit were the textiles and footwear industries which failed to compete. The majority of the people were forced to buy/wear imported 'MITUMBA', i.e. second hand products especially clothes and shoes.

With economic liberalisation, the pressure and need for political reforms intensified. There were forces both inside and outside Tanzania that called for political democratisation and reforms and an end to the one-party political system. Thus, at the end of the 1980s, the trade union movement in the country operated under a situation characterised by the above mentioned socio-economic and political situation. The new winds of change of liberalisation and democratisation of the economic, political and social sectors were blowing through in Tanzania.

As was pointed out earlier, demands for trade union autonomy were made within the trade union movement by the JUWATA Congress as early as 1982. However, the first General Secretary of JUWATA (Mr. A. Tandau) who was also the Minister for Labour, had complained to the President that it was too much for him to combine both jobs. The President asked him to recommend somebody to the position of JUWATA's General Secretary. Among those recommended for the post was Mr. J. Rwegasira who was then Tanzania's Ambassador in Zambia. The President recalled him and appointed him to be the General Secretary of JUWATA in October 1980. Then came the 1982 resolution by JUWATA Congress which requested the Government permission to elect its own General Secretary and Deputy General Secretaries, formulate its own constitution, end political affiliation to the CCM and hold free elections without interference from the CCM. This request, as already pointed out, was rejected by the CCM National Executive Committee.

The same demand for workers' autonomy became even louder at yet another JUWATA Congress of 1984. Again the demand was rejected by the Party but this time the Party directed that instead of the chief executives of JUWATA being appointees of the President of the Party they would be appointed by the Central Committee of the Party (chaired by the President) subject to approval by the National Executive Committee of the CCM.

In 1985 Mr. Rwegasira was appointed by the Party to continue being the General Secretary of JUWATA for another five-year term. Mr. H. Kolimba was elected Chairperson. The two leaders urged the JUWATA General Council to press for the right to choose/elect its own chief executives including the post of General Secretary rather than them being CCM appointees. With the support of the leadership, demands for the right to have its own constitution and to choose its own leaders without interference from the party intensified. As a result, the government gave in to the latter demand in 1989. Yet the CCM reserved the right to screen candidates' names; in other words, they had to send their names to JUWATA which in turn would submit them to the CCM for screening before releasing a number of names for each post for election by union members. In the same year JUWATA held elections to elect its own leaders.

The elections were conducted in accordance with the CCM constitution. For the post of General Secretary, JUWATA sent several names to the CCM for scrutiny, among them that of J. Rwegasira. The Party approved the name of Rwegasira and two other names: Mr. Elias Mashasi (who was the Deputy General Secretary for Tanzania Mainland) and Mr. Issa Mohammed Issa (the Deputy General Secretary for Zanzibar). But these two did not apply for the post and actually they were Rwegasira's Deputies. By picking the three top executives of JUWATA, it is obvious that the CCM did not want changes in trade union leadership or was afraid of changes. Anyway, the two withdrew their names at the last moment and Rwegasira became the sole candidate. He was elected on the basis of Yes/No vote. The previous Chairperson Mr. H. Kolimba (by then the Regional Commissioner of Coast region) was also elected Chairperson of JUWATA. Both of them were members of the National Executive Committee of the CCM. In the same year Rwegasira was appointed Minister for Industries and Trade while in the following year (1990) Kolimba was appointed Secretary General of the CCM and Minister of State, Presidents' Office. The demand for trade union autonomy continued to be raised by trade union members even after the 1989 election. With the advent of the multiparty political system in the country, this autonomy was granted in 1990.

Following this, the Executive Committee *(Kamati ya Usimamizi)* of the General Council of JUWATA which met in August 1990 directed JUWATA to prepare a circular on Reforming the workers union in Tanzania, given the political situation in the country. Thus, the Secretariat of JUWATA appointed a committee of seven people under the Chairperson (Deputy General Secretary Mr. Cyprian Manyanda) to prepare the draft circular.

The proposed changes or new structure aimed to achieve the following: (JUWATA, 1990: 4)
- widening democracy for workers and their organs;
- bringing about a rapid development in the national economy;
- promoting social development, especially high standards of living for the workers; and,
- maintaining the unity of workers.

The committee sought and collected views and opinions from Secretaries and Deputy Secretaries at JUWATA Headquarters, from participants of four seminars organised by JUWATA to brainstorm on the issue, and from minutes of previous JUWATA meetings. The proposed reforms were presented to the Executive Committee for discussion and the following, *inter alia,* were agreed upon:
- one trade union in the country has promoted workers' unity, cooperation and financial strength of the union. Therefore, in the new structure there should be only one trade union in the country;
- within the new structure there will be nine sectors of work for Tanzania Mainland and eight for Zanzibar;
- in order to expand democracy the workers union will have the following meetings/organs:
  *At National Level:* National Congress; General Council; National Executive Committee; and, Executive Committees of each National Sector.
  *At Regional Level:* Regional Congress; Regional Executive Committee; and, Executive Committees of the Regional Sectors.
  *At District Level:* District Congress; District Executive Committee; and, Executive Committees of the District Sectors.

*At the Workplace:* Annual General Assembly; and, Branch Executive Committee.
- to continue with the check-off system;
- the trade union to be allowed to have 10 representatives in the Union Parliament and 4 in the House of Representatives in Zanzibar. These should be in the form of reserved seats for the trade union;
- if any JUWATA executive leader is given an executive job/position in the government, then he must resign or apply for leave without pay for the entire period he/she will be in government office; and
- the government should legalise strikes including solidarity strikes.

These proposals were discussed by the Executive Committee and formed the basis for preparing the constitution of the new organisation. According to trade union officials interviewed, the constitution was prepared under the direction of Mr. Kolimba, a lawyer by profession. The draft constitution contained most of the above proposals including that of having only one trade union to be known as the "Organisation of Tanzania Trade Unions" (OTTU). However, a few changes were made as follows: i) no reference was made to the proposal for having trade union representatives in Parliament; ii) the various sectors to form trade unions which however have to be under OTTU, but each union to have its own constitution which has to be approved by OTTU's General Council; iii) no OTTU executives should be allowed to hold an executive post in any other institution (s). If he/she is elected or appointed to be an executive in any office outside OTTU he/she will be considered to have resigned from his/her OTTU office/post.

The proposed constitution was discussed and adopted by the Executive Committee and as a result, both the General Secretary and the Chairperson (who were Cabinet Ministers) had to resign. Consequently, JUWATA convened an emergency meeting of the Congress on 20 August 1991 to elect new leaders. But again the elections were held under the CCM constitution and Mr. B. Mpangala and Mr. Paul Kimiti, all members of the CCM National Executive Committee were picked by the CCM to compete for the post of General Secretary. But before the elections the Congress first adopted the OTTU constitution and accepted the candidates. Mr. B. Mpangala was elected the new General Secretary of OTTU and Mr. P. B. Nyamuhokya was elected to the post of Chairperson. It was also decided that all other persons who were leaders under JUWATA to continue with their posts under the new union (OTTU) until such time as sectoral trade unions were formed and new elections held. Thus, OTTU was formed on August 20 1991, at a time when the JUWATA Act was still in place.

As a result of the above developments, an Act of Parliament (the OTTU Act No. 20 of 1991) was passed in December 1991. It took into account many of the suggestions made by OTTU and provides for the deregistration of JUWATA, repeal of the JUWATA Act, and the establishment of OTTU.

Section 4.- (1) of the Act states categorically that *'OTTU shall be the sole trade union body representative of all employees in the United Republic'* while section 5.- *(2) provides that 'every person who is, immediately before the effective date, a member of JUWATA, be deemed to have become... a founder member of OTTU'*. Section 5.- (1) opens OTTU membership to other persons in accordance with OTTU's constitution. Section 8 allows for the formation of other trade unions by OTTU or otherwise; however, any trade union so formed shall not only be affiliated to OTTU but shall also be (i) known as an 'OTTU Union' and (ii) deemed to have been registered as such along with OTTU. Thus, according to this Act OTTU is both a trade union and a federation of trade unions. Indeed, according to OTTU's constitution the organisation is understood to be composed of different industrial/sectoral trade unions. The sectors identified were: Industries and Trade/Commerce; Mining and Construction; Communication and Transport; Railways; Agriculture; Teachers; Central Government and Hospitals; Local Government; Hotels, Residential and Allied Workers, and Institutions of Higher Learning and Research. However, the formation of these other trade unions had to await the formation of OTTU, whose leadership would oversee the formation of sectoral trade unions to be affiliated to it. After their formation a general assembly would be called to elect new leadership. The process of forming OTTU unions started in 1992 and was completed in 1995.

Elections for OTTU leadership took place in August, 1995 in Dodoma. There were 11 sectoral trade unions which met in Dodoma; all of them were affiliated to OTTU. At this meeting they decided to change the name of the umbrella organisation from OTTU to TFTU (Tanzania Federation of Trade Unions). The election of TFTU leadership was held and both the former Chairman and General Secretary of OTTU were elected to the same posts in the new umbrella organisation.

The registration of TFTU is, however, doubtful unless the OTTU Act is repealed. Yet, the statrade unions of OTTU as a trade union is now unclear, and individuals who constituted its membership have now joined the sectoral trade unions. Its statrade unions as a federation of trade unions is also open to question since the other trade unions have no separate registration and their affiliation to OTTU/TFTU was not by choice but by law. OTTU leaders tried without success to have separate registration of the sectoral trade unions. As a result, they are now waging a struggle to have the OTTU Act repealed and replaced by another Act which will provide for the establishment and registration of TFTU as well as the separate registration of the existing trade unions.

What emerges from our discussion so far is that the state-centred approach to development (in Tanzania, at least up to the mid 1980s) did not encourage or promote self-activity of the common working people. Within that context, civil society lost its power, initiative and independence as mass organisations and peoples associations were either abolished or brought under direct party or state control. Development cannot be achieved by destroying the initiative of the masses to organise themselves through associations independent of the ruling party and the state, in short without democratic participation. Without real democratic involvement and participation of the people, the working masses, in socio-economic and political decisions, the new economic policy and measures will fail to bring about sustainable development. In the next section we will examine trade unions and democracy in Tanzania.

## Trade unions and democracy

As pointed out earlier, Tanzania, like many African countries, introduced economic reforms from the mid 1980s onwards; these transfer power from the state to the individual, to the private sector and to market forces. These were followed by political reforms that allowed democracy to blossom and the state and its institutions and instruments to become accountable to the people. In this section, we discuss the process of political democratisation in the country, the role played by the trade union in this process, the effects of political reforms on the trade union movement and on workers' participation, and democracy within the trade union movement itself.

### The process of political democratisation

The process of political democratisation in Tanzania started after the resignation of the first President of Tanzania, Mwalimu J. K. Nyerere. After relinquishing his Presidential post he still remained the Chairman of the CCM up to 1989 and his major concern was to strengthen the party. Thus, in 1986/87 he toured all over Tanzania in what he called efforts to revive the CCM. Throughout his tours he urged people (both CCM and non-CCM members) to speak freely and frankly on the good as well as bad things about the CCM and its leadership. He occasionally made statements opposed to the ERP/SAP reforms sponsored by the IMF. This encouraged people to air their views openly for or against the CCM and/or government policies, and on ills brought about by the CCM leadership including corruption. In February 1990, he opened the multiparty debate in the country through a press conference in which he stated that the political leadership should not regard open discussion on multiparty politics as a crime or a sin. Indeed, Nyerere was of the view that the situation in Tanzania was not safe without political liberalisation (Mmuya et al, 1992: 97).

Again in May 1990 while addressing CCM Youths in Mwanza in a speech broadcast by Radio Tanzania, Nyerere argued, that because political changes were inevitable, 'the CCM must be at the forefront in bringing about those changes, including the CCM overseeing the process of change to multiparty politics' (ibid).

Following this, the next stage in the process of political liberalisation was taken on 27 February 1991 when a Presidential Commission (the Nyalali Commission) was appointed *inter alia* to coordinate the views and opinions of the people on the one-party and the multiparty systems, and recommend and advise the government on the expediency and consequences of retaining or restructuring the political system. The commission was given one year to complete its task. The report of the commission, which was submitted to the President in February 1992, recommended formal adoption of a multiparty political system in Tanzania and constitutional amendments to accommodate the new system.

The multiparty political system in Tanzania officially started on 1 July 1992 when the 8 constitutional amendments (Act no. 4 of 1992) came into force. This was followed by the mushrooming of many political parties, many private newspapers, television stations and private radio stations. By October 1995 when the first multi-party general elections were held, Tanzania had 13 fully registered political parties which took part in the 1995 general elections, 41 newspapers (one state-owned), 10 radio stations (two state-owned), and 4 television stations (all of them privately owned). The first local government elections took place in October 1994. Seven political parties took place, and 97% of the councillors elected came from the ruling party, the CCM; this showed the weakness of the opposition, especially because of lack of unity within it.

It is important to note here that the blossoming of the independent press, was not without cost to the masses. The limitations of the media became more pronounced as the general elections approached. Many newspapers carried chapters that were both critical and supportive of the government. Some were either owned by or agents of a particular political party. True, the various newspapers and television and radio stations covered the general elections but each had its own perspective, and some provided information either in favour or against a particular political party with little objectivity. Some were neutral or fairly objective in their analysis and coverage and others were highly biased and at times even dared to carry completely distorted information. The public was highly confused as to which one (s) to believe. Many people ended up either listening to the radio stations, or watching the television stations, that provided information that was in line with their own socio-political and economic beliefs, and buying and reading newspapers that supported their personal opinions. Thus, instead of educating the masses, the media ended up confusing them. Lack of unity within the opposition may have led most people to the conclusion that the devil you know is better than a devil you don't know. As a result, the CCM won the general elections by a landslide majority.

*Involvement of the trade union movement in the political reforms*

One of the main activities of all trade unions is to protect the rights and interests of their members (workers) and, if needs be, to take industrial action. To accomplish this, they have no choice but to defend the political rights of assembly, association and speech. Thus, trade unions are/should be the first to go onto the attack once human rights are violated. In this regard, trade unions often find themselves in alliances with other groups (e.g. students, journalists, lawyers and professional organisations) in their struggle for rights and freedom. In short, trade unionists have to fight for the existence of a strong framework of civil liberties; the absence of such a framework will make it impossible for them to carry out their work effectively. Seen in this light, trade unions are expected to be in the forefront of the struggle for political democratisation in their respective countries.

Having been under the direct surveillance of the 1964-1977 government as well as under the control of the ruling party, the CCM between 1977 and 1992, the trade union movement in Tanzania did not take an active part in the struggle for political reforms. Even so, as a result of these reforms the trade union was freed from political control, and for the first time since 1964 organised a general workers' strike in March 1994; the aim was to increase the pressure for wage increases against the interests of the state which used every means in its disposal to suppress the strike.

But it is important to recall that the trade union movement was freed of party political control as a result of the political democratisation process. In fact, with the advent of the multiparty era in Tanzania, 'the CCM offered official representation to the national organisation of trade unions, the national cooperative movement, the youth league and the women organisations. The youth and women organisations are still part and parcel of the CCM. The cooperative movement and the organisation of trade unions declined the offer (JUWATA became OTTU as a result) and are, therefore, independent bodies' (Kasilati, 1994: 65). It is important to point out here that some political parties in the country have formed their own Youth and Women's organisations, and they should be referred to accordingly. Furthermore, although OTTU is not under the influence of any political party, 'it has reiterated many times that it will cooperate with any political party whose policies are directed towards the furtherance of workers' interest. So far, the CCM Party Programme for the 1990s seems to be attractive to OTTU leadership' (ibid).

Apart from trade union autonomy, another gain is that the Union enjoys statutory benefits related to its income: the OTTU Act provides for the Union to collect periodic or regular membership subscription fees, known as OTTU dues. To obtain these, the General Secretary or his/her representative is required to issue every employer of OTTU members with a notice requiring the employer to deduct specified dues from such members and remit the same to OTTU (s.11 (2)). It is also empowered to use the same means to collect a monthly levy known as a service charge from every person who is not a member of OTTU, but is employed at any place of work where at least 50% of the total number of employees are OTTU members (s. 12 (1) and (3)). The sum of money payable as the OTTU service charge shall be determined in the same manner as the sums of money payable by members of OTTU as OTTU dues (s. 12 (2)). However, the number of OTTU members and even the total number of employees in the formal sector is very small (Table 2); it is also declining because of the ongoing worker retrenchment exercise within the public sector due to SAP reforms.

Table 2:    Trade union membership rates in the formal sector in East African countries in 1988/89

| Country | TU Membership | As % of Formal Sector Workers | As % of Total Labour Force |
|---------|---------------|-------------------------------|----------------------------|
| Tanzania | 470 000 | 58 | 4 |
| Kenya | 300 000 | 35 | 4 |
| Uganda | 57 000 | 16 | 1 |

*Source*: Kasilati (1994: 58)

The OTTU act is not without its flaws. Firstly, workers are still compelled to organise through OTTU; this may be to OTTU's advantage, but the requirement is still contrary to Freedom of Association as provided for in the constitution. Secondly, and to the disadvantage of OTTU for that matter, OTTU cannot dissolve itself; however, the Registrar can order the cancellation of registration of OTTU and specify some other trade union body which shall operate as representative of all employees in the place of OTTU (for details see s. 9 (1) through 9 (5)). OTTU and the other trade unions affiliated to it have to live and work together, but they do not need to die together (s. 8 (2) and 10 (1)). Anyway, the point being stressed here is that further reforms of the existing labour legislation in the country are needed to remove the above and other shortcomings (Rutinwa, 1995: 33-36).

## Political reforms and workers' participation

In the field of employment, workers' participation seeks to apply the principle that people (workers or otherwise) who are substantially affected by decisions made by others should be involved in, and participate in, the making of those decisions. The underlying assumption is that people's involvement and participation in the making of decisions that would affect them promotes democracy and human dignity. In the case of workers' participation, the assumption is that it promotes industrial democracy or democracy at the workplace, workers' commitment and harmonious labour relations, and also reduces industrial conflicts (ILO, 1994: 34). Seen in this light, workers' participation is a form of democracy.

In Tanzania, workers' participation was elaborated in Presidential Circular No.1 of 1970. It directed that in every public (state-owned) institution, or in those enterprises where the government was the majority share-holder, with at least 10 employees must establish the following:
- Workers' Council
- Workers' Council Executive Committee, and
- Board of Directors.

The Workers' Councils were to be the main bodies through which workers' participation would be promoted. It was envisaged that through Workers' Councils, workers would participate in discussions and in making decisions related to the running of the enterprises, as well as their own welfare. Thus, management should not regard workers as tools like machines but rather as owners and equal partners in the management of the enterprises (Maseko, 1976: 234).

The directive spelled out five main objectives behind the establishment of Workers' Councils:
- to promote the humanisation and dignity of the workers;
- to promote the participation of workers in the decision-making process at enterprise level;
- to develop and promote a sense of discipline and responsibility among the workers;

- to establish harmonious relations between workers and management thereby avoiding and reducing conflicts at the workplace; and
- to facilitate greater productivity by improving the skills of the workers and making them more conscious of their contribution to national development.

The Workers' Council was to meet at least twice a year and advise the Board of Directors on the following (these also constitute its functions):
- the requirements of the wages and income policy as announced by the government from time to time;
- marketing aspects as well as on matters related to quality and quantity of the product/s produced;
- matters of planning; and,
- other aspects of productivity such as workers' education.

Another function of the Workers' Council is to receive and discuss the 'balance sheet'.

Workers' Councils were/are supposed to draw representatives from the workers, and also on the Board of Directors of each Parastatal organisation there was a union representative nominated at the national level (Mapolu, 1976: 153 - 158). The Workers' Councils were supposed to combine workers and management in decision-making and make recommendations to the Boards of enterprises. The composition of the councils, according to the directive, was supposed to be worker-dominated. Up to 75% of the members of the Workers' Council were therefore workers; this group also included union representatives. The remaining 25% was shared between the management including all heads of departments, the General Manager and the Chairman of the party branch.

This composition of Workers' Council could be split into two types of membership. One type was made up of members by virtue of their positions; these included the branch party chairman (before 1992), the whole branch committee of the trade union and heads of departments or sections and the top level leaders in the management structure. The second type comprised elected representatives to each of the departments or sections of the enterprise.

The Workers' Council Executive Committee comprised the chief executive/General Manager as Chairperson, heads of departments or sections and not more than one-third of the total workers' representatives elected by Workers' Council. Its functions include:
- scrutinising financial and production estimates as prepared by management;
- scrutinising labour, financial, production, equality, export and marketing programmes;

- advising on the execution of the general policy as proposed by the Workers' Council and/or approved by the Board of Directors; and,
- advising on the day-to-day running of the enterprise.

This circular, it should be noted, came from above and was in fact meant to complete the socialisation process in the country; it was considered that nationalisation of the means of production in 1967 was insufficient without socialisation of the managerial functions (Kinyondo, 1984). However, it is worth mentioning here that socialisation becomes a futile exercise if the workers do not have full control over the nationalised means of production as was/is the case in Tanzania.

However, APADEP research in Tanzania shows that most of the officially stated objectives of workers' participation have been attained to a large extent. Issues normally discussed in Workers' Councils include: production targets/plans, budget and investment plans, work problems (including enterprise and workers' problems), and incentives for employees and social welfare. The achievements and/or importance of workers' participation in Tanzania are as follows:
- promoting good industrial relations (stability and harmony), thereby contributing to increased worker productivity;
- providing a forum for workers to air their views and grievances;
- solving some problems facing workers and the enterprise;
- helping management in making sound decisions;
- increased material benefits to workers.

Even so, workers' participation in Tanzania has had the following limitations.

Firstly, the limited mandate/powers of workers' council: that it had only an advisory role, that all its deliberations were to be approved by the Board and that the councils had no obligation to consult with their constituencies or report to them. Actually minutes of Workers' Council meetings were confidential, as were those of the Board of Directors.

Secondly, although Workers' Councils were worker-dominated in terms of numbers, they were dominated by management in terms of influence. This situation has been compounded by two factors: i) in many workplaces, the trade union branch committee members (all of them members of the Workers' Council as worker representatives) were subordinated to management; ii) in most cases the chief executive was also the chairperson of the Workers' Council. In such a situation his/her opinion or those of the management tended to dominate.

To reiterate the foregoing explanation, when CCM branches were still dominant at places of work, the management tended to fear the former more than it feared JUWATA. In fact, before anything was brought to the Workers' Council for discussion it had to get the sanction of the CCM. This situation continued to exist even after the formation of OTTU in 1991, and it was not until the CCM branches were abolished in workplaces in 1992 that OTTU became independent of the party.

Thirdly, there was/is lack of effective participation in the Workers' Council by the elected worker representatives from departments or sections. Those from the management dominated discussions in the meetings. The lack of effective participation in discussions by the elected worker representatives from departments/sections was because of two reasons (Chambua et al, 1994).

- The majority of these workers representatives had low level of education which implied that their capacity to understand the technical issues discussed in Workers' Council meetings was very low.
- The presence of the workers' representatives and their heads of departments/sections at the same meeting made it difficult for the former to air their views freely, particularly if and when they were called upon to give their views or criticisms relating to the running of departments and sections. This undermined the stipulation in the contract that "all members of the Workers' Councils have equal statrade unions, with the exception of the Chairman, and that every member is free to speak and air his/her views without any fear".

Another reason behind the lack of effective participation by workers' representatives in Workers' Council meetings was the use of English language. Documents and information in many workplaces were/are in English, and the majority of workers' representatives were not able to express themselves fluently in this language.

Another limitation of workers' participation is that it is not backed by law, but by a Presidential directive; this also further limits workers' participation to enterprises and institutions in both the private and public sectors. There is therefore the danger that it might disappear with the privatisation of public enterprises. Indeed, in efforts to speed up privatisation of public enterprises, the requirement to have workers' representatives on the Board of Directors has now been removed. But given the importance of workers' participation in promoting industrial democracy and increased productivity, there is a need to enact a law to enforce workers' participation and extend it to private enterprises as well. Moreover, workers' participation should also be seen as a fundamental human right.

The reading that we get from the above explanation is that they all were, or became, possible because of the post-independence historical processes whereby, through legislation and administrative practice, labour organisations were subordinated to the state and ruling political party; even at enterprise level, trade union branch committees were subordinated to the party and management.

The effects of political changes on workers' participation thus far have been minimal but significant: abolition of the political party's representation in Workers' Council meetings (positive) and also removal of the requirement of workers' representation at meetings of Boards of enterprises (negative). In addition, new forms of workers' participation are now being encouraged: these include profit-sharing and/or ownership of the enterprise through shareholding. Otherwise, workers' participation in the country is still as undemocratic (though as useful) as it used to be.

## Gender, trade unions and workers' participation

It is appropriate to treat the question of gender, and particularly the role of women, in workers' participation in a separate sub-section. This is essentially because women's position in the trade union movement, both as leaders and as members, has been greatly marginalised.

Women workers' participation at the place of work can be looked at from two particular angles; firstly, it can be viewed from the point of view of the number of women workers who have joined the existing trade unions and whether, as members, they participate effectively in the issues that concern their welfare particularly, and the welfare of all workers in general; secondly, their participation can be reflected in the position that they hold in leadership of the trade unions. The belief here is that the more women we have in leadership positions, the more chances they have for speaking on behalf of the rest of women in general.

It has been argued by one trade unionist (Kasungu, 1992) that although one third of all workers in Tanzania are women, very few of them are active in the trade union movement. This is so, the argument goes, despite the fact that 2% of their salaries was being deducted as trade union dues. In fact, while these dues are deducted, very few know that they are not trade unionists. Kasungu, adds that membership helps in giving women the right to vote and be voted for, participate in all union issues and be represented by union officials in grievance procedures and industrial courts.

The low level of women's participation at the workplace has a lot to do with the nature of the employment system that dates from the colonial period. The employment system during the colonial era recruited mostly men as labourers in mining industries, settler farms, and later in manufacturing industries. In fact, even employment in government services was also confined mainly to men. This kind of situation continued after independence and the result was that, when women began to be employed as workers in different industries, companies, parastatal organisations and government services, their number was very small compared to that of men. The criteria used to employ workers at different levels included education, skills and experience, and these weighed heavily against women. Not only was the number of women workers in trade unions small but their position in leadership was also minimal even after independence.

When we look at the leadership positions in JUWATA at almost all levels in terms of gender, we find that the percentage of women in leadership is very small. Research done by the OTTU Directorate of Women and Youth in 1994 revealed that, by 1988, the number of women in various leadership positions in JUWATA at national level was as follows (OTTU, 1994): all positions: 9%; General Council members: 12%; Executive Committee members: 15%; Heads of department/sections: 13%; Regional secretaries: 5%; District secretaries: 3%. At branch level the situation was as follows: all positions: 16%; Chairpersons: 4%; Secretaries: 14%; Committee members: 18%.

It is obvious from these figures that there has been under-representation of women workers at the different levels of trade union leadership and that, this being the case, there has been little progress among women workers.

There are a number of reasons for this under-representation. Some are historical, as we have indicated in this section, but others could include the following reasons which were given to us by some of the women we interviewed:

- lack of education, skills and experience;
- lack of confidence, which is a result of (a) but also because of being looked down upon by men;
- domestic responsibilities because of their gender position in the household;
- societal norms and traditions which relegate women to an inferior position when compared to men;
- little attempt by JUWATA to mobilise women for participation in the trade union movement and leadership.

Following the policy of liberalisation, and particularly after 1985, attempts were made systematically to expand the extent of women's participation and leadership at places of work. It was felt that in order for the union to reach rank-and-file women members and raise their awareness, a women's directorate had to be established. This took place in 1986. It seems that there was a push both from the very few women who had leadership positions in the union at national level and from the donor community.

The General Council Meeting held in February 1987 in Arusha adopted a resolution to create a Women's Committee network from workplace to national level. This resolution was finally accepted, and it implied the formation of Women's Committees as part of the trade union structure to support the work of the Union.

A firm decision to form these women's committees at Branch, District, Regional to National levels was made by JUWATA in Arusha on 27 July 1990. These Committees were to consist of representatives from different/ major trade union branches.

In our opinion the reasons for the formation of these Committees include the fact that they would:
- be a way for the union to collate women's issues and demands at branch level and send them all the way up to national level;
- be able to make women aware of their rights;
- be able to encourage women's participation by making them more aware.

Before the 1992 OTTU elections, the JUWATA directorate of women and youth went to different workplaces around the country urging women to participate not only in voting but also in standing for elections themselves. The women directorate also proposed that, at all levels where elections were to be held, women should be given 25% of the leadership positions which were being contested; this was accepted. It would be very useful to follow this up to see if, by having 25% of the leadership positions given to women, their participation has become better and more effective.

## Democracy within the trade union

To date, OTTU and its affiliates constitute a democratic organisation. The leadership at all levels consists of elected persons, and even workers' representatives at branch level are elected by all trade union members in that branch through a secret ballot. The system is as follows. At national level, the OTTU Congress elects the General Secretary, the Chairperson, the two Vice Chairpersons, and members of the General Council; the General Council in turn appoints the Deputy General Secretary. In addition to this, leaders and other members alike are allowed to join the political party of their choice and compete for political positions in their respective political parties. During the October 1995 General elections, for example, two OTTU leaders contested the same Parliamentary seat representing different political parties, and one of them (the junior of the two) won the election. Of course this raises other questions, especially those related to unity of vision within the leadership of OTTU and its affiliates. Of course, democracy has its costs but, if the leadership is divided ideologically and politically, this will certainly jeopardise the unity and strength of the trade union movement.

## Trade unions democracy and structural adjustment/economy

In the years that followed political independence, most, if not all, African countries greatly increased state spending in the following areas:

- education and infrastructure, because they lacked even the minimal levels of skills and infrastructure needed to develop their economies/societies;
- the development of export agriculture to pay for expanded imports;
- import substitution industrialisation.

'Many aimed to attract foreign private investors, especially for industrial development. But most found them less interested in investing their own funds than in loan-funded joint ventures where donor and African states guaranteed the loan and the latter also guaranteed the market by imposing protection. Thus, much state intervention arose less from efforts to supplant private business than from the conditions imposed by business for its involvement.' (Centre for Development Research, 1995: 3)

In Tanzania, the situation was as is described briefly below. For the first five years after independence (December 1961 - February 1967), the emphasis was on an expansion of health and education, the production of export agricultural crops, and private foreign investment for industry and infrastructure. Although average annual growth rates of GDP and agriculture were high (about 5%) by present standards, they were considered unsatisfactory at the time. By the end of 1966, agricultural policy was considered to have failed, and attempts at the same time to raise foreign funding and/or attract foreign investment also failed.

In February 1967, partly because of the above situation, the government announced the Arusha Declaration which committed the country to the policy of *ujamaa* (socialism) and self-reliance. This was followed by nationalisation of the major means of production. Paradoxically, this move attracted a lot of foreign funding instead of discouraging it. Those foreign firms which were unwilling to invest their own funds found it profitable and risk-free to enter into joint ventures (the Tanzanian state being the majority share-holder) and management and construction agreements with Tanzania - in other words, to establish and construct industries, and provide management of the same, for a specified period of time (normally five years). These agreements were financed through loans guaranteed both by Tanzania and by their home governments. Another major feature of the post-1967 period was the encouragement of peasants to form and live in ujamaa villages. This culminated in a programme of forced resettlement of the rural masses in what were called 'development villages'. These developments led to the restriction of more and more goods for sale through state and parastatal agencies; high rates of investment, under heavy state control, were financed through foreign aid. External financing multiplied all these trends, especially since the then President of the World Bank singled out the country's post-Arusha declaration policies as an inspiring example on how to develop Africa. This expanded investment and activity in all sectors of the economy took a major toll on efficiency since it severely overstrained the capacity and morale of the state and parastatal workers whose real wages were falling (ibid, 10).

Towards the end of the 1970s, Tanzania, like many African countries, was faced with a severe economic crisis caused by both internal and external factors. The donor community attributed this to bad policies, especially heavy state control of the economy. As has already pointed out the crisis became severe in early 1980s. Thus, Tanzania, as a well known example of socialist development, became a particular target of the international financial institutions which imposed a severe lending policy from 1980 to 1985, which brought the country to its heels. Consequently from 1986 to the present time, the country has been implementing IMF/World Bank-sponsored structural adjustment programmes (SAPs).

The economic situation that prevailed in Tanzania and in many sub-Saharan African countries meant that structural adjustment measures were essential if economic growth was to be revived. The issue was not whether there should be economic adjustment, but rather what kind. However, when economic adjustment measures become necessary, society requires strong institutions supported by the majority of the population in order to handle the process successfully to the advantage of the working masses. To this end, there must be an emphasis on poverty alleviation and the maintenance of basic living requirements for the whole population. The implication of this is that the involvement of all socio-economic interest groups, including trade unions as partners in development, is mandatory. Unfortunately this did not take place. Indeed, the structural adjustment policies of the IMF/World Bank disregard the needs and interests of working people and have led not only to large-scale unemployment but also to poverty aggravation. They are also openly hostile to trade union organisations.

As social partners in the development process of their country, trade unions should be consulted and take an active role during the design and implementation of structural adjustment programmes (SAPs). They can and should provide SAPs with the social dimension by explaining to governments their consequences to workers, and also proposing viable alternatives that will eliminate or reduce adverse effects. Unfortunately, this did not take place. True, the trade union movement in Tanzania opposed some of the SAP's measures, especially those relating to the entrenchment of workers and the privatisation or sale of competently performing public firms, but were found wanting when it came to suggesting viable alternatives. There is still mistrust between the government and trade unions. The government is reluctant to encourage the emergence of a strong and autonomous trade union movement, and actually fears such a development. But there can be no democratic participation and sustainable development either if the trade unions are weak and dependent or if the government is weak. Thus, trade unions should ensure that they become strong and independent, and work together with a strong government; likewise, governments should promote the emergence of a strong and autonomous trade union movement, and work closely with it. Only then will it be possible to resist adaptation and the implementation of externally and narrowly conceived policy reforms which disregard the needs and interests of working people.

The effects of SAPs on the economy have been mixed. There was an immediate improvement in growth of around 4% per annum from 1986 to 1994 (see Table 1), but export performance has not been impressive and the balance of payments has continued to deteriorate (Table 3). Agricultural growth started to improve with the country's own SAP (1984-5), and continued under the IMF/World Bank-sponsored SAP, but this growth "is quite modest in relation to the import support funds poured in and improvements in the weather, and is certainly not an 'agricultural boom' as asserted in one World Bank publication" (Centre for Development Research (1995: 34). Annual average growth rates of manufacturing output improved from - 4.7% (1980-85) to 4.3% (1985-93) although it slowed down from 12% in 1991 to 1.9% (1992) and 2.1% (1993) (ibid, 39). Declining rates of growth during the 1990s reflect the closure or running-down of parastatal enterprises prior to sale or liquidation, the increased cost incurred (and difficulty encountered) in obtaining to credit due to high interest rates, and failure to compete with imports as protection is removed. SAPs have thus been the causes both of improvements in industrial performance during the late 1980s and of its decline during the early 1990s by failing to sustain that initial growth.

## Table 3: Balance of payments, 1980 - 1994 (US$ millions)

| | 1980 | 1981 | 1982 | 1983 | 1984 | 1985 | 1986 | 1987 | 1988 | 1989 | 1990 | 1991 | 1992 | 1993 | 1994 |
|---|---|---|---|---|---|---|---|---|---|---|---|---|---|---|---|
| Trade Account | -712,8 | -607,3 | -697,4 | -434,8 | -485,7 | -713,6 | -699,9 | -798,8 | -812,2 | -834,8 | -956 | -1 115 | -1 113 | -1 026 | -985,6 |
| 1. Exports | 505,8 | 553,7 | 415,4 | 379,7 | 388,3 | 285,6 | 347,6 | 353,2 | 380,2 | 395,8 | 389,3 | 362,2 | 400,6 | 439,89 | 519,4 |
| 2. Imports | 1 218,6 | 1 161,0 | 1 112,8 | 814,5 | 874,0 | 999,2 | 1 047,5 | 1 150,0 | 1 192,4 | 1 230,0 | 1 346 | 1 476,7 | 1 513,3 | 1 465,4 | 1 505 |
| Services (net) | 19,0 | 69,9 | 38,8 | 23,2 | -43,2 | -68,1 | -85,1 | -98,1 | -196,1 | -219,3 | -1622 | -160,9 | -217,7 | -96 | -150,9 |
| 1. Receipts | 178,9 | 195,7 | 117,2 | 109,1 | 107,4 | 108,1 | 110,0 | 108,6 | 119,7 | 122,3 | -141,1 | 150 | 155,6 | 290,2 | 441,4 |
| 2. Payments of | 159,9 | 125,8 | 78,4 | 84,9 | 150,6 | 176,2 | 195,1 | 207,7 | 315,8 | 341,8 | 303,4 | 310,9 | 373,3 | 386,2 | 592,3 |
| which interest | 27,6 | 32,2 | 27,6 | 18,0 | 89,3 | 97,3 | 112,8 | 99,4 | 187,8 | 206,4 | 210,1 | 192,1 | 233,5 | 167,4 | 153,4 |
| Transfers (net) | 128,7 | 130,2 | 119,3 | 103,3 | 159,5 | 366,7 | 473,0 | 583,0 | 531,3 | 652,2 | 693,5 | 823,4 | 905 | 719,7 | 746,7 |
| 1. Inflows | 154,2 | 153,4 | 137,3 | 128,3 | 180,9 | 394,3 | 501,0 | 610,0 | 643,0 | 688,0 | 723,5 | 856 | 940 | 749,7 | 779,2 |
| 2. Outflows | 25,5 | 23,2 | 18,0 | 25,0 | 21,4 | 27,6 | 28,0 | 27,0 | 29,8 | 29,8 | 30 | 32,6 | 35 | 30 | 32,5 |
| Current account (net) | -565,1 | -407,2 | -539,3 | -308,3 | -369,4 | -415,0 | -312,0 | -312,9 | -387,0 | -401,8 | -426,1 | -452 | -425,4 | -401,81 | -390 |
| Current account (net) | 226,8 | 258,7 | 193,4 | 208,0 | 35,7 | -50,5 | -49,4 | -7,0 | 33,5 | 32,3 | 137,2 | 103,4 | 59,4 | 34,4 | -28,47 |
| 1. Receipts | 256,9 | 284,9 | 214,7 | 270,0 | 292,6 | 200,0 | 165,0 | 213,0 | 226,0 | 245,6 | 311,1 | 249,1 | 296 | 372,4 | 316,3 |
| 2. Payments | 30,1 | 26,3 | 21,3 | 62,9 | 256,9 | 250,5 | 214,4 | 220,0 | 186,4 | 313,3 | 173,9 | 145,7 | 236,6 | 338 | 344,8 |
| Exeptional Financing | 122,9 | 90,8 | 177,1 | 153,5 | 49,1 | 60 | 83 | 47,1 | 96 | 143,7 | 20,3 | 98,2 | 64,1 | 92,5 | 111,5 |
| Overall Balance | -178,1 | -101,7 | -109,3 | -137,5 | -158,7 | -394,6 | -383,6 | -281,1 | -257,9 | -248,6 | -277,4 | -260,8 | -224,4 | -295,1 | -164,4 |

*Source:* Economic Surveys and Bank of Tanzania: Economic and Operation Report (various years)

Table 4:    Trends of external financing of the government budget
            (Annual averages)

| Year | External Finance as % of Development Expenditure | External Finance as % of Total Budget |
|---|---|---|
| 1971-1973 | 40 | 12 |
| 1974-1976 | 47 | 18 |
| 1977-1979 | 52 | 19 |
| 1980-1982 | 60 | 16 |
| 1983-1985 | 47 | 10 |
| 1986-1988 | 132 | 26 |
| 1989-1991 | 146 | 24 |

*Source*: Extracted and calculated from A. Danielson, F. Mndeme and G. Mjema
       (1993: Table 2), Aid and Debt Issues in Tanzania: Past Trends and Future
       Prospects, Sweden: University of Lund

Another effect of SAPs has been the deepening of external financial
dependence. If we look at the financing of the country's government budget,
we see that the contribution of foreign aid increased considerably during
the SAP period (Table 4). This again creates doubts as to whether this kind
of development will be sustainable once external financing is removed or
reduced significantly.

Turning to the social scene, the point has already been made both
implicitly and explicitly that the economic reforms being carried out in
Tanzania were of more benefit to the already entrenched small group of
rich people. The hardest hit group is made up of workers and poor peasants
who now have to pay for education (at all levels), health and other social
services while their incomes continue to decline in real terms and subsidies,
which one benefited them, have been removed. Workers' wages are still
too low to meet their daily basic needs, while at the same time prices for
virtually everything - house rents, transport, food and other commodities -
have gone up. Retrenchment and rising unemployment have increased the
crime rate in urban areas, and many live in fear and cannot even enjoy a
good sleep lest they are robbed of the little they have acquired and own.
Surely, this is not the kind of development they want; nor is it conducive to
the promotion either of productivity or of democratic participation.

The economic reforms have also led to the sale or privatisation of public
enterprises with negative consequences for workers' participation. Many

parastatals and enterprises in Tanzania are being sold to foreign individuals and transnational/multinational corporations, or else they coming under joint ownership between the state and private proprietors mostly from outside the country. Consequently, not only is the organisational structure and the line of management hierarchy fast changing, but also top management consists predominantly of foreigners. Since workers' participation in the country lacks a legal basis, and was confined to a public sector that is now shrinking, it is doubtful if it will thrive under these conditions. At all events, the concept of workers' participation including ownership and control of the means of production has to acquire a new and different dimension.

This requires a follow-up study that would reveal how government parastatals, nationally and privately owned companies, joint state-privately owned businesses, and wholly foreign privately owned companies are organised and run and whether there is room for workers' participation in their management. Indeed, the new ownership structures might be antagonistic to workers' participation.

## Institutionalisation of democracy

Democracy is more than simply the right to vote or to be elected to form a government. This is a necessary, but not sufficient, condition. It is about a whole set of rights which citizens must enjoy if a government is to be open, accountable and participatory. These rights include freedom of speech, especially for those critical of government policies/measures; freedom to form and associate, for example, in trade unions, political parties or any pressure group; an independent press; the rule of law, and respect for the law by all including the top political leaders and rulers; access to state information, particularly about specific state plans for those directly affected by them, and the right to be consulted on, and involved in, such decisions; and freedom from discrimination on grounds of sex, race, colour, religion or creed (Clark, 1991: 16). These are the necessary conditions for sustainable democracy.

Tanzania now has an independent press, as has already been mentioned, and even the other human rights/freedoms are provided for in the current country's constitution. However, their provision is subjected to a number of caveats including clauses like "... provided that one does not break the laws". Some of these laws violate the constitution; the Nyalali Commission listed 40 such laws, and many of them are still in force.

For example, where as freedom of association is provided in the constitution:
- workers are still compelled by law to organise through OTTU;
- Tanzanian trade unions are compelled by law to be OTTU affiliates;

- the Registrar has powers to order that the registration of OTTU be cancelled, and specify some other trade union body to operate as representative of all employees in the country in its place;[3]
- registration of any political party is dependent of getting members from both parts of the Union - the Mainland and Zanzibar;
- in order to be elected by the people to any political post at any level (councillors, members of Parliament, or even President of the country) one must first belong to a political party; independence is not allowed, again by law.

Another example is that although Tanzania has legislation providing for the right to strike, dispute settlement procedures are interventionist, complex, lengthy and the interests of workers are not given the weight they deserve.[4] According to one trade unionist, "the extremely long period needed to comply with the compulsory pre-strike procedures makes legal strikes virtually impossible" (Kasilati, 1994: 56).

Pressure for change in Tanzania has come, and continues to come, from various social groups such as political parties, the trade union movement, teachers, university students and intellectuals. However, as was pointed out earlier, the formalisation of the process of transition was championed by the CCM. The opposition parties did take an active role in pressuring for political restructuring, but they were not able to participate in deciding how future competitive politics should be conducted. This was definitely because the opposition was weak because it was fragmented. Weak or not, democratic participation implies that they should have been fully involved in the preparation and implementation of the democratisation process.

In conclusion, we note that although Tanzania has taken the necessary reforms to promote democracy - an independent press, a constitution that provides for human rights and freedoms, further reforms are needed to address the limitations discussed above. Moreover, sustainable democracy will only be possible if, in addition to economic prosperity, the rule of law obtains and there is respect for the law, for it was largely the hard economic conditions that intensified and justified the struggle for socio-economic and political liberalisation. If these are to persist, a return to dictatorship is not an impossibility.

## Notes

1   The main sources of data/information contained in this chapter are APADEP research reports: Questionnaire Surveys for workers' representatives conducted between 1992 and 1995, Case Studies and Trend Studies on

workers' participation and Development; and published and unpublished materials in libraries and/or documentation rooms.

2   The Trade Union Ordinance (Amendment) Act No. 51 of 1962.

3   But before ordering the deregistration of OTTU, the Registrar has first to consult with all such parties as he/she deems necessary in the public interest and obtain prior approval in writing of the Minister responsible for labour matters. The order is also subject to the approval by resolution of the Parliament (see OTTU Act s. 9 (1) through 9 (5)).

4   See B. Rutinwa (1995: 29-32); and The Industrial Court Amendment Act, no. 2 of 1993 (especially s.4 - s.11).

# 14 Togo
# The Logic of History

NADEDJO BIGOU-LARÉ

*The slogan 'No to the Eyadema dictatorship' is regularly seen on placards at Togolese demonstrations; indeed, since 1991 it has become something of a commonplace. However, as little as six years ago, such a slogan was unimaginable or, at the very least, illegal. This turnaround reflects the large number of transformations that the country has undergone since late 1990. Democratic transition is taking place, but in a troubled period marked by divisions in the trade union movement.*

How has this situation come about? The ground swell that rocked African societies, and Togo in particular, in the early 1990s had originated in faraway places only a short period of time before, and manifested itself in many different ways. Moreover, the interrelation between a number of issues - economic (mainly Structural Adjustment Plans) and social factors, the need for populations to participate increasingly in the government of their countries, and action by trade unions - produced movements that were identified (perhaps too hastily) as having something to do with democracy.

For a better understanding of the phenomenon, we need to look back at how these factors came together; in the specific case of Togo, it is worth recalling some historical facts that have manifestly contributed to the present situation. Togo is geographically tiny, covering an area of 56,000 km , that is to say 1/10 the size of France, the former colonial power. It has a population of 3.6m, and is one of the least advanced countries in the world: in 1991, per capita GNP stood at USD 391. Between 1881 and 1960, Togo lived under colonial rule, but after independence in 1960 political life was shaped by a succession of short-lived governments: an emergency government from 1967 to 1979, a monolithic system of administration from 1979 to 1990, and then a series of stormy, politically-motivated social uprisings starting in 1991.

The Togolese trade union movement was born in 1947 with the formation of the Union des Syndicats Confédérés du Togo (USCT - Union of Confederated Workers of Togo); this federation brought together unions representing employees in several sectors such as the civil service, post and telecommunications, railways and docks, customs and health. The USCT was initially affiliated to the French CGT (Confédération Générale du Travail -

317

General Confederation on Labour), but broke away in 1951 to join the Union Générale des Travailleurs d'Afrique Noire (UGETAN - General Union of Black African Workers); in 1959, the USCT became the Union Nationale des Travailleurs togolais (UNTT - National Union of Togolese Workers).[1]

It is interesting to note that all trade unions at this time were much more engaged in the independence struggle than in the defence of workers' interests or in dealing with matters strictly related to employment. However, this strategy had its reward after the April 1958 election when, following independence, the UNTT General Secretary, who was already a Deputy, became Minister of Labour and the Public Sector. This first instance of trade union participation in government was initially welcomed by workers, but it soon ran into difficulties; these stemmed from political intrigues that the trade union centre had inherited during the struggle for independence.[2]

For a time, relations between government and trade unions alternated between complicity and divorce, but this changed when the army seized power in January 1967. There then followed an 'observation' period between State and unions that lasted until November 1969. It came to an end with the formation of a single political party, the Rassemblement du Peuple Togolais (RPT - Togolese People's Rally). The new party wanted a single trade union structure, and at once began to interfere actively in the way the various unions were run.

This chapter aims to analyze the role of the political system, the role of the trade unions, and the impact of economic policies that have been introduced over the last 20 years or more as Togo has gradually embraced democracy. The last point is seen as a dependent variable, the first three as independent variables.

The overall aim of this analysis is to determine the extent to which the combination of the three independent variables led in the direction of democracy. In other words, might it have been possible to predict the advent of democracy in the early 1990s from observing them?

The variables are defined as follows:

- the political system currently in place may be assessed according to two parameters: political pluralism and the degree of civil society's participation in the management of the State (we describe the latter as the space for freedom);
- the action of trade unions is measured by the participation of the unions - or the role played by unions and union leaders - in the management of the State. We do not look at workers' participation in decision-making at the workplace;
- economic policy is restricted to the following indicators: the standard of living measured by per capita GDP and per capita GNP, the rate of inflation, balance of trade figures, and servicing of the public debt;

- lastly, the dependent variable (the democratic phenomenon) is understood to mean people's articulated need for more freedom.

We consider indicators of this variable to be the number of publications in the news media and the number of political parties and associations.

With regard to interdependence between the variables, we shall study them in due course under headings that refer to the situation in a general way over a given period of time. Our study covers the period from independence to the present day, that is to say from 1960 to early 1996, and is divided into four phases: hesitancy in finding a way of managing the State (1960-1967), euphoria (1967-1979), crisis (1980-1990), and the democratic process (1990 to the present day).

This approach allows us both to clarify the impact of the independent variables on the dependent variable over time, and to observe continuously the influences of certain variables from one period to the next.

## Hesitancy in finding a way of managing the State: 1960-1967

After independence was won, everyone set great store by political, social and economic advance, and development plans were put in place to enable the country's economy to take off. In the event, the period was principally marked by political instability which included fierce struggles for a share in the spoils of victory, and a military takeover in 1963 that led to the abrupt suspension of political institutions; this inevitably affected all development programmes implemented during that time.

The political, social and trade union organisations that made an impact in the period 1960-1967 had been set up during the struggle for independence (1947-1958); they included the Comité pour l'Unité Togolaise (CUT - Committee for Togolese Unity) and the UNTT's Juvento, and they combined their activities to produce the overall political action that took place between 1960 and 1963. However, long before the military seized power in January 1963, these organisations had been racked by internal dissent about the position they should adopt on the government (it was dominated by the all-conquering CUT) and the political line it was taking. A concrete manifestation of this dissent was a breakdown in relations between the CUT and Juvento. The military takeover of January 1963 brought the situation into even sharper relief, and any progress on political, social and economic plans was halted in consequence.

Any examination of statistics for the first seven years of independence is difficult because the civil service was still at embryonic stage of development and only had limited means of collecting and preserving data. Where data do exist, for example on Gross National Product (GDP), Gross Domestic Product (GNP), imports and exports, they are not complete; numerical data relating to economic aggregates are only available from 1967 onwards. For that year, nominal GNP stood at CFAF 55,296.4m while GDP came to CFAF 57.025.9m (Directorate of Statistics, National Accounts Office of Togo).

It is hard to identify instances of interdependence between players in the social and political arenas during the period 1963-1967. The 1963 coup d'état left trade unions temporarily inactive, although it was not long before arguments between the various tendencies at leadership level surfaced and became public knowledge; these arguments were exacerbated by the fact that the union leaders in question still bore traces of their previous political alliances. This gave the government an excuse to start meddling in trade union affairs, and the whole history of Togolese trade unionism at this time is a sorry tale of government interventions (described as 'mediations') aimed at achieving a single trade union structure (Natchaba, 1981: 49).

In short, the period from 1960 to 1967 is mainly remembered for a brutal interruption to the fledgling democracy in 1963, and the search for a new way of managing the State.

## Euphoria: 1969-1979

The period of hesitancy had been marked by a troubled pluralist government that offered the prospect of no freedom, and therefore no democracy. The army takeover of 1967 and the establishment of a single party in 1969 then brought the democratic experiment to a decisive close. In fact, the hesitation which followed the seizure of power in 1963 - and other hesitation that beset the political class (unpredictable intrigues and alliances) and trade unions - also laid the ground for the army's second incursion into politics.

In political terms, the period of hesitancy extended into 1969 following indecision about which system to adopt after the military takeover in January 1967. All political institutions were banned, and the emergency government outlawed political activity of any sort, even going so far as to suspend the Constitution and dissolve the Assembly. However, in November 1969, Togo's political void was challenged by the setting up of the Rassemblement du Peuple Togolais (RPT - Togolese People's Rally) as the single political party of 'national union'. The lives of Togolese citizens were thereafter circumscribed by the single party, and freedom of expression was limited to an articulation of RPT ideals. All social groups complied with the party's principles; in other words, they went about their business in the normal way, but strictly within the limitations set by the party. The RPT's tentacles already stretched deep into all social structures.

*Relative political stability*

The country's most stable period in political, and perhaps economic, terms lasted from 1969 to 1979. The incorporation that inevitably accompanied one-party government meant that all views expressed by the people had to comply with Party principles. While protest was not 'allowed' because of the way in which the political system operated, it is equally true to say that there was not any demonstration of discontent indicating that the people did not support the government.

This 'total support' of the Togolese people was reflected in a proliferation of groupings at all socio-professional levels (except peasants) as active elements of the Party. Organisations formed at this time included the Jeunesse du Parti (JRPT - Party Youth), the Union des Femmes du Togo (UNFT - Union of Togolese Women), the Union Nationale des Chefs Traditionnels du Togo (National Union of Traditional Togolese Chiefs) and the Mouvement National des Etudiants et Scolaires du Togo (MONESTO - National Movement of Students and Pupils).[3] Interestingly, it appears that young students in colleges and high schools and teachers at all levels of the education system were the only groups that refused to be incorporated.

This relative political stability inevitably affected the state of the economy. The Togolese economy is dominated by agriculture; the industrial sector at the time consisted solely of a few factories processing agricultural products such as cassava and soap. Unlike the period 1960-1966 which saw the establishment of a coherent development policy, this time round only a few scattered development projects were undertaken; these included building works in the port and the construction of a brewery, the 'Brasserie du Bénin'. The first five-year development plan was implemented from 1966 to 1970, and altogether three of the four five-year plans were introduced between 1969 and 1979. Although these plans were not systematically assessed before their abandonment in 1985, most observers accept that the first one was relatively well managed.

The failure of the second plan (1971-1975) stemmed largely from the sharp price rise in phosphates during 1972-1973 - from USD 30 to USD 70, an increase of approximately 105%. As phosphates constituted Togo's sole export product, the State then conducted a vast, if uncoordinated, investment programme, but it later put public finances under serious strain.

However, GDP grew by an average of 12% during the period, this aggregate climbing from CFAF 57,025.9m (nominal prices) in 1967 to CFAF 212,880m in 1979, while GNP rose from CFAF 55,296.4m to 208,800m (Directorate of Statistics, National Accounts Office of Togo).

Table 1:    Rate of increase of GDP and GNP in Togo (1967-1979)

| Years | 67-68 | 68-69 | 69-70 | 70-71 | 71-72 | 72-73 | 73-74 | 74-75 | 75-76 | 76-77 | 77-78 | 78-79 |
|---|---|---|---|---|---|---|---|---|---|---|---|---|
| Aggregates | (%) | (%) | (%) | (%) | (%) | (%) | (%) | (%) | (%) | (%) | (%) | (%) |
| GPD | 5 | 16 | 5 | 9 | 8 | 6 | 42 | -6 | 9 | 22 | 15 | 13 |
| GNP | 5 | 17 | 6 | 9 | 8 | 6 | 45 | -22 | 6 | 42 | -4 | 13 |

*Source*: Directorate of Statistics, National Accounts Office of Togo

Table 1 shows GDP and GNP both falling around 1974-1975, and GNP falling again in 1977-1978. The economy was already running out of steam following a number of conjunctural events; these included the implementation of an over-ambitious investment policy in 1974-1975 and the effects of the world economic crisis on all our economies in 1977-1978.

The balance of trade was favourable from 1967 to 1969 before going into the red from 1970 to 1973; there was a deficit of CFAF 7bn in 1973. Figures for 1974 showed a profit of 22bn as a result of the phosphate boom, but the second half of the 1970s was again marked by a deficit; the shortfall for 1979 was CFAF 58bn, or 28% of GNP for that year.

Figure 1:    Balance of trade figures (1969-1979)

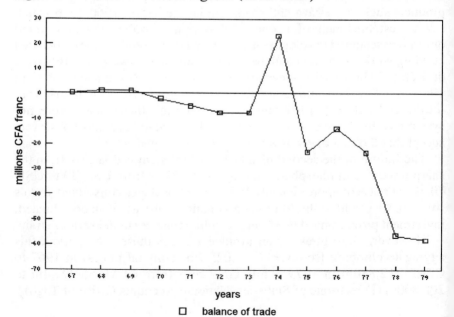

Figure 1 shows how the economic situation, as measured by the balance of trade, began to deteriorate in 1975; the result was considerable pressure on public finances (due to a year-on-year increase in imports), and therefore on the newly introduced development policies. The government went deeper and deeper into debt in its attempt to finance this deficit, and the Togolese public debt soared from USD 47.4m (i.e. 16% of GNP) in 1970 to USD 1058.3m (95.5% of GNP) in 1979.

**Table 2:**   Togolese public debt and debt servicing (1970-1979)

| Year | Public Debt in $ millions | Debt/GNP % | Debt Servicing in $ millions |
|------|---------------------------|------------|------------------------------|
| 1970 | 47,4 | 16 | 2,3 |
| 1974 | 144,3 | 26,56 | 8,5 |
| 1975 | 172,8 | 28,96 | 16,6 |
| 1976 | 369,8 | 65,1 | 23 |
| 1978 | 976,3 | 119,21 | 47,7 |
| 1979 | 1058,3 | 107,81 | 42 |

*Source*: World Debt Tables - BCEAO Agence de Lomé

As with other indicators, the increase in the overall public debt coincided with the phosphate boom years when several public investment programmes relied on phosphate prices maintaining their 1973-1974 levels at least in the medium term. Sadly, these investments, which came to be known as 'white elephants', were failures.

By contrast, inflation hovered around 1% between 1967 and 1969 before stabilising at about 12% until 1976; over the period generally, it averaged 9.27%. That was a relatively small increase by comparison with the experiences of other countries, and followed the rise in GNP quite closely (see Table 1); however, closer examination of these rates of inflation reveals that the peak years coincide with the sharpest rises in GNP.

Despite the paucity of economic data, it is still possible to identify trends which explain subsequent events. In fact, during this decade, the years 1973-1975 were a turning point in economic terms. There were certainly grounds for optimism at this time, but the conjunctural rise in the price of phosphates was swiftly followed by an era of reckless investments; it was these that led to a deterioration in the GNP and balance of payments for

1975-1976, and to a 20% inflation increase in 1976. From this point onwards, Togo's public debt began to grow slowly; this put further strain on the servicing of the national debt, which jumped from USD 2.3m in 1970 to USD 42m in 1979 (see Table 2).

The position of the trade unions in relation to these indicators is very revealing in the context of their involvement in the management of affairs of State.

## The trade union position

Firstly, we need to remember that, politically speaking, the decade 1969-1979 coincided with the first ten years of Togo's single-party government. They were also decisive years for the Togolese trade union movement, now that the era of colonial rule and the period 1960-1972 were things of the past. The RPT was founded in 1969; then, in 1971, the two national centres that had survived the army takeover in 1967, the UNTT and the CSTT, together with the autonomous union of teachers, formed an 'intersyndicale' (inter-union structure), the Comité National Intersyndical du Togo (CONISTO - National Inter-union Committee of Togo).

However, the Committee had little time to engage in activities of any significance; as early as 1972, the political authorities were already interfering in the affairs of individual unions, and it eventually dissolved both CONISTO and the centres. A commission was then set up to prepare for the Constitutive Congress of a new single union; the Conference took place between 5 and 8 January 1973 in Lomé, and culminated in the foundation of the Confédération Nationale des Travailleurs du Togo (CNTT - National Confederation of Togolese Workers).

From the outset, the CNTT made no secret of its wish to be an active element of the RPT; the Preamble to the Rules makes this crystal clear. It also argued for a participative form of trade unionism that 'guaranteed workers' participation in the management of national enterprises and institutions of the State, and in the drafting and implementation of, and control over, economic plans'.

The implication was that the kind of trade unionism which submitted claims and demands was being replaced by one that was 'essentially constructive and objective'. The CNTT's policy certainly enabled it to wring substantial gains out of the government; these included the setting up of a consumers' cooperative in 1976 and the doubling of family allowances in 1977. Indeed, this concept of participation trade unionism was later clarified at the Extraordinary Congress in 1977 and described as 'responsible' participation. According to the then General Secretary of the CNTT, responsible participation meant that the CNTT should be 'represented at all levels of all political and socio-economic bodies' (lecture by CNTT General Secretary, Study Day, August 1976).

In practice, this definition gives us little idea of what responsible participation actually meant; it seems to have had more to do with a state of mind than with a structure that set down rules. However, responsible participation emerged a little more clearly from the way the centres actually behaved towards the government, and from the ideals of the single party. Every action that the national centre carried out within the framework of participation had to be guided by the wishes of the Head of State; more accurately, 'each person must contribute his/her stone to the construction of the nation' (Barnabo, 1981: 16).

However, do these gains made by the unions satisfactorily explain their silence on the economic difficulties that were beginning to affect the country? Given the extent to which trade unions were involved in the management of affairs of State at all levels, one might have expected them to adopt some sort of position; after all, everyone could see the crisis approaching, and they could not fail to have been very concerned. The process of 'responsible participation' meant that unions were not in a position to claim they did not know what was going on economically. However, union announcements - mostly contained in speeches given at seminars and other trade union gatherings, particularly May Day festivities - referred solely to the benefits that had been won (Barnabo, op cit: 48-51).

To be fair, expressions open to the people generally - for instance, the Party and other civil organisations such as women's and youth groups - were just as silent as the trade unions had been over imminent economic dangers. The fault lay with the monolithic political structure, which excluded any opposition or viewpoint that pinpointed any weaknesses in the system.

All in all, the period from 1969 to 1979 was of critical importance to the establishment of the political system that was to rule the country for almost 30 years. For all that the political monolith and the systematic compromising of social groups had a negative influence on the dependent variable (i.e. the phenomenon of democracy), they appeared nonetheless to allow the country to enjoy relative political stability; this is particularly true if we bear in mind the period in question (1960-1967) and the situation prevailing in neighbouring countries. However, most economic indicators (e.g. inflation, servicing the public debt and balance of trade figures) were starting to go into the red at this time, and the country's leading players could have drawn attention to this if they had been given the opportunity.

The result was that life continued in a climate of relative political stability, and this lulled people into a sense of false security. In reality, deteriorating economic indicators were having an increasingly serious effect on the daily lives of Togolese citizens.

## Crisis: 1980-1990

The 1980s were a period of crisis for Africa generally. For countries that depended for more than 50% of their export revenue on staple products (Fisher, 1991), the generalised fall in world prices for these products led to a major shortfall in receipts. The result was that governments had to go deeper and deeper into debt if they wanted to finance development projects, and this had a knock-on effect on certain macro-economic imbalances.

Draconian corrective measures were introduced to correct the imbalances, although these prompted social protest in many cases. The outcome was that the whole continent lurched from a late 1980s crisis that was essentially economic to another different, political crisis marked by social unrest. This time, however, this crisis was accompanied by demands for more democracy and freedom, and governments came under pressure to take the road to political opening ('Jeune Afrique Économie', May 1990, pp 108-111).

Although it was possible to detect a degree of popular discontent with the Togolese government following the measures taken to check the crisis, no substantial social unrest was observed at any time during the period under examination. For example, in 1982-1983, the government realised that various deficits (e.g. debt, budgetary deficit and privatisation) were growing, and introduced harsh, draconian measures to correct these deviations. One was a halt to public sector recruitment; another involved the introduction of supplementary taxes, including a national solidarity tax that was voted in by the 6th RPT Congress in 1982. At the time, it was still possible to introduce such measures without unleashing social unrest; the reason was that the political system obliged people to give unquestioning support to the actions of a government which in turn only carried out decisions taken by the State-Party.

In political terms, the first half of the 1980s was somewhat reminiscent of period 1969-1979. The monolithic structure prevailed, and even 'touching up' the RPT to give it a semblance of legitimacy handed the Party even more control over the State. Other legislation passed at this time concerned:
- voting on a new Constitution in December 1979 (promulgated in January 1980);
- calling the first-ever elections.

The 1980 Constitution brought in a Presidential government which was notable for the primacy of the State-Party. This strengthened the powers of the President of the Republic, who was also the Founder-President of the RPT, by making him Head of State and government, and giving him full executive powers. The aim of the new Constitution was to institutionalise the government as the RPT's Extraordinary Congress in November 1979 had suggested (Report of the Commission of General Policy and of the Administrative Reform of the Congress).

In addition to the Draft Constitution, the 1979 Congress had recommended that a list of candidates be produced for the first legislative elections since 1967. This single list was to be drawn up by the Party's Political Bureau, and candidates had to be activists who worked for the single party; the aim was to elect new-style Deputies who were 'vigilant and responsible' (Report of the Political Commission to the 3rd RPT Congress, Lomé, 27-29 November 1979).

The referendum and the legislative elections of December 1979 were therefore the régime's first 'political opening', and enabled it to move from emergency administration to constitutional government. This opening did not mean that democracy reigned in all corners of the Party and throughout the country as a whole; for that, the Party's principles and working methods had to undergo a root-and-branch transformation.

In practice, these consultations did not bring about any change in the single party's principles and methods. On the contrary, at the very time the Party was recommending this 'opening', the 1980 Constitution was reinforcing and centralising the Party's powers by confirming its primacy over the State. For civil society, therefore, what appeared to be a political opening did not translate into more freedom (e.g. freedom of expression, a diversity of publications and freedom of association) at all; in fact, the existence of an organisation outside the framework of the single party was still beyond the bounds of possibility. What is more, there continued to be only one legally authorised newspaper: the daily, 'Togo-Presse'.

Everything seemed to go swimmingly for the Party and the country generally from 1980 to 1985, but from 1986 onwards the relative political stability that Togo had hitherto experienced was put to the test by indirect manifestations of protest; they included a bomb blast, the distribution of subversive tracts, and even an armed attack by 'elements from beyond the country's borders'. These protests persisted until the end of 1990. However, the government was able to brush aside these 'minor disorders' - they were most unlikely to undermine the State anyway - and it profited from the relative political stability to introduce further draconian measures. These were necessary because of the national and international economic situation, but they had also been recommended by the Bretton Woods Institutions. The RPT's 6th National Council in December 1982 then endorsed decisions that the Party's Central Committee had taken the previous month. They were:
- the introduction of a solidarity tax to 'build up a fund designed to guarantee self-sufficiency in food for the immediate future' (Report on the economic situation to the 6th National Council: 24);

- the winding up of six State-owned companies and the privatisation of one of them (Special Resolution of the Synthesis Commission on State-owned Companies, RPT 6th National Council).

The latter decision to close the State-owned companies was widely accepted as 'normal', despite the social problems that would flow from it, but the solidarity tax was deemed authoritarian, and anyway conjunctural; it was felt that it should therefore be withdrawn in the short term, and no later than the medium term. The perpetuation of this tax was later used as a stick with which to beat the government.

In conclusion, despite the adjustments that were made at a political level, the 1980s were a transitional period when measures taken by the Party were seen as unpopular, even though some of them were dictated by external economic factors.

The 1980s brought the curtain down on the five-year development plans. The last of them (the fourth), which ran from 1980 to 1985, had been expected by the government to give Togo economic lift-off, but in the end it was terminated early for financial reasons (Kpetigo, 1992).

Most of the significant economic indicators had already declined during the 1970s and, to head off any further deterioration, the government initially brought in a package of austere economic policies; then in 1979, on the recommendation of the IMF and World Bank, Togo had its first SAP. Three more were introduced before they were eventually abandoned in 1986-1988. The various economic recovery plans failed because of the serious errors that had been committed during the 1970s, the period of euphoria; these included major public works programmes, and disastrous, ill-thought out investments.

*Economic mistakes*

The period 1974-1978 was characterised by a public works policy which enabled the country to acquire the infrastructures (e.g. roads, hotels and the foundations of an industrial base) it badly needed for economic development, but many economic mistakes were also made during this time. As a report presented to the RPT's 6th National Council in December 1982 pointed out, 'Investments have not produced the best results in all sectors; this is due to a lack of management capacity and a poor assessment of economic information' (Report on the economic, social and cultural situation in Togo, RPT 6th National Council).

The following analysis of trends in the various economic aggregates during this ten-year period highlights the peaks and troughs. The GNP and GDP grew by approximately 7% between 1980 and 1990; this represented a net improvement over the previous period.

**Table 3:** **Trends in GNP and GDP in USD millions (1980)**

| Year | Aggregates | |
|------|------|------|
| | GPD | GNP |
| 1980 | 1128,36 | 1091,44 |
| 1981 | 949,47 | 900,15 |
| 1982 | 820,75 | 771,15 |
| 1983 | 782,01 | 736,1 |
| 1984 | 718,15 | 677,88 |
| 1985 | 752,79 | 710,5 |
| 1986 | 1054,86 | 1004,62 |
| 1987 | 1237,43 | 1184,2 |
| 1988 | 1378,88 | 1322,14 |
| 1989 | 1351,36 | 1311,87 |
| 1990 | 1637,77 | 1607,78 |

From this Table, it is possible to extrapolate a graph showing the growth rates of both aggregates, and so provide a clearer explanation of trends over the period.

**Figure 2:** **Growth of GNP and GDP from 1979-1980 to 1990 (%)**

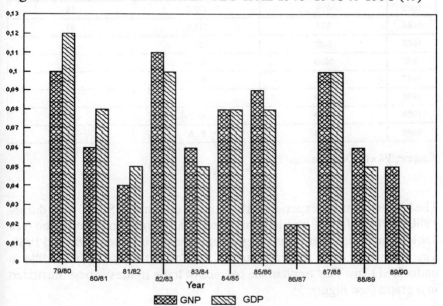

Forewarning of the crisis came in the form of falls in GNP and GDP in 1981-1982, 1983-1984 and 1986-1987, but the decline was even more remarkable from 1989-1990 onwards, with growth in both aggregates slipping from +10% in 1988 to +3% in 1990.

As Table 4 below shows, debt servicing rose from USD 52m in 1980 to USD 145m in 1876, before falling back to USD 86m in 1990 (World Debt Tables). After 1981, the total public debt accounted for much more disturbing proportions, even outstripping GNP (107.21% of GNP in 1981) until 1988 when it dropped back to 93.4%.

The ratio of debt servicing to export revenue[4] (this measures a country's capacity to honour its short-term commitments through export revenue) grew substantially from 1984 to 1986, indicating a serious drain on this revenue which was used exclusively to pay back interest and the principal; it rose from 16.2% in 1983 to 28.7% in 1986, after dropping to 9% in 1980 (World Debt Tables). Altogether, debt servicing grew at an alarming rate during this period (see Table 4).

Table 4:     Trends in total public debt (1984-1990)

| Year | Debt in $ Millions | Debt/GNP % | Debt Servicing in $ Millions |
|------|--------------------|-----------|------------------------------|
| 1980 | 1045 | 95,5 | 52 |
| 1981 | 965 | 107,22 | 64 |
| 1982 | 956 | 123,97 | 55 |
| 1983 | 915 | 126,6 | 59 |
| 1984 | 807 | 118,8 | 91 |
| 1985 | 940 | 131,7 | 111 |
| 1986 | 1069 | 106,5 | 145 |
| 1987 | 1239 | 103,3 | 90 |
| 1988 | 1229 | 93,4 | 130 |
| 1989 | 1186 | 91,7 | 91 |
| 1990 | 1296 | 81,8 | 86 |

*Source*: World Debt Tables

The balance of trade experienced an average deficit of USD 10.91m during 1980-1990. In fact, it was in permanent deficit throughout the period (see Table 5), although there was a slight improvement between 1983 and 1985. The balance of trade settled around USD 6m, but fell sharply in 1984 to under USD 1m. This trend in the balance of trade figures is best illustrated in a graph (see Figure 3).

**Table 5:**   Imports and exports (USD millions) (1980-1990)

| Year | Imports | Exports | Balance |
|------|---------|---------|---------|
| 1980 | 68,77 | 55,18 | -13,58 |
| 1981 | 56,45 | 47,65 | -8,79 |
| 1982 | 54,07 | 43,28 | -10,77 |
| 1983 | 40,67 | 34,4 | -6,27 |
| 1984 | 37,32 | 36,77 | -0,54 |
| 1985 | 47,13 | 36,9 | -6,23 |
| 1986 | 51,25 | 38,46 | -12,79 |
| 1987 | 55,43 | 42,78 | -12,64 |
| 1988 | 70,47 | 54,08 | -16,38 |
| 1989 | 66,54 | 53,97 | -12,57 |
| 1990 | 74,04 | 54,54 | -19,5 |

*Source*: Our own work based on data supplied by the National Accounts Office
of Togo and CFAF-USD rates of exchange
*Série*: Moyenne de la période, IMF, Statistiques financières internationales.

**Figure 3:**   Togolese imports and exports (1980-1990)

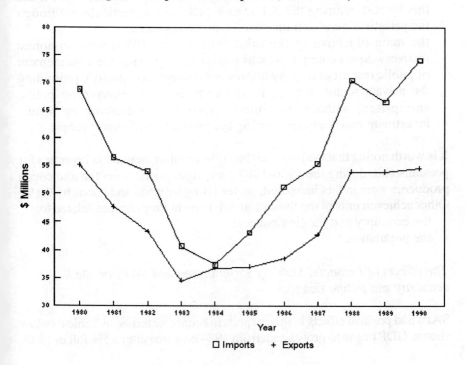

The condition of the aggregates as illustrated in the Tables and Figures above led to the various economic recovery measures already referred to. The most important were:
-   the levying of a solidarity tax;
-   the introduction of several SAPs;
-   a halt on public sector recruitment (despite the fact that the State was the country's biggest employer).

In practice, most of the measures taken to correct the economic imbalances were implemented within the framework of Finance Stability Programmes and Structural Adjustment Programmes that the IMF and the World Bank promoted in order to reduce budget deficits and debts. An example was the decision by the State to limit staffing costs and other current expenditure starting in 1983.

Togo implemented three Structural Adjustment Programmes in addition to the Financial Stability Programmes:
-   the first, which ran from 1980 to 1984, was mainly aimed at reducing the costs of public enterprises; this led to the closure of a number of non-profitable State-owned and parastatals in 1982;
-   the second Structural Adjustment Programme, which commenced in 1985, sought to consolidate the 'gains' made by the first SAP; it did this by restructuring the public enterprise sector, particularly through the privatisation of certain State-owned companies;
-   the main objective of the third Programme (1988) was economic recovery. Special emphasis was placed on improving the management of public resources (e.g. by improving absorption capacity), promoting the private sector (e.g. by removing monopolies enjoyed by public enterprises, withdrawing import licences and drawing up a new investment code) and developing the production of export crops.

It is worth noting that the first SAP brought about an increase in revenues for peasants and, during the 1986-1987 campaign, prices to coffee and cocoa producers were in fact increased, coffee rising by 9.6% and cocoa by 9.1%. Other achievements of the Structural Adjustment Programmes related to:
-   the economy and public finances;
-   the population.

*The effects of Financial Stability Programmes and SAPs on the economy and public finances*

SAPs had positive effects in this respect; in economic terms, as Table 6 below shows, GDP began to grow again from 1984 onwards after a 5% fall in 1983.

Table 6:    Nominal GDP growth 1984-1989 (CFAF millions)

| Year | GDP | % Variation |
|------|-----|-------------|
| 1984 | 313,8 | - |
| 1985 | 338,2 | 7,77 |
| 1986 | 365,3 | 8,01 |
| 1987 | 371,9 | 1,8 |
| 1988 | 410,7 | 10,43 |
| 1989 | 431,1 | 4,96 |

*Source*: Directorate of Statistics, National Accounts Office of Togo

Recovery stemmed partly from the funds that supported these programmes and were injected into the economy, and partly from a range of economies in public expenditure and a revitalisation (albeit timid) of the private sector.

As far as public finances were concerned, the various closures and privatisations of State-owned companies cut back the financial cost that these enterprises represented to the State. In fact, the ratio of budgetary deficit to GDP fell during the period from 7.6% in 1983 to 5.4% in 1989 (Macro-economic Unit, Ministry of the Plan).

It is hard to find anything positive to say at all about the impact that structural programmes had on other economic partners.

*The effect on economic partners*

Positive effects included the settlement of back pay owed by State and State-owned companies, speeded-up procedures for the settlements of public markets, and the adoption of a new investment code allowed by these Programmes. However, enterprises experienced generally negative effects due to:
-   increased tax and customs pressure;
-   higher cost prices caused by steeper water and electricity charges;
-   compression of demand brought about by a wage and recruitment freeze, and a limit on public investment.

Although the adjustment programmes caused growth to pick up from 1984 onwards, households experienced negative effects as follows:
-   decreased purchasing power resulting from the solidarity tax, the wage and promotion freeze in the public sector, an increase in public sector charges (e.g. water and electricity), and higher medical and education costs;

- higher unemployment because the modern sector was doing little in the way of recruiting, and the public sector none at all or limiting recruitment to the filling of vacancies. The workforce in the modern sector, as opposed to the informal sector, fell dramatically between 1987 and 1989 (0.23% in 1987-1988, 7.05% in 1988-1989) (Ministère de l'Enseignement Technique et de la Formation Professionnelle (METFP - Ministry of Technical Education and Vocational Training)), 1993: 36);
- a fall in revenue experienced by small business people and artisans in the informal sector; this was the result of a slowdown in production and shrinking incomes in the towns and cities;
- limited purchasing power for farmers growing food products, mainly because of a small rise in food prices compared with consumer prices.

At the beginning, SAPs were seen as the only way of limiting and containing the economic crisis engulfing SSA countries, but most experts now consider them to have been a failure. In the case of Togo, the economic situation was already unfavourable in the late 1970s, and the implementation of SAPs in the 1980s only accentuated the decline of workers' purchasing power; more particularly, it aggravated a sense of frustration and discontent among those living in the towns and cities. For example, between 1977 and 1989, 42% of urban dwellers were living below the poverty threshold, compared with a rate for all developing countries of 25% (Human Development Report, 1993, Table 18, p 193).

Nonetheless, there were no signs of social disapproval of this situation until late 1990. Only then did the government really have any idea of the level of popular discontent.

*What are the trade unions doing?*

For the CNTT, now the only recognised trade union centre still in existence, the status quo reigned throughout the 1980s despite the crisis. Its leadership acquired an unsavoury reputation nationwide, and at an early stage, the General Secretary was even offered a seat on the Party's Central Committee, a key body with responsibility for taking high-level decisions; he subsequently joined the Political Bureau, the Party's most senior committee. The centre also took a key role in a number of economic recovery measures and the various SAPs, most of these policies having been ratified by the Central Committee. This may well explain why during that time - and certainly not before 1990 - the CNTT failed to react to the crippling effect that SAPs were having on workers' purchasing power; the government's 5-10% pay rise had been granted long before in 1986.

The considerable support that the CNTT gave to government action left it in a parlous position in 1990 when Togolese people began to articulate general concern about the political system in general.

The period 1980-1990 may be described as a period of decline for Togo's one-party system. True, the single party slowly tightened its grip on the apparatus of the State between 1980 and 1985-1986, but from 1987 onwards the system's 'popularity' fell away to such an extent that it had completely evaporated by 1990. However, it is difficult to see how the increasing hold that the Party had over the management of the country actually led to its decline, or that people's living conditions were in any way to blame for the system's failure.

One way and another, after 20 years of monolithic rule, people were clearly beginning to feel they had had enough. The gloomy economic situation of the time certainly reinforced this sentiment, particularly as unfavourable economic results were now being adduced as proof that the system was failing.

To conclude, the winds of democracy that had begun to blow across Africa towards the end of the 1980s acted as a catalyst for this 'sudden' appearance of anti-government protest. A growing desire for free expression in late 1989 on the part of the people, and journalists and lawyers in particular, also persuaded the government to agree to the founding of a private sector press.

## The democratic process: 1991 to the present day

Even in the last few months of 1989, Togo's political and economic situation was such that changes were clearly inevitable if the country was ever to make a fresh start. In the political arena, voices were raised for a review of the Party's methods and practices (RPT 7th National Council); as for the economy, the grim effects of the SAPs had worked their way down to ordinary people, and it was now widely acknowledged that nothing short of a clean sweep at the top was acceptable if a new economic policy was to be put in place.

The fall of the Berlin Wall and the collapse of Communism are often credited with the upheavals that have shaken the world so decisively since the late 1980s. However, in Africa, and francophone Africa in particular, more frequently cited causes of political change are President Mitterrand's speech at La Baule in 1990, and what have been called the 'winds from the east'. Just the same, as we have seen from earlier developments, internal factors, such as an authoritarian political system and unpopular economic measures aimed at halting the crisis, also contributed to discontent among the people, and it was this discontent that triggered the protests.

The first manifestation of this unrest occurred on 5 October 1990 during the trial of a group of young people accused of writing and distributing subversive tracts;[5] in defiance of police authority and while the hearing was still in progress, the accused sang 'Terre de nos aïeux' (Land of our ancestors), the national anthem of independence that had been replaced by the Party's anthem, 'Unité nationale' (National unity) at RPT Congress on 27-29 November 1979.

Thereafter, protests proliferated until February or March 1991; then, after the inhabitants of Lomé, the capital, and the suburbs joined in a series of demonstrations calling for more freedoms - including freedom of expression and freedom of association - the government gave way and signed an agreement with the opposition on 12 June. This brought the one-party system to an end and suspended the National Assembly in mid-term. The establishment of other political parties was also legalised,[6] and the principle of calling a National Conference was at last won. A National Conference in fact took place on 8 July 1991 (Decree N 91/179 of 25 June 1991 as amended by Decree N 182 of 2 July 1991), and provided people with an opportunity for voicing their dissatisfaction; all the institutions that had been set up by the one-party system came in for heavy criticism.

## Trade unions and the democratic process

The single trade union centre, the CNTT, was denounced and its leaders made almost unqualified confessions. The CNTT's capitulation was all but complete:
- most local unions opted to disaffiliate;
- both private sector and public sector workers refused to pay their compulsory dues any more (this entitlement, which had been granted by the previous government, was now renounced by the CNTT itself);
- there was a change in the national centre's leadership, and an Extraordinary Congress broke off relations with the RPT;
- new unions were formed and proclaimed themselves independent from the CNTT;[7]
- a large number of pay and conditions claims were submitted by these new unions, which now formed themselves into new centres. The most important of these were the Union Nationale des Syndicats Indépendants du Togo (UNSIT - National Union of Independent Togolese Unions), the Confédération Syndicale des Travailleurs du Togo (CSTT - Trade Union Confederation of Togolese Workers), and the Groupe des Syndicats Autonomes (GSA - Group of Autonomous Trade Unions); the latter included the unions for bank staff and post and telecommunications employees (SYNBANK and SYLPOSTEL respectively).

These three organisations later came together in the Collectif des Syndicats Indépendants (CSI - Collective of Independent Trade Unions), which took an active role in the industrial action and political activities that preceded the National Conference in July-August 1991. In addition, it rapidly became a powerful pressure group during pay and conditions negotiations covering the majority of jobs (e.g. teachers and post and telecommunications staff) and on popular demonstrations calling for more freedom (freedom of expression and freedom of association). In political terms, these unions were also active participants in the National Conference, and most of their leaders chaired the various committees associated with it (e.g. the Conference Presidium) or served as members of the High Council of the Republic.[8]

Towards end of 1992, the Togolese trade union movement presented a very diversified picture, but one nonetheless dominated by two organisations: one was the CSI, which concealed none of its distaste for the previous government and the former single party, the RPT; the other was the CNTT, which was yet to give any unambiguous sign, through concrete actions, of having distanced itself from the RPT. This bipolarisation of the trade union movement was to play an important role in subsequent political and social events that accompanied the democratic process in Togo. One of them was the general strike in November 1992.

When the CSI called an indefinite General Strike for 16 November 1992 in protest against the sense of insecurity pervading the country (in conjunction with the opposition parties, it also demanded the formation of a new government), the CNTT responded in a way that gave the impression of being weak and undecided about which way to turn. The situation was made all the more embarrassing for the CNTT by the fact that the strike call was obeyed by the majority of its members.

The CNTT came out in support of the strike after it had been running for two weeks, but it was opposed to the action continuing indefinitely. Accordingly, it called for a return to work, but no one took any notice. However, new 'free' unions were now being formed, and they argued openly against the strike on the grounds that it was 'political'. In fact, 'free' trade unions sprang up in all socio-professional sectors and, in December of the same year, they formed themselves into the Union Générale des Syndicats Libres (UGSL - General Union of Free Trade Unions). This new body also described itself as independent of the CNTT, which now found its leadership role in the trade union movement under attack.

There were two lessons to be learned from this situation: firstly, it spelled the end of the single trade union structure in Togo; secondly, it posed a general question about the role that African trade unions should play in the democratic processes in their countries.

When the indefinite General Strike was over, the trade union stage was dominated by the UGSL, CNTT and CSI.[9] In October 1993, in the course of this study, we carried out a survey of all the trade union centres to identify grass roots unions and determine their relative size in terms of membership. Unfortunately, only the UGSL responded to our questions; the others were unavailable or else refused to take part.

Of the 43 trade unions which senior UGSL officials say are affiliated to that centre, 23 sent back completed questionnaires. The most important conclusions were as follows:
-   56% of them were formed between 16 November and late December 1992;
-   they have an average membership of 200;
-   local unions cover almost all socio-professional categories.

CSI activities were curtailed in February 1993, and the union did not resume its work until after the electoral consultations of February 1994.

The key feature of the Togolese trade union movement is the pluralism that came out of the political protests of 1990-1991.[10] In Togo, the trade union (the CNTT in this case) opted simply to let democracy happen, and decided against being a key player. Furthermore, the CNTT was slow to identify its members' aspirations, and it is now trapped between those who held power in the former government and the trade unions that sprang up during the democratic process (i.e. the CSI and the UGSL).

All three trade unions, the CSI, CNTT and UGSL, claim independence from the various political parties, but the facts suggest that the UGSL and the CNTT are closer to the RPT; the CSI, for its part, is quite open about its affinity to pre-February 1994 opposition parties. These various 'alliances' of unions and political parties may explain the lethargy in social affairs since the indefinite General Strike was called off in August 1993.

The devaluation of the CFA franc in January 1994 was one of the most important devaluations in Black Africa since the Second World War, but Togo was one of the very few countries affected where the unions took a relatively long time before announcing their post-devaluation position. Indeed, some unions did not even start organising study seminars and study days until after March of that year; for example, the CNTT ran its first study day on 'The 50% devaluation of the CFA franc: advantages and disadvantages for economic and social life in Togo'[11] that month, and the UGSL organised a seminar on 'How should workers respond to the devaluation of the CFA franc?' on 7 April 1994.[12]

In fact, it was not for another year, when an inter-union structure was founded in January 1995, that the trade union movement organised any concrete actions; these were aimed at forcing the government to introduce assistance measures and counter-balance the reduction in workers' purchasing power caused by devaluation.

*Trade union activity since January 1995*

Trade union lethargy since the end of the General Strike in August 1993 is partly explained by trade union pluralism, and partly by the alliances that the various unions have formed with political parties. This is sometimes reflected in the hesitancy about the appropriate action to take. Such unwillingness on the part of trade unions to make a move was challenged in 1994 by the establishment of a new national centre, the Confédération Générale des Cadres du Togo (CGCT - General Confederation of Togolese Executives). This body, which proclaims political neutrality and seeks to operate on a pragmatic and responsible basis, played an active role in setting up the intersyndicale (inter-union structure) in January 1995.[13]

Under Article 1 of its Internal Regulation, the inter-union structure (intersyndicale) comprises:
-   the Confédération Nationale des Travailleurs du Togo (CNTT);
-   the Confédération Syndicale des Travailleurs du Togo (CSTT);
-   the Union Générale des Syndicats Libres (UGSL);
-   the Confédération Générale des Cadres du Togo (CGCT).

The intersyndicale had been set up 'to bring together the active citizens (les forces vives) of the country for the defence of workers' material and moral interests' (Article 1 of the Internal Regulation); however, of the centres that had been in existence since 1992, only the UNSIT and GSA were not members.

The structure of the intersyndicale is set out in Article 6 of the Regulation:
-   a General Assembly of seven members per trade union centre;
-   a Coordination Committee of three members per national centre, including the most senior official;
-   a secretariat run by an appropriately skilled member;
-   a Finance Committee made up of one representative per trade union centre.

The intersyndicale's sources of finance are not identified in the constitution; Article 13 of the Internal Regulation states merely that, 'expenses incurred by the organisation's activities shall be shared equally among affiliated trade union centres, and bills shall be settled promptly'.

Since April-May 1995, the inter-union structure has been taking part in tripartite negotiations (involving government, the employers' national council and trade unions[14]) on union platforms of demands. These negotiations were the unions' first concrete actions after their long period of silence, and this is reflected in their claims:
- settlement of back pay;
- settlement of the backlog of pension contributions;
- review of, and revaluation of, salaries.[15]

Preliminary agreement between the parties on these demands had already established priorities. Then, in March 1996, the intersyndicale took part in more detailed negotiations with State-owned companies engaged in the delivery of particular services (e.g. electricity, water and telephones), and with the government on the rates that these companies charged. After implementation of the economic recovery programmes that came in the wake of the 1992-1993 political crisis and devaluation, these rates were revised upwards (with the specific addition of VAT) although salaries stayed where they were. Finally, on 26 March, the negotiations produced a 5% reduction in the cost of electricity for domestic use (down from CFAF 75/Kwh to CFAF 71/Kwh with effect from September 1996).[16]

The setting up of the inter-union body clearly relaxed tensions in the Togolese trade union movement following a long period of hesitancy and mutual distrust. In addition to the various gains that the intersyndicale won, its leaders also made progress on trade union involvement in government decision-making.[17] However, the platform of demands submitted to the government on May Day 1996 shows how much remains to be done if the unions are to build on the consensuses reached in April-May 1995 and March 1996.

The devaluation of the CFA franc has been presented as a penalty for the disastrous economic situation our countries were in; however, what really accentuated the country's already deteriorating economic situation were the socio-political problems that marked the democratic process in Togo; this explains the difficulty that the government experienced in getting the economy moving again.

The SAPs were abandoned in 1989 because the conditions laid down by the IMF were not observed. The balance of trade remained in deficit until 1992, falling from CFAF 40.1bn in 1989 to CFAF 53.1bn in 1990, before climbing back to CFAF 44.9bn in 1992. The total debt went from CFAF 352.8bn in 1990 to CFAF 326.76bn in December 1993 (Directorate of the Economy); this relative decrease in the debt is partly due to the fact that funders had withdrawn credit facilities in 1991.

*Price spiral*

It is too early to estimate the real impact of the devaluation of the CFA franc on the economy and on workers' purchasing power; what is certain, however, is that the economic situation of most of the countries affected is going to deteriorate in the short term at least. For the Togolese consumer, for example, this will result in certain vital products doubling in price. Broadly speaking, in the weeks that immediately followed devaluation in 1994-1995, retail prices of most imported goods rose 30%, and some by over 100% (see Table 7). These increases also found their way into food shops where prices of local products went up by 30-40%.

Table 7:    Comparison of prices of vital products

| Product | Origin or Brand | Qty | Price prior to devaluation of CFA Franc | Price after devaluation | Variation (%) |
|---|---|---|---|---|---|
| Rice | Thailand | 50 kg | 7 220 | 11 943 | 65,4 |
| Rice | VietNam | 50 kg | 5 872 | 12 744 | 117 |
| Rice | Pakistan | 50 kg | 5 670 | 13 250 | 133,7 |
| Sugar | EU powdered sugar | 50 kg | 6 667 | 14 100 | 111,5 |
| Sugar | St Louis | 1 kg | 275 | 493 | 79,3 |
| Goutte d'or Oil | NIOTO17 | 25 l | 7 565 | 11 500 | 52 |

*Source*: Directorate of the Economy (March 1994)

Prices spiralled during 1994 and 1995, but some locally produced goods, food in particular, became relatively cheaper towards the end of 1995. The period from 1991 to the present time appears to be terminating the interaction between the independent variables (i.e. the political system, trade union activity and implemented economic policies); the state of these variables from 1980 onwards seems to have had a considerable impact on the dependant variable (i.e. democracy). In fact, it was precisely during this time that the RPT had a stranglehold over the State through the primacy of the single party; by the same token, it may well have encouraged the people to reject the government altogether. It was also during this period that the economy's poor international showing caused growth policies at home to be abandoned in favour of Structural Adjustment Programmes; these in turn had a crippling and direct effect on people's purchasing power.

If we examine the upheavals that ushered in the democratic process in the majority of francophone African countries, two factors stand out:

- the various political changes that introduced political pluralism and democratic freedoms into francophone African countries were not achieved by revolution. Democracy really came to these countries as a result of negotiations and agreement - although, as in the case of Togo and Mali, the process was sometimes accompanied by violence. In the main, social structures were preserved;
- francophone Africa seems to have been most affected by democratic fever, with anglophone Africa remaining largely untouched. In practice, even though political change in the English-speaking countries led to pluralist elections, the level of protest never attained the virulence of their francophone neighbours. Might one infer from this observation that the governments in francophone Africa were more authoritarian? This could suggest that the governments on the receiving end of protest in francophone Africa were more authoritarian.

## Conclusion

The yearning for democracy that has gripped francophone Africa over the last few years was largely unexpected, particularly as there was no sign of any such development at all until as late as 1987. For an explanation of this, several economic and socio-political factors need to be addressed. It would be hazardous to try and understand this phenomenon on the basis of too small a sample; however, of all the players in the various democratic processes that have been set in motion throughout Africa, trade unions, the army, youth, women and political parties have played roles of the greatest importance.

In this study, we have focused on the role of the trade unions, the political system and the economic situation in our explanation of democracy in Togo. In order to understand the dynamic of these factors, we have observed them over a period over 30 years divided into three shorter periods of 10 years each. Our observation of these factors over the entire period points to a certain concordance in the way they have evolved; for example, we have noted that each political system in each period was matched by a particular form of trade unionism - political pluralism going hand in hand with trade union pluralism.

Similarly, the establishment of the single party in 1969 led to the disappearance of the various trade union centres then in existence; they were then replaced by a single centre, the CNTT. However, the concentration of power within the monolithic structure occasioned certain slippages which the CNTT, speaking in the name of responsible participation, was unable to do anything about. Perfect identification of the trade union with the single party in 1973, at a time when the democratic process was about to get under way, meant that the former was unable to distance itself from the latter (or anyway was not able to do so in time) when the one-party system came under fire and was rejected in favour of political pluralism.

In the economic arena, growth in the early 1970s, during 1979-1980 and then from 1982 to 1983 was partly due to the relative political stability that the country enjoyed during these periods. However, the persistent economic crisis of the 1980s proved more lasting than political stability because the effects of the crisis, and the decisions taken to contain it, inevitably promoted discontent, particularly among those living in the towns and cities. The result was that the dissatisfaction, which had been economic in origin, led to political protest towards the end of the 1980s.

Did the economic crisis, the political system and trade union action provide the basis for demonstrations calling for more freedom of expression in Togo? In answering this question, we first attempted to identify the role that each of the independent variables (the economic situation, the political system and the trade unions) has been able to play in the advent of the democratic process. We then tried to show chronologically how the cumulative interaction of these variables was able to lead to the democratic process of the 1990s.

## Notes

1  For more on the history of the Togolese trade union movement, see Natchaba, 1982, 1983.
2  See also Jean-Maurice Verdier, 1987: 105.
3  Although supporting most of the Party's ideals, MONESTO later refused to be included as an active element of the Party.
4  Here, export revenue includes all revenue from goods and services.
5  Until this time, ideas could only be published by the one existing (State-owned) press.
6  Over 60 political parties were established and recognised between June 1991 and the end of 1992; the period between October 1990 and July 1992 also

saw the foundation of about 150 civil associations, of which at least 100 were women's organisations.

7  For example, the 15 new unions established between October 1991 and August 1992 exactly replicated the organisations that had previously been affiliated to the CNTT (Ministry of Territorial Administration and Security).

8  The General Secretary of Synbank was a member of the Presidium, and the General Secretary of UNSIT was on the High Council of the Republic; in the transitional period, this was a senior body with legislative powers.

9  When CSI leaders were sent into exile following the events of January 1993, virtually all of the union's activities were left on hold from February to August 1993.

10 Interestingly, freedom of association has always been protected under Togolese law, and under the 1980 Constitution in particular. However, there was a de facto single trade union structure throughout the period from the CNTT's foundation until 1990.

11 'Togo-Presse', Monday 21 March 1994: 4.

12 'Togo-Presse', Friday 8 April 1994: 3.

13 Règlement intérieur de l'intersyndicale (Internal Inter-union Regulation), Workers' Education Centre, Lomé.

14 These include centres that are intersyndicale members and others, such as the GSA and UNSIT, that are not.

15 In the main, the issues of back pay and pay reviews refer to the time of the indefinite General Strike of November 1992 and to the consequences of the devaluation of the CFA franc.

16 Report of Government-Intersyndicale-CEET negotiations of 26 March 1996. Intersyndicale headquarters, Workers' Education Centre, Lomé.

17 Only a year after the intersyndicale was set up, two of its leaders were promoted to executive positions in the State, one as a member of the Presidential cabinet, and the other to a Ministerial post ('Togo-Presse', 28 August 1996).

# Bibliography

Abeyasekera, C. (1977), 'Participative Models for Employee Motivation in Public Enterprises in Sri Lanka'. Paper, Asian Centre for Development Administration: Kuala Lumpur.

Adam, H. and K. Moodley (1993), *Negotiated Revolution: society and politics in post-apartheid South Africa*. Jonathan Ball: Johannesburg.

Adégbidi, F. (1993:64-79), 'Promouvoir l'Engagement au Travail: une approche judicieuse pour l'étude de l'entreprise africaine?', in: *Cahiers de Sociologie Economique et Culturelle*, Le Havre, N 20.

Adégbidi, F. (1994), *Culture et Développement: l'engagement au travail dans l'industrie africaine*. Essai de Psychosociologie du Travail. Thèse de Doctorat (Ph. D), Université du Québec à Montréal: Montréal.

Adler, G. and E. Webster (1995), 'Challenging Transition Theory: the labour movement, radical reform, and transition to democracy in South Africa', in: *Politics and Society*, March 1995, Vol. 23, N 1.

African Charter for Popular Participation in Development and Transformation. International Conference on popular participation in the process of recovery and development in Africa, Arusha, 12-16 February 1990.

African Development Bank (ADB) (1995), *African Development Report*. Addis Ababa.

African National Congress (1994), *The Recontruction and Development Programme: a policy framework*. Umanyano Publications: Johannesburg.

African Workers' Participation and Development Programme (APADEP) (1985), 'Etude Exploratoire sur la Participation des Travailleurs en Relation avec les Structures Syndicales'. Rapport de l'Etude de Cas. PADEP: Togo.

African Workers' Participation and Development Programme (APADEP), International Workshop, Bamako et Mopti (1993), 'Mopti Syndicalement'. Rapport de l'Etude de Cas à Mopti. PADEP: Mali.

African Workers' Participation and Development Programme (APADEP), Mali, Centre Regional (1993), 'Les Nouveaux Vents qui Souflent en Afrique... Le Défi Syndical'. Rapport d'un séminaire de l'Atelier International: syndicats à l'épreuve démocratique en Afrique. 1er février au 11 mars 1993 au Mali, Mopti/Bamako.

Agbanglanon, F. (1993:5), 'Grèves d'Avertissement des Centrales Syndicales: vers une profonde crise sociale', in: *FORUM de la semaine*, N 145, Cotonou.

Agbokou, M. et A. Shadé (1991:4-5), 'Les Réactions de la Rue', in: *FORUM de la semaine*, N 74, Cotonou.

Agossou, J. (1988), 'La Participation en Question', in: *Quotidien Ehuzu*, N 62, Août, Cotonou.

Ake, C. (1995:79-100), 'Approches et Orientations Socio-Politiques pour le Développement Durable en Afrique', in: *Afrique 2000*, N 22, Août.

Akwetey, E.O. (1994), *Trade Unions and Democratisation: a comparative study of Zambia and Ghana*. University of Stockolm: Stockholm.

Albert, M. (1991), *Capitalisme contre Capitalisme*. Seuil: Paris.

Allen, C. (1992:42-58), 'Restructuring an Authoritarian State: democratic renewal in Benin', in: *Review of African Political Economy*, N 54.

Anyang'Nyong'o, P. (ed.) (1987), *Popular Struggles for Democracy in Africa*, Zed Books: London.

Anyang'Nyong'o, P. (1995:27-40), 'Discours sur la Démocratie en Afrique', in: E. Chole et J. Ibrahim (eds.), *Processus de Démocratisation en Afrique: problèmes et perspectives*. CODESRIA, Khartala: Paris.

Asante, S. (1994), *Processus de Démocratisation et Syndicats en Afrique*. Solidarité mondiale: Belgique.

Baah-Nuakoh, A., O. Barfour, N.K. Sowa and K.A. Tutu (1992), *Small Enterprises and Adjustment: The Impact of Ghana's Economic Recovery Programme*. Chameleon Press Ltd.: London.

Bakhiet, A.A. (1992), 'Trade Unions Freedom and the Trade Union Act'. Khartoum, Sudan.

Banégas, R. (1995:25-44), 'Mobilisation Sociale et Opposition sous Kérékou', in: *Politique Africaine*, N 59.

Bangura, Y. (1989:177-190), 'Crisis and Adjustment: the experience of Nigerian workers', in: B. Onimode (ed.), *The IMF, the World Bank and the African Debt: the social and political impact*. Institute of African Alternatives. Zed Books: London.

Bangura, Y., P. Gibbon and A. Ofstad (eds.) (1992), *Authoritarianism, Democracy and Adjustment: the politics of economic reform in Africa*. Scandinavian Institute of African Studies: Uppsala.

Barnabo, N. (1981), *La CNTT et la Participation Responsable*. Maison Tancsico: Budapest.

Barrett, J. (1994:84-88), 'Trade Unions in Nigeria: the temperature is rising', in: *South African Labour Bulletin*, Vol.18, N 4.

Baskin, J. (1991), *Striking Back: a history of COSATU*. Verso: London.

Bayat, A. (1991), *Work, Politics and Power*. Zed Books: London.

Bio, G. (1993:9), 'La Querelle des Centrales Syndicales Profite-t-elle aux Travailleurs Béninois?', in: *FORUM de la semaine*, N 114.

Blardone, G. (1990), *Le Fonds Monétaire International, l'ajustement et les coûts de l'homme: dégager de nouveaux chemins*. Editions de l'Epargne: Paris.

Boateng, K. (1995), 'Employment, Unemployment and the Labour Market', in: *The State of the Ghanaian Economy in 1994*. Legon, Accra.

Botswana Federation of Trade Unions (BFTU), International Confederation of Free Trade Unions (ICFTU) (1991), 'Joint BFTU / ICFTU Panafrican Conference on Democracy, Development and the Defence of Human and Trade Unions Rights'. Gaborone, 9-11 July 1991.

Bourguignon, F. and C. Morrison (1992), *Adjustment and Equity in Developing Countries: a new approach*. OECD Development Centre: Paris.

Bowles, S. et H. Gintis (1987), *La Démocratie Post-Libérale: essai critique sur le libéralisme et le marxisme*. La Découverte: Paris.

Buhlungu, S. (1994:7-17), 'COSATU and the Elections', in: *South African Labour Bulletin*, Vol. 18, N 2.

Buijtenhuis, R. et E. Rijnierse (1993), *Démocratisation en Afrique au Sud du Sahara 1989-1992: un aperçu de la littérature*. African Studies Centre: Leiden.

Buijtenhuis, R. et C. Thiriot (1995), *Démocratisation en Afrique au Sud du Sahara 1992-1995: un bilan de la littérature*. Centre d'Etude Africaines / Centre d'Etudes d'Afrique Noire: Leiden / Bordeaux.

Cahen, M. (1991:347-92), 'Archipels de l'Artenance: la victoire de l'opposition aux îles du Cap Vert et à São Tomé e Princípe', in: *Année Africaine* 1990/91.

Cassen, B. (1991:22), 'Pour une Démocratie Vraiment Participative', in: *Le Monde Diplomatique*, Août.

Centrale Générale des Travailleurs du Bénin (CGTB) (1994), 'Rapport du Séminaire National sur la Participation des Femmes au Mouvement Syndical et au Processus de Démocratisation'. CGTB: Porto-Novo.

Centre for Development Research (1995), *Structural Adjustment in Africa: a survey of the experience*. Danish Ministry of Foreign Affairs: Copenhagen.

Chambua, S.E. (1991), 'Beyond State-Centred Development', in: B. Turok (ed.), *Alternative Strategies for Africa: debt and democracy*. Vol.3. Institute for African Alternatives: London.

Chambua, S.E. (1995), 'Workers' Participation in Tanzania: the case of Kilombero and Mtibwa Sugar Companies'. APADEP: Dar es Salaam. Forthcoming.

Chambua, S.E. and H.H. Semkiwa (1994), 'Undemocratic Workers' Participation in Tanzanian Public Enterprises: the case study of Morogoro Canvas Mills Ltd'. Case study report. APADEP: Dar es Salaam.

Chesneaux, J. (1991:22), 'Pour une Démocratie Vraiment Participative', in: *Le Monde Diplomatique*, Août.

Clark, J. (1991), *Democratizing Development*. Earthscan Publications Ltd.: London.

Clegg, I. (1971), *Workers' Self-Management in Algeria*. Allan Lane: London.

Coetzee, J.K. and J. Graaff (eds.) (1996), *Reconstruction, Development and People*. Tomson Publishing: Johannesburg.

Cohen, R. (1974), *Labour and Politics in Nigeria: 1945-1971.* Heinemann: London.

Commission of the European Communities (1994), 'Community Support for Structural Adjustment in the ACP countries: towards the consolidation and strengthening of a realistic and concerted approach'. Communication from the Commission. COM (94) 447 final. Brussels.

Commission of the European Communities (1995), 'Reformulating Conditionality in Economic Reform Programmes in Sub-Saharan Africa: an operational approach'. Paper prepared for the meeting of the Special Programme for Africa-Working Group on Economic Reform in the Context of Political Liberalisation, Paris 10-11 November.

Cornia, G., R. Jolly and F. Steward (eds.) (1987), *Adjustment with a Human Face.* (2 vols) Clarendon Press: Oxford.

Coulibaly, M., S. Seydou et S.M. Sissoko (1993), 'Etude de Cas aux Usines SADA-SA'. Rapport de l'Etude de Cas. PADEP: Mali.

Coulibaly, M., F. Maïga, O.O. Sidibé, D.M. Sissoko, S.M. Sissoko et O.M.D. Tacko (1994a), 'Etude de Cas Huicoma'. Rapport de l'Etude de Cas. PADEP: Mali.

Coulibaly, M. et S.M. Sissoko (1994b), 'Autogestion n'est pas Participation: étude de cas à Sukala'. Rapport de l'Etude de Cas. PADEP: Mali.

Coulson, A. (1982:39-40), *Tanzania - a political economy.* Clarendon Press: Oxford.

Council for the Development of Social Science Research in Africa (CODESRIA) (1992:12-26), 'Conference on: Democratization Processes in Africa: Problems & Prospects', in: *CODESRIA Bulletin,* N 1&2.

Crankshaw, O. and D. Hindson (1990), 'New Jobs, New Skills, New Divisions: the changing structure of South Africa's work force', in: *South African Labour Bulletin,* Vol. 5, N 1.

Dahoun, M. (1995:5), 'Femmes et Activités Syndicales', in: *Journal Le Phare,* N 004, Mars.

Dahrendorf, R. (1996:229-49), 'Economic Opportunity, Civil Society and Political Liberty', in: *Development and Change,* Vol.27, N 2.

De Brie, C. (1991:22-23), 'Champ Libre au Modèle Libéral et Démocratique', in: *Le Monde Diplomatique,* Novembre.

Delors, J. (1994), *L'Unité d'un Homme.* Entretiens avec Dominique Wolton. Editions Odile Jacobs: Paris.

Diallo, M., M. Dopavogui et G. Kester (1992), *Guinée: pour un nouveau syndicalisme en Afrique.* PADEP/ L'Harmattan: La Haye/Paris.

Dicko, O, O.O. Sidibé et T. Touré (1985), *Participation des Travailleurs et de leurs Organisations Syndicales en tant que Stratégie de Développement.* Fondation Friedrich Ebert/Union Nationale des Travailleurs du Mali: Bonn/ Bamako.

Diejomaoh, V.P. (1993), 'Effects of Structural Adjustment Programmes on Labour Markets in Africa: the challenge of public sector retrenchment and redeployment programmes'. Paper presented to the OATUU High Level Policy Conference on Structural Adjustment and African Trade Unions, Cairo, 16-18th April, 1993.

Direction de la Statistique, Togo (1967-1992), 'Comptes Nationaux'. Lomé.

Direction de l'Economie, Togo (1994), 'Incidences de la Dévaluation du FCFA sur l'Activité Economique au Togo'. Lomé.

Dodji, S. (1991:4), 'De la Légalité ou de L'Illégalité des Grèves au Bénin', in: *FORUM de la semaine* N 77, Cotonou.

Economic Intelligence Unit (EIU), Country Profiles: Congo, São Tomé and Princípe, Guinea-Bissau, Cape Verde 1995-96. Country Reports: Congo, São Tomé and Princípe, Guinea-Bissau, Cape Verde, 1993 4th quarter (1993), 1994 1st quarter (1994), 1995 4th quarter (1995). The Economic Intelligence Unit Limited: London.

El-Jack, A.H. and C. Leggett (1980), 'Industrial Relations and the Political Process in the Sudan', in: *Research Series* N 49, International Institute for Labour Studies: Geneva, Switzerland.

El-Sayed, S. (1978), *Workers' Participation in Management: the Egyptian Experience*. The American University in Cairo Press: Cairo.

El-Soudan El-Hadieth (February 1996), Daily Newspaper. Khartoum, Sudan.

El-Soudani International (March 1994), Daily Newspaper. Khartoum, Sudan.

Ela, J.-M. (1995), 'Démocratie, Culture et Développement: contextes et enjeux sociologiques en Afrique aujourd'hui'. Communication présentée au Colloque de l'Association Internationale des Sociologues de Langue Française, Cotonou.

Elie, B. (1994:A7), 'Le Fond de l'Histoire: le tiers monde, terre d'expérimentation', in: *Quotidien le Devoir*, N du 10 Août, Montréal.

Elson, D. (1991), *Male Bias in the Development Process*. Manchester University Press: Manchester.

Eritrea Profile (May 1995), Weekly Newspaper. Asmara, Eritrea.

Espinosa, J. and A. Zimbalist (1978), *Economic Democracy: workers' participation in Chilean industry 1970-1973*. Academic Press: New York.

European Confederation of Trade Unions (ETUC) (1994), 'The Lusaka Trade Union Declaration: trade union proposals for a more effective Lomé convention'. Conclusions of the EU/ACP trade union conference on 'The Trade Union Role in the Lomé IV Convention'. Lusaka, Zambia 29 to 31 August 1994.

Fall, M. (1987), *L'Etat et la Question Syndicale au Sénégal*. L'Harmattan: Paris.

Fashoyin, T. (1986:174), 'Management of Industrial Conflict in Africa: a comparative analysis of Kenya, Nigeria and Tanzania', in: U.G. Damachi and H.D. Seibel (eds.), *Management Problems in Africa*. Macmillan Press: London.

Fashoyin, T. (1994), *Economic Reform Policies and the Labour Movement in Nigeria.* Nigerian Industrial Relations Association. University of Lagos: Lagos.

Fashoyin, T. and S. Matanmi (1996), 'Democracy, Labour and Development: transforming industrial relations in Africa', in: *Industrial Relations Journal.* Blackwell Publishers: Oxford.

Fincham, R. and G. Zulu (1980:171-90), 'Labour and Participation in Zambia', in: *Labour and Society*, N 5.

Finley, M. (1976), *Démocratie Antique et Démocratie Moderne.* Payot: Paris.

Fisher, B. (1991:169: 24-27), 'From Commodity Dependency to Development', in: *The OECD Observer,* April/May.

Fox, A. (1971), *A Sociology of Work in Industry.* Collier-Macmillan Limited: London.

Foy, C. (1988), *Marxist Regimes. Cape Verde: politics, economics and society.* Pinter: London.

Free Labour World (November 1993:2), 'The African Saga of IMF Structural Adjustment'. Brussels, Belgium.

Fukuyama, F. (1992), *The End of History and the Last Man.* Hamish Hamilton: London.

Ghana Trades Union Congress (GTUC) (1996), 'Policies of the Trades Union Congress adopted at the 5th quadrennial Congress of TUC'. GTUC: Accra.

Giri, J. (1986), *L'Afrique en Panne.* Karthala: Paris.

Global Coalition for Africa (GCA) (1995), *Africa: 1990-1995 and Beyond.* Document prepared for the 2nd plenary in Maastricht, GCA/SC-J5.4/no.2/06/ 1995, Washington.

Gnancadja, L.-M. (1995:16-18), 'Voeux de Nouvel An de la Société Civile au Chef de l'Etat', in: *La Lettre d'ABUS*, N 000, Janvier, Cotonou.

Godbout, J. (1983), *La Participation Contre la Démocratie.* Editions Saint-Martin: Montréal.

Gogué, A.T. (1997a), 'Impact des PAS sur les Effectifs Scolaires: cas du Togo', in: *La Revue Canadienne d'Etudes de Développement.* A paraître.

Gogué, A.T.(1997b), 'Impact des PAS sur le Secteur de la Santé: cas du Togo', in: *Nouvelles Pratiques Sociales.* A paraître.

Gogué, A., G. Kester and F. Nangati (1992:167-86), 'Trade Union Education and Research for Workers' Participation in Africa', in: T. Fashoyin (ed.), *Industrial Relations and African Development.* Int. Book Cy, Absecon: New York.

Gouvernement Révolutionaire de l'Epoque, Burkina Faso (1983), 'Discours d'Orientation Politique'.

Haggard, S. and S.B. Webb (eds.) (1994), *Voting for Reform: democracy, political liberalisation and economic adjustment.* World Bank, Oxford University Press: Oxford.

Herbst, J. (1991), 'Labour in Ghana under Structural Adjustment: the politics of acquiescence', in: D. Rotschild (ed.), *Ghana: the political economy of recovery.* Lynne Rienner Publishers: Boulder/London.

Hirst, P. (1993), 'Associational Democracy', in: D. Held (ed.), Prospects for Democracy. Polity Press: Oxford.

Hoeven, R. van der (1996), 'Policies for Economic Growth and Development in Southern Africa'. Presentation paper for the 'Seminar for Labour Union Leaders in Southern Africa', Harare, 1-3 April 1996. ILO: Geneva.

Ikiara, G.K. and N.S. Ndung'u (1996), 'Employment and Labour Market during Adjustment: the case of Kenya'. Paper prepared for the seminar on Adjustment Policy, Employment and Labour Market Institutions in Kenya jointly organised by ILO and the Institute of Policy Analysis and Research (IPAR), Nairobi, Kenya, 24th April 1996.

Imam, A. (1991:5-6), 'Democratization Processes in Africa: Problems and Prospects', in: *CODESRIA Bulletin*, N 2.

International Confederation of Free Trade Unions (ICFTU) (1993), 'Les Dimensions Sociales de l'Ajustement au Mali'. Document du Conférence. CISL/UNTM/FFE: Bamako, Mali.

International Confederation of Free Trade Unions (ICFTU) (1993), *The Harare Trade Union Declaration on Equity, Democracy and Development.* April. Harare.

International Confederation of Free Trade Unions (ICFTU) (1995), 'Droits Syndicaux et Relations de Travail en Afrique Francophone: l'impact de l'ajustement structurel', in: *Droits syndicaux et legislation du travail*, N 1, Septembre 1995.

International Confederation of Free Trade Unions (ICFTU) / ICFTU African Regional Organisation (AFRO) (1995), *Trade Unions, Civil Society and Democracy in Africa.* ICFTU/AFRO Pan-African Conference on the Democratisation Process in Africa, Kampala, Uganda 7-10 November 1995.

International Confederation of Free Trade Unions (ICFTU) / World Confederation of Labour (WCL) (1995), 'Evaluation of World Development Report 1995'. Circular N 40. ICFTU: Brussels.

International Confederation of Free Trade Unions (ICFTU) (various years), 'Les Dimensions Sociales de l'Ajustement Structurel au Burkina Faso, Côte-d'Ivoire, Gabon, Ghana, Kenya, Mali, Mozambique, Niger, Ouganda, Sénégal, Tchad, Zambie'. Documents de référence et conclusions du Conferences Nationales du CISL sur les dimensions sociales du PAS. CISL: Brussels.

International Labour Organisation (ILO) (1987), 'Tripartite Preparatory Meeting on Employment and Structural Adjustment'. Report of the meeting. ILO: Geneva, 27-29 April.

International Labour Organisation (ILO) (1989), 'Tripartite Symposium on Structural Adjustment and Employment in Africa: the challenge of adjustment in Africa'. ILO: Nairobi, 16-19 October.

International Labour Organisation (ILO) / Jobs and Skills Programme for Africa (JASPA) (1989), *From Redeployment to Sustained Employment Generation*. ILO/JASPA: Addis Ababa.

International Labour Organisation (ILO) / Jobs and Skills Programme for Africa (JASPA) (1990), *African Employment Report 1990*. ILO/JASPA: Addis Ababa.

International Labour Organisation (ILO) (1992), *World Labour Report*. N 5 of 1992 ILO: Geneva.

International Labour Organisation (ILO) / Jobs and Skills Programme for Africa (JASPA) (1993), *African Employment Report 1992*. ILO/JASPA: Addis Ababa.

International Labour Organisation (ILO) (1994), 'Political Transformation, Structural Adjustment and Industrial Relations in Africa: English speaking countries', in: *Labour Management Relations Series*, N  78, ILO: Geneva.

International Labour Organisation (ILO/EMANO) (1994), 'Document d'Objectifs au Cap Vert'. Bureau de BIT à Dakar, Décembre 1994.

International Labour Organisation (ILO) (1995), 'Impact of Structural Adjustment in the Public Services (efficiency, quality improvement and working conditions)'. Joint meeting on the impact of structural adjustment in the public services. Sectoral Activities Programme, ILO: Geneva.

International Labour Organisation (ILO) (1995), *World Employment 1995, an ILO Report*. ILO: Geneva.

International Monetary Fund (IMF) (1993), 'Structural Adjustment in Sub-Saharan Africa: programme design, recent experience and challenges 1'. Statement by the Fund Staff representative OATUU/ILO High-Level Policy Conference on Structural Adjustment and African Trade Unions. Cairo, Egypt April 16-18, 1993.

Jebuni, C.D., A. Oduro, and K.A. Tutu (1992), 'Trade Liberalization and Economic Performance in Ghana'. AERC: Nairobi, 1992.

Jeune Afrique (diverses années), Le Temps du Monde. Hebdomadaire International Independant. Le Groupe Jeune Afrique: Paris.

Jeune Afrique (17 au 23 janvier 1996), Le Temps du Monde. Hebdomadaire International Independant. Le Groupe Jeune Afrique: Paris.

Jolly, R. and R. van der Hoeven (1991:1801-21), 'Adjustment with a Human Face: record and relevance', in: *World Development* 19, N 12.

Jong, J.A. de (1993), 'Beweging in Afrika: vakbonden van Panafrikaanse eenheid naar pluriformiteit'. Christelijk Nationaal Vakverbond (CNV): Utrecht.

Julien, C. (1991:1 et 7), 'La Démocratie Blessée par les Injustices du Système Economique', in: *Le Monde Diplomatique*, Juin.

Kabashima, H. (1984:309-38), 'Supportive Participation with Economic Growth: the case of Japan', in: *World Politics*. N 3, April.

Kabeya, M. (1989), *Syndicalisme et Démocratie en Afrique Noire: l'experience du Burkina Faso*. Editions Khartala: Paris.

Kaboré, N., 'Une Tradition Pluraliste'. En voie de publication.

Kakwani, N. (1995:469-502), 'Structural Adjustment and Performance in Living Standards in Developing Countries', in: *Development and Change*, Vol. 26, N 3, July.

Kankwenda, M. (1992), 'Processus de Démocratisation en Afrique: problèmes et perspectives'. Paper. CODESRIA: Dakar.

Kasilati, T.M. (1994:65), 'The Role of Political Parties in Democratic Civil Society', in: ESAURP, *The Cost of Peace: views of political parties on the transition to multiparty democracy*. Tanzania Publishing House: Dar es Salaam.

Kasungu, H. (1992), 'Participation of Women in the Trade Union Movement in Tanzania'. Mimeo. OTTU: Dar es Salaam.

Kester, G. (1992:234-41), 'Development Strategy', in: G. Széll (ed.), *Concise Encyclopaedia of Participation and Co-Management*. de Gruyter: Berlin/New York.

Kester, G. (et al) (1994:65-83), 'Les Chantiers de la Democratisation en Afrique', in: G. Kester et O.O. Sidibé (eds.) (1994), *Democratie et Concertation Nationale: la mise en oeuvre du Conseil Economique, Social et Culturel du Mali*. PADEP/l'Harmattan: La Haye/Paris.

Kester, G. (1995:56-71), 'Principes Directeurs pour une Stratégie en Matière de Participation Démocratique', in: G. Kester et H. Pinaud (eds.), *Syndicats et Participation Démocratique: scénario pour le 21ème siècle*. L'Harmattan: Paris.

Kester, G. (1995), 'Towards Effective Worker Participation in South Africa', in: NALEDI, *Opinions on the New Labour Relations Bill*. Progress Press: Johannesburg.

Kester, G. and F. Nangati (1987), 'Trade Unions, Workers' Participation and Education: trends and challenges', in: G. Kester, *Trade Union Education in Africa Reviewed*. APADEP: The Hague.

Kester, G. et O.O. Sidibé (eds.) (1994), *Democratie et Concertation Nationale: la mise en oeuvre du Conseil Economique, Social et Culturel du Mali*. PADEP/l'Harmattan: La Haye/Paris.

Ki-Zerbo, C. L. (1992:375-82), 'l'Entreprise et la Societé', in: J. Ki-Zerbo (et al.), *La Natte des Autres: pour un développement endogène en Afrique*. Codesria, Karthala: Paris.

Kiduanga, J.R., H.S. Msola, E.A. Musa and J. Shaidi (1994), 'Workers' Participation under Structural Adjustment: for whose interests? The case study of a Tanzanian private enterprise'. Case study report. APADEP: Dar es Salaam.

Killick, T. (1995:305-31), 'Structural Adjustment and Poverty Alleviation: an interpretative survey', in: *Development and Change,* Vol. 26, N 2, April.

Kinyondo, S.R. (1984), 'Appraisal of Workers' Participation Policy in Tanzania'. 4th Annual Parastatal Manpower Symposium Arusha. Unpublished.

Konaté, S. (1994), 'Etude sur la Capacité d'Adaptation des Entreprises au Contexte Post-Dévaluation'. Ministère de l'Economie, des Finances et du Plan, Burkina Faso. Coopération Technique Allemande-Ouagadougou.

Konings, P. (1993:113-17), 'Vakbonden, Structurele Aanpassing en Democratisering in Afrika', in: *Internationale Spectator* 47, N 2.

Kotoudi, I. (1993), *Transition à la Nigérienne: récit.* Nouvelle Imprimerie du Niger: Niamey.

Kpétigo, E. (1992: 3 et 9), 'Radioscopie de l'Economie Togolaise: bilan de trente années', in: *Repères,* Jeudi 20 Février.

Kwakye, J. and N.K. Sowa (1992), 'Inflationary Process in Ghana'. AERC: Nairobi, 1992.

L'Observateur (15 Juillet 1996), N 1200. Burkina Faso.

L'Observateur Paalga (24-25 Mars 1993). Burkina Faso.

Lachaud, J.P. (1994), *The Labour Market in Africa.* International Institute for Labour Studies (IILS): Geneva.

Le Monde, 7 février 1995. Paris.

Le Pays (20 Décembre 1993), N 552. Burkina Faso.

Lefebvre, H. (1974), *Le Droit à la Ville. Espace et Politique.* Le Seuil: Paris.

Lemarchand, R. (1992:178-85), 'African Transitions to Democracy: an interim (and mostly pessimistic) assessment', in: *Africa Insight,* Vol. 22, N 3.

Lew, R. (1991:7), 'Démocratie ou Technocratie', in: *Le Monde Diplomatique,* Juin.

Limmen, N. (1996), 'Trade Unions and Structural Adjustment in Africa: the ICFTU approach'. FNV: Amsterdam.

Lodge, T. (1994), 'South Africa: democracy and development in a post-apartheid society'. Unpublished. Department of Political Studies, University of Witwatersrand.

Lorino, P. (1991:24), 'Etre Citoyen dans l'Entreprise', in: *Le Monde Diplomatique,* Septembre.

Lowenthal, A. (ed.) (1975), *The Peruvian Experience: continuity and change under military risk.* Princeton University Press: Princeton/London.

Mafeje, A. (1995:1-25), 'Théorie de la Démocratie et Discours Africain: cassons la croûte, mes compagnons de voyage!', in: E. Chole et J. Ibrahim (eds.), *Processus de Démocratisation en Afrique: problèmes et perspectives.* CODESRIA, Karthala: Paris.

Malik, E.M. (1988), *The Role of the Labour Movement in the Political and Economic Development in Sudan.* Sudan Worker's Trade Unions Federation: Khartoum, Sudan.

Mallé, Y., O.O. Sidibé et S.M. Sissoko (1992), 'Etude de Cas Somapil'. Rapport de l'Etude de Cas. PADEP: Mali.

Mana Kâ (1991), *L'Afrique va-telle Mourir? Bousculer l'Imaginaire Africain*. Editions du Cerf: Paris.

Mandela, N. R. (1994:24-25), *Long Walk to Freedom*. Little, Brown and Company: Boston.

Mapolu, H. (ed.) (1976:153-158), *Workers and Management*. Tanzania Publishing House: Dar es Salaam.

Marktest, C.V. (1995), *Informar cem Riger para Decidir Melhor*. Estudo de Representatividade Sindical nas Empresas. Principais Conclusões.

Martens, G. (1996), 'Trade Unions and Africa's Future'. Forthcoming.

Maseko, I.J. (1976:234), 'Workers' Participation: the case of Friendship Textile Mill and TANESCO', in: H. Mapolu (ed.), *Workers and Management*. Tanzania Publishing House: Dar es Salaam.

Mboweni, T. (1992), 'The Role of the Trade Union Movement in the Future of South Africa', in: *South African Labour Bulletin*, Vol. 16, N 8.

Meister, A. (1981), *l'Autogestion en Uniforme*. Privat: Paris.

Meyns, P. (1992/93:582-99), 'Civil Society and Democratic Change in Africa: the cases of Cape Verde and Zambia', in: *African Development Perspectives Yearbook*, Vol.3.

Michael, G.M. (1988), 'The Role of Trade Unions and Employer's Organisations in the Social and Economic Development of Africa: an overview'. First African Regional Congress on Industrial Relations, Lagos, Nigeria, November 9-11.

Michalon, T. (1993:26), 'Légitimité de l'Etat et Solidarités Ethniques', in: *Le Monde Diplomatique*, Novembre.

Mihyo, P.B. (1983), *Industrial Conflict and Change in Tanzania*. Tanzania Publishing House: Dar es Salaam.

Mihyo, P. and F. Schiphorst (1995:169-200), 'Africa: a context of sharp economic decline', in: H. Thomas (ed.) (1995), *Globalization and Third World Trade Unions: the challenge of rapid economic change*. Zed Books: London.

Ministère de l'Economie des Finances et du Plan, Burkina Faso (1995), 'Impact de la Dévaluation du Franc CFA sur l'Economie à Moyen Terme'. Burkina Faso.

Ministère de l'Enseignement Technique et de la Formation Professionnelle (METFP), Direction des Etudes de la Recherche et de la Planification, Togo (1993), 'Aperçu de l'Evolution de l'Emploi dans les Entreprises du Secteur Moderne au Togo. Données de Base', Lomé.

Ministère du Plan, Togo (1989), 'Cadre Macro Economique. 1990-1995', Lomé, Togo.

Ministry of Finance, Ghana (1993), 'Government Budget Statement'. Accra, Ghana.

Ministry of Finance, Sudan (1990), 'Disposal of the Public Enterprise Sector Act', Khartoum, Sudan.

Ministry of Finance, Sudan (1990), 'The Three-Year Economic Salvation Programme', Khartoum, Sudan.

Ministry of Finance, Sudan (1992), 'The National Comprehensive Strategy', Khartoum, Sudan.

Mmuya, M. and A. Chaligha (1992:97), *Towards Multiparty Politics in Tanzania.* Dar es Salaam University Press: Dar es Salaam.

Moção de Estratégia e Estatutos do MPD (1993), II Convenção do Movimento para a Democracia. Praia.

Monga, C. (1994), *Anthropologie de la Colère: societé civile et démocratie en Afrique noire.* L'Harmattan: Paris.

Monga, C. (1995:63-77), 'l'Indice de Démocratisation: comment déchiffrer le nouvel aide-mémoire de l'autoritarisme', in: *Afrique 2000*, N 22, Août.

Mtukulo, A. (1995), 'Malawi - Structural Adjustment Programmes Hurt the Poor', in: *Southern Africa Political and Economic Monthly*, Vol. 9, N 2.

Musa, E.A. (1992), 'The Role of the State in Industrial Relations Systems in Africa: the case of Sudan', in: *The Role of the State in Industrial Relations*, Vol.1. 11RA 8th World Congress, Sydney, Australia, August.

Musa, E.A. (1992:63-69), 'Privatisation in the Less Developed Countries: the case of Sudan', in: *Journal of African Administrative Studies*, African Training Research Centre in Administration for Development (CAFRAD). Tangier, Morocco.

Musa, E.A. (1994:354-99), 'Privatisation in the Least Developed Countries', in: T. Clarke (1994), *International Privatisation: strategies and practices.* De Gruyter: Berlin, Germany.

Musa, E.A. (1995), 'Privatisation, Workers' Participation and Social Consequences in Africa: the case of Sudan'. Paper prepared for the International Conference on Privatisation-Participation-Social Consequences in the East and in the West. Chemniz, Germany, September 26-28.

Musa, E.A. and M.K. Khaliel (1989), 'Trade Unions and Workers' Participation Development in Sudan'. Paper prepared for the international workshop on workers' participation in Africa, Harare, Zimbabwe, March-April.

Natchaba, O. F. (1982:32-72), 'L'Unité du Syndicalisme Togolais', in: *Revue Penant*, Juillet-Décembre, 777-778.

Natchaba, O. F. (1983:36-65), 'L'Unité du Syndicalisme Togolais. 2ème Partie', in: *Revue Penant*, Janvier-Mars, 779.

National Union of Tanzanian Workers (JUWATA) (1990), *Waraka kuhusu Mageuzi katika Umoja wa Wafanyakazi.* JUWATA: Dar es Salaam, Tanzania.

Newbury, C. (1994:1-8), 'Introduction: paradoxes of democratization in Africa', in: *African Studies Review*, Vol. 37, N 1.

Olukoshi, A.O. (1993:75-97), *The Politics of Structural Adjustment in Nigeria.* James Curry: London.

Onimode, B. (1992), *A Future for Africa: beyond the politics of adjustment.* Earthscan: London.

Organisation for Economic Cooperation and Development (OECD) (1993), *DAC Orientations on Participatory Development and Good Governance.* OECD: Paris.

Organisation of African Trade Union Unity (OATUU) (1992), 'What is Structural Adjustment'. OATUU paper. Accra.

Organisation of African Trade Union Unity (OATUU/ILO) (1993), 'High Level Trade Union Policy Conference on Structural Adjustment and Trade Unions'. Summary Report. Cairo, Egypt, April 16-18, 1993.

Organisation of African Trade Union Unity (OATUU) (1995), 'Report of Activities, January 1994 - May 1995'. 18th session of the General Council: Accra - Ghana, 20 May, 1995.

Organisation of African Trade Union Unity (OATUU) (1996), 'Report of Activities, June 1995 - December 1995'. 19th session of the General Council: Cairo - Egypt, 15 - 16 May, 1996.

Organisation of Tanzania Trade Unions (OTTU) (1994), *Gender Research on Workers' Participation in the 1992 Trade Union Elections.* OTTU Headquarters: Dar es Salaam.

Ouattara, D. (1996), 'The IMF and Trade Unions'. Speech by the Deputy Managing Director of the IMF at the Seminar on Economic Growth and Development in Southern Africa, Harare, April 1.

Park, Y.C. (1990), in: Moustapha Kasse, *Sénégal: crise économique et ajustement structurel.* Editions Nouvelles du Sud: Paris.

Pateman, C. (1970), *Participation and Democratic Theory.* Cambridge University Press: Cambridge.

Pinaud, H. (1995:33-48), 'Le Rôle des Acteurs Sociaux dans l'Evolution Récente de la Participation des Salariés dans dix Pays de l'Europe de l'Ouest', in: G. Kester et H. Pinaud (eds.) (1995), *Syndicats et Participation Démocratique, Scénario 21: scénario pour le 21ème siècle.* L'Harmattan: Paris.

Pisani, E. (1988), *Pour l'Afrique.* Odile Jacob: Paris.

Plant, R. (1994), *Labour Standards and Structural Adjustment.* ILO: Geneva.

Ponte, S. (1994:539-58), 'The World Bank and 'Adjustment in Africa'', in: *Review of African Political Economy,* N 66.

Prasnikar, J. (1991), *Workers' Participation and Self-Management in Developing Countries.* West View Press: San Francisco.

Pratt, C. (1976:189), *The Critical Phase in Tanzania 1945 - 1968: Nyerere and the emergence of a socialist strategy.* Cambridge University Press: London.

Przeworski, A. (1991), *Democracy and the Market: political and economic reforms in Eastern Europe and Latin America.* Cambridge University Press: Cambridge.

Public Services International (PSI) (1994), 'Structural Adjustment Programmes and the Public Sector in Africa'. 8th African Regional Conference, Abidjan 19-24 September 1994.

Raftopoulos, B. (1992:57-66), 'Beyond the Hose of Hunger: democratic struggle in Zimbabwe', in: *Review of African Political Economy*, N 55.

Rakner, L.G. (1992), *Trade Unions in Processes of Democratization: a study of party labour relations in Zambia*. Report N 6. Chr. Michelsen Institute: Bergen.

Raptis, M. (1974), *Revolution and Counterrevolutiuon in Chile*. Allison: London.

Rasheed, S. (1995:333-354), 'The Democratization Process and Popular Participation in Africa: Emerging Realities and the Challenges Ahead', in: *Development and Change*, Vol. 26, N 2.

Rasheed, S. (1996), 'New Approaches to Partnership', in: *Development*. N 2, June 1996.

Research and Development Training Programme (RDTP) (1994a), 'Trade Union Research in Central and West Africa on Structural Adjustment'. ICFTU/ AFRO: Nairobi.

Research and Development Training Programme (RDTP) (1994b), 'Trade Union Research in English-Speaking West Africa and in East and Southern Africa on Structural Adjustment'. ICFTU/AFRO: Nairobi.

Robin, J. (1991:21), 'Pour une Démocratie Vraiment Participative: l'ère des ruptures', in: *Le Monde Diplomatique*, Décembre.

Rolland, D. (1992:63-81), 'La Politique Régionale à la Suédoise: le cas Uddevalla', in: *Revue Interventions Economiques*, N 24.

Ross, N. (1969), *Constructive Conflict*. Oliver and Boyd: Edinburgh.

Rutinwa, B. (1995:29-32), *Legal Regulation of Industrial Relations in Tanzania: past experience and future prospects*. Labour Law Unit, University of Cape Town: Cape Town.

Saby, H. (1991:56-60), 'La Dignité Humaine est une Valeur Universelle', in: *Le Courier*. N 128, Juillet-Août.

Sandwidi, K., 'Evolution de l'Histoire du Mouvement Syndical Burkinabé'. En voie de publication.

Sankara, T., 'Burkina Faso: CNR AN II, Programme Populaire de Développement Octobre 1984 - Décembre 1985'.

Schiphorst, F. (1995:215-32), 'The Emergence of Civil Society: the new place of unions in Zimbabwe', in: H. Thomas (ed.), *Globalization and Third World Trade Unions: the challenge of rapid economic change*. Zed Books: London.

Schutte, G.R. (August 1995), 'Report of the ICFTU mission to Cape Verde'. Federatie Nederlandse Vakbeweging (FNV): Amsterdam.

Secretariat Administratif du RPT (1976), *Rapport du Premier Conseil National du RPT.* 10, 11, 12, et 13 Novembre, Sokodé. Togo.

Secretariat Administratif du RPT (1978), *Rapport du Troisième Conseil National du RPT.* 6, 7, 8, et 9 Novembre, Lomé. Togo.
Secretariat Administratif du RPT (1979), *Rapport du Troisième Congrès Statutaire du RPT.* 27, 28, et 29 Novembre, Lomé. Togo.
Secretariat Administratif du RPT (1982), *Rapport du Sixième Conseil National du RPT.* 3 et 4 Décembre, Lomé. Togo.
Shao, F. and G.M. Naimani (May 1995), 'Development of Workers' Participation in Tanzania: an APADEP longitudinal study report'. Unpublished. Institute of Development Studies, University of Dar es Salaam: Dar es Salaam.
Sidibé, O.O. et S.M. Sissoko (1995), 'Etude pour un Projet de Formation Syndicale en Afrique Francophone'. Document de Reference. Internationale des Services Publics (ISP): Ferney Voltaire.
Simutanyi, N.R. (1992), 'Trade Unions and the Democratization Process in Zambia', CODESRIA paper. Septième Assemblée Générale, 'Processus de Démocratisation en Afrique: Problèmes et Perspectives', 10-14 février, 1992.
Sirianni, C. (ed.) (1987), *Worker Participation and the Politics of Reform.* Temple University Press: Philadelphia.
Skarstein, R., K.J. Havnevik and W.D.S. Mbaga (1988:90-104), *Norwegian Commodity Import Support to Tanzania: background, design and implications.* Institute of Economics, University of Trondheim: Trondheim, Norway.
Sklar, R. (1987:696-98), 'Developmental Democracy', in: *Comparative Studies in Society and History,* 29, 4.
Sowa, N.K. (1991), 'The Social Effects of Adjustment in Ghana', Legon.
Sparks, A. (1994), 'The Secret Revolution', in: *The New Yorker,* April 11.
Statistical Service of Ghana (1964, 1977-80, 1993), 'Economic Survey'. Accra.
Statistical Service of Ghana (1985, 1989, 1992), 'Quarterly Digest of Statistics'. Accra.
Statistical Service of Ghana (1988), 'Ghana Living Standard Survey'. Accra.
Stephens, E.H. (1980), *The Politics of Workers' Participation: the Peruvian approach in comparative perspective.* Academic Press: New York.
Stryker, D. (1990), *Trade, Exchange Rate and Agricultural Pricing Policies in Ghana.* World Bank: Washington, D.C.
Sudan Workers' Trade Unions Federation (SWTUF) (1990), 'Trade Union Dialogue Conference: proceedings and recommendations'. August. SWTUF Publications: Sudan.
Sudan Workers' Trade Unions Federation (SWTUF) (1993), 'Recommendations of the Founding Meeting'. February. Khartoum, Sudan.
Sudan Workers' Trade Unions Federation (SWTUF) (1993), 'General Information Department'. March. Khartoum, Sudan.
Tedga, P.J.M. (1991), *Ouverture Démocratique en Afrique Noire?* L'Harmattan: Paris.

360    *Trade Unions and Sustainable Democracy in Africa*

Thomas, H. (ed.) (1995), *Globalization and Third World Trade Unions: the challenge of rapid economic change.* Zed Books: London.

Todjinou, P. (1994:65-80), 'Le PAS et la Justice Sociale: l'action syndicale', in: 'Rapport Séminaire National sur Le Programme d'Ajustement Structurel et les Effets de la Dévaluation du F. CFA'. CGTB: Cotonou.

Toit, du D. (1996), 'Industrial Democracy in South Africa's Transition'. Paper presented at the 8th Conference of the International Association for the Economics of Participation, Prague, Czech Republic, August 1996.

Torres, L. (1995), 'South African Unions: schools or agents for democracy', in: *The Journal of Contemporary African Studies,* Vol. 13, N 1.

Touraine, A. (1994), *Qu'est-ce-que la Démocratie?* Editions Fayard: Paris.

Toye, J. (1995), *Structural Adjustment and Employment Policy: issues and experiences.* ILO: Geneva.

Tungaraza, F.S.K. (1991), 'The IMF/World Bank Programmes and Social Policy', in: B. Turok (ed.), *Alternative Strategies for Africa: debt and democracy.* Vol.3. Institute for African Alternatives: London.

Turshen, M. (1994), 'The Impact of Economic Reforms on Women's Health and Healthcare in Sub-Saharan Africa', in: N. Aslanbeigui, S. Pressman and G. Summerfield, *Women in the Age of Economic Transformation: gender impact of reforms in post-socialist and developing countries.* Routledge: London.

Tutu, K.A. (1995), *Structural Adjustment Programmes and Their Effects on Ghanaian Workers.* Friedrich Ebert Stiftung: Accra.

Uca, M.N. (1983), 'Workers' Participation and Self Management in Turkey: an evaluation of attempts and experiences'. Research Report Series, Institute of Social Studies: The Hague.

União Nacional dos Trabalhadores de Cabo Verde - Central Sindical (UNTC-CS), 'Movimento Sindical em Cabo Verde'. Documento apresentado no Seminário da AJOC de 26 de Marco 1993.

United Nations Development Programme (UNDP) (1990), *Human Development Report 1990.* Oxford University Press: New York.

United Nations Development Programme (UNDP) (1993), *Rapport Mondial sur le Développement Humain 1993.* Economica: Paris.

United Nations Development Programme (UNDP) (1994), *Human Development Report 1994.* Oxford University Press: New York.

United Nations Economic Commission for Africa (UNECA) (1991), 'African Alternative Framework to Structural Adjustment Programmes for Socio-Economic Recovery and Transformation (AAFSAP). UNECA: Addis Ababa.

Vandermoortele, J. (1991), 'Labour Market Informalisation in sub-Saharan Africa', in: G. Standing and V. Tokman (ed.), *Towards Social Adjustment: labour market issues in structural adjustment.* ILO: Geneva.

Verdier, J.M. (1987), *Droit du Travail Syndicats et Droit Syndical.* Vol. I, Tome 5, Dalloz 2è. éd., Paris.

Viveret, P. (1991:29), 'Réintégrer la "Zone" dans la Ville', in: *Le Monde Diplomatique*, Octobre.

Wapenhans, T. (1994:36-52), 'The Political Economy of Structural Adjustment: an external perspective', in: R. van der Hoeven and F. van der Kraaij (1994), *Structural Adjustment and Beyond in sub-Saharan Africa*. James Curry: London.

World Bank (1983-1984), *Commodity Trade and Price Trends*. The World Bank: Washington, DC.

World Bank (1989), *Sub-Saharan Africa: from crisis to sustainable development*. The World Bank: Washington, DC.

World Bank (1991), *Ghana: Structural Adjustment for Growth*. The World Bank: Washington, DC.

World Bank (1993), *The World Bank Annual Report 1993*. The World Bank: Washington, DC.

World Bank (1994), *Adjustment in Africa. Reforms, Results and the Road Ahead*. Oxford University Press: New York.

World Bank (1994), *Reducing Poverty in South Africa: options for equitable and sustainable growth*. The World Bank: Washington, DC.

World Bank (1995), *World Development Report 1995: workers in an integrated world*. The World Bank: Washington, DC.

World Confederation of Labour (WCL) (1992), 'Africa: a new start', in: *Labor Events* N 3.

World Confederation of Labour (WCL) (1992), 'International Economic Seminar' with the IMF and the World Bank. A joint initiative of WCL, ICFTU and IMF, the World Bank. Washington, November 3rd - 6th.

World Confederation of Labour (WCL) (1993), '23rd Congress of the World Confederation of Labour'. WCL: Republic of Mauritius, November 22nd to 27th.

Zimbabwe Congress of Trade Unions (ZCTU) (1996), 'Beyond ESAP: framework for a long-term development strategy in Zimbabwe beyond the economic structural adjustment programme'. ZCTU: Harare.

# Abbreviations

| | |
|---|---|
| AAFSAP | African Alternative Framework to Structural Adjustment Programmes |
| ACP | African, Caribbean and Pacific States |
| ADB | African Development Bank |
| ADEMA | Alliance pour la Démocratie au Mali (Alliance for Democracy in Mali) |
| ADIDE | Association des Initiateurs et Demandeurs d'Emploi (Association of Job Providers and Job Seekers) |
| ADP | Assemblée des Députés du Peuple (Assembly of People's Deputies) |
| AEEM | Association des Elèves et Etudiants du Mali (Association of Malian School and College Students) |
| AFRO | African Regional Organisation of the ICFTU |
| AJDP | Association des Jeunes pour le Développement et le Progrès (Youth Association for Development and Progress) |
| ALO | Arab Labour Organisation |
| ANC | African National Congress |
| APADEP | African Workers' Participation Development Programme |
| ASP | Afro-Shiraz Party |
| BFTU | Botswana Federation of Trade Unions |
| CCM | Chama Cha Mapinduzi (Political Party in Tanzania) |
| CCS | Conselho de Concertação Social (Social Consultative Council) |
| CCSL | Confederação Caboverdiana dos Sindicatos Livros (Cape Verdean Confederation of Free Trade Unions) |
| CCT | Commission Consultative du Travail (Consultative Labour Commission) |
| CDR | Comités de Défense de la Révolution (Committees for the Defence of the Revolution) |
| CDTZ | Confédération Démocratique du Travail du Zaïre (Zaïre Democratic Confederation of Labour) |
| CFDT | Confédération Française Démocratique du Travail (French Democratic Labour Confederation) |
| CGCT | Confédération Générale des Cadres du Togo (General Confederation of Togolese Executives) |

| | |
|---|---|
| CGT | Confédération Générale du Travail (General Confederation on Labour) |
| CGTB | Centrale Générale des Travailleurs du Bénin (General Trade Union Centre of Beninese Workers) |
| CGTB | Confédération Générale du Travail du Burkina (General Confederation of Burkina Faso Labour) |
| CILSS | Comité permanent Inter-états de Lutte contre la Sécheresse dans la Sahel (Permanent Inter-State Committee on Drought Control in the Sahel) |
| CISA | Confédération Internationale des Syndicats Arabes (International Confederation of Arabic Trade Unions) |
| CMLN | Comité Militaire de Libération Nationale (Military Committee for National Liberation) |
| CMRPM | Comité Militaire de Redressement pour le Progrès National |
| CNE | Comissão Nacional de Eleicões (National Elections Committee) |
| CNID | Congrès National d'Initiative Démocratique (National Congress for Democratic Initiative) |
| CNM | Commission Nationale des Médias (National Commission for Media) |
| CNR | Conseil National de la Révolution (National Revolutionary Council) |
| CNT | Convention Nationale du Travail (National Labour Agreement) |
| CNTB | Confédération Nationale des Travailleurs Burkinabé (National Confederation of Burkina Workers) |
| CNTG | Confédération Nationale des Travailleurs Guinéens (National Confederation of Guinean Workers) |
| CNTS | Confédération Nationale des Travailleurs du Sénégal (National Confederation of Senegalese Workers) |
| CNTT | Confédération Nationale des Travailleurs du Togo (National Confederation of Togolese Workers) |
| CNTV | Confédération Nationale des Travailleurs Voltaïques (National Confederation of Upper Volta Workers) |
| CNV | Dutch Christian National Union |
| CODESRIA | Council for the Development of Social Science Research in Africa |
| CONISTO | Comité National Intersyndical du Togo (National Inter-union Committee of Togo) |
| COSATU | Congress of South African Trade Unions |
| CRN | Comité de Réconciliation Nationale (Committee for National Reconciliation) |

| | |
|---|---|
| CSA | Centrale des Syndicats Autonomes (Confederation of Beninese Autonomous Trade Unions) |
| CSAP | Coordination des Syndicats de l'Administration Publique (Coordination Committee of Public Sector Unions) |
| CSB | Confédération Syndicale Burkinabé (Burkina Trade Union Confederation) |
| CSC | Confédération Syndicale Congolaise (Congolese Trade Union Confederation) |
| CSI | Collectif des Syndicats Indépendants (Collective of Independent Trade Unions) |
| CSR | Caisse de Solidarité Révolutionaire (Revolutionary Solidarity Fund) |
| CSTB | Centrale des Syndicats des Travailleurs du Burkina (Trade Union Centre of Burkina Workers) |
| CSTB | Centrale des Syndicats des Travailleurs du Bénin (Trade Union Centre of Beninese Workers) |
| CSTT | Confédération Syndicale des Travailleurs du Togo (Togolese Trade Union Confederation) |
| CSV | Confédération Syndicale Voltaïque (Upper Volta Trade Union Confederation) |
| CTC | Comité Tripartite de Concertation (Tripartite Concertation Committee) |
| CTSP | Comité de Transition pour le Salut du Peuple (Transitional Committee for People's Welfare) |
| CTUC | Commonwealth Trade Union Council |
| CUT | Comité pour l'Unité Togolaise (Committee for Togolese Unity) |
| CVT | Cabo Verde Telecom |
| DAC | Development Assistance Committee |
| DNSI | Direction Nationale de la Statistique et de l'Information |
| ECOWAS | Economic Community of West African States |
| EI | Education International |
| EIU | Economic Intelligence Unit |
| EPI | Effort Populaire d'Investissement (People's Investment) |
| ERP | Economic Recovery Programme |
| ETUC | European Trade Union Confederation |
| EU | European Union |
| FAIMO | Frentes de Alta Intensidade de Mão de Obra (Labour-Intensive Manpower Fronts) |
| FASR | Facilité d'Ajustement Structurel Renforcé |
| FEN | Fédération de l'Education Nationale (National Education Federation) |

| | |
|---|---|
| FENSAMEV | Fédération Nationale des Syndicats des Personnels de la Santé et de la Médecine Vétérinaire (National Federation of Health and Veterinary Medicine Workers) |
| FENSAP | Fédération Nationale des Syndicats Administration (National Federation of Public Sector Unions) |
| FIET | International Federation of Commercial, Clerical, Professional and Technical Employees |
| FNV | Dutch Confederation of Trade Unions |
| FP | Front Populaire (Popular Front) |
| FRELIMO | Mozambican Liberation Front |
| FRTU | Federation of Revolutionary Trade Unions |
| GATT | General Agreement on Tariffs and Trade |
| GCA | Global Coalition for Africa |
| GD | Groupes de Dynamisation (Dynamising Group ) |
| GDP | Gross Domestic Product |
| GNP | Gross National Product |
| GRN | Gouvernement de Renouveau National (Government of National Revival) |
| GSA | Groupe des Syndicats Autonomes (Group of Autonomous Trade Unions) |
| GSI | Grupo de Dinamização de Sindicatos Independentes e Democráticos (Trade Union Pressure Group) |
| GTUC | Ghana Trades Union Congress |
| HDI | Human Development Index |
| ICATU | International Confederation of Arab Trade Unions |
| ICEM | International Confederation of Chemical, Energy and General Workers' Unions |
| ICFTU | International Confederation of Free Trade Unions |
| IFBWW | International Federation of Building and Wood Workers |
| IILS | International Institute for Labour Studies |
| ILO | International Labour Organisation |
| IMF | International Monetary Fund |
| INPS | Institut National de Prévoyance Sociale (National Social Welfare Institute) |
| INSD | Institut National de la Statistique et de la Démographie (National Statistics and Demography Institute) |
| ITF | International Transport Workers' Federation |
| ITS | International Trade Secretariat |
| IUF | International Union of Food, Agriculture, Hotel, Restaurant, Catering, Tobacco and Allied Workers' Associations |
| JASPA | Jobs and Skills Programme for Africa |
| JLD | Jeunesse, Libre et Démocratique (Free Democratic Youth) |

| | |
|---|---|
| JUWATA | National Union of Tanzanian Workers |
| METFP | Ministère de l'Enseignement Technique et de la Formation Professionnelle (Ministry of Technical Education and Vocational Training) |
| MFJ | Movement for Freedom and Justice |
| MMD | Movement for Multi-Party Democracy |
| MNR | Mouvement National pour le Renouveau (National Movement for Revival) |
| MONESTO | Mouvement National des Etudiants et Scolaires du Togo (National Movement of Students and Pupils of Togo) |
| MPD | Movimento Para a Democracia (Movement for Democracy) |
| MURC | Manpower Utilisation and Redeployment Committee |
| NACTU | National Council of Trade Unions |
| NCCE | National Commission on Civic Education |
| NCG | Commission Nationale pour l'Education Civique (National Commission on Civic Education) |
| NDA | National Democratic Alliance |
| NEDLAC | National Economic Development and Labour Council |
| NES | National Electoral Commission |
| NESP | National Economic Survival Programme |
| NGO | Non Governmental Organisation |
| NLC | Nigerian Labour Congress |
| NMC | National Media Committee |
| NUTA | National Union of Tanganyika Workers |
| OATUU | Organisation of African Trade Union Unity |
| OAU | Organisation of African Unity |
| ODA | Official Development Aid |
| OECD | Organisation for Economic Cooperation and Development |
| OJM | Organisation des Jeunes du Mozambique (Youth Organisation of Mozambique) |
| OMM | Organisation des Femmes du Mozambique (Women's Organisation of Mozambique) |
| OMOE | Office National de la Main-d'Oeuvre et de l'Emploi (National Manpower and Employment Office) |
| ONSL | Organisation Nationale des Syndicats Libres (National Organisation of Free Trade Unions) |
| OTM | Organizaç o dos Trabalhadores de Moçambique (Workers' Organisation of Mozambique) |
| OTTU | Organisation of Tanzania Trade Unions |
| OVSL | Organisation Voltaïque des Syndicats Libres (Upper Volta Organisation of Free Trade Unions) |
| PAC | Pan African Congress |

| | |
|---|---|
| PADEP | Programme Africain pour le Développement de la Participation des Travailleurs (African Workers' Participation Development Programme) |
| PAICV | Partido Africano de Independência de Cabo Verde (Cape Verdean African Independence Party) |
| PALOP | Pays Africains de Langue Officielle Portugaise |
| PCD | Partido de Convergencia Democratica (Party of Democratic Convergence) |
| PCT | Parti Congolais du Travail (Congolese Labour Party) |
| PE | Public Enterprise |
| PNDC | Provisional National Defence Council |
| PPD | Programme Populaire de Développement (Popular Development Programme) |
| PPS | Progressive Party of Sudan |
| PRE | Structural Adjustment Programme of Mozambique |
| PSI | Public Services International |
| PTI | Portugal Telecom Internacional |
| PTTI | Postal, Telegraph, and Telephone International |
| RDA | Rassemblement Démocratique Africain (African Democratic Assembly) |
| RDP | Reconstruction and Development Programme |
| RDP | Révolution Démocratique et Populaire (Democratic and Popular Revolution) |
| RDTP | Research Development and Training Programme |
| RNTC | Régie nationale des transports en commun (National Public Transport System) |
| RPT | Rassemblement du Peuple Togolais (Togolese People's Assembly) |
| SACP | South African Communist Party |
| SAP | Structural Adjustment Programme |
| SFCB | Société des Chemins de Fer du Burkina Faso (Burkina Faso Railway Company) |
| SLIM | Free and Independent Trade Unions of Mozambique |
| SNEAHV | Syndicat National des Enseignants Africains de Haute-Volta National Union of African Teachers in Upper Volta) |
| SNEC | Syndicat National de l'Éducation et de la Culture (National Education and Culture Union) |
| SNES | Syndicat National de l'Enseignement Supérieur (National Higher Education Union) |
| SONAPHARM | Société Nationale d'Approvisionnement Pharamaceutique (National Pharmaceutical Supply Company) |

| | |
|---|---|
| SONAR | Société Nationale d'Assurance et de Réassurance (National Insurance and Reinsurance Society) |
| SSA | Sub-Saharan African Countries |
| STCT | Sindicato dos Transportes, Comércio e Turismo (Union of Transport, Commerce and Tourism Workers) |
| SWTUF | Sudan Workers' Trade Unions Federation |
| SYLCAD | Syndicat Libre des Cadres (Free Union of Managers) |
| SYLPOSTEL | Syndicats des Postes et Télécommunications (Union of Post and Telecommunications) |
| SYNBANK | Syndicats des Banques (Union for Bank Staff) |
| SYNCAB | Syndicat National des Banques et Assurances (National Bank and Insurance Union) |
| SYNUTRAP-TP | Syndicat National des Travailleurs des Travaux Publics (National Union of Public Works Employees) |
| TANU | Tanganyika African National Union |
| TFL | Tanganyika Federation of Labour |
| TFTU | Tanzania Federation of Trade Unions |
| TNA | Transitional National Assembly |
| TPR | Tribunaux Populaires de la Révolution (Popular Revolutionary Courts) |
| UCID | União Caboverdiana de Independência e Democracia (Cape Verdean Union of Independence and Democracy) |
| UDF | United Democratic Front |
| UDPM | Union Démocratique du Peuple Malien (Democratic Union of Malian People) |
| UGSL | Union Générale des Syndicats Libres (General Union of Free Trade Unions) |
| UGTA | Union Générale des Travailleurs Africains (General Union of African Workers) |
| UGTAN | Union Générale des Travailleurs d'Afrique Noire (General Union of Black African Workers) |
| UGTB | Union Générale des Travailleurs Burkinabé (General Union of Burkina Workers) |
| UGTCI | Union Générale des Travailleurs de la Côte-d'Ivoire (General Union of Côte d'Ivoire Workers) |
| UGTV | Union Générale des Travailleurs Voltaïques (General Union of Upper Volta Workers) |
| UNCTT | Union Nationale des Chefs Traditionnels du Togo (National Union of Traditional Togolese Chiefs) |
| UNDP | United Nations Development Programme |
| UNECA | United Nations Economic Commission for Africa |

| | |
|---|---|
| UNFT | Union Nationale des Femmes du Togo (Union of Togolese Women) |
| UNSIT | Union Nationale des Syndicats Indépendants du Togo (National Union of Independent Togolese Unions) |
| UNSTB | Union Nationale des Syndicats des Travailleurs du Bénin (National Union of Beninese Trade Unions) |
| UNTC-CS | União Nacional dos Trabalhadores de Cabo Verde - Central Sindical (National Union of Workers of Cape Verde-Trade Union Centre) |
| UNTM | Union Nationale des Travailleurs du Mali (National Union of Malian Workers) |
| UNTT | Union Nationale des Travailleurs du Togo (National Union of Togolese Workers) |
| USAID | United States Agency for International Development |
| USCT | Union des Syndicats Conféderés du Togo (Union of Confederated Workers of Togo) |
| USHIRIKA | Cooperative Union of Tanzania |
| USN | Union des Scolaires Nigériens |
| USR | União Sindical Regional (Regional Union) |
| USRDA | Union pour le Rassemblement Démocratique Africain (Union for African Democratic Assembly) |
| USTB | Union Syndicale des Travailleurs du Burkina (Trade Union of Burkina Workers) |
| USTC | Union Syndicale des Travailleurs de Centrafrique |
| USTN | Union des Syndicats des Travailleurs du Niger (National Union of Niger Workers) |
| USTN-USN | Union des Scolaires Nigériens (Niger Union of Teachers) |
| USTV | Union Syndicale des Travailleurs Voltaïques (Trade Union of Upper Volta Workers) |
| UTB | Union des Travailleurs du Burundi (Union of Burundi Workers) |
| UTM | Union des Travailleurs Mauritaniens (Union of Mauritanian Workers) |
| UWT | Union of Women in Tanzania |
| VAT | Value Added Tax |
| VIJANA | National Youth Association |
| WAZAZI | Tanzania Parents Association |
| WCL | World Confederation of Labour |
| WFTU | World Federation of Trade Unions |
| ZCTU | Zambia Congress of Trade Unions |
| ZCTU | Zimbabwe Congress of Trade Unions |
| ZEDC | Zimbabwe Economic Development Council |